William M. Sloane

The French War and the Revolution

William M. Sloane

The French War and the Revolution

ISBN/EAN: 9783337227593

Printed in Europe, USA, Canada, Australia, Japan

Cover: Foto ©ninafisch / pixelio.de

More available books at **www.hansebooks.com**

THE AMERICAN HISTORY SERIES

THE FRENCH WAR

AND

THE REVOLUTION

BY

WILLIAM MILLIGAN SLOANE, Ph.D., L.H.D.

PROFESSOR IN PRINCETON UNIVERSITY

WITH MAPS

NEW YORK
CHARLES SCRIBNER'S SONS
1893

DEDICATED

WITH GRATEFUL DEVOTION

TO

MARY ESPY SLOANE

PREFACE

This book is the second of a series of four, each of which, while complete in itself, is to form part of a connected history of the United States down to our own time. The limits of this volume are the years 1756 and 1783. This period has a unity in many ways. From the beginning of the "old French War" to the end of the Revolution the English commonwealths in America were both learning the necessity of union and growing conscious of a common destiny. It might even be said that while in one of the two conflicts they were hostile to France and in the other allied with her yet nevertheless such a connection is in itself substantive. Both illustrate phases of French history. A still stronger mark of the epoch is the continuous development in action of common exertion for the common welfare. But the strongest and most philosophical unity is in the evolution of a new theory of government during these years by the application of English principles to American conditions. The author hopes that while the narrative in the following pages is necessarily brief it is full enough to illustrate this essential conception in American history.

The colonies, united in discontent by a general military

control, nevertheless combine in measure to loyally fight the American portion of the Seven Years' War, and by their victory free themselves both from fear of Indian savagery and the menace of a hostile French civilization. Thus emancipated, their next concern is commercial liberty and freedom of trade. To this end is formed, first, the idea of allegiance, not to Parliament but to the Crown, as the expression of sovereignty; then the notion of representation as the necessary antecedent of internal taxation, a concept which, in the form of No representation no taxation, awakens the interest of English liberals and produces eventually a new idea of representation. The next stage destroys the false distinction between imperial and internal taxation, displays the impossibility of American representation in Parliament, and announces the new doctrine of No representation no legislation. The collapse of the colonial governments in the struggle for independence necessitates the substitution of new ones, very like the old, but different in one essential feature, which contains the germ of what is called congressional, to distinguish it from parliamentary, government. This is the erection of the executive on one hand into an active power in government, and on the other into a regulative force in controlling legislation. That the governor may not be tyrannical he must be elective, and thereby directly responsible to the people. This device was in the following period applied in federal as well as state government.

The chief end of this volume is to present a reasoned account of all the facts. During my studies I have had access to many original sources, some of them unpublished copies from the English and French archives. At the same time I have diligently used the results of trustworthy investigators wherever found.

The ever-present question in writing a book like this is how best to present the subject as a whole, and it will be found that many details not essential to the central idea have been omitted.

PRINCETON, January, 1893.

CONTENTS

CHAPTER I.

THE ENGLISH PEOPLE IN THE EIGHTEENTH CENTURY—1688-1756, ... 1

Nature of the European Struggle—Position of the Powers—Changes in English Politics—Party Struggles—Gains and Losses in Public Morality—Pitt and Wesley—Influences in America — Character of Colonial Civilization — The Americans as Political and Religious Dissenters—Dangerous Elements in the Population.

CHAPTER II.

INSTITUTIONS OF THE ENGLISH COLONIES—1688-1756, . 10

Influence of the English Revolution—The Colonial Governments—Political and Legal Speculation—Political Theory—Contemporary Speculation in Europe—The Free-thinkers of England—Roman Catholic Disabilities — Scotch-Irish Presbyterians—Irish Emigration to the Continent—Influence of the Protestant Irish in America — Roman Catholics in America — Causes of American Loyalty — France in America—The Fisheries Question.

CHAPTER III.

THE ENGLISH AND FRENCH IN NORTH AMERICA—1688-1756, 22

The Mississippi Valley—French Possessions and Ambitions—Continental Lines of Communication—Contrast between the Strength and Aims of England and France—Divergent Institutions of the Two Peoples—The Conflict to be

Decided in America—Preparatory Negotiations and Measures—The Aborigines of the South—The Algonquins and Iroquois—Their Institutions and Religion—Their Character and Domestic Economy—Their Relations to the Colonists—Indian Alliances—Character of English Intercourse with the Red Men—William Johnson and the Iroquois—Summary of the Situation.

CHAPTER IV.

OUTBREAK OF THE FRENCH AND INDIAN WAR—1755-1756, . 38

European Complications — The Combination against Frederick the Great—The Newcastle Ministry—General Braddock—French Preparations—Demand for Colonial Taxation—The English Regulars and American Militia—Braddock's Advance—The French and Indian Ambuscade—The Battle — Defeat of the Expedition—Acadia—Treatment of the French Farmers—Capture of the French Forts—Dispersion of the Natives—Fort Niagara—Johnson's Successes—Fort William Henry—Plans for Taxing America.

CHAPTER V.

SUCCESSES OF THE FRENCH AND INDIANS—1756-1758, . 52

English Inactivity—Montcalm and the French Leaders—Capture of Oswego by the French—Armstrong ejects the Indians from Kittanning—Winter Warfare—Plan against Louisburg Abandoned—Outrages of Montcalm's Indians—The Massacre at Fort William Henry—Results of Intrigue in Canada—Partisan Activity—Loudon Recalled—Pitt in Power—His Influence and Plans—Amherst, Howe, and Wolfe.

CHAPTER VI.

SUCCESSES OF THE ENGLISH AND AMERICANS—1758-1759, . 62

England and Prussia as Allies—Success of Frederick and Pitt—Influence of Prussian Success in America—Fall of Louisburg — Pitt Arouses American Enthusiasm — Abercrombie before Ticonderoga — Topography — Death of Howe—Montcalm's Preparations—Failure of the Attack—

Retreat of Abercrombie—Recapture of Oswego—Effect of the Success—The Middle Colonies and Forbes's Expedition—Washington and Bouquet—Defeat at Grant's Hill—Illness of Forbes—Weakness of the Garrison at Fort Duquesne—Advance of Washington and Armstrong—Seizure of Fort Duquesne—Pitt's Monument.

CHAPTER VII.

NIAGARA AND QUEBEC—1759, ... 75

Quarrels and Disaffection among the French—Course of the War in Europe—The Height of England's Military Grandeur—Pitt's Plan for the Campaign in America—Wolfe—Enthusiasm in the Colonies—Capture of Niagara—Important Results—Evacuation of Ticonderoga and Crown Point by the French—Futility of Amherst's Campaign—Montcalm at Quebec—Measures of Defence—The English Fleet in the St. Lawrence—Disposition of the Land Forces—French Fire-ships—Desultory Operations during July—Wolfe at the Falls of Montmorency—Defeat of the English—Movements during August—The Plan for Scaling the Heights of Abraham.

CHAPTER VIII.

THE PLAINS OF ABRAHAM—1759-1760, ... 89

Movement of the English—French Precaution—Feints and Alarms—Wolfe's Preparations for Landing—His Presentiment of Death—Wolfe's Cove and the Heights of Abraham—Preparations for Battle—The French Unready—Montcalm Bewildered—The Battle—Death of the two Leaders—Surrender of Quebec—Operations during the Winter—Ste. Foy—Relief of Quebec by the English Fleet—Canada Conquered.

CHAPTER IX.

THE PEACE OF PARIS—1760-1763, ... 99

Affairs in the Southern Colonies—Expedition against the Cherokees—New Territory Opened for Settlement—Indian Discontent—Revolt of Pontiac—Relief of Detroit and

Suppression of the Rebellion—Naval Supremacy of England—The War Continued in Germany—Death of George II.—Accession of George III.—His Character and Policy—Pitt and Frederick the Great—Fall of the Ministry—Bute and the New Tories—Frederick and Russia—England and Spain—The Terms of Peace—Effect of the Seven Years' War on the Continent—Its Character in America and India—Determinative Results in the American Colonies—Its Relation to American Nationality and Independence.

CHAPTER X.

A NEW ISSUE IN CONSTITUTIONAL GOVERNMENT—1760-1762, 116

Disunion between America and England—Their respective Forms of Administration—Political Theories in Vogue—The Terms Provincial and Colonial—Theory of Grenville—Restrictions on American Trade—Practice of the Age—Royal Requisitions—The Plea of Gratitude—Legal Argument for the Taxing Power—Inconsistency of Claim and Conduct—Inadequacy of the English Constitution—The New Question—Writs of Assistance—James Otis and the Spirit of the Constitution—New York and the Appointment of Judges—The same Question Elsewhere.

CHAPTER XI.

THE STAMP ACT—1762-1766, ... 127

The Ministries of Newcastle and Bute—Grenville and Townshend—Ministerial Responsibility—Wilkes and the *North Briton*—General Warrants and the Freedom of the Press—Proposition for a Stamp Act—Prosperity and Education in America—Colonial Unity and the Name American—Failure of Franklin's Protest—Enactment of the Stamp Act—Discussion of its Illegality—Its Reception in America—The Patriots and the Masses—Measures of Nullification—Taxation by Consent of the Governed—Call for a Congress—Significance of the Assembly—Inconsistency of its Memorials—Gadsden's Plea and the First Steps toward Union—Change in New England Opinion—The Rockingham Ministry—Attitude of English Factions—The Repeal and the Declaratory Act.

CONTENTS xv

CHAPTER XII.

CONFLICT OF TWO THEORIES—1766-1768, ... 142

Charles Townshend—The Chatham-Grafton Ministry—Consolidation of the New Toryism—Enforcement of its Policy—The Billeting Act in New York—A New Tariff—The King his own Prime Minister—The Constitutional Crisis—The Attitude of France—Change in Colonial Doctrine—The "Farmer's Letters"—America Indignant—The Colonial Officials—The Circular Letter from Massachusetts—Parliament Demands its Withdrawal—The other Colonies Support its Principle—Outbreak of Armed Resistance in North Carolina—New Orleans, St. Louis, and the New West.

CHAPTER XIII.

THE CONSTITUTIONAL REVOLUTION—1770-1774, . . . 154

Reply to the "Farmer's Letters"—The Colonies United in Purpose—Disorganization of Colonial Government—New York Suggests a Congress—New Opinions in Great Britain—Loyalty in America—The Boston Riots—The Battle on the Alamance—Burning of the Gaspee—Effects of Oppression—Failure of the non-Importation Agreements—Committees of Correspondence—Final Collapse of Colonial Administration — Constitutional Changes in England — Benjamin Franklin—The Hutchinson Letters—Franklin before the Council—His Conduct.

CHAPTER XIV.

RESISTANCE TO OPPRESSION—1773-1774, ... 166

The Tea Tax—Resistance to Importation—Boston Resorts to Force — Lord North Retaliates—The Boston Port Act—Changes in the Massachusetts Charter—The Quebec Act—American Tories and Patriots—Respective Propositions of New York and New England — The "Continental" Movement—Passive Resistance of New England—Movement to Convene a Congress—Alexander Hamilton—Character of the Delegations—Royal Officials Menaced—The Savage to Fight against the Americans—The First Continental Congress—Dramatic Opening—Last Appeal for Justice—Two Assertions of Sovereignty—Significance of the Fight at Point Pleasant.

CHAPTER XV.

THE BEGINNING OF HOSTILITIES—1774-1775, . . . 179

Dissensions in Parliament and Cabinet—Chatham's Plan of Conciliation—Burke the Friend of America—Duplicity of the King—War Measures of the Administration—Return of Franklin—Burke on the Spirit of the Constitution—Effect of the News in America—Approach of the Crisis—The Gathering on Lexington Green—The Conflicts at Lexington and Concord—Retreat of the English—Boston Besieged by the American Farmers—The Colonies Organize for Armed Resistance—Overthrow of the Colonial Governments—Seizure of Ticonderoga—War Measures of Parliament and the King—Attitude of Europe.

CHAPTER XVI.

THE BATTLE OF BUNKER HILL—FEBRUARY-JULY, 1775, . 192

Self-reliance of the Americans—Their Attitude Toward England—Conservative Elements—Patriotic Impulses—The Mecklenburg Declaration—The Second Continental Congress—Its Apparent Inconsistencies—Results of Moderation—The Virginia Burgesses and Lord North's Proposals—George Washington—Appointed Commander-in-Chief—Character of the New England Army—Fortification of Bunker Hill—The Battle—The Result Indecisive—Washington at Cambridge.

CHAPTER XVII.

OVERTHROW OF ROYAL AUTHORITY—1775-1776, . . 203

The Expedition against Canada—Siege of Quebec—Failure of the Campaign—Siege of Boston—The English Withdraw—Bombardment of Norfolk—Overthrow of Royal Govern-

CONTENTS xvii

ment in the South and in New England—Anomalous Situation in the Middle Colonies—Beginnings of United and Independent Action—Paper Money—John Adams and the Conduct of Congress—The First American Flag—Trade Notions of Congress—The Petition to Parliament Rejected—The Americans Proclaimed Rebels—Purchase of Troops by George III.—Congress Petitions the King—Action of the Patriots—" Common-Sense "—Effect on Congress and the Country—Final Overthrow of Royal Authority.

CHAPTER XVIII.

THE MOVEMENT FOR INDEPENDENCE — JANUARY-JUNE, 1776, ... 216

Parliament Declines Redress—The Ministry Proposes Pardon—Danger to English Institutions—The Colonies Temporize—French Agents in America—France Had Two Motives for Interference — Plan of Vergennes — English Strength in New York—Sears and Charles Lee—The City Fortified—North Carolina Tories Routed—The British before Charleston—Bombardment of the City—Success of the Defence — New Commonwealths — Virginia—Debates in Congress—New York Hesitates—Overthrow of the Proprietary Assembly in Pennsylvania.

CHAPTER XIX.

INDEPENDENCE AND CONFEDERATION—JULY-AUGUST, 1776, 227

Congress and the State Governments—Diversity of Opinion—Debate on the Declaration of Independence—Jefferson's Document Adopted—Adams and Witherspoon—Popular Enthusiasm—Character of the Paper—Real Nature of the Confederation—The Appearance of a Separatist Temper—Congress to be Stripped of Power—Conflict between Southern and Northern Opinion—Local Ideas of Independence Expressed in the Articles of Confederation—The Western Lands and True Union—Inefficiency of Congress—Fickleness of the Masses.

CHAPTER XX.

THE LOSS OF NEW YORK CITY—APRIL–DECEMBER, 1776, 238

Three Divisions of the War—Importance of New York City—Arrival of Washington—The System of Defence—The Opposing Forces—The Battle of Long Island—Inefficiency of the American Militia—Evacuation of New York—Encampment on the Bronx River—The Battle of White Plains—Capture of Fort Washington by the British—The American Army in New Jersey—Retreat of Greene—Need of a Regular Army—Treachery of Charles Lee—Congress Authorizes Long Enlistments—Washington's Retreat across New Jersey—His Army Reinforced—His Successful Strategy—Lee Captured by the British—His True Character.

CHAPTER XXI.

TRENTON AND PRINCETON—DECEMBER, 1776, . . . 251

Congress Leaves Philadelphia—The Winter Quarters of the English on the Delaware—Washington's Plan for a Surprise—The Battle of Trenton—Courage and Activity Revived—Preparations to Assume the Offensive—The English March to Trenton—Camp on the Assanpink—Washington's Flank Movement — Battle of Princeton — The Americans at Morristown — The Delaware and Hudson Safe—Plans for Reorganizing the Army—Thwarted by Localism—Timidity of the States—American Success Justified the American Revolt.

CHAPTER XXII.

BENNINGTON AND THE BRANDYWINE — JANUARY–SEPTEMBER, 1777, ... 262

Secret Assistance from France—Franklin in Paris—French Volunteers—Lafayette and De Kalb—Success of Franklin's Negotiations—England and the Coming Campaign—Expedition of the Howes against Philadelphia—Preliminary Movements in New Jersey—Schuyler and Gates in the North—Danbury and Sag Harbor—Burgoyne Takes Ticonderoga—Indian Barbarities—Increase of Schuyler's

CONTENTS xix

Force—Fort Stanwix—The Fight at Oriskany—Stark at Bennington—The English Defeated—General Howe at Elkton—Washington's Army—The Battle on the Brandywine—Loss of Philadelphia—The Americans at Germantown.

CHAPTER XXIII.

SARATOGA AND THE FRENCH ALLIANCE — SEPTEMBER-DECEMBER, 1777, ... 275

The Army of the North—Its Position near Stillwater—The First Day's Battle at Bemis's Heights—The English Pass the Highlands—The Battle of Freeman's Farm—Retreat of Burgoyne—Surrender at Saratoga—The Battle of Germantown—Affairs near Philadelphia — Summary of the Year's Campaign—Congress and the Cabal— Continental Money and Valley Forge—Prosperity of the People—Success of the State Governments—Weakness of the Confederation—The Public Finances—The News of Saratoga in France—The Compact of Friendship.

CHAPTER XXIV.

RECOGNITION OF AMERICAN INDEPENDENCE — JANUARY-JULY, 1778, ... 288

National Sentiment in England—The Rockingham Whigs—British Supremacy Endangered—Conciliation as a Political Expedient—Proposal to Yield Independence—Public Reception of Franklin at the French Court—Congress Ratifies the Treaty—Collapse of the Cabal—Reorganization of the Army — Conciliation Offered — Failure of the Mission—The English Abandon Philadelphia — Their March Impeded—The Battle of Monmouth—Incidents of the Fight—The Massacre of Wyoming.

CHAPTER XXV.

EVIL EFFECTS OF THE FOREIGN ALLIANCE—1778-1779, . 300

Arnold at Philadelphia—The Government Returns—D'Estaing's Failures—The Expedition Against Newport—Situation at the North — Humiliation of the Confederacy—

Straits of the English Ministry—Ambitions and Fears of
Spain—Spain Joins the Alliance—Western Settlement—
Clark's Expedition—Louisiana and Florida Lost to England—France Expects Peace — Movements of Clinton—
Stony Point—Sullivan's Campaign Against the Iroquois—
The Fiasco of Castine—The Exploits of Paul Jones.

CHAPTER XXVI.

CAMDEN AND KING'S MOUNTAIN—1779-1780, . . . 312

Hostilities in Georgia—English Authority Re-established—
Lincoln and D'Estaing Fail before Savannah—Proposition to Arm Slaves—Fall of Charleston—English Policy
in the South—Measures Taken by Cornwallis—The Reign
of Terror in South Carolina—The Patriots Prepare for
Resistance—Gates Defeated at Camden—The Frontiersmen Meet the Crisis—Battle of King's Mountain—Moral
Effect and Character of the Victory—Greene Relieves
Gates—Bankruptcy and Mutiny in the North—Failure of
Plans for Co-operation between Washington and D'Estaing
—Arrival of Rochambeau.

CHAPTER XXVII.

THE SOUTHERN INVASION REPELLED—1780-1781, . . 325

Washington Reprimands Arnold — Arrest of André — His
Character and Guilt—Insubordination in the Army—Robert Morris and the Finances of the Confederation—Arnold
in Virginia—Lafayette and Steuben—Greene Creates a
Southern Army—Morgan at Cowpens—Greene's Retreat—
The Forces at Guilford—Cornwallis Victorious but Thwarted—Groton Heights—Effect of Rawdon's Cruelties—Greene
Marches Southward—Defeat at Hobkirk's Hill—Sumter
and Marion—Battle of Eutaw Springs.

CHAPTER XXVIII.

YORKTOWN—1781, ... 337

Plans of Cornwallis—His Advance against Lafayette—The
Pursuit and Retreat—Steuben Creates an Army—Disagree-

CONTENTS xxi

PAGE

ment between Clinton and Cornwallis—Position of the Latter at Yorktown—Arrival of the French Fleet under De Grasse—Washington's Plans—Sectional Feeling among the States—Events in the North during 1780—Conferences of Washington and Rochambeau—Clinton Expects an Attack on New York—The Combined Armies March Southward —The Threatened Mutiny at Philadelphia—Defeat of the English Fleet in the Chesapeake—Investment of Yorktown—Cornwallis Surrenders—Disposition of the American and French Forces—Closing Events of the War.

CHAPTER XXIX.

THE PEACE OF VERSAILLES—1782-1783, ... 348

American Independence and European Politics—England and the Bourbon Powers—International Law—Blockade and Contraband—The Continental Neutrals—The Armed Neutrality—William Lee and the Amsterdam Proposal— Position of the Netherlands—The News of Yorktown— Fall of the North Ministry—State of English Parties—The Rockingham Ministry—American Peace Commissioners— The Terms proposed by Congress—Oswald and Franklin— Grenville and Vergennes—Cross Purposes in the Negotiation—The Shelburne Ministry—Position of Jay and Adams —Franklin's Attitude—The Wishes of Vergennes—Secret Mission of Rayneval—Jay's Proposals—Final Negotiations —Character of the Treaty—The General Pacification— Fall of Shelburne's Ministry—The Coalition Ministry— Final Ratification of the Treaty.

CHAPTER XXX.

WEAKNESS AND STRENGTH, ... 370

American Independence and European Politics—The Former and Later Generations—The American Navy—Its Achievement—Its Gradual Diminution—Privateering—Morris and the Finances—Expense of the War—Congress and the Army—Washington Allays the Discontent—The Army Disbanded—The Cincinnati—Washington's Political Insight

—The Southern States —The Middle States—Their Occupations and Educational Institutions—New England—Massachusetts and Virginia—Character of the Revolution—Effect on Ecclesiastical Movements—Slavery—Tendencies toward Union in State Administrations—Importance of the New Forces—Literature of the Revolution—Signs of a National Spirit—Political Writers—The New Society.

APPENDIX

I. Chronological Table, ... 380
II. Bibliography, ... 393

INDEX, ... 397

LIST OF MAPS

1. The Territory Now in the United States, As it was in 1756, ... *Frontispiece*
2. The Northern Colonies and Canada, Illustrating the French and Indian War, *Page* 38
3. The Northern Colonies, Illustrating the First Half of the Revolution, . . " 179
4. The Southern Colonies, Illustrating the Second Half of the Revolution, . " 312
5. The Territory Now in the United States, as it was after the Peace of 1783, ... *At the end of volume*

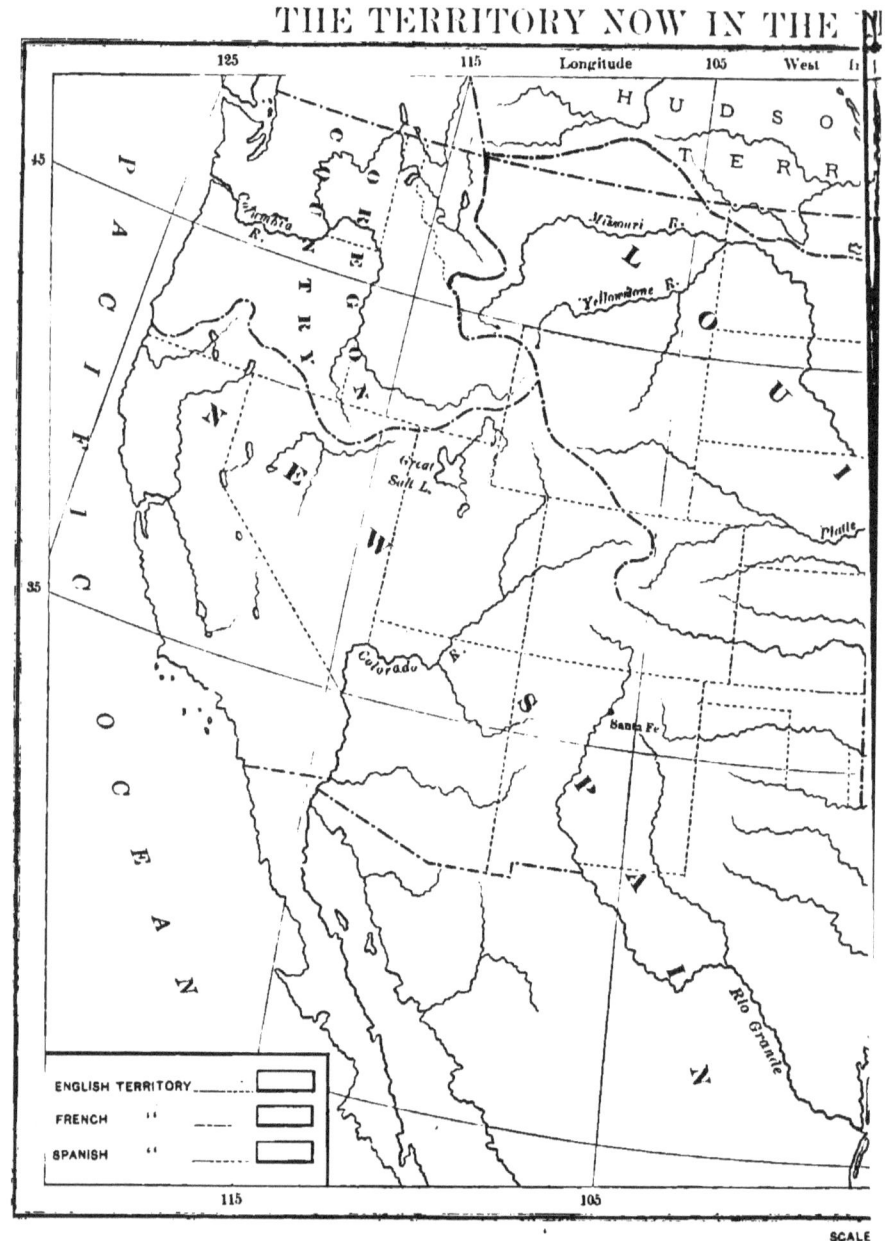

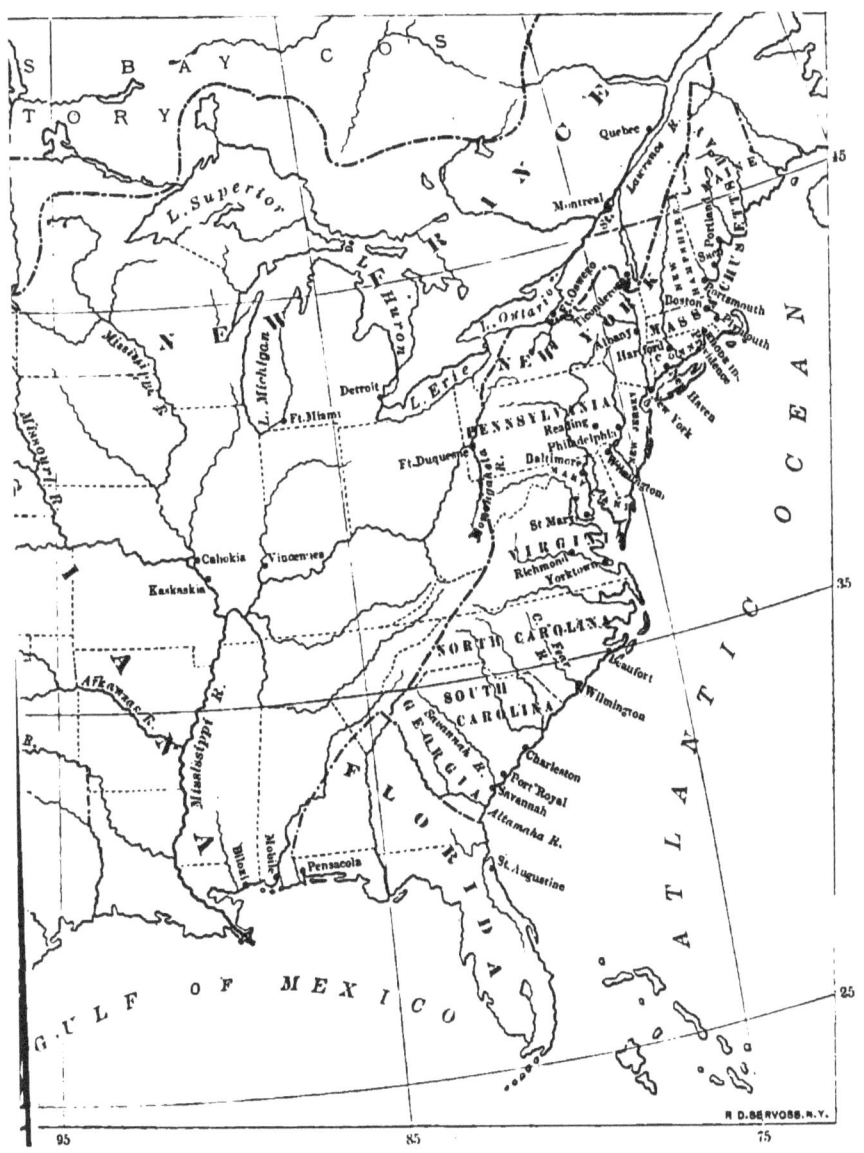

THE

FRENCH WAR AND THE REVOLUTION

CHAPTER I.

THE ENGLISH PEOPLE IN THE EIGHTEENTH CENTURY—
1688-1756

Nature of the European Struggle—Position of the Powers—Changes in English Politics—Party Struggles—Gains and Losses in Public Morality—Pitt and Wesley—Influences in America—Character of Colonial Civilization—The Americans as Political and Religious Dissenters—Dangerous Elements in the Population.

THE interval between the English and the American Revolution was full of intellectual ferment and military activity both throughout Europe itself and in the colonial settlements of her various political divisions. Absolute monarchy as a system of government had done its work in the establishment of powerful and permanent nationalities. Boundary lines, however, were as yet unsettled even at home, the relations of the masses to their rulers were undetermined, and the warfare of the time had for its object the decision of a double question, that of political theory and actual control both on the continent and beyond the seas. A few great men understood that free institutions and a territorial expansion which might be more than ephemeral, were corollaries one of the other. In the great Euro-

Nature of the European struggle.

pean struggle for religious liberty the leaders of the opposing forces had been William the Silent and Philip II., of Spain. In this renewal of European hostilities the forces arrayed on either side were substantially the same. Now, however, the commander for absolutism was the King of France, while the general of those who stood for political liberty and who had ascended the English throne by the choice of the English parliament as a protest against tyranny in both religion and politics was a lineal descendant of William the Silent.

By the middle of the eighteenth century the contest had seen many phases, none of them conclusive for any of the parties engaged. The peace of Ryswick, in 1697, effected little change as regards sovereignty, although it gave Strasburg to France; but it secured a great moral victory for England by compelling Louis XIV. to acknowledge the constitutional title of William III. as King, and of Anne as his successor. The peace of Utrecht, in 1713, enforced a renewal of the broken promise, definitely confirmed both for the Continent and for the disaffected at home the Protestant succession to the English throne, established the great power of Prussia as a Protestant kingdom, and wrenched from France Nova Scotia, Newfoundland, and the Hudson's Bay territory. It also prevented the union of France and Spain under an absolute government, and gave Gibraltar to England. The peace of Aix-la-Chapelle, in 1748, was a sorry affair. Avowedly it was to turn Prussia into a great power by giving her Silesia, and to sustain Maria Theresa on the Austrian throne, restoring all conquests to those who had held them by the peace of Utrecht. In reality it was but an armistice which gave the contesting powers an opportunity to re-arrange in secret diplomacy their dynastic alliances, so that with recruited strength they might once more renew the mortal combat.

Position of the powers.

In all these years English politics had steadily developed on liberal lines. At the close of the Revolution there was but one supreme power in the state, and that was resident in Parliament. Still further, it was the House of Commons which was now predominant, its members being elected by a very limited suffrage, and representing the three interests of the landed aristocracy, the powerful trading classes, and the equally influential body of lawyers who were the corner-stone of the new system. The powers of the crown were so limited by the Bill of Rights that government was carried on by party organization, and except in a few comparatively short periods the Whigs were in control. The new extra-legal plan of cabinets led by a prime minister with undefined but commanding authority, had been fully developed and put into effective operation. The judicial system had been emancipated by making the tenure of office dependent, not on the good will of the crown, but on the good behavior of the incumbent; free speech was assured, the censorship of the press abolished, and a measure of religious liberty had been guaranteed in the authorization of assemblies for worship outside of the organization of the Anglican Church, although none but its conforming members might hold office. By the Act of Union the legislatures of the two kingdoms of Scotland and England had been amalgamated, and the nations themselves welded into one.

Change in English politics.

The aim of William was to destroy the military supremacy of France. But the Whigs carried on the costly continental wars with the determination of establishing their domestic policy, and sometimes forgot the dictates of prudence in refusing advantageous terms of peace. Thus, out of elements which were living though dormant, was formed again the Tory party. But they in turn were intoxicated by power, and

Party struggles.

in the prosecution of a domestic policy subversive of all that the Revolution had accomplished lost their hold upon the nation. It was therefore an unpartisan and national movement which by the Act of Settlement confirmed the Protestant succession and brought the House of Hanover to the throne. George I. at once gave his confidence to the Whigs. The extreme Tories promptly turned to the support of the desperate Stewart cause, and thereby not only abandoned party lines, but became virtual rebels and outlaws, leaving the Whigs in undisputed predominance for over thirty years.

The time was productive of some good and much evil to England. Two attempts were made to bring back the Pretender, but they failed, partly through the indifference of his professed supporters. The nation then understood that absolutism was forever ended in England, and turned its attention to commerce, trade, and the discussion of constitutional questions. Walpole's long ministry and his peace policy were to the people as the calm of the winter solstice to the fabled halcyon, a time of building, refitting, and propagating. In this period the political expedients of the past grew into permanent institutions; the expression of the popular will, which had been regarded as the extreme remedy for public evils, became more and more frequent and was found to be, not an exceptional and violent antidote, but an excellent and regulative habit. But, on the other hand, public morality fell lower than ever before or since, and dragged with it the conduct of individuals. Statesmen found that in following the line of least resistance, the easiest system of parliamentary tactics was the use of bribes. Walpole, Pelham, and Newcastle seem to have forgotten the existence of public virtue, and practised corruption with an effrontery which the plain people among their contemporaries

Gains and losses in public morality.

were willing to accept for the boldness of innocence. It will be remembered also that this was a so-called age of reason. In the reaction against the Puritan reformation, many felt that the only counterpoise to the authority of the infallible Bible was in the authority of the human reason. Every ancient belief was thrown into the crucible. Religion and unbelief alike came forth dispassionate and unsympathetic. Loftier minds contented themselves with entertaining but fruitless speculation, while the lowly fell into timid formalism and carelessness. It was the day of the bluff and tipsy squire, of the fox-hunting parson, of general vulgarity and coarseness, of unimaginative materialism and mere expediency in high places. By the middle of the century the state of the nation was mirrored in the inglorious ministry of Henry Pelham, in the utter insignificance of England, in the moderatism of the established Kirk of Scotland, in the lukewarmness of the national Church of England, in the feebleness of the army which a little later was displayed by the poltroonery of the Duke of Cumberland at Closter-Seven, in the cowardly inactivity of Abercrombie in America, in the supineness of Byng at Minorca.

But behind the mask of political baseness, of unmilitary conduct, and of apparent impiety was another national spirit. The emotions and imagination of the people could not forever smoulder without fuel; on the contrary, they grew in intensity, burned for an object, and one was found. The great outburst of earnestness which followed is connected with the name of Pitt in politics, and with that of Wesley in religion; and striking parallels have been drawn, although in matters of detail the contrasts are far more pointed than the resemblances. The religious revival was begun by preaching, appealed to the emotional nature, and in the end permeated the entire nation. The extreme form

<small>Pitt and Wesley.</small>

which was typical of the whole was Methodism, a conception of religious life based on conviction of sin, conversion to a higher life, and the realization through careful living of the Creator's image in each of his human creatures. To secure and confirm the converted sinner an organization was devised so perfectly adapted to its end that the sect thus initiated is now the most numerous and one of the most fervent in the Reformed Church. In a certain sense there was also a political revival which addressed and awakened the emotions. Pitt fired the imagination of men, appealed to their patriotism and prejudice by his scorn of Hanoverian influence in English politics, swayed their minds by eloquence, inspired them with trust, and with pardonable ostentation gave them in his own person an example of personal purity and public virtue. Thus was moulded that important element which has been, down to our own time, the savor of English life, distasteful often to outsiders in its extremes of talk and conduct, but correcting the richness of English luxury and the heaviness of British conservatism. As yet it was neither coherent nor consistent. Pitt's first ministry was too short and unsuccessful to subvert old parties or form new ones, and for a long weary while he and his followers fought under the Whig banner, beside comrades who still used the old disreputable weapons.

There was therefore a real liberal party in England itself, characterized by tolerance and acuteness, concerned for the sanctity of those constitutional principles which had been reasserted in the Revolution, and sympathizing with the dumb yearnings of the people for emancipation and self-government as they grew more intense and struggled for utterance. But its adherents were far less numerous and influential in England than they were proportionately among the English in America. We use the designation broadly but advisedly, because

<small>Influences in America.</small>

although there were people of other nationalities in the colonies who left their mark in many a virtuous habit or curious idiosyncrasy upon their respective neighborhoods, yet it was nevertheless a fairly homogeneous population of about a million and a half, bearing a civilization thoroughly English as that word was used in Great Britain, which dwelt along the Atlantic seaboard from the Bay of Fundy to Florida. The initial differences between the colonies had been very great, some of them still survive in unfortunate completeness. But, politically at least, they were less distinct from each other than could have been foreseen by their founders, and in their theory of government they were vastly more congruous than the various schools of Englishmen at home. The widest separation was in ecclesiastical matters, for every form of polity known in England had been transplanted to America in the interest of religious liberty, and the sects being free from state control, had under the voluntary system developed and retained a strong individuality each for itself. But wide as it was, it was not so wide as the social gulf which the insular prejudice of the English aristocracy had opened between themselves and their relations beyond the sea. Nor was it comparable to the divorce of sentiment and interest caused by the navigation acts and the enforced monopoly of the slave-trade. In spite, therefore, of the division in America between Whig and Tory, Calvinist and Arminian, Puritan, Presbyterian, and Churchman, there existed quite as strong a basis for national unity on one side of the Atlantic as on the other.

But while there was another England in America, it was by no means the same England as that in Britain. The very presence of the colonists on foreign soil was in great measure a protest. They were still monarchical in theory, but their king was three thousand miles away, they obeyed laws of their own making, the Test Act had no validity in their commonwealths, and their immediate allegiance was to a taxing power instituted and controlled by themselves. Neither feudalism nor priestcraft had made the voyage, and would have been stifled in the air of the wilderness if they had. Labor too was free; no mediæval craft or guild could survive in a society where every man's labor was directed to what he must do, and not to what he wished to do or could do. Being in the main of Germanic blood, whether from England, Germany, Holland, or Scandinavia, they were likewise of one religion. They were Christians in the highest sense of that word, for the sensualism of the school of Locke and the deism of Shaftesbury had left them untouched. They had crossed the seas for a principle which they still cherished as their most valuable possession, and their lives were guided and fashioned under the influence of ideals which had long since disappeared or changed among their kinsfolk. Excepting the few Roman Catholics in Maryland, the colonists belonged almost exclusively to the Reformed Church. They held the Calvinistic confessions of Scotch or English Presbyterianism and Puritanism, of the Huguenots, or of Holland, adhered to the Lutheran creeds of Scandinavia and Germany, or to the comprehension of Calvinism and Arminianism in the Episcopalians and Methodists. One central thesis they all maintained, the right of private judgment, of freedom in belief, of liberty in practice.

They were capable, moreover, of holding such a doctrine. Common minds could neither apprehend it nor practise it. But the colonists at the middle and close of the eighteenth century were either the children of religious and political refugees, or themselves exiles for conscience sake. Their intellects having been sharpened in theological discussion and trained by the study of the

Scriptures in the vernacular, their language was consequently moulded by the eloquent and adequate diction of the King James translation. Their courage had been hardened by suffering, whether in Ulster or in Salzburg, and the enterprise of transatlantic colonization was not then, as now, a matter of a few dollars and still fewer days. *The Americans as political and religious dissenters.* It may at once be granted that they were even yet self-willed and intolerant, but the other older world had lately seen the bigotry of the Sacheverell incident, and was yet to see the worse fanaticism of the Gordon riots. The very limitations of the American settlers constituted an important virtue. Energy in action is not the quality of those who are open to all influences and sensitive to all shades of thought. It is the man with an eye single to one end who displays promptness and tenacity of purpose.

In 1688 there were about 200,000 Europeans under the twelve colonial governments; in 1755 they had, by natural increase and an ever-growing immigration, risen to about 1,425,000. While most of the new-comers were of the same sturdy character as the original colonists, there was also a proportionate increase in the refuse element. With the ever-increasing prosperity of the plantations, adventurers in greater numbers were attracted to our shores, many of those turbulent men who haunt European seaports were kidnapped and sold in America for menial service, convicts were encouraged to cross the seas and trouble the criminal courts of Europe no more, and many did so; but above all, of the more than two million negroes carried in English slave-ships to all the American colonies, including the West Indies, during the period from 1680 to 1766, it is likely that in the year 1755 not less than 260,000 were in the English colonies of the North American continent. *Dangerous elements in the population.*

CHAPTER II.

INSTITUTIONS OF THE ENGLISH COLONIES—1688-1756

Influence of the English Revolution—The Colonial Governments—Political and Legal Speculation—Political Theory—Contemporary Speculation in Europe—The Free-thinkers of England—Roman Catholic Disabilities — Scotch-Irish Presbyterians—Irish Emigration to the Continent—Influence of the Protestant Irish in America—Roman Catholics in America—Causes of American Loyalty—France in America—The Fisheries Question.

THE English Revolution had been productive of most important results in this large number of men subject to the English crown. At home the people had not carefully analyzed the underlying theory of that event. There had been no demand for liberty and equality abstractedly considered, the watchword, if there was one, could better be phrased as liberty and property, or better yet, liberty and privilege. The privileges of the aristocracy and the great merchants were at stake, and the weakness of the Stewarts had lain in their attack on private property. In America there was neither social nor mercantile privilege, but there was the same jealousy as to property and taxation. The King now stood not for the invasion of free charters, but for English rights and liberties. His vetoes of certain acts were not received in the old rebellious spirit. Massachusetts got a new charter, which partly satisfied her people ; Rhode Island and Connecticut received again the old ones as they had been before the infractions of James II.

Influence of the English revolution.

South Carolina representatives banished Colleton, the proprietary governor. Virginia restored the democratic institutions which Culpepper and Effingham had threatened, for her first assembly after William and Mary ascended the throne elected a treasurer subject only to its own orders; in Maryland an armed gathering proclaimed King William, and a convention which had been summoned for the defence of Protestantism assumed the government.

So it came about that the distinctions between the crown, charter, and proprietary colonies had been reduced to a minimum. The freemen had all the power under the charters; in the crown colonies there was a royal governor, a council, and a judiciary appointed by the crown, but the assembly was elected by the freemen, and as the members of the council were chosen from the chief citizens of the colony, the government of the crown colonies was almost as popular and free as that of those which had a charter. The proprietaries in Pennsylvania, Delaware, Maryland, and Carolina nominated governors with the right and duty of calling assemblies to make laws. These assemblies were elected by the people, and in Maryland, under a charter granted by the proprietary, chose the governor. The general direction of changes was theoretically to give greater control to the crown, which was understood for a long time to be virtually in commission to parliament and the ministry. At first there was some interference in the assertion of royal sovereignty, but both Walpole and Newcastle treated the American colonies with a happy neglect under which they came to regard themselves as subject to the crown, but virtually independent in legislation and taxation. The franchise was ordinarily limited to property owners, especially those who were landed proprietors. The initiative was with the people, the judiciary had much the same function as

The colonial governments.

under the English constitution, and while, presumptively, administration was in the hands of the crown, yet, because in all cases some executive officers were elective, and in some cases all of them, the conduct of affairs was in reality nearly as popular as legislation.

The American colonists were also much given to political and legal speculation. Being a religious people trained in the principles of the Reformation, they were educated from earliest childhood to examine and discuss the most abstruse and difficult questions of theology, and to give a reason for the faith they held. Their ecclesiastical affairs were conducted in the popular assembly of the congregation, or in representative bodies with supreme control, and the public interest in such gatherings was even more intense then than now. In New England, at least, local government was carried on by town meetings, in which every free man had the right of discussion and a vote. In a system so purely democratic the speaker is the man of influence. Hence the leaders, many of them lawyers, were the educated men, and the people were accustomed to hear and weigh both evidence and argument, and to decide after deliberating on questions put with nice discrimination and passionate fervor.

Political and legal speculation.

In the field of political theory, therefore, the results of the English Revolution were more definite even than in the matter of political forms. The convention parliament which declared the flight of James II. to be abdication, and called William and Mary to the throne, sat without royal or executive sanction, stated the existence of an original contract between the monarch and his subjects and held the king responsible. Kingship or the supreme executive, therefore, is not an hereditary possession, but an office resting on the consent of the governed; it is a trust which can be and is

Political theory.

INSTITUTIONS OF THE ENGLISH COLONIES 13

destroyed by unfaithfulness; the legitimacy of a government depends on its success in securing the general welfare; questions of taxation and the public credit can be decided only by those who pay; if the aristocracy and merchants assert and secure these privileges, why not all other English people; if vested rights are sacred in England, so are those of the colonial legislatures and the people whom they represent. The confirmation of such views in America was easy because of the absence of tradition, which was as yet so strong in England.

Sentiments like these were, of course, not peculiar to colonial radicals, nor were they entirely due to the English Revolution. The age was one of intellectual ferment. All Europe had felt the influences of the Reformation. Prussia was rapidly coming forward under Frederick the Great as the exponent of religious and philosophical liberty, giving also complete civil rights to Roman Catholics; Catherine of Russia perverted the new tenets into an apology for hideous license. Joseph II., of Austria, was a reformer in his way, and his partial, though ill-starred, success, showed that even in the stormy days of his mother, liberalism had been abroad in Austria. Philip V., of Spain, stupid and obdurate as he was, made use of the flowing tide to set limits to papal power and overawe the arrogance of the Jesuits, while introducing many administrative reforms and softening the criminal law. In France there was every degree of liberty and license of opinion, while an extreme scepticism was laying the mine to destroy eventually all existing institutions. As the authority of the Church in matters of faith and behavior faded, the belief in all authority, even political, disappeared in the same mist. Voltaire alone sought to set his scoffing philosophy as a prop to monarchy; cringing and fawning before George II. and Lewis XV.,

[margin: Contemporary speculation in Europe.]

14 THE FRENCH WAR AND THE REVOLUTION

he saw in the former a sage and hero ruling the universe by his virtues, the latter he designated a Trajan to whom not the least infamous of his three mistresses was an Egeria. There was also a brotherhood possessing just views and a fine philosophical spirit of inquiry which chose the middle path, finding truth by investigation and justice in moderation. No more brilliant galaxy sparkles in any literary sphere than that composed of Montesquieu, Quesnay, and Turgot. But while their influence was potent in England and America, a more baleful star controlled the thought of the French masses. Rousseau was an uncontrolled tempest with passionate, ignorant, but eloquent zeal; he painted in vivid colors the impotence of a decayed past, the hopelessness and despair of the present, and then declared himself the prophet of a new dispensation, that of nature, the oracle of a new era, that of the people. The social compact, popular sovereignty, the renovation of society from the lowest stratum, these were his engaging and seductive teachings. But he forgot the personal worth of man in the exaltation of men; civil power with him was a religion, dissenters were to be killed or banished, revolution must be a devastation, the new democracy a despotism. Unfortunately there were a few in America who also listened to his siren voice and laid up his teachings in their hearts to work mischief, small indeed, but yet, at a critical moment, mischief.

Even in England itself there was a movement akin to that on the Continent. Free-thinkers of every shade had sought a historic confirmation of their views in the English Revolution and its consequences. A just or perverted interpretation of English institutions was the stock in trade of every political philosopher, and most felt that for a rounded system the metaphysic and theology of the past must also

The free-thinkers of England.

be denied or replaced. The English deists attacked the Bible and Christianity as part of a worn-out system. Locke converted thought into substance, Hartley held the soul to be flesh and blood, and others followed Hume in reducing the sensuous theory of knowledge to an absurdity in the conclusion of nescience. They had their school largely among the Great, so called, but a conservative and loyal devotion to their old institutions in church and state characterized the people, both English and Scotch, and prevented the general spread of radical views. Nor was America as yet directly affected by them. Indirectly, however, a work was accomplished of vital importance to the political and religious feeling of the colonists. Materialism is always the last worn-out phase of a philosophical epoch, and with intellectual apathy there is always physical inactivity. The harvest of free institutions raised by the events of 1688 was reaped in both England and Scotland. But in Ireland what gleanings there were had been gathered by the Anglican establishment, while the Irish themselves were, through the indifference of the English ruling classes, thrown into even lower depths than those into which the conquests of Cromwell had cast them.

Generations of oppression had numbed all enterprise in the Roman Catholic inhabitants of Ireland, and if it had been otherwise the very intensity of Protestant feeling in England would have made it impossible for them to secure the religious liberty which the Scotch had wrung from the sister kingdom. No one but members of the English establishment could hold office under the Test Act, and to one-tenth of the population was thereby entrusted the entire control of government. Their methods were identical with those by which the landed gentry of England ruled at home. Boroughs were so constituted and the people

_{Roman Catholic disabilities.}

so overawed, that the great proprietors were able to nominate two-thirds of its members to the Irish House of Commons. It was the least of the disabilities of Roman Catholics that they were disfranchised. The truth sounds to us as if it must be a lying fiction. But it is a fact that, among many other outrages, they were disbarred in courts of law and thus hampered in the enjoyment of civil rights; that they were forbidden to hold even the lowest office of trust or profit, and thus robbed of possible influence; that they were so restricted in trade and manufactures as to quench all enterprise and prevent the creation of a powerful mercantile class. If a priest married a Romanist to a Protestant he was to be hanged; for a Roman Catholic to teach was felony; to seek an education abroad subjected all concerned to forfeiture of land and goods. The training of priests, and religious worship according to the Roman rite, were subject to painful and disgraceful restrictions. Since the beginning of English control, six-sevenths of the land had come into the possession of landlords representing a foreign and despotic civilization. The antipathy to them felt by their tenants created a system of oppression and extortion for the collection of rents. None but a Protestant might purchase land, or lease it, or lend money on a mortgage. If the oldest son were a Protestant he inherited the entire landed estate of his father, otherwise it was equally divided. Catholic children could have only a Protestant guardian. It is impossible to exaggerate the shamefulness of English misrule in Ireland in the middle of the eighteenth century.

There was another class in Ireland, about equal in number to the ruling oligarchy, which fared only a little better than the Roman Catholic natives. Under James I. six counties of Ulster had escheated to the crown and were settled by Scotch Pres-

Scotch-Irish Presbyterians.

byterians. This settlement had steadily grown in numbers and importance. Its loyalty had been intense until under Queen Anne. By the influence of the Episcopalians, who then began to feel stronger and more independent, a statute was enacted, the notorious Test Act, which forbade them to hold any magistracy or engage in the public service unless they should receive the sacraments according to the English rite. Their business enterprise was limited in the most harassing way. The restriction put by Parliament on the sale and manufacture of wool, ruined the most promising industry of Ireland ; her merchants were also shut off from the colonial trade, and as the Presbyterians were chiefly farmers, their prosperity was diminished almost to the vanishing point. Their temper would, however, brook no tyranny. In a foreign land they had cherished the traditions of their race, and were in their exile more tenacious of the doctrine and system of Calvin and Knox than their co-religionists in Scotland. Their church organization was quite as perfect as that of the Kirk, and more active, because of the defiant attitude it was compelled to assume toward the High Church establishment which touched them at every point because the Toleration Act had not been enacted for Ireland. They were unlike the Roman Catholics in that they could and did openly and regularly celebrate their sacraments, perform their worship, and discharge all ecclesiastical functions at marriage and death. Their judicatories, too, sat regularly and transacted their business successfully. The ministers received also a kind of legal recognition in the Regium Donum, which was a pittance of twelve hundred pounds sterling per annum. But a large minority, if not a majority, of the Scotch-Irish resembled the Roman Catholics in one vital point, a bitter hatred of the British Government.

One and the same door of escape was open to the better and more energetic men of both sorts, and they used it in enormous numbers. The Roman Catholics naturally emigrated to lands where their own confession was dominant, and in France, Spain, Austria, and even in Russia, the number of Milesian names distinguished in the public service attests the superb qualities of intellect, endurance, and enterprise with which their owners were endowed. They were alike famous in church and state, illustrious in the chancery and at the bar. In Russia there were Browne and Lacy; in France, Clare, Dillon, Tyrconnel, and Lally; in Austria, Browne, Maguire, Lacy, Nugent, and O'Donnell; in Spain, O'Mahony, O'Donnell, O'Gara, and Bowles. One wonders which is the more eminent fact: the natural leaders of a people so small and oppressed as the Irish overcoming all the disadvantages of alienage, and acquiring distinction in the great nations of Europe; or a people deprived of its finest minds, retaining its individuality and institutions almost intact under a misrule the aim of which was annihilation.

[Sidenote: Irish emigration to the Continent.]

A few Protestants also went to Roman Catholic lands, notably to France, and a few settled in Germany, but by far the largest number followed the lines of newly awakened Scotch enterprise. The American commerce of Glasgow had been created by the Union, but it was already enormous. It was estimated that for some years after the famines of 1740 and 1741, twelve thousand persons annually left Ulster alone in Scotch ships, while, as late as 1773, as many as half that number left Irish ports each year for the West Indies and the North American continent. Virginia, Carolina, and Georgia took the largest number, although in Pennsylvania they eventually became one of three foremost elements in the population, and

[Sidenote: Influence of the Protestant Irish in America.]

many important districts of New England were exclusively settled by them. On every side they disseminated their views of the relation between the civil magistrate and the Church, their hatred of oppression, and their particular indignation with the English Government as they knew it. They quickly displayed an aptitude for settlement, for public life, and for fighting when it was necessary. Throughout the latter half of the eighteenth century they were one of the most important formative influences in colonial society—an influence which was, it is needless to say, distinctly antagonistic to interference by Parliament.

From the very beginning there had been a spirit of intolerance to all Roman Catholics in every colony except three : Maryland, Pennsylvania, and New Jersey. In the latter colony they were granted civil and religious rights, but were not permitted to perform the duties of citizenship. In Maryland they had shown a spirit of the largest tolerance to the Protestants. Although the administration was in their hands they were in a minority, and the spirit of the colony had always been strongly for religious liberty. In 1689 the Association for the Defence of the Protestant Religion seized the political power, and for a short time persecuted the Roman Catholics. Two years later a royal governor was appointed and the Church of England established by law, but their condition was not ameliorated. In New York the laws against them were most harsh. Taking the population of the colonies as a whole, the Roman Catholics were comparatively very few in number, their power slight, and it was asserted that where they could, they instigated the Jesuits to strengthen French influence with the Indians. The charge had little or no foundation in fact. [margin: Roman Catholics in America.]

And yet the colonists were loyal Englishmen. Such

discontent as there was smouldered beneath the surface and diminished in intensity as its causes lost directness through distance from their source. The prosperity of the people was unexampled, the subjugation of a rich land which, though a wilderness, yielded ample returns to every exertion, gave abundant outlet to all their energies; the more ardent spirits had ample scope for enterprise in exploration and amid the dangers of pioneer life. For, above all other considerations one was ever present: the existence of the aborigines on every side, and on two sides, to the north and west, of a civilization apparently in league with the savage, and hostile in every element to the democratic institutions most cherished in the continental colonies of the English crown.

Causes of American loyalty.

The unknowable factor in their destinies was the immediate neighborhood, both in Canada and in the valley of the Mississippi, of the power which still stood in Europe for mediævalism and despotism, and which would, if successful in America, perpetuate a system of society hostile to their development and their destiny. Another France was at their door menacing their industrial and social empire, and it was not unnatural that the centuries of English and French rivalry should be recalled to inspire the feeling that they were the England, as Canada was the France, of America. On this side, moreover, there was between the two no natural barrier of ocean, narrow or otherwise. They were aspirants for the same continent with no stormy arm of the sea to keep them apart. Physical causes were not conspicuous in the evident separation of two nationalities with distinct territories and different tasks. On the contrary, the conformation of the continent and its adjacent seas but served to make the conflict of interests more desperate.

France in America.

INSTITUTIONS OF THE ENGLISH COLONIES 21

⌈The fisheries on the high seas near Newfoundland, in the Gulf of St. Lawrence, and about the eastward peninsulas and islands, ⌈were of great importance, first in the actual value of the fish caught, and second, to a still higher degree, in the practice of seamanship secured to those who engaged in them.⌋ There never was a question as to the right of fishing in the high seas, but it was held that the fisheries within the limit of territorial waters belonged to the power which held the shore. Even now certain questions in international law as to capes, headlands, and the included waters, are open; in those days the men of New England had, unforbidden and for generations, pursued their calling in the great expanse of waters, itself an inland sea, where the St. Lawrence debouches into the Atlantic; they felt themselves, therefore, to have a prescriptive right in waters not a portion, according to our modern definition, of the high seas; but the right was even then disputed. The question, in many of its forms and consequences, is still a subject of international negotiation, and is so difficult and nice that it sometimes threatens the peace of the world. At the time of our narrative the contention lay between the French and English in America; after our independence the United States and England were chiefly concerned. It is a curious instance of the return of an old historic phase, that English colonies and France have lately been once more the parties in interest.

The fisheries question.

CHAPTER III.

THE ENGLISH AND FRENCH IN NORTH AMERICA—
1688-1756

The Mississippi Valley—French Possessions and Ambitions—Continental Lines of Communication—Contrast between the Strength and Aims of England and France—Divergent Institutions of the Two Peoples—The Conflict to be Decided in America—Preparatory Negotiations and Measures—The Aborigines of the South—The Algonquins and Iroquois—Their Institutions and Religion—Their Character and Domestic Economy—Their Relations to the Colonists—Indian Alliances—Character of English Intercourse with the Red Men—William Johnson and the Iroquois—Summary of the Situation.

GEOGRAPHICAL influences and physical causes in general are too often over-estimated in determining political and other moral results. But it is impossible to understand the course of American history without noticing the configuration of the North American continent and its relations to Europe. The great Mississippi Valley, which The Mississippi Valley. by its wide outstretched arms binds together the mountain chains and seaboards of the east and west into a strangely assorted but powerful union, was the prize for which England and France were contesting in America. At the headwaters of the Ohio the English colonies were nearer to its limits, but there intervened a long stretch of forest wilderness not perfectly explored. There was a circuitous route by the Hudson and Mohawk Valleys into the more level forest lands which extended to the headwaters of the Allegheny River, but the tract of country was the home of the powerful Indian confederacy of the Six Nations. Around by the water-shed and the Gulf of Mexico, Spain blocked the way, and the southern Indians were quite as unreliable, though not as fierce, as those to the north. The few and scattered English settlements in the Mississippi Valley had been made by the mountain pioneers, therefore, and were in the main at the headwaters or in the intervales of the great streams tributary to the Father of Waters.

The French were in possession of the valley of the St. Lawrence. By way of the great lakes, which they discovered and explored, they had a waterway to the threshold of the Ohio Valley and to the very headwaters of the Mississippi itself. *French possessions and ambitions.* Their explorations had been vastly more extended in the heart of the continent than those of the English colonists, their mission stations and factories were more numerous and better equipped. The mouth, too, of the great central river was under their control through the settlement of New Orleans, and it was a natural desire that led them to establish a chain of stations connecting the countries claimed by them around the great lakes with their possessions on the Gulf of Mexico. The watersheds therefore of the St. Lawrence system, including the inland seas which feed it, and of the Mississippi, seemed to the French their destined empire. This would, of course, have given them such a territorial preponderance on the continent as to reduce the English to insignificance. They had had singular success in their dealings with the Indians. It seemed probable that, as in Central and South America, the Latin race would here again commingle its blood with that of the native races, to introduce an imperfect though persistent civilization throughout lands capable of sustaining an enormous population, and as favorable to a high civilization as Europe itself.

The established track of communication between the eastern sea-shore and the seat of French control was by the Hudson Valley, Lake Champlain, and the Richelieu River. Along these lines took place every movement of settlement and conflict, but the French had a decided advantage in their ownership of the St. Lawrence, which was at the same time the easiest thoroughfare and also, in actual distance, closer to the European base of supplies than any point in the colonies. It was, to be sure, for many long months in the winter blockaded by ice, but in summer, when the operations of trade and colonization were most active, the nearness of its mouth both in latitude and longitude to the great seaports of Europe, combined with the navigability of its mighty stream for a long distance inland, gave to its harbors a marked advantage over those in the South. As yet the victories of enterprise in building roads and canals to outweigh natural disadvantages, had not been won, and are not in this narrative to be taken into account.

Continental lines of communication.

The territorial expansion of France had an object quite different from that of England. In both there was much religious zeal, but in the English colonies it took the form primarily of a desire to secure liberty of worship for the settlers; the conversion of the heathen followed as a corollary. In New France the latter was ostensibly the main object, and the colonists were men enlisted for a purpose rather than volunteer emigrants. In both there was a strong commercial element, but the English looked for permanency to agriculture and the development of large communities, while the French, concerned for the fur trade, the exigencies of which kept their depots small, scattered their immigrants over a wide extent of country, and made their posts dependent on military garri-

Contrast between the strength and aims of England and France.

sons for security. These diverging policies had kept New France in the most intimate connection with the centralized, hierarchical, and despotic administration of a government and court thousands of miles away, while the English had enjoyed a substantial autonomy and had developed democratic institutions. The French had all the strength of an ever-active political power immediately supporting, supplying, and directing them, as long as that power was itself strong. But when its attention and energies were monopolized elsewhere, it was seen that they were weak as children are when suddenly deprived of parental sustenance and guidance. The English were weak also in their divided interests and lack of harmonious action under one organization, but they were strong in their self-reliance, in the mutual help of neighboring communities, and in a commerce which had grown up, not by artificial forcing but in spite of the disfavor of the home government.

Since 1688, moreover, the whole spirit of each of the two peoples, on both sides of the ocean, had been changed. In one there had been created popular institutions, new force had been infused into constitutional government, the industrial classes had been recognized as an independent element in society, and the emphasis in the distribution of power had been laid on a legislature which was in part, at least, representative, and the controlling rather than the regulating arm of monarchical rule. In the other the crown had absorbed every public function, the people were mere taxpayers, every activity of society had its origin from above, and the spontaneity of the masses was more and more limited to the sphere of private life.

Divergent institutions of the two peoples.

In this way the question of supremacy in America had acquired a significance transcending the sphere of local interests and national aggrandizement. The interest of the whole world of thought and letters was also awakened, and a few men of prophetic vision began to see and say that the destinies of European civilization were to be determined in America. The preliminaries to the solution of this momentous problem lay partly in diplomacy, but to a greater extent in the question of possession. The clearer apprehension of those on the spot disregarded negotiation as futile, and turned to the latter as alone conclusive. After the treaty of Aix-la-Chapelle a commission sat for three years to weigh the respective claims of England and France in America. Those of France included the immense territories of Louisiana and Canada, and were based on discovery, exploration, and occupation. England referred to the original charters and maps which extended the east and west lines of the colonial grants through to the Pacific Ocean, and to the language of the treaty of Utrecht. The text was "the five nations are subject to the dominion of England," and this was interpreted by the British to mean not only the hereditary lands of that confederacy, but also the Ohio Valley and the lands north of it as far as the Mississippi, which they declared had been conquered by the Iroquois in 1672. The outcome of negotiations conducted with such pretensions was of course nothing at all, and the Paris commission separated without accomplishing anything. In the meantime, however, agents of the respective nations in America were wide awake. The French governor La Jonquière made a request for ten thousand immigrants to settle the Ohio Valley, for he saw that if he should fail to occupy it that of the Mississippi would also be lost; but owing to the state of French finances and the condition of European politics, the demand was unheeded. Virginia, Pennsylvania, and the Ohio Company remitted

The conflict to be decided in America.

Prefatory negotiations and measures.

nothing of their enterprise in trade and exploration west of the Alleghenies. The French began in 1750 to stir up the Indians of New York to marauding raids westward, strengthened their fleet on Lake Ontario, and built new works at Niagara. In 1752 they commenced to attack the English pioneers in Ohio, and in 1753 they descended the Allegheny in force, disregarded the summons sent by Virginia, drove off the English backwoodsmen who had begun to fortify the naturally strong point at the confluence of the Allegheny and Monongahela, and on that commanding position themselves erected a fort which was called, in honor of the new governor of Canada, Fort Duquesne. As far as the white population of North America was concerned, everything was ready to topple the unstable equilibrium of claim and counterclaim at a moment's notice.

The relation of the aborigines to the impending struggle was a matter of vital importance. It may not be amiss to recall that, among the primitive inhabitants of America, climate seems to have had a determining influence in the formation and fixity of social life. The most complex civilization was that in Central America and Mexico. The Florida Indians—Seminoles, Cherokees, Chickasaws, Choctaws, and Creeks—were less subject to customary law, and were therefore receptive to the example of the settlers. With the exception of the Cherokees, they spoke various dialects of the same tongue, but, including these, all were by this time in great measure a settled agricultural people, giving only an occasional exhibition of their former nomadic tendencies. But there was no true kindness between them and the English, nor mutual confidence. Self-interest was as certainly their ruling principle as it was among their congeners to the north. Life was easy under southern skies, and the immense territory over

The aborigines of the South.

which they ruled, extending as it did from the Gulf to the Tennessee, was scarcely to be called inhabited, for their numbers did not probably exceed fifty thousand at any time, and were not sufficient for effective occupation. Their country was not in dispute between the English and French, their contact with Europeans was not very close, and as there were few mutual injuries, there were correspondingly few exhibitions of ferocity or savagery. When, many years later, they were wronged by the United States, their display of courage, guile, and persistence was second to no other in the history of border warfare.

To the north of these southern natives, known as the Gulf, Florida, or Mobile Indians, lay what was now and had long been the debatable land of the Algonquins, stretching eastward from the Mississippi and northward to the limits of the Hyperboreans or Esquimaux. Within it were two peoples, differing in origin, habits, and speech. The Algonquins themselves, or Delawares, had been the original owners and were a homogeneous people, divided into confederacies and tribes speaking modifications of one language. But in their very heart, occupying the district immediately south of Lake Ontario and Lake Erie, was a people of altogether different origin, if speech and appearance are trustworthy indications, the Iroquois. They were known at first as the Five Nations, from their tribal division into the Mohawks, Oneidas, Onondagas, Cayugas, and Senecas. In 1713 another tribe, the Tuscaroras, from North Carolina, joined the confederacy and formed "The Six Nations." In the course of time the Delawares had succumbed to the superior race. The Iroquois combined in a higher degree than any others the qualities of craft, energy, courage, and intelligence. The name of the best known of their tribes, the Mohawks, has passed

The Algonquins and Iroquois.

into literature as a symbol of ferocity and treachery. The poetic fancy of our fathers saw in the combination of personal independence and successful organization which they secured by their social system, an ideal for the rising white democracy, and adopted many of their national and tribal names as characteristic of American life. [They stand in our fancy as the type of the Red Indian; stern, cruel, and desperate in the face of foes; ambitious, politic, and eloquent in diplomacy; endowed with the primitive virtues of self-respect, self-control, and honor in dealing with each other; physically erect, well-proportioned, and beautiful; familiar with the secrets of nature, conversant with the woods, using the forest, plain, and stream with equal ease for purposes of travel, concealment, or warfare; thus approaching somewhat our visions of man in a golden age.

The truth is perhaps far enough from such conceptions, but with all our modern coldness we are forced to admit, even in the light of more accurate knowledge, that there was an intensely heroic element in the story of the Hodenosaunee, as they called themselves. (Conservative estimates place their numbers at about seventeen thousand, of whom never more than four thousand were warriors. Their origin is unknown, but their historic seat was a place whence waters flowed in one direction to the Atlantic, both through the lakes by the St. Lawrence and by the headwaters of the Hudson, in another to the Gulf by the Allegheny and the Ohio; while the watersheds of the Susquehanna and the Delaware enabled them to reach yet a third important district with ease. It was not accident but the highest intelligence which put them in such a centre of radiating lines of control. Their organization was at the same time close-knit and elastic, being a combination of two primitive institutions, the tribe and the totem.

Their institutions and religion.

The former was an association based largely on expediency and consent. There was but one official, the sachem, whose position was hereditary, but was also, by a reversion to the very earliest custom, in the female line, and could not therefore reside in one family long enough to create privilege. The tribal relation was useful for holding councils, which took place in houses built of bark for the purpose ; but there seems to have been no law except custom, no force except of a moral nature, and no obedience to formal results of deliberation except by individual consent. Personal liberty was absolute, even to the exercise' of a caprice dangerous to others. On the other hand, there was a bond of natural union more powerful in such a society than we can conceive. If the nation sprang originally from one pair to whom were born eight sons, each having as a device a plant or a familiar animal like the turtle, wolf, bear, or eagle, the descendants of each one might form a clan, every member of which would feel a superstitious reverence for the device of his ancestor, and would perhaps in time come to believe himself descended, in dim ages long since past, from this totem. Two conceptions of the strongest nature would thus unite—a religious or superstitious one, making him feel binding obligation to every man or woman under the same protection, and that of kinship, showing that his highest duty was toward those whose blood relation was evident from their possession of the same totem. Among the Iroquois this system of clan totemism survived in perfection, creating an eightfold division, but the clan and the tribe were entirely different, every clan being represented, probably by intermarriage, in every tribe. The national bond was far stronger than the tribal, because based, as we would say, upon a common worship and religion, though it degrades and violates the words to apply them to totemism. The darkest form of fetichism, which some would dignify by the name of ancestor-worship, was the cement of their society, but their spiritual strivings were somewhat higher in character, being a form of nature-worship. Each object had its spirit or manitou, and among these spiritual essences were orders, some regulated by locality, some by inherent inferiority or superiority, but the prevalent notion that they had a conception of one supreme personal spirit is false.

In the arts of life the Iroquois were on a low level. They built and inhabited structures of beams and bark which were generally large, averaging eighty by sixteen feet in dimensions, while some were more than a hundred feet in length. These were to them the chief feature of their life, because they often designated their splendid territory as The Long House. *Their character and domestic economy.* Within these buildings were numerous and ingenious arrangements for sleeping and eating, for the storage of fuel and provisions. Each sheltered several families in compartments constructed under the eaves, the floor-space beneath the peak being reserved for the several fires. Their vessels were of coarse earthenware, their knives and arrow-heads of stone; their pursuits in time of peace were for the men hunting, and for the women agriculture, which they brought to a high perfection. They had apple orchards of mature growth and extensive fields of maize, beans, and pumpkins. For protection the dwellings were built in clusters, and around them, in the shape of an oval, were erected palisades pierced with loop-holes, under which on the interior stood platforms from which arrows could be shot or stones hurled at the intruder. In some cases these palisades were double and even threefold. One early French writer states that the loop-holes were also furnished with water-pipes to extinguish the fires which an enemy might build against the wooden wall. Their amusements were gambling, feasting, the recital of witch and ghost tales, the practice of a gallantry which was offensive even to their own remnants of morality, and the torture of victims taken in war, which more completely than anything else filled them with joy. They inured themselves to the necessary fatigues of their long marauding expeditions, which extended over hundreds of miles, by the practice of many admirable out-door sports, archery, riding, and games of ball. What we call the treachery of the Indian was to him the easiest means of gratifying the passion of the moment, revenge, desire, or envy. Labor, menial or otherwise, he felt in his overweening and childish pride to be beneath his station; his passions were those of an animal, and the qualities which under our code are virtues—reverence for age, admiration of heroes, the endurance of hardship—sprang from the patriarchal system beyond which he had not advanced.

It is worth while to contemplate these features of Iroquois life, because they were, in a debased form and lower degree, the characteristics of all the northern tribes between the Mississippi and the Ocean, who differed from their conquerors only in the imperfection of their institutions, being more nomadic, less completely organized, and not so highly endowed with natural gifts. They stood in terror of the more vigorous and ruthless power which struck with the swiftness of lightning, and as unexpectedly. This Algonquin people, however, played a more important rôle than even the Iroquois, because it was on their land that our ancestors settled in the largest numbers, with their tribes that the earlier Indian warfare was waged and the later alliances were consummated with them. Some investigators think that at one time they may have numbered all told ninety thousand,

Their relations to the colonies.

others go as low as forty thousand in their estimate. Their great tribes were the Lenni Lenape, with whom Penn held his famous council, the Shawnees of Ohio, the Miamis, the Illinois, the Ojibwas, the Pottawattamies, Ottawas, Sacs, Foxes, and Menomonies, together with the Pequots and other tribes in what is now New England. With the fourth great family of Red Indians, speaking a fourth tongue, the Dakotahs, our early history has nothing to do. They are now, as they were then, more savage, more restless, more wild than any of the others. They assimilate with difficulty the arts of peace, bid defiance to European civilization, and occupy toward the other Indians and the whites of to-day, much the same position as the Iroquois had a century and a half ago.

The condition of Indian affairs at the outbreak of what was called in the colonies the Old French and Indian War was a matter of great importance. In a word, and for the most part, the Algonquins were allies of the French and the Six Nations of the English. For this there was a double reason. The French policy of conciliation had turned their Algonquin neighbors into hearty friends. It was easy for them to humor Indian fondness for display. In the course of trade large numbers of the red men paid an annual visit to the Canadian ports, bringing their peltries for barter. They were welcomed by rolling drums and booming cannon, their festivities while trading were shared by their hosts, and the day of their departure was again a festival. It is said that no less a personage than Frontenac himself donned their uncouth but picturesque costume and engaged in their dances. Religious zeal sent the missionaries in turn into the remotest bounds of the wilderness, where they dwelt among the savages, founded settlements which were often turned into military posts, and kept the nations constantly familiar with the thought of French interest and favor. The whole Canadian system seemed suited to create the intimate relations of the two races. A petty feudal nobility easily made place for red retainers among a white peasantry who felt no degradation in the intercourse. To an extreme ecclesiastical organism like that of Roman Catholicism in Jesuit hands, the importance of the savage was not less than that of the civilized man, and the child-like vanity of the former was gratified by the zeal of the priest for his salvation. [And finally the light-hearted, adventurous spirit of the French settlers, soldiers, and traders had a kind of natural affinity to the better side of their allies, the Algonquins.]

The second reason for this double alliance was simply the hostility between the two Indian stocks contending for the same possessions. There was no fondness, no unity of advantage, no affinity, social or religious, between the Iroquois and the people of the colonies. In fact, between the English and all savages whatsoever,

<small>Character of English intercourse with the Red Men.</small> there was a relation of mutual suspicion in many places, and nowhere, not even in Pennsylvania, a thorough understanding between the colonists and the aborigines. William Penn had first paid the Iroquois and then the Lenni Lenape for the lands they both claimed. His intercourse with the latter was just, wise, and amicable, but their behavior toward him had a wholesome restraint in their terror of the fierce enemies who held their own prior bargain with the Quakers to be conclusive. But as generations passed the still subjugated descendants of Penn's friends were crowded into the outlying valleys of the Delaware, the Susquehanna, and even of the Juniata; such encroachments on the hunting grounds of the Delawares produced first irritation and then bitter hatred toward the intruders. Finally ill-feeling was created even among the Iroquois,

who had repeatedly given their broken-spirited subjects successive assurances of peaceable possession, as they in turn occupied and abandoned the tracts assigned them. When, therefore, the French had approached the new seats of the Delawares on the Muskingum and Allegheny, they found the Lenni Lennape as ready to treat with them as they had once been with the Pennsylvania English. In the earliest days, before history, the hostile relations of the Iroquois and Algonquins had been established. The French often accompanied the Algonquin war parties in their raids into Iroquois territory. On one occasion Champlain appeared in front of the lines in shining corselet and helm, armed with an arquebuse, and shot two opposing chiefs already exulting in victory. To the ignorant savages he appeared a supernatural being. At first they fled in dismay to cherish their hate, but with increasing knowledge they came to scorn the chicken-hearted enemy who were dependent on such support. Similar occurrences fanned their natural hatred, until at the opening of the century it was at its height. But for thirty years the French had been using their diplomacy with the Iroquois, while the English had been indifferent or proudly insulting in their behavior. The contempt of suffering, the endurance, the lofty courage of the French emissaries, though most barbarously and inhumanly entreated, seem finally to have moved the Iroquois' heart. Their forays into the country of the Cherokees and Catawbas in Carolina and Virginia, were often thwarted by the advancing lines of English pioneers, and the French knew how to fan the fires of discontent thus lighted. Finally, in 1749, the missionary Picquet boldly advanced into their land, and from his fortified station where Ogdensburg now stands, so wrought and schemed that nearly half the nation seemed to be under his sway.

The entire defection of the Iroquois was thwarted by

William Johnson, an Irishman of high birth, from the County of Meath, who had settled in the Mohawk Valley near the site of Schenectady, to manage estates already in the family and acquire new ones for himself. His character and conduct resembled the French model much more closely than the English. He acquired the language of the Six Nations, traded with them in honesty, and endeared himself to them by his courtesy and perfect good faith. He became at last so familiar with their whole social structure, their traditions, and their motives, that the Mohawks adopted him and gave him the rank of sachem. In 1744 Governor Clinton appointed him colonel of the Six Nations, in 1745 the province made him commissary for Indian affairs, and in 1748 he was set over all the frontier defences. In 1750 the King gave him a seat in the colonial council. His influence was, of course, constantly exerted against the French, and with great success, while there was an ever-growing good-will on the part of the Iroquois. In 1753 the colony changed its Indian policy and angered the tribes. After effecting a reconciliation with the savages at the famous council fire of Onondaga, he resigned. The next year saw the colonial congress at Albany to which he was a delegate. The Indians were summoned to deliberate and came. But it was to charge the English with neglect and rapacity, and they were so urgent that Johnson should be re-appointed as their superintendent that, in 1755, Braddock consented and gave him his commission at Alexandria. He was also made a major-general, and put in command of the expedition to Crown Point, the post from which Canada hoped to control the country which is now Vermont and New Hampshire, a territory which was for the Puritan frontiersman much what the Ohio Valley was to the Virginian.

Such then was the Indian situation : the Iroquois, few

in number, living in a small country of the highest strategic importance, fierce and enterprising beyond all their fellows, the hereditary foes of the Algonquins, allied to the English by slender ties, and honeycombed with disaffection; on the other hand the Algonquins, bound to the French by every tie of long hereditary friendship, scattered over a splendid and extended territory and outnumbering the Six Nations four to one, but inferior to them in courage, while at the same time they were consumed by a sense of weakness and wrong which they traced to the English influence, and of course thirsted for revenge. To complete the situation at the opening of 1755, we must remember that the French and English forces were at loggerheads in Acadia, the commissioners having failed to agree on the limits of what was ceded by the peace of Aix-la-Chapelle. From Fort Frederic or Crown Point the French menaced New England and New York. We must also recall that they had fortified places at Ogdensburg to control the Iroquois, at Niagara to command the western waterway, at Presqu'Isle, Le Bœuf, and Venango to regulate and retain the line of trade southward from Lake Erie, and Fort Duquesne to command the whole Ohio Valley. While in the far West their posts were in a wilderness and separated from each other by hundreds of miles, yet by means of Detroit, St. Joseph, Vincennes, Cahokia, Kaskaskia, and New Orleans, they dominated the expanse of Louisiana. There had been numerous minor collisions and one of some importance at Fort Necessity, near the forks of the Ohio, when George Washington, on July 4th, 1754, after a stubborn resistance to a superior French force, had capitulated with the honors of war. In the conference at Fort Le Bœuf and in the leadership of this expedition, that memorable name appears for the first time in the records of history.

Summary of the situation.

CHAPTER IV.

OUTBREAK OF THE FRENCH AND INDIAN WAR—1755-1756

European Complications—The Combination against Frederick the Great—The Newcastle Ministry—General Braddock—French Preparations—Demand for Colonial Taxation—The English Regulars and American Militia—Braddock's Advance—The French and Indian Ambuscade—The Battle—Defeat of the Expedition—Acadia—Treatment of the French Farmers—Capture of the French Forts—Dispersion of the Natives—Fort Niagara—Johnson's Successes—Fort William Henry—Plans for Taxing America.

THE strained relations and conflicting interests of France and England in North America made it impossible for events to await a formal declaration of the war on this side of the sea, and while hostilities did not formally begin according to diplomatic rite until 1756, the preceding year saw the threatened outbreak. This state of affairs had also a counterpart beyond the sea in the international complications consequent to the artificial and incomplete treaty of Aix-la-Chapelle. Two years before the articles of that document were signed the sovereigns of Austria and Russia had concluded a defensive alliance, and in secret articles provision was made for a possible restoration of Silesia to Maria Theresa. Four years later, George II. acceded to the treaty for the sake of preserving his hereditary principality of Hanover, while Saxony was won over to the entire agreement, secret articles and all.

The adroit and brilliant Kaunitz, for many years Aus-

THE NORTHERN COLONIES AND CANADA II.

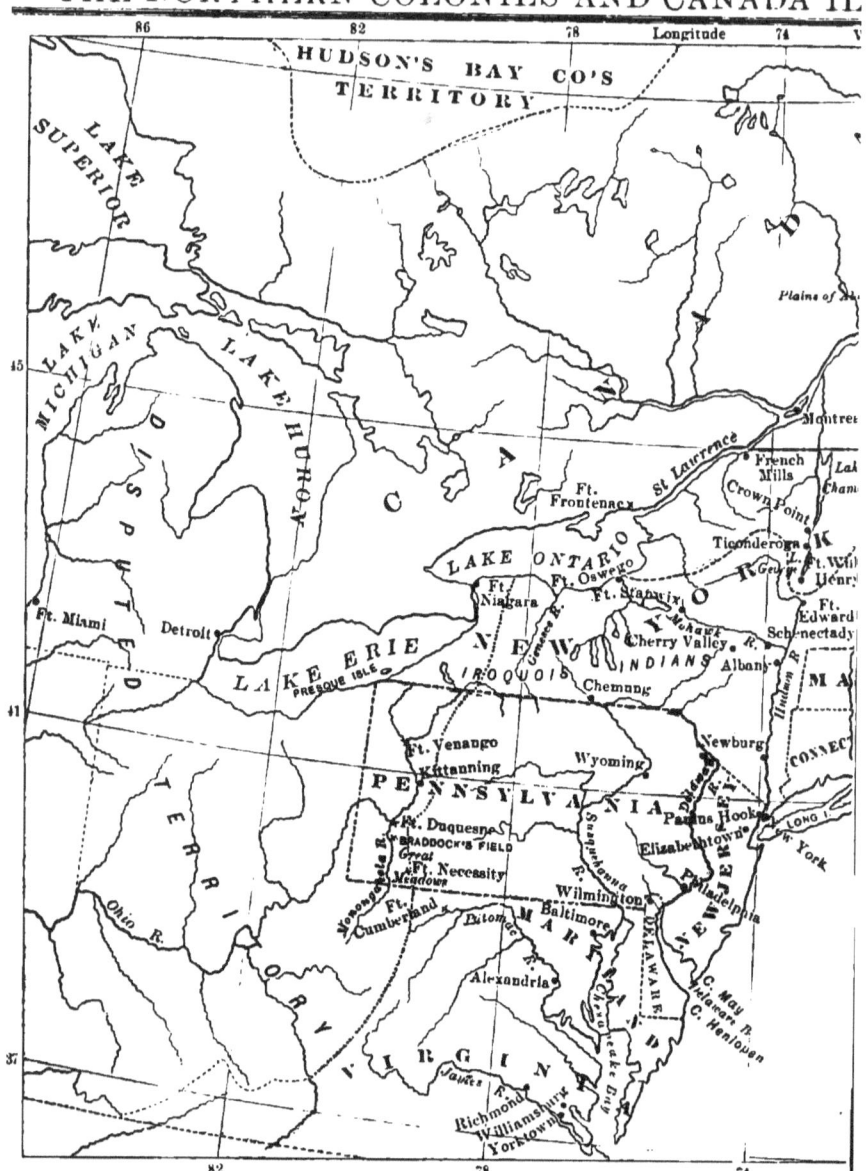

ILLUSTRATING THE FRENCH AND INDIAN WAR.

OUTBREAK OF THE FRENCH AND INDIAN WAR 39

trian ambassador in Paris, now chancellor of the empire, had meanwhile accomplished the unexpected, in reconciling, through the influence of Madame de Pompadour, the two great powers which had so long been deadly rivals, the houses of Bourbon and Hapsburg. In 1755, after Frederick the Great had been intriguing with the Jacobites in the hope of securing Hanover, the Newcastle ministry made a subsidy treaty with Elizabeth of Russia, who cherished resentment against Prussia on account of the bitter witticisms by which Frederick had exposed her character. But already in the next year there was a re-arrangement, because of the menace by the Austro-French league to the very existence of the new military power, and a renewal of partial friendship between the two great Protestant nations was shown in a treaty forbidding the troops of any nation to cross German territory. This of course alienated Russia from England, and four months later, in May, 1756, France and Austria completed their defensive alliance. Frederick found himself, therefore, confronted by the combined strength of Russia, Sweden, Austria with the German princes, and France. His only ally was England. *The combination against Frederick the Great.*

Never in modern times had England known deeper humiliation. Newcastle was now in power; the spirit of dull, incapable rapacity was all-pervasive in public life. The officials under the cabinet shared the sloth and feebleness of their superiors, and what ability was available looked rather to the immediate and apparently inevitable, than to the larger measures of real statesmanship. When, therefore, open conflict in America made procrastination impossible, the measures taken were of a very clumsy and dubious character. In the Pelham cabinet, which lasted from 1746 to 1754, Pitt had only a subordinate position, *The Newcastle ministry.*

but his influence was very great. The plan which that cabinet had formed to thwart the French in America is believed to have been his. At all events, when he finally came into full power, he promptly renewed its fundamental conception and fought on its lines. It was an admirable one, but while the Newcastle ministry did not change it, they nullified it through the general incapacity of the creatures chosen to carry it into operation, and by the orders given to them. Acadia, or Nova Scotia, was to be made entirely secure, and three expeditions were to be organized to proceed against Fort Duquesne, Niagara, and Crown Point, respectively.

In the first months of 1755 a fleet was despatched from Cork to Virginia with two regiments under command of Major-General Braddock, who was to be commander-in-chief of the English forces in America. He was a soldier of forty years' standing, and had gained distinction in the career to which he had been devoted, but on the other hand he was conceited and headstrong, ignorant of every problem in frontier fighting, and wedded to the martinet forms and discipline of what was then considered civilized warfare on the continent of Europe. His habits and general view of life were diametrically opposed to the simplicity and straightforwardness of the colonial leaders, upon whose co-operation he would be dependent for success. There was a strong sentiment for war in England, but the king was absent in Hanover and the feeble, vacillating ministry, distracted by indecision, feared to take the step, but gave instead piratical orders to Hawke, the commander of the Channel fleet, to destroy every French ship between Capes Clear and Ortegal.

In contrast with the commingled feebleness and desperation of Newcastle was the direct and capable course of France. By means of diplomacy she succeeded in

OUTBREAK OF THE FRENCH AND INDIAN WAR 41

gaining time for extensive preparation. A few months after the departure of Braddock's army a fleet with four thousand troops left Brest for America. Boscawen, with an English squadron, started at once in pursuit, overtook the French who were making for the Gulf of St. Lawrence, and captured two vessels. The others, with Vaudreuil, the new governor appointed to supersede Duquesne, and the commander of the forces, Baron Dieskau, came safely to land. Vaudreuil was a Canadian by birth; Dieskau was a German who had been aide-de-camp to Marshal Saxe, and had gained a high reputation in the Netherlands. Meantime the wretched policy indicated by the orders to the Channel fleet was further carried out by sending privateers to sea under letters of marque, and before the end of the year, war not yet having been declared, about three hundred French merchantmen and seven thousand French sailors were captured. France, by way of ostentatious rebuke, set free one English vessel which had been illegally taken, but on receipt of the news from the Banks of Newfoundland recalled her ambassador from London. French preparations.

Braddock's first official act on reaching Virginia was to convene a congress at Alexandria. There were present the governors of Massachusetts, New York, Pennsylvania, Maryland, Virginia, and Commodore Keppel. He himself was, of course, the presiding officer. The determination had long since been formed in official circles that a general fund for the immediate necessities of the impending war should be raised in the colonies. The royal governors had found their assemblies difficult to convince, and there was an almost universal consensus of opinion among the agents of the crown that the people would not move of their own accord, but would acquiesce if taxed by an act Demand for colonial taxation.

of Parliament. Braddock, in explaining his instructions, angrily expressed his disappointment that the money had not been raised. The governors retorted by explaining the colonial reluctance and renewing their advice that Parliament should enact a tax. This is the first appearance in positive form of the constitutional question which was later to occupy the entire energies of England and her colonies.

But just then there were more urgent and immediate matters of detail, as to the colonial troops and the attitude of the Iroquois. Most of them were satisfactorily arranged. One regulation which had been promulgated before Braddock's arrival was enforced, that the general and field officers of the American soldiers should have no rank when those of the regular army were in the field. The result was to anger and dishearten at the outset the very flower of Braddock's command; and to make matters worse, he declared that the savages might be formidable to the raw American militia, but upon the king's regulars and disciplined troops it was impossible they should make any impression. Both Pennsylvania and Virginia, however, disregarded his insulting attitude and promptly furnished the necessary supplies; numbers of the "raw militia," from those colonies and from New York, two thousand in all, joined the expedition, and Washington accepted a position as one of the aides-de-camp.

<small>The English regulars and American militia.</small>

The march through the settlements to Will's Creek, which was then first named Fort Cumberland in honor of the Duke of Cumberland, Braddock's patron, was itself long and weary. After twenty-seven days it was reached in May; the militia, who had already assembled there, were put under rigorous discipline, and some time was spent in drills and other preparations before the hundred and thirty miles of

<small>Braddock's advance.</small>

OUTBREAK OF THE FRENCH AND INDIAN WAR 43

wilderness from that point to Fort Duquesne were attacked. The whole of June and eight days of July was consumed in the desperate march. The very road had to be built; trees were felled, such bridges as were absolutely necessary were constructed over morasses, and in general, the route was over the hills, in disregard of the natural course by the streams. At last the banks of the Monongahela were reached at the confluence of the Youghiogheny. The line, extended sometimes to four miles but marching as if on a turnpike, forded the river at the mouth of Turtle Creek to the left bank on the ninth of July, and a few miles further down recrossed to a spot which still retains the ill-omened name of Braddock's Fields, but defies the omen with thronged and prosperous workshops, huge furnaces, and all the clangor of a throbbing industrial life. All the severity of rigorous discipline had been enforced, even in a forest path but twelve feet wide, between the river bank on one side, and ground which rose first gradually and then abruptly to a high ridge, on the other. There were guides, flanking parties, all the regular divisions of a marching army, but no scouts. By the line of the river they were within ten miles of their goal.

But they had long been watched by the keen eyes of French and Indian scouts. Within the walls of the fort there was great dismay; reinforcements had been sent, but the troops were only some hundreds in all. There were gathered, how- *The French and Indian ambuscade.* ever, at its gate a considerable number of Indians from the Ojibwas, Ottawas, Delawares, and other Algonquin tribes. Nevertheless Contrecœur, the commandant, thought only of retreat; the enemy were upon him with a well-equipped and disciplined force of over fifteen hundred near at hand, and the main army close behind. But Beaujeu, one of his captains, was a daring spirit,

44 THE FRENCH WAR AND THE REVOLUTION

and an offer made by him to advance and form an ambuscade in two well-known ravines athwart the English line of march was accepted. Three times the bold French adventurer laid his reckless scheme before the stolid savages, and at last they consented.

Early on the morning of July 9th, 1755, two hundred and thirty French and Canadians, in the garb of backwoodsmen, and six hundred and thirty-seven red men in all the tawdry horror of paint, grease, and feathers, left Fort Duquesne under command of Beaujeu, Dumas, and Ligneris. The apparently unequal forces met at a moment unexpected to both. But the French and Indians were fresh, alert, and excited to a pitch of frenzy. Attacking their enemy with spirit, they availed themselves of all the arts of forest warfare, pouring in on front and flank a deadly fire from behind the trees, and using the hill-crests or any natural obstacle as shelter. The savages made the air ring with yells and war-whoops. The English sought to form in due old-world order; they poured their fusilade and artillery fire in all directions, but their foe was scarcely visible, while they themselves, in scarlet uniform and compact ranks afforded a too prominent target. The regulars had been disheartened by unaccustomed hardships, the militia were soured by the rigors of an unaccustomed discipline, which they knew unfitted them for their task. But the militia force stubbornly contested their ground for two hours under a galling fire, forbidden to answer the enemy by his own tactics, exposed to the fury of a July sun, in the face of an unseen foe. Their officers displayed prodigies of courage, five horses were shot under the general before he succumbed to his wounds. Washington, likewise, had four bullet holes through his coat and lost two chargers in the desperate struggle. His two fellow-aides were early disabled, and he was the

The battle.

OUTBREAK OF THE FRENCH AND INDIAN WAR   45

only active one during the whole engagement. Of the English and colonial forces twenty-six officers were killed, thirty-seven wounded, and seven hundred and fourteen privates were slain or wounded. The regulars fired while ammunition lasted; the militia stood until the last; of one Virginia command comprising three companies, it is related that not thirty men survived. On the victorious side three officers and thirty men were killed and about the same number wounded.

The retreat was a mere rout. There was no pursuit, for the savages stopped to plunder the fallen, and the French returned to their fort. Braddock died   Defeat of the
the second day of his wounds, and was buried   expedition.
by the wayside. Dunbar, who had been in command of the rear, abandoned Fort Cumberland, destroyed all his stores and ammunition, and joined the columns hurrying eastward. Thus ended the first effort to overturn French influence in the Ohio Valley. The affair produced dismay in England and roused the middle colonies from their lethargy. The Virginia burgesses gave forty thousand pounds, and Pennsylvania voted fifty thousand, refusing to exempt the property of the proprietaries from taxation. The others made ready to supply men and arms according to their ability. But the narratives of the survivors fostered distrust of the English troops among the colonists, and embittered them against the Indians wherever found. The frontier settlements being left defenceless, those of the savages who still wavered were confirmed in their allegiance to France, for they now felt that on that side was not only friendship but safety for their lands. Nor was their least inducement the immediate chance to plunder the white intruders. The advancing line of pioneers, in both Virginia and Pennsylvania, was checked and driven back, their rude homes being given over to pillage and desolation.

46 THE FRENCH WAR AND THE REVOLUTION

The French patent of 1603 claimed for Acadia the territory between the present sites of Philadelphia and Montreal, granting liberty of worship to Huguenots within those boundaries. The following year an expedition of which Champlain was a member founded Port Royal and St. Croix, and discovered the St. John's River. This was the first attempt at settlement, and though occupation was precarious and the colonists were subjected to serious hardship, it continued until 1614, when the Virginians, basing their claims on a discovery by the Cabots in 1497, drove out the French. Sir William Alexander obtained a patent in 1621 for the peninsula now known as Nova Scotia, but his attempts at permanent occupation, in 1623, were rendered unavailing by the French. Cromwell sent out a powerful expedition in 1654, but by the treaty of Breda the territory was ceded to France. Henceforth it was known as Acadia or Nova Scotia, although its boundaries were utterly uncertain and no attempt was made to settle them until 1750; the other claims of the French in North America were designated New France. The English colonists never regarded the treaty obligations of their government, and so harassed the French settlers that, in 1713, England regained possession under the treaty of Utrecht.

Acadia.

For thirty years the English rule was nominal. The industry, thrift, and piety of the people created an unexampled prosperity in an ideal pastoral life. In 1749, evidence began to accumulate that France would once again enforce her pretensions. Accordingly, four thousand settlers were sent out and the city of Halifax was founded. But the French inhabitants were still a majority, and although ostensibly neutral they now courted the Indian alliances, drew closer to their religious rulers than ever, and rendered the

Treatment of the French farmers.

English administrative measures well-nigh futile. The English were stern, and in their helplessness the Acadians became hopelessly intractable. Measures of an unwonted severity seemed to them tyranny; the English assumed the guardianship of their titles and laid heavy taxes, while burdensome contributions of labor and of produce were enforced under threats of martial law. That they might neither fly nor fight, they were stripped of both boats and fire-arms. Throughout the colonies the feeling prevailed that a life struggle with popery and tyranny, as embodied in French supremacy, had begun, and passions were inflamed to a high pitch. We deprecate the bigotry and ruthlessness of the time, but the principle of resistance to encroachment was the same from 1755 down to the Declaration of Independence. The wrong was in the savage application of it. Step by step the English officials interpreted the laws of their mother land against Roman Catholics with more unjustifiable stringency, until they came to regard the meek and unresisting people as rebels and an obstacle to peace and progress. At last the Acadians one day refused the oath of entire allegiance to the crown, and then having repented their determination the next, were refused permission to take it. Finally the fatal decision was reached that their splendid possessions must be forfeited, and they themselves with their families exiled into other parts of the continent.

Two French fortresses had been erected on the isthmus after the surrender of the peninsula to England, one small and scarcely more than an outpost, Fort Gaspereaux, so named from the little river at the mouth of which it stood; the other, Fort Beau Séjour, well constructed, well equipped, and occupying a position of strategic importance at the narrowest part of the isthmus, north of the River Messa-

Capture of the French forts.

gouche. From a levy of over seven thousand Massachusetts troops, some fifteen hundred had been despatched early in the year under Winslow against these strongholds. The men, like others of the colonial forces, were animated by both religious and political bitterness, and the skill of their leaders was in marked contrast to the incapacity of Vergor, the French commander. They were supported also by three hundred regulars and a company of artillery. Both places were taken in June almost without an effort. Any resistance by the peasantry would therefore have been futile and desperate. Their doom had gone forth and the Americans were unfortunately foremost in its execution, although the real stigma of the measures rests on the Lords of Trade and the supple judiciary of the province, willing tools in interpreting the constitution according to the rapacious desires of the authorities.

In September the Acadian men were taken prisoners by an artifice which could only have imposed on simple minds, and the forced emigration began. The embarkation was not completed until December, the season was most inclement, and cruelty went hand in hand with incapacity to torture the paralyzed and helpless victims. Wherever they were finally deposited, in Georgia, Pennsylvania, or Canada, they were left to their own misdirected and feeble efforts for sustenance. The strange absence of the paternal hand to which they had been accustomed, in both politics and religion, induced a numbing home-sickness, under the influence of which many blindly sought to regain their former seats. But all effort was vain, fate seemed to overpower them in every movement, for they were forlorn and the government relentless. So their dispersion was accomplished. Seven thousand in all were carried away. Their houses and barns were burnt, their cattle

Dispersion of the natives.

sold, their land became not only a solitude but a desert: for the ocean beat down the neglected dikes and resumed for many long years its ancient sway over the low-lying meadows, which had been the pride of the country. "This poor, innocent people," said Burke, "whom our utter inability to govern or to reconcile, gave us no right to extirpate."

The French fortress at Niagara was weak and half-dismantled, but as the centre of a fur trade which carried French men, French influence, and French speech into the unmeasured boundaries of the far West, it was the support of the French claim to supremacy in North America. William Shirley assumed the leadership of an expedition to capture this important place, and expected there to receive with his two thousand troops the army of Braddock after its hoped-for victory at Fort Duquesne. But fetters of indolence and delay hampered the movement from the outset; the defeat on the Monongahela disheartened all; obstacle succeeded obstacle until in the late season the entire project was abandoned for the poor substitute of an English stronghold at Oswego, which was built and garrisoned.

Fort Niagara.

But for one success the gloom of the year 1755 would have been without any relief. The highway into New France was commanded by the fortification at Crown Point, and both French and English looked on the undertaking commanded by William Johnson as the most arduous enterprise of the whole campaign. Vaudreuil gave Dieskau every available man, seven hundred regulars, sixteen hundred Canadians, and seven hundred Indians for a garrison. The raw levies of colonists and Indians under Johnson were about three thousand four hundred, outnumbering slightly the French forces, though we are ignorant of the proportion of savages to white men. No great capacity was shown on

Johnson's successes.

4

either side, though many choice men from New England were under the English flag, and Dieskau showed both craft and courage. The whole summer had been consumed in trifling negotiations with Indians and a purposeless bustle among the colonials. It was September 8th before their advance produced a collision. The decisive combat took place on the shores of the Lake of the Holy Sacrament, the French engaging with fourteen hundred men, the colonials with but a thousand. But in the crisis the white troops under Lyman, of Connecticut, fresh from their farms, undrilled and poorly equipped, fought with a hitherto unseen coolness and effectiveness. The loss was numerically equal on both sides, but the French regulars were annihilated, and Dieskau was wounded and captured.

The victory was complete and ended the possibility of French aggression for the year, but it resulted in nothing substantive, for Johnson feared or said he feared " a more formidable attack." He built, however, a new and useless fort which he named William Henry, for one of the king's grandsons. Fort Lyman was renamed Fort Edward, for another, and the Lac St. Sacrement has ever since been called, as he wished, Lake George, for the king. The real failure of the great plans which had been formed was to be concealed, if possible. The attention of the English public was therefore concentrated on the affair by a grant of five thousand pounds to Johnson with the title of a baronet, and for the short hour he was the hero of the nation in both America and England.

Nevertheless, no year in the history of our continent was more pregnant with ultimate good than the ill-starred year 1755. The home government had been profoundly affected by the news of one disaster after another, and recognized the necessity of raising by some general plan a permanent fund to carry on the war which was before them. During the winter the project broached at the Braddock conference was renewed, and schemes were put forward by the governors of Massachusetts and Virginia. The former, Shirley, actually suggested all the forms which became subsequently so hateful to the colonists, stamp-duty, excise, land and poll tax. He foretold the growth of a feeling for union among the colonies, and suggested parliamentary control. This was the origin of the conviction prevalent among so many influential Englishmen, that Parliament must regulate American revenue. But neither the time nor the ministry was suited to so radical a measure, although the removal of Shirley himself as commander-in-chief and the appointment in his place of a typical aristocrat holding extreme views of colonial subordination was a step in the direction of parliamentary supremacy. The next chief of the now well-established military power was the Earl of Loudon, with General Abercrombie as second in command. Their powers were independent of the colonial governors, and by orders in council authority was given to quarter soldiers without consent of the colonial assemblies. Other encroachments there were also, which though petty, showed the intention of the cabinet in treating American questions. The policy thus initiated and persistently followed for twenty years was the cause of the American Revolution.

Plans for taxing America.

CHAPTER V.

SUCCESSES OF THE FRENCH AND INDIANS—1756-1758

English Inactivity—Montcalm and the French Leaders—Capture of Oswego by the French—Armstrong ejects the Indians from Kittanning—Winter Warfare—Plan against Louisburg Abandoned—Outrages of Montcalm's Indians—The Massacre at Fort William Henry—Results of Intrigue in Canada—Partisan Activity—Loudon Recalled—Pitt in Power—His Influence and Plans—Amherst, Howe, and Wolfe.

THE formal declaration of war on May 18th, 1756, was made by Great Britain, but the course of her failures was not even for a moment interrupted. It is true that in June a vessel with one hundred thousand pounds was despatched to reimburse the colonists for the extraordinary contributions they had made to carry on hostilities, and thus renew their energies for the future. But in the same month Abercrombie arrived and at once billeted his troops on the people of Albany. It is true that Oswego was provisioned, equipped, and garrisoned with admirable skill and judgment by Bradstreet under the advice of Shirley. But Loudon did not arrive until late in July. The majority of the Iroquois, aware of the activity and energy shown on all sides by the French, sought and obtained neutrality from Vaudreuil; and the English, with five thousand men in Oswego and ten thousand at Albany, did nothing.

English inactivity.

Such inactivity appears even more inexplicable in contrast with the French restlessness. The old régime in France, led by Pompadour, was given over to lewdness, philandering, and plots. Conceit and folly were at the helm even in Russia and Austria. The grandees of the French court would therefore be employed in the continental convulsions of the Seven Years' War. So it happened that a man of the old sound stock, then as ever uncorrupted by the intrigues of an over-centralized government, was chosen to lead in America, where the war had opened and the greatest issue was to be decided. Montcalm, though of noble family, small in stature, and mercurial in temperament, was strong and healthy in body, of an active, intelligent, capable mind, and had served with distinction in the wars of the eighteenth century from 1741 onward. His second in command, De Lévis, and his adjutant Bougainville, were men of the same stamp. The expedition reached Quebec in May. Of three important posts, Carillon or Ticonderoga, Niagara, and Frontenac, the first had been planned and built, the others had been carefully strengthened by the best French engineering skill, and in March Fort Bull, an insignificant English post on the road from Albany to Oswego, had been captured with great and unwarranted acclamation. The spirits of both Canadians and French were raised to the highest point when a garrison was finally thrown into the new post of Ticonderoga, which was further advanced toward the English colonies than even Crown Point.

Montcalm and the French leaders.

Quick to perceive the sluggishness of Loudon, Montcalm devised an attack on Oswego and its outpost, Fort Ontario. Such was the swiftness of his movements that by August 5th he had collected at Frontenac some three thousand troops, with which, on the 12th, he began a regular siege. It lasted but eighteen hours before the outworks fell, and on the fourteenth the whole garrison of Oswego surrendered. The French were in ecstasy, and to win the affections of

Capture of Oswego by the French.

54 THE FRENCH WAR AND THE REVOLUTION

the suspicious Indians razed the entire structure, leaving only two boastful trophies on its site. Loudon, fearing an attack, withdrew to New York, after putting what obstacles he could between himself and his enemies by felling trees across the trails. But he strove to quarter his officers for the winter on the people of both New York and Philadelphia. The people pleaded their rights as Englishmen, the officer replied with threats of force, and a collision was only prevented by compromise in Philadelphia and virtual surrender in New York. The irritation was of course intense. Montcalm remained inactive because his inferior strength, five thousand four hundred to Loudon's ten thousand, compelled him to keep the safe position of Ticonderoga.

So far there was but a single item on the credit side of the English account for the year 1756, the construction of Fort Loudon on the Tennessee, to guard Georgia and Carolina against the French posts which were springing up to the east of the Mississippi. Otherwise all was loss and disgrace. The autumn was brightened by one success, that against the Delawares of Kittanning, who, from their lair within fifty miles of Fort Duquesne, were ravaging the frontier of Pennsylvania. Again it was the Provincials who gained the scanty laurels. Captain John Armstrong, a Scotch-Irish Covenanter of Cumberland, set out across the wilderness of the Alleghenies with a party of men as fearless and determined as himself. With consummate skill they threaded the trackless woods, came on the Indians unawares, and virtually exterminated the settlement, destroying their carefully collected ammunition, and rescuing eleven whites who were held in captivity.

Armstrong ejects the Indians from Kittanning.

When the seat of war is a virgin wilderness, densely wooded, and for the most part covered with matted undergrowth as well, the passage of troops and store-trains is difficult enough even in the summer months. The cessation of hostilities in winter was not, therefore, as on the continent of Europe, a mere conventionality, but a necessity; and in our north country the rigors of winter render even the waterways impassable. Fierce blasts, deep snows, and severe cold heighten the stern aspect of nature. But there were classes of men on both sides who dared to challenge her, forbidding as she was. During the autumn months savages from Ticonderoga were ubiquitous, and from Fort William Henry scouts and rangers threaded their ways where stray enemies might be captured, and occasionally a smart blow was struck by partisans from New England, hardened by exposure and ready for any venture. The notorious Rogers and his band were typical adventurers, making forays into the enemy's country, cutting off supplies, burning homesteads, destroying cattle, taking prisoners, and even daring to approach the hostile works near enough to sketch rude plans. Familiar with the use of skates and snowshoes, the heart of winter had no terrors for them, and in January they advanced to the very threshold of the new French fort, fought a short, sharp engagement which dismayed their foes, and returned with many wounded, but successfully, to the head of Lake George. In March a French party of the same character, *coureurs de bois*, Indians and some regulars, equipped at a cost of a million francs, sixteen hundred men in all, endeavored to strike a retaliatory blow. Over snow and ice they reached the English fort. Attempted surprises, alarms, and strategic marchings were plenty, but they failed to dismay the little garrison of some three hundred and forty-six effective men. The ice-bound boats in the lake, a sloop-of-war on the stocks, the out-houses and barns around the fortress were

Winter warfare.

burned, but a bold sortie dismayed the attacking force, and the costly expedition retreated without further success.

Throughout all these long months the European combatants, in their respective quarters at Montreal and New York, were eagerly emulating the gayety, hospitality, and luxury which reigned at such seasons in Paris and London. Montcalm wasted his energies in squabbles with the jealous and boastful Vaudreuil. Loudon languidly dreamed of an expedition against Louisburg, and his languor was seen in his inadequate and tardy preparations. It was said at the time that, like St. George on a tavern sign, he was always on horseback but never advancing. He and his troops were, however, finally embarked and reached Halifax in June. A squadron from England with additional forces had sailed in May, but arrived at the rendezvous only in July. It was then found that the French had learned the whole matter through spies, and that no less than twenty-two ships of the line were united in Louisburg harbor waiting the attack. The ten thousand troops, the sixteen ships and frigates, were thought to be of no avail against such a force. Loudon and his forces returned to New York, the squadron from England was disabled by a September storm, and the disaster of the season was crowned by a horror perpetrated on the abandoned garrison at Fort William Henry, which was made possible by the withdrawal of the English forces from the seat of war.

Plan against Louisburg abandoned.

The disputes of Montcalm and Vaudreuil about the respective merits of the Canadian militia and the French regulars, who loved each other as little as did the English colonials and their commanders from beyond the ocean, did not prevent active and effective co-operation, bitter and imprudent as they were on both sides. As soon as

Loudon's movements were certain, Montcalm went to
"sing the war song" and hold the war feast with surrounding Indians. By the end of July a strong and well-provisioned force was gathered at Ticonderoga, Indians, Canadians, and French troops, eight thousand in all, a quarter at least being savages gathered from near and far, as far even as the banks of the Des Moines River, in Iowa. Almost immediately the Red Men began warfare in their own way, nor could the polite and fastidious Frenchmen restrain them. Scouting parties captured prisoners, and forming lines with but a narrow interval between them, made their unhappy victims run in the midst to be beaten with clubs even to death. At other times, in open orgies they practised the foulest cannibalism, roasting, boiling, and eating human flesh without a thought of concealment, at the very tent-door, in one instance, of a French missionary. And their numerous petty successes made them every day more insolent and unmanageable. Montcalm used skill and diligence to bridle their passions both for blood and for indulgence in intoxicating drink. His success was partial, and on August 1st the picturesque and unruly expedition set out from Ticonderoga.

Outrages of Montcalm's Indians.

Four days later, after a preliminary skirmish and a summons to surrender, the investment of Fort William Henry was begun. Munro, the commander, had five hundred men within the bastions and seventeen hundred in an entrenched camp near by. He wrote for reinforcements to Webb who was fourteen miles away at Fort Edward with twenty-six hundred men ; Webb sent two hundred regulars, refused further assistance, and in dreary terror despatched messengers in turn to distant New York and New England for help, fearing an attack on his flank. For five days the intrepid garrison held out, three hundred were killed, many

The massacre at Fort William Henry.

were disabled by wounds and more by an epidemic of small-pox; the cannon burst and were useless. On the ninth, therefore, Munro made honorable terms and capitulated, marching out on the following day with the honors of war. The gallant Montcalm had extorted from his Indians a promise to keep the conditions of surrender faithfully. But the last man of the garrison had not left the fort before the treacherous crew clambered with yells and hideous whoops through the embrasures into the interior. The sick were murdered and their corpses mutilated. Plunder there was none, and the savages turned at once to the camp from which on the morrow the English were to march under escort to Fort Edward. The French guards held the greedy creatures in check for a time, and Montcalm moved among them cajoling, threatening, and praying. They seemed to yield to his entreaties, but in the early dawn of the next day they could no longer be restrained. The English were paralyzed by the sudden and awful attack, and there ensued, under the very eyes of Montcalm and his officers, the atrocious massacre which more than any other event clouded his reputation, inspired the English with rage and horror, and partly fixed on the conflict the name of French and Indian war. The Indians massacred in cold blood upwards of seventy, including the sick in the hospital, and carried away two hundred prisoners whom the French could not then rescue, although they afterwards redeemed most of them. The worthless wooden works of the fort were razed, the bodies of the dead piled on them, and the whole burnt to ashes.

The autumn and winter were almost a repetition of the preceding ones. Montcalm failed to follow up his victory; colonial militia rushed in from all sides to Fort Edward, but owing to lack of equipment and employment, turned again to their homes. In November, a

SUCCESSES OF THE FRENCH AND INDIANS 59

helpless German settlement on the Mohawk was burned and sacked by the French and Indians. The wretched intrigues and gayeties of New York and Montreal began again with the winter. The unhappy Canadians had not been able either to sow or reap according to their necessities, the French troops were pinched in their supplies by the knavery of Bigot and other royal agents, and as the English were masters at sea, half rations and actual famine filled regulars and natives with dismay. But the crafty leaders found means to feast the Indians who were again practising cannibalism under their very eyes, and to load their uncertain allies with gifts.

Results of intrigue in Canada.

Partisan activity about the region of Lake Champlain and Lake George was constant. At one time Rogers and his men ventured into the very moat of Ticonderoga, at another they approached so near as to snatch prisoners and cattle from under its guns. In March, however, the rangers suffered a serious repulse, eight of their officers and a hundred of their men being killed.

Partisan activity.

Loudon was as usual fertile in inventions and busy with plans which never left the paper they were sketched on. At last he came to be regarded as a mere trifling busybody, and in the spring he was recalled. Under his leadership the depth of degradation had been sounded. The French were in successful occupation of five-sixths of the continent, while England held less than half of the remaining portion. Lewis XV. and his Indian allies controlled not only the two great waterways of the St. Lawrence and Mississippi, but they actually held every portage between them ; by way of Waterford to Fort Duquesne, by way of the Maumee to the Wabash, and by way of what is now Chicago to the Illinois. The unsuccessful general

Loudon recalled.

returned to England, sure that the colonies had been the root of his failure, and that the first necessity was for Parliament to assume administrative and fiscal control. A stamp act for America would have been one of his remedies.

It seems impossible to explain the imbecility of the Englishmen then in America, except by the worthlessness of the Newcastle ministry. The ruinous politics of its premier led to indecision and the ultimate choice Pitt in power. of second-rate men for leadership. In April, 1757, Pitt, having put himself at the head of a sentiment strongly opposed to the Hanoverian policy of the king, was deprived of office. It was soon seen that a cabinet without him was impossible. For eleven weeks all compromise with the old aristocratic régime was firmly refused, while the Great Commoner, as he was now called, received from the towns and the nation such assurances of enthusiastic regard as were never given to another public servant. At last, in June, court and aristocracy yielded and the great representative of the people came into power.

Though he had been nominally leader of the Commons, and Secretary of State in the last cabinet, yet Newcastle was ever busy with his old tactics of parliamentary control, and the Duke of Cumberland had charge of the His influence war. His generous plans for the colonies had and plans. therefore been largely thwarted, although he successfully resisted every proposition for a stamp act. Now he was the real ruler of England. He stood for no faction, neither for the king nor for the Prince of Wales, nor for the falling Whig oligarchy. The nation had been morally quickened by the great Wesleyan movement and the preaching of Whitefield. He was first known to them by his disinterested refusal to accept interest on the public moneys, or even a percentage on subsidies ; their devotion was intensified by his zeal for better representation, for the total overthrow of the brazen venality which Newcastle practised, and for every wholesome reform. He had, and was for four years to keep their undivided loyalty in his liberal and enlightened policy. The results were soon seen. His old plan for the redemption of America was not changed, for it was the best, but men of a new stamp were selected for the various enterprises. Louisburg was first to be reduced, and in the sequel Quebec. The northern colonies were to be liberated by the destruction of Ticonderoga, and the great avenue of enterprise toward the west was to be opened by the capture of Fort Duquesne.

Amherst, Wolfe, Forbes, and Howe were to be the leaders. Not one of them was a man of mediocre power. Amherst was calm, cold, prudent, but most capable. Forbes, the Head of Iron, as his soldiers nicknamed him, was a tried soldier, destined to give his master's name to the metropolis of the metal which was thought to be in his own veins. Lord Howe, a man of the loftiest birth, had endeared himself to everyone by his judicious, manly, and unassuming character. The greatest of them all was Wolfe, already a hero who had won laurels and successive promotions on the fields of Dettingen, Fontenoy, and Lauffeld, although he was now only in his thirty-first year.

Amherst, Howe, and Wolfe.

CHAPTER VI.

SUCCESSES OF THE ENGLISH AND AMERICANS—1758-1759

England and Prussia as Allies—Success of Frederick and Pitt—Influence of Prussian Success in America—Fall of Louisburg—Pitt Arouses American Enthusiasm — Abercrombie before Ticonderoga—Topography—Death of Howe—Montcalm's Preparations—Failure of the Attack—Retreat of Abercrombie—Recapture of Oswego — Effect of the Success — The Middle Colonies and Forbes's Expedition—Washington and Bouquet—Defeat at Grant's Hill—Illness of Forbes—Weakness of the Garrison at Fort Duquesne—Advance of Washington and Armstrong—Seizure of Fort Duquesne—Pitt's Monument.

THE Seven Years' War, in which the intrepid Frederick faced single-handed the secret coalition of the great Catholic powers, was no less England's affair than his own. The King of Prussia had inherited from his Calvinistic father a splendid army, and the use he had made of it was nothing short of wonderful. In 1756 he had perfect knowledge of the negotiations which had united nearly all Europe against him. In August, therefore, without a word of warning he entered Saxony, captured Dresden, and pushing on, defeated the Austrians at Lobositz. In January, 1757, England became his ally. In May Frederick re-opened his victorious career at Prague, but in June the Austrians under Daun overwhelmed him at Colin. In July the French defeated the auxiliary force of Hanoverians, Brunswickers, and Hessians which England had furnished under the Duke of Cumberland. In August

England and Prussia as allies.

SUCCESSES OF THE ENGLISH AND AMERICANS 63

the Russians overpowered a Prussian army under Lehwald, and in September the allied troops were pledged to neutrality by their English commander in the disgraceful treaty of Closter-Seven. The humiliation of Great Britain was as complete in Europe as in America ; even the elegant Chesterfield gave way to a most ungentlemanlike despair.

Fortunately the treaty of alliance with Frederick had in April been widened by a promise of subsidy. When Pitt came into power he began to support his great ally at the rate of seven hundred thousand pounds a year, worth about seven millions of our money in these days. The convention of Closter-Seven was denounced, and the trifling Duke of Cumberland was replaced by Ferdinand of Brunswick, who at once relieved the Prussian monarch from anxiety about western Germany. On November 5th Frederick crushed the French and imperialists at Rossbach in a battle so important that many German historians date the opening of all modern history from it. Exactly a month later the Austrians met a similar fate at Leuthen, where Frederick gave an exhibition of daring and brilliant strategy which is unsurpassed in military history. First and last, he had thus far fought against odds of three to one in soldiers who actually took the field.

<small>Success of Frederick and Pitt.</small>

It is not merely from the standpoint of general history that the Prussian successes are connected with American affairs. Their moral influence was direct throughout the colonies. The devout prayed for the Protestant champion, and with the answer to their prayers came new life and energy into their disheartened minds. The unbroken experience of reverses was to be relieved moreover by important victories at home, although the tide was only turning and did not reach its flood until the following

<small>Influence of Prussian success in America.</small>

year. Early in the spring Pitt despatched his fleet under Boscawen, with Amherst and Wolfe on board. On May 28th, 1758, they reached Halifax after a long, and tempestuous voyage. There were twenty-two line-of-battle ships, fifteen frigates, and about ten thousand effective troops. Adverse weather still attended them on their departure from Halifax, but after six days of beating against opposing winds, on June 7th the frigates opened a protecting fire and the troops were landed before Louisburg through a raging surf. They were met by a skilful fusillade from behind the French ramparts, but with characteristic spirit Wolfe, who had waded through the shoal water before the boats touched land, rallied the troops, captured the outposts, and drove in the enemy's lines. The same day the town was invested.

The French had put forth many efforts for the fortress which seemed to them the key of their supremacy. The works were well constructed, the garrison ample, but of all the vessels they had despatched only twelve lay within the harbor, misfortune of various kinds having overtaken the others. Of those six were sunk at the mouth of the port to prevent the entrance of Boscawen's fleet. Day by day the cannon boomed on both sides from fleet and port, while the English lines were drawn closer and closer. The usual incidents of a regular siege were varied by the interchange of unusual courtesies between Amherst and Drucour. At short intervals Wolfe kept performing some striking deed of valor. Finally the buildings behind the French lines were rendered useless and untenable, and on July 26th a breach was made by the English cannon in the walls themselves. There was nothing left for the brave garrison but to capitulate. Terms of surrender honorable to both sides were arranged. The prisoners, five thousand six hundred and

Fall of Louisburg.

thirty-seven in number, officers, soldiers, and marines, were sent to England, and though the place itself was abandoned the neighboring French lands, Cape Breton and Prince Edward's Island, were occupied. One success only Drucour had gained, he had protracted the siege until it was now too late for Amherst to co-operate with Abercrombie in the attack on Ticonderoga by an advance into Canada. In his extraordinary exertions Wolfe had been the soul of affairs, but he was weakened by exposure and his feeble constitution seriously impaired. Accordingly, he first obeyed the distasteful orders of Amherst to destroy the French fishing villages of Gaspé and Miramichi, and then sailed for England. Amherst himself started with six regiments, by way of Boston, to join the expedition against Ticonderoga.

Hitherto the exertions of the colonists had been lamed by two considerations : first, the knowledge that every aid they gave to the permanent military power which had been established among them was to strengthen the only menace to their liberties ; second, the haughty contempt with which they had been treated on the field and the disrespect shown to their officers, who were generally elected by themselves. But enthusiasm for the courage and capacity of Pitt lifted them for the time above all considerations of expediency, and they obeyed his summons with alacrity. *Pitt arouses American enthusiasm.*

In the early summer, while the English bombs were bursting over doomed Louisburg, there assembled on the shores of Lake George what is said to have been the largest number of white soldiers hitherto gathered on the continent, an army of fifteen thousand men, six thousand three hundred and sixty-seven British regulars and nine thousand and twenty-four American provincials, chiefly from New England, New York, and northern New Jersey. Its nominal *Abercrombie before Ticonderoga.*

commander was Abercrombie, the former lieutenant of Loudon. He was a survivor from a régime now happily passed away and was dubbed by the rustic wit of the colonies "Nabbiecrombie." The real leader was intended to be Lord Howe, regarded by penetrating men like Wolfe and Pitt as the mirror of military virtue. He had the same peculiar power which Wolfe had shown of inspiring enthusiasm and energy in every member of his expedition. His discipline was most severe, but he shared it with every common soldier, and his easy grace commanded respect and affection from every grade. Among the colonial officers were Captain Stark, of New Hampshire, and Major Israel Putnam, of Connecticut. Every preparation which human foresight could suggest had been made; Lord Howe and his regulars had thoroughly drilled themselves in the tactics of forest fighting, there were nine hundred bateaux and one hundred and thirty-five whale-boats for the troops, with stout barges for the artillery. The expedition moved down the lake on July 5th. The equipments were in good order, officers and men in high spirits. Early next morning they landed near the foot on the west shore, at a point still known as Howe's Cove.

The outlet is a rapid stream, four miles long and full of cataracts, emptying into Lake Champlain. For half its length it flows north and then makes a sharp turn to the east. The thoroughfare from the landing-place followed the stream a short distance on the left bank, passed over to the right by a bridge, and leaving the great bend far to the west, crossed the outlet once more by a second bridge about a mile from the fort. To the east of the second bridge, on both sides of the river, were morasses and low meadows, and just below it were a waterfall and saw-mills. On its left bank, at the mouth, stood Ticonderoga, upon a

Topography.

promontory protected on three sides by water, and on the fourth by strong outworks and an abattis, the only access being from the northwest.

Montcalm had made his dispositions with care, a picket was at the landing-place and three hundred skirmishers had been thrown out to annoy and observe the enemy. Both bridges were burnt, and the English force, under incompetent guides, began its march on the sixth through the wilds on the west bank, crossing ravines and climbing steep banks without even a wood-path to diminish their pains. Though keeping their general course they were soon lost, their ranks broken, and after two hours' weary marching but a semblance of regular advance in columns was maintained. At the head of the foremost body were Howe and Putnam, scrambling over the fallen trunks and crashing through the underbrush, when suddenly a body of the French skirmishers, in even worse disorder, appeared on the left, having also lost their way. The collision was short and sharp, the French stragglers were soon overpowered, but Lord Howe fell dead at the first onset. All courage and what little order was left seemed to vanish immediately, such had been the reliance of all on their young leader. The army bivouacked for the night where it was, and returned next day to the landing. *Death of Howe.*

Irresolution and fatuity marked the course of the expedition almost from the moment of Howe's death. Abercrombie was a timid elderly man, appointed through political influence, who seems to have had little confidence in his own judgment, and to have felt that others had none at all. Montcalm's force, even with reinforcements which were to come up under Lévis, was less than a quarter of Abercrombie's. The venality of the French officials in Canada had become a *Montcalm's preparations.*

scandal, and Vaudreuil's jealousy of the commander was intolerable. Between these two disasters the effective fighting force was reduced to the lowest limit, and the soldiery was ill-fed, ill-equipped, and dispirited. But they had unbounded faith in their leader. On July 8th, early in the morning, his final arrangements were made, and his entire army of three thousand six hundred and fifty men, including Lévis, were under the walls of the fort, busy strengthening the log entrenchments, which stretched across the central ridge from bogs on one side to wet meadows on the other. They were rendered impregnable to infantry by an abattis of tree-tops formed by the frontiersman's simple device of felling the trees for the distance of a musket-shot, with their butts to the breastwork and their bushy crowns to the enemy. Bradstreet, lieutenant-colonel of the Sixtieth Royal American Regiment, had promptly occupied the abandoned French positions on the road and rebuilt both the bridges. On the afternoon of the seventh, the whole English force advanced and camped at the falls by the second bridge, a mile and a half from the enemy's position. The same day Sir William Johnson arrived with four hundred and forty Iroquois braves, who climbed the slopes of Mount Defiance, on the right bank of the stream, overlooking Ticonderoga. There they remained, uninterested spectators of the sequel, amusing themselves by the occasional discharge of their firearms.

About noon on the eighth the English troops appeared before the outworks. No artillery was brought to

Failure of the attack. break through the light breastwork, nor set to rake the fort from Mount Defiance. No flank movement was attempted, nor any attempt made to cut off the French base of supplies and starve out the enemy. To the blank amazement of their foes the English marched, left, centre, and right, direct into the

SUCCESSES OF THE ENGLISH AND AMERICANS 69

leafy tree-tops, with orders to carry the breastwork at the point of the bayonet. They were met by an appalling and deadly fire of balls and grape-shot from muskets and swivel-guns, and driven back. Abercrombie himself was esconced at the saw-mills, whence he attempted, by a flotilla despatched down the outlet, to turn the enemy's left, but the cannon of the fort made it impossible. From that safe retreat he despatched his orders to charge again. Six times, between one and seven o'clock of the afternoon, the dauntless British and provincials dashed their ranks against the bristling entrenchment, only to be driven back with ever-increasing slaughter. The American rangers and colonial militia fought a few skirmishes to the left of our lines, but at twilight nineteen hundred and forty-four brave Englishmen lay dead on the field, the survivors of the charging columns were at length withdrawn, and the frightened general, with his thirteen thousand men and unused artillery, set out in full retreat, after setting fire to the saw-mills which had sheltered his own person during the long disastrous day.

A braver or more stupid conflict is not recorded on the page of history. The French, behind their stanch woodland defences, lost about four hundred men. Their partisans and savages were at once unleashed on the surrounding country, while Abercrombie with his entire army lay stunned at the head of Lake George, until Amherst reached him with his useless reinforcements in October. Abercrombie, like Loudon, returned to a seat in Parliament to vote in due season against the colonists, to whom he likewise attributed his failures.

<small>Retreat of Abercrombie.</small>

The sloth of the general, his timidity, and the wretched retreat were severely criticised by many in his army; but it gave the opportunity for the dashing Bradstreet to take up again a design he had repeatedly opened to both Loudon and Abercrombie, that of an attack on Fort Frontenac. If successful it would cut the French line of communication at a vital point. Even now the commander would not listen, but a council of war authorized the enterprise. With three thousand provincials, among whom were the Clintons from New York, the expedition set out from the Oneida portage, then in command of General Stanwix. Forty-two Iroquois accompanied it. They reached Oswego in safety and crossed Lake Ontario in a flotilla of open boats, whale-boats, and bateaux, and landed on August 25th a short distance from the walls of Frontenac. On the twenty-sixth the commander, with his little garrison of a hundred and ten men, surrendered to the superior force.

Recapture of Oswego.

The place was packed with supplies for Fort Duquesne and the west — guns, ammunition, stores, and goods for barter. Nine armed vessels, too, were there, some of them mounting eighteen guns. Their crews escaped, but the boats themselves were captured with their armament. The Indians were consoled for the scalps they were forbidden to take by abundant booty; the little flotilla, increased by two of the captured vessels, was loaded to the water's edge with useful spoils. What could not be transported was destroyed, and the walls of the fortress were razed. The expedition returned in high spirits to Lake George, leaving a portion of its numbers to garrison the new fort at Oneida portage, which Stanwix was building to take the place of Oswego. The effect of this success, easily as it was achieved, was very great. The wavering Indians were taught to observe a strict neutrality or give their allegiance to the English, and Fort Duquesne was rendered virtually untenable by the French.

Effect of the success.

Hitherto the middle colonies had used but one line of

communication with the far west, Braddock's route, which followed the Potomac to Cumberland, and crossed by an easy carry to the head-waters of the Youghiogheny, an affluent of the Mononga- hela. The English ministry threw itself al- most entirely on the support of Pennsylvania, Maryland, Virginia, and Carolina for the men and supplies with which Forbes was to reduce Fort Duquesne. The previous year had seen a sharp dispute between the governor of Pennsylvania and the assembly, which had demanded as a right his signature to a bill taxing the proprietary lands as well as other real estate. And yet such was her ardor that she furnished twenty-seven hundred men under the famous John Armstrong. A similar dispute was the constant occupation of the Maryland delegates, but they did little for the cause. Virginia sent nineteen hundred men under Washington, whose fame had suffered nothing from his disputes with the touchy governor Dinwiddie concerning the number of troops needed to defend three hundred miles of frontier against the savage allies of France. The new governor gave him more aid. There were also some provincials from North Carolina, twelve hundred and fifty highlanders from South Carolina, and a corps of royal Americans commanded by an admirable Swiss officer, Bouquet.

The middle colonies, and Forbes's expedition.

Forbes reached Philadelphia in April, but his force did not move until June was nearly over. His delay in starting was diplomatic, for he knew how the leaven of savage disaffection, with the weakness of the French and their inability to fulfil their promises, was working. But the still greater delay after the march was begun arose from a mortal illness, which grew worse with every stage, and confined him to a litter carried by his troops. In July Washington was at Cumberland, and Bouquet, with

72 THE FRENCH WAR AND THE REVOLUTION

an advance guard at Raystown, now named Bedford, from the fortification then erected there.

Each represented one of the two opinions held concerning the further route of march. Washington, both from conviction and loyalty to the interests of his colony, upheld the advantages of Braddock's road. Bouquet put forward the superior claims of an entirely new line, up the headwaters of the Juniata, across the transverse ridges and valleys of the Allegheny and Laurel Ridge mountain chains to the Loyal Hanna, a tributary of the Allegheny. This was the more direct road, though the more difficult, and as the expedition hoped forever to rout the French from the Ohio Valley, Forbes, supported by the Pennsylvania influence, determined to take it, and thus add a new highway to the old ones, between the seaboard and the Mississippi Valley. Washington therefore yielded, and joined the main force.

Washington and Bouquet.

Bouquet advanced with two thousand men to the Loyal Hanna River, whence he threw out eight hundred skirmishers under Grant, to reconnoitre the heights above Fort Duquesne. They reached what has since been known as Grant's Hill, overlooking the post, on September 14th. The leader's plan was to decoy a portion of the garrison from their shelter, and capture them. But the expectation of inferior numbers was based on false information, a mad rush of numbers far superior to the assailants threw the latter into confusion, and while the loss was terrible, no less than two hundred and seventy-three killed, wounded, and prisoners, there would have been an actual massacre but for the coolness of the Virginians, who had been carefully equipped and trained for frontier warfare by Washington.

Defeat at Grant's Hill.

The commanding general did not reach Bedford until September. He had grown weaker in his painful progress, but, with courage and persistence, pressed on to the camp of Loyal Hanna, where he arrived on November 5th. A council of war was held, and the decision to go no farther was taken. *Illness of Forbes.*

A few weeks later the Delawares, and some other Indian tribes, renounced the French alliance in a meeting with Frederick Post at Easton, which had been planned by Forbes. The same influence must have been at work in the French fort, for the savages from Detroit and the Wabash departed, and Ligneris, the commander, learning that no supplies could be expected from Frontenac, sent away a number of his white soldiers. This news reached Washington on the twelfth, and knowing how to conduct such affairs by reason of his past experience, as no other could, he was at once despatched with twenty-five hundred picked men. *Weakness of the garrison at Fort Duquesne.*

Armstrong, who was expert in woodland manœuvres, was sent ahead with a thousand of them. On the twenty-fourth the entire expedition bivouacked on Turtle Creek, ten miles from the confluence of the two great rivers which form the Ohio. The pace had been severe, for snow lay on the ground and the paths grew soft and sticky with the moisture. That night the French force of but five hundred men, seeing themselves outnumbered and destitute of provisions wherewith to maintain a siege, fired the fort and departed, some up the Allegheny to Fort Machault, some to Presqu' Isle toward Lake Erie, and some sailed away down the river. The next day the troops of Washington reached the place. Nothing was left but smouldering ruins. *Advance of Washington and Armstrong.*

The English flag was raised on a staff by Armstrong's

hand. The next day was observed as a thanksgiving festival. On the twenty-eighth a party pushed up the Monongahela to Braddock's Fields, and buried the whitened skeletons they found still lying where they had fallen. A young officer, Major Halket, recognized in two, which were locked in a firm embrace, the remains of his father and brother, the former having some marked conformation of the teeth. Such supplies as were available were then collected, and a rude stockade was hastily built around a few huts. Two hundred men, the largest garrison which could sustain itself during the winter with the provisions which could be spared, were then installed in the quarters. The rest reached Philadelphia without adventure, carrying their iron-hearted leader in a litter from stage to stage, exactly as they had brought him. He died the following March, having taken from France her hopes of savage support in that quarter, and the golden opportunity of occupying the valley of the Ohio.

Seizure of Fort Duquesne.

The site of Fort Duquesne still bears the name of Pittsburgh, which he gave it in honor of the man whose ideas had inspired him. It is the poetry of history that the great commoner, to whom the interests of the colonies were so dear, who stood then and afterward in defence of their liberties, at the risk of popularity and power, should have found, in the great city which commands that fertile western land, a monument such as no sovereign prince has ever had reared in his memory.

Pitt's monument.

CHAPTER VII.

NIAGARA AND QUEBEC—1759

Quarrels and Disaffection among the French—Course of the War in Europe—The Height of England's Military Grandeur—Pitt's Plan for the Campaign in America—Wolfe—Enthusiasm in the Colonies—Capture of Niagara—Important Results—Evacuation of Ticonderoga and Crown Point by the French—Futility of Amherst's Campaign—Montcalm at Quebec—Measures of Defence—The English Fleet in the St. Lawrence—Disposition of the Land Forces—French Fire-ships—Desultory Operations during July—Wolfe at the Falls of Montmorency—Defeat of the English—Movements during August—The Plan for Scaling the Heights of Abraham.

AFFAIRS in Canada had come to a crisis. The quarrel between Vaudreuil and Montcalm was so bitter that it was carried home to the court. The latter was supported, himself and friends were loaded with new honors, but substantial aid in men and supplies was withheld. A few hundred recruits and some absolutely essential munitions were embarked and reached Quebec in safety, but the condition of the province was no less desperate. The officials were so recklessly dishonest that even the scanty supplies afforded never reached those for whom they were intended. From Bigot, the intendant, down to the meanest commissary in Fort Duquesne, not excepting the commander Ligneris, every man through whose hands they passed stole a portion, until the troops, half-starved and revengeful, became mutinous as well. The Indians, too, found the articles they wanted few and dear, and became so

Quarrels and disaffection among the French.

disaffected that the example of the powerful Delawares in abandoning the French grew more and more contagious. The Canadians themselves had thus far been deceived in every respect by the gasconade of Vaudreuil, and having sustained their courage by faith in a glory which was fictitious, suddenly found themselves with half-tilled fields and scanty crops, large contributions from which were often exacted for the king, while an angry and licentious soldiery were quartered in their cabins at the munificent rate of fifteen francs a man per month. It was evident that the rottenness and intrigue so successfully imitated from Paris and Versailles would quickly finish their work in Montreal and Quebec. Montcalm lost the buoyant cheerfulness natural to his southern blood, and with a secret desperation, but half-veiled by his assumed and pathetic courage, prepared to obey the instructions from home, to confine operations for the coming season to posts close together and with easy intercourse one with the other. And all the time Vaudreuil blustered, threatened, and plotted ; nor was the tide of official corruption stayed even for an instant. Many expected and some desired the overthrow of New France, hoping to escape detection and punishment.

The course of the Seven Years' War on the Continent was far from uniform. In the west the able and determined Ferdinand defeated the French at Crefeld, forcing them across the Rhine. Frederick spent much time at Olmütz, where he was unsuccessful. But in August he won a fierce and bloody battle over the Russians at Zorndorf. Hastening thence to aid his brother Henry against the Austrians, he was in turn beaten at Hochkirch by Marshal Daun. At the opening of 1759 Ferdinand likewise suffered a reverse at the hands of De Broglie, but on August 1st he took summary vengeance at the battle of Minden. The

Course of the war in Europe.

day was a signal victory, and would have been an utter rout for the enemy, if Lord George Sackville had used the turn of affairs by hurling the English cavalry against the faltering lines of his opponents. It was not a mere error of judgment, and he was punished later for cowardice. On that day a new revelation was made to the student of the art of war. Six English infantry regiments, through a mistake in interpreting an order, charged the French cavalry opposite them, and regardless of a raking artillery fire, successfully broke through the lines. Twelve days later Frederick was defeated by the combined Austrians and Russians at Kunersdorf. The possible consequences were averted by the dissensions of his foes. The road to Berlin was open, but they did not take it. Dresden, however, surrendered and a part of Saxony was lost. Yet this, his darkest hour, was marked by the same unsurpassable qualities of greatness which illuminated his whole career. The winter found him still master of Silesia and much of Saxony.

The year 1759 seemed in England to atone for the past. Her career of victory both by land and by sea was almost unbroken. To herself and to others she seemed to be a world power of the first importance, and in the sphere of general history she has never since outdone the achievements of that wonderful time. France, in the last effort of exhaustion, made a feint of invading England, and began ostentatious preparations in the harbors of Toulon and Havre. In July Rodney bombarded Havre, and rendered ineffective whatever had been done there; Boscawen fell upon the Toulon fleet off Lagos, and scattered it; while Sir Edward Hawke gained a decisive victory over Admiral de Conflans, near Quiberon. A little British squadron during the same summer conquered Senegal. Keppel after a short struggle seized Goree. Pococke

The apogee of England's military grandeur.

kept the upper hand in East Indian waters; and although the West Indian fleet failed against Martinique, it nevertheless captured Guadeloupe. Byng's defeat at Minorca had stung the nation to hasty injustice, for they saw themselves stripped of naval supremacy. It was felt that Quiberon had restored that mastery. There was in all English history no agreement so pusillanimous as that of Closter-Seven. Men saw in Minden the restoration of England's military honor. No less than twelve millions of supplies was voted by parliament during the year.

But the highest lustre shines in Pitt's ministry for none of these things. It is remembered in the story Pitt's plan for the campaign in America. of the world for deeds quite as illustrious in another quarter of the globe, and more lasting in their influence on human destinies than any of these. The American campaign was again laid out on a complete and far-sighted plan. The frontier between the newly founded Pittsburgh and Lake Erie was to be secured and held by Stanwix; Sir William Johnson and Prideaux were to collect Indians and provincials, and advance by Niagara and Lake Ontario on Montreal. Amherst had been appointed commander-in-chief. With the main army he was to march as far as Lake Champlain, and there seize the chance, if it offered, to unite with the army of the St. Lawrence for the capture of Quebec. Into this latter purpose the moral strength and nervous vitality of the whole movement were thrown. Admiral Saunders, in command of the fleet, was a thorough officer, a man of noble and generous personality, great enough to co-operate without jealousy or to rise independently to the height of an emergency.

Of Wolfe, Pitt's general, as he was called, we have already spoken. His form was feeble and his face uncomely, but the fire of his energy glowed in his fine eyes. After the dashing exploits of the preceding year he had spent the winter in London, where he won the affections of a noble woman whom he was destined never to see again. He was a devotee of that learning which is its own end and reward, and though a soldier at heart, often found refuge from the throng of camp and court in the avocation of quiet study. He had from the beginning been assigned to posts not ordinarily given to youth, and now, in the zenith of his power, he was but thirty-two years old. He fully realized the confidence placed in him, and the importance of the command which had been given to him. To one of his friends he had used these words: "I feel called upon to justify the notice taken of me by such exertions and exposures of myself as will probably lead to my fall." _{Wolfe.}

The colonies were inferior to no other part of the British dominions in self-denying enthusiasm. In some of them, as in Massachusetts, fifteen per cent. of all able bodied men were under arms; in others, as in New Jersey, taxes amounting to five dollars for every man, woman, and child, were imposed in support of the war. Provincials and regulars together, there were about fifty-two thousand effective men in the field; Montcalm's forces were upward of twelve thousand, excluding the savages. _{Enthusiasm in the colonies.}

The campaign opened by the successful execution of the plan regarding Niagara. Prideaux had two regiments of English troops with artillery, a battalion of royal Americans, and two of New York provincials. Sir William Johnson brought his quota of Iroquois. A large garrison was left at Fort Stanwix, on the great carrying place, and still another considerable body was detached at Oswego to rebuild the fort. Early in July the small remainder sailed from _{Capture of Niagara.}

Oswego, and reached Niagara in safety. The fort stood on the promontory where the river sweeps into Lake Ontario, and as befitted its importance, had been entirely rebuilt and strengthened by its commanding officer, Pouchot. But after some blunders, it was invested in due form and the English batteries set. Almost at the first discharge Prideaux was killed by the bursting of a small mortar. But Johnson took command immediately, and pursued the work so successfully that in a short time the works were breached. Meantime the French along the frontier had gathered the largest possible force to retake Fort Pitt, as the English had named the reconstructed Fort Duquesne. The force contained but few soldiers, being chiefly bushrangers and Indians. Such as it was, however, its leaders, Aubrey and Ligneris, were ordered to bring it up for the aid of the beleaguered garrison at Niagara. They arrived, eleven hundred whites and two hundred Indians, on the twenty-fourth, but were almost at once engaged by the British forces and Johnson's Indians. The conflict was short but decisive. Many of the French forces were killed, and the rest fled, most of the fugitives continuing their retreat as far as Detroit. The leaders were all taken prisoners. There was nothing left for the brave garrison but surrender. Johnson made honorable terms for them, and though his Indians were permitted to plunder the fort, no massacre revenged the unforgotten slaughter at Fort William Henry.

By this success Stanwix was enabled to occupy the entire frontier, and the whole upper valley of the Ohio passed into undisputed English possession. The posts of the French at Presqu' Isle, Venango, and Lebœuf had been destroyed by the fugitives, and those further distant in the wilderness were entirely cut off from their eastern support. The only outlet for them was to Louisiana. The colony of New York claimed

Important results.

NIAGARA AND QUEBEC 81

the hitherto debatable lands about the river and lakes. Amherst hoped to gain still further advantage by sending General Gage to take Prideaux's command and secure the upper St. Lawrence. Lévis had been sent by Montcalm to prevent just such a movement. He had but eight hundred men, a number insufficient for his purpose. Gage would have had still fewer in all probability, if he had sufficiently garrisoned Niagara and Oswego. In any case he made no effort to carry out his orders, and reported that the plan was not feasible.

Holding Ticonderoga only as an outpost, the French had established themselves for real resistance on the Isle-aux-Noix, in the middle of the river Richelieu below Lake Champlain. Bourlamarque was in command, "intrenched," as he said, "to the teeth, and armed with a hundred cannon." His garrison numbered thirty-five hundred, and behind him was Lévis, whose very name was a tower of strength to the Canadians. Nothing was more desired than an attack by Amherst. The English army was entirely disproportionate to its task, five thousand seven hundred and forty-three regulars and as many provincials with artillery and perfect equipments. By June they were assembled at Lake George, on July 21st they sailed down the lake, next day there was a skirmish under the walls of Ticonderoga, and the French retreated finally from that famous spot on the twenty-sixth, and from Crown Point on August 1st. *Evacuation of Ticonderoga and Crown Point by the French.*

It is useless to speculate on the motives of Amherst, or to call him dull and slow, for the sequel seems incomprehensible on any hypothesis. He at once began a costly and massive fortress, and spent the remaining months of the season, August, September, and part of October in its construction, while a little navy of three vessels was building. The four *Futility of Amherst's campaign.*

6

French vessels made no stand, and three of them were rendered useless by their crews. Thereupon the regulars embarked in open boats, but a wintry storm arose and after five days the expedition returned to Crown Point. In August the general had sent a messenger, promising effectual assistance, who reached Wolfe by a long detour after a month's journey ; a second letter was despatched in September by the directer route of the Abenakis on the St. Francis River, but the messengers were seized by them and carried to Montreal. In revenge Robert Rogers, with a party of rangers, destroyed the village, but the generals remained ignorant of each other's movements. This was the end of Amherst's campaign, and the result of all his extravagant preparation. [The decisive blow was struck elsewhere, with fewer men and less expenditure of money, but with a lavish consumption of energy and brains. There was to be no co-operation, and Wolfe had therefore, after waiting in vain, dauntlessly undertaken his task, the most difficult hitherto assigned to any of the English generals.]

In pursuance of the policy of concentration, Montcalm had gathered into the army around Quebec what was substantially the effective fighting force of Canada, between sixteen and seventeen thousand men, exclusive of the Indians, who were by this time disheartened and worthless. The city stands on a promontory formed by the great river of the St. Lawrence on the southwest, and the St. Charles, which directs its current into the main stream in a direction almost due east, on the north side of the town. At short intervals along the north shore, minor rivers, as the Larry and the Beaufort, flow down from the highlands of the interior, until the rushing torrent of the Montmorency with its famous waterfall is reached at a distance of about seven miles. Quebec itself had two

Montcalm at Quebec.

ports, the lower town on the alluvium of the St. Charles, and the upper on a cliff, the slopes of which were crowned by the ramparts ; and these in turn were overtopped to the riverside by the citadel. The majestic flood is here crowded into a narrow strait thirteen hundred yards in width. The left bank on the north is the more precipitous, and on its summit, level with the upper town, lie the plains of Abraham, the end of a tableland which stretches southwest some eight miles to Cape Rouge.

Montcalm had done everything to deserve success. There were one hundred and six pieces of artillery on the walls of the stronghold. Above the place as far as Cape Rouge, batteries and mortars were disposed on the heights, and off the low shores lay five rafts. Below the confluence of the rivers the low shores, as far as the intervals of Beaufort, were defended by earthworks, behind which were the headquarters of Vaudreuil. Beyond Beaufort the land was much higher, and along the natural escarpment strong ramparts were thrown up as far as the falls of Montmorency. At the upper end of these Montcalm had his quarters, at the lower Lévis. Within this long and strong line the troops were placed to the best advantage, two thousand in the city, the remainder in camps stretching up and down the river. The channel at the mouth of the St. Charles was closed by a chain and guarded by armed hulks. *Measures of defence.*

The English fleet, with Wolfe and his army of eight thousand men, had reached Louisburg in May, and on June 26th they anchored below the isle of Orleans, some miles from their objective point. There were many men on board whose names were to become either famous or notorious, among them Cook, the navigator ; Monckton, George Townshend, Isaac Barre, William Howe, and Guy Carleton. The *The English fleet in the St. Lawrence.*

army was safely disembarked. Much time must, of course, be spent in reconnoitring, some arrangements were made only to be changed, and there were occasional skirmishes of no importance. The fleet commanded the waters; batteries were accordingly posted on the eastern point of the Isle of Orleans, and across the south channel of the river, at Point Levy, were built redoubts protected and strengthened by frigates at anchor; the shore guns were able to throw red-hot balls into the lower town, which they burned. The citadel was beyond their range.

The chief camp was established on the left bank of the Montmorency, where the land is higher than that occupied by the French across the river, and to the northeast of them. Higher up the stream, four miles in the interior, a ford was found, but there was a strong entrenchment on the French side which rendered its passage impossible. Such, in short, had been the vigilance and capacity of the coolly desperate Montcalm, that from the Montmorency on one side to the St. Charles on the other, every possible means of approach from either one of the three rivers had been examined and fortified. His confidence that the citadel would be found impregnable was, moreover, not ill-founded. It must have appeared to him that his most dangerous foe was starvation. July was spent by Wolfe and the officers of the fleet in industrious but unavailing examination of the ground.

Disposition of the land forces.

The French had begun, as early as June 21st, to use their favorite device of fire-ships. They tried it again on the twenty-eighth, and on July 27th despatched an ingeniously constructed raft consisting of numerous vessels against the fleet. This last infernal engine consisted, according to their own account, of over seventy different boats and rafts together,

French fire-ships.

on which were erected old cannon, swivels, muskets, and mortars, all loaded to the muzzle with powder, ball, and grapeshot. The whole was daubed with pitch and fired. In this, as in every other case, however, the effort was nugatory, because, while the flames roared and the worthless firearms exploded and burst, the brave English sailors grappled the craft from small boats, and as the blaze lighted the sky either towed them into channels through which they passed picturesquely furious but harmless on toward the sea, or else ran them ashore.

The long month was not without exciting events. Day and night the heavens were torn by hissing bombs and the thunder of artillery. The camp on the heights of the Montmorency shelled the French under Lévis across the intervening chasm; a portion of the fleet bombarded the French works below Beaufort; the batteries of Point Levy sent ruin and havoc into the lower city; another part of the squadron ran the batteries of Quebec citadel in safety, and compelled Montcalm to send troops for the defence of the highlands above the town; a sharp, short fight occurred at the ford of the Montmorency between Canadian Indians and provincial rangers, and there was scarcely a day without an encounter between savages and soldiers in the precincts of the various English camps, either on the north side, or on the island, or on the point opposite the city. This long line of six miles or more, with two great arms of a mighty river crossing it, was further lengthened when the squadron of Admiral Holmes passed the strait and anchored above. A land force followed and made the British position still more scattering and weak, although their raids rendered a still greater expanse of country unsafe and greatly weakened the moral courage of the Canadians, who were unable to appreciate the Fabian policy of Montcalm.

Desultory operations during July.

Such inconsequential bustle was abhorrent to Wolfe's character. He longed for action and a downright trial of strength with his enemy. As a relief, therefore, to his feverish impatience, he planned a sortie from his headquarters. Below the beautiful falls of the Montmorency, where it plunges two hundred and fifty feet in one grand leap from the heights above into a gorge with regular and perpendicular walls, the stream itself widens, and spreading its shallow waters over a broad bed, forms at its mouth a great muddy shoal, fordable at low tide. Between the heights and the high-water mark of the river the shore is but a few hundred feet wide, and at the flood the bed of the tributary is impassable. On the French side there were redoubts below, and the whole slope was commanded by earthworks above. The morning of July 31st opened with an artillery fire directed across the chasm against the works commanded by Lévis. The result was very slight, as was expected, but toward midday an English force of about fifteen hundred appeared in the river off Beaufort. For some hours they passed up and down in their boats, making several feints to land. Suddenly, in the early evening, at the very ebb, the English renewed their cannonade, this time not only from the main camp, but from ships in the river and from Point Levy, and the French returned the fire. In the midst of the uproar the British, with Wolfe at their head, landed above the shoal, and almost simultaneously another party from the camp below, two thousand strong, began the passage of the shallows.

[marginal note: Wolfe at the Falls of Montmorency.]

But the adventure was too delicate for the headstrong grenadiers of the landing party. No sooner did their feet touch the shore than with a headlong rush, and without orders, they charged the French redoubt. Repulsed once by a deadly fire they charged again, but shaken by the same bloody and fearful shock, they reeled and fell back. At that instant the elements burst on them in a pouring rain, and though the succor of their friends was at hand, ammunition was drenched, all firing was at an end, the tide was on the turn, and the commander ordered a retreat. The dejection of the departing soldiers was heightened by the jeers of their successful foe, who quickly regained the works above. Four hundred and forty-three brave Englishmen had fallen victims to their own impetuous disobedience, and the savages on the Canadian side defiantly rushed down to scalp the dead and dying. *Defeat of the English.*

Early in August a force of twelve hundred men was despatched up the river to the south shore, to destroy the enemy's shipping which had been anchored there for safety while the sailors manned the citadel batteries, and to effect if possible a landing on the north shore. There were hopes as well of a junction with Amherst. Two ill-starred attempts at a landing were made, a third was more successful; and the news of the inglorious successes of the commander-in chief came through hostile channels, but of the longed-for arrival of his splendid army there was no word. As day by day the precious weeks passed on, Wolfe's impatient disappointment developed into an actual physical fever, and in his worried brain one plan succeeded another only to be rejected by his cooler subordinates. His dominant idea was a landing below Quebec, theirs was to scale the heights above the town with four or five thousand men, and compel a general engagement. Any plan was better than the deadening inactivity of the English, for a corresponding hopefulness apparently began to invigorate the enemy. The instinct of the besiegers was untrustworthy, but it seemed as if the Indians returned more *Movements during August.* *The plan for scaling the heights of Abraham.*

and more vigorously to their pestilential occupations, the soldiery in their daily skirmishes saw among the Canadians boys of fifteen and men of seventy, fighting with equal buoyancy and vigor, and Montcalm they felt was steadily growing stronger in the decimation of their own army, which had lost since June eight hundred and fifty men, and was further weakened by prevailing disease. Accordingly Wolfe acquiesced. He knew now, by the arrival of Amherst's first messenger, that whatever was to be done must be done by himself, and he was strengthened probably in his resolve by information from those in command of the fleet, that they dared not much longer brave the approaching stormy season. He would have been more cheerful had he known the realities of the situation and the despair of the French, their scanty supplies threatened by his movements up the river, their undisciplined levies frightened and deserting in hundreds, and Lévis absent in Montreal with eight hundred men to prevent Amherst, the expected foe, from seizing the fortifications of the valley above Montreal.

CHAPTER VIII

THE PLAINS OF ABRAHAM—1759-1760

Movement of the English—French Precaution—Feints and Alarms —Wolfe's Preparations for Landing—His Presentiment of Death —Wolfe's Cove and the Heights of Abraham—Preparations for Battle—The French Unready—Montcalm Bewildered—The Battle—Death of the two Leaders—Surrender of Quebec— Operations during the Winter—Ste. Foy—Relief of Quebec by the English Fleet—Canada Conquered.

THE prospect of action revived Wolfe's failing powers for a time. "To be without pain for a few days and able to do my duty," such was his desire. On August 31st he was able to be abroad once more, and once again, as of old, he passed from post to post rallying the ebbing spirits of his men. On September 3d began the evacuation of the fortified camp above the Montmorency, a difficult feat, only accomplished by a feigned attack on Beaufort which drew off the enemy from his rear; on the fourth the stores were safely floated up the current. Brigadier Murray, with four battalions, forced his way under the fire of batteries on the opposite side, farther up the south shore than the English had yet gone, beyond the Etchemins River; next day three battalions followed under Monckton and Townshend, and that night the entire body of men were safely embarked on the vessels of Holmes's squadron with Wolfe himself in command.

The movement was not unknown, of course, to the

Movement of the English.

90 THE FRENCH WAR AND THE REVOLUTION

enemy, but they believed it was preliminary to the embarkation of the whole army and the departure of the fleet. Nevertheless their vigilance was not relaxed. The steep sides of the plains above the city seemed unsurmountable, but at every little cove a force was set in extraordinary precaution. The shores farther up were less inaccessible, and larger bodies of troops under Bougainville were sent to guard the places where attack was therefore more possible. Montcalm, with the residue of his men, who were a motley assemblage which neither he nor his enemies would dignify by the name of army, confronted Saunders behind the old earthworks of Beaufort.

<small>French precaution.</small>

Immediately the plan adopted by Wolfe began to unfold. An attack was made on September 7th, at Cape Rouge, but it was only to excite and mislead his opponents. For the next five days the entire fleet passed backward and forward on the tide opposite the plateau which stretched between that point and Quebec, as if ready at any moment to detach a landing party. The French dashed hither and thither by land to forefend a surprise, and thus exhausted their strength. Although they were untrained men, many of them but "disorderly peasantry," they yet outnumbered Wolfe's army two to one, including the reinforcement of twelve hundred which was coming up under Burton from Point Levy.

<small>Feints and alarms.</small>

On the twelfth the climax was to come. With his acute mind and keen eyesight, Wolfe had discerned what neither friend nor enemy suspected, that it was feasible not merely to scale the heights higher up but those of Abraham near the city and surprise the foe. While reconnoitring he had found and chosen as his landing the little cove, since known by his name, from which a zigzag path on which

<small>Wolfe's preparations for landing.</small>

but two men could climb abreast wound to the top. He had fortunately learned that French supply-boats were ordered to pass down in the darkness under the north shore that very night. Accordingly the fleet as usual floated above Cape Rouge, and although boats for the leaders of the desperate enterprise were lowered in full sight of the French, Bougainville thought nothing of it, expecting a repetition of the usual barren events of the past few days. It so happened also that the commanders on the plains above had carelessly given furlough to a considerable number of their scanty force, and that a Guienne regiment, which was to have encamped there, had inexplicably remained in its old quarters on the St. Charles River. Down below Admiral Saunders showed an ostentatious activity in taking soundings off Beaufort and in other meaningless preparations for attack, which completely deceived Montcalm.

As the evening hours slowly passed, Wolfe proceeded from ship to ship to assure himself that everything was ready, and to inspire his troops with courage. A presentiment of death had overpowered him. Before leaving the cabin of the flag-vessel he had given to his friend and schoolmate, Jervis, a miniature of his affianced bride, Miss Lowther, and a farewell message. In the boat, during one of the intervals of inspection, he spoke of Gray's Elegy, quoting with deep pathos the verse:

<blockquote>
"The boast of heraldry, the pomp of power,
And all that beauty, all that wealth e'er gave,
Await alike the inexorable hour.
The paths of glory lead but to the grave."
</blockquote>

His presentiment of death.

It needs little imagination to realize the solemnity with which he repeated the last line. According to the midshipman who was present and told the touching story, he said he would rather have written that poem than take Quebec on the morrow. It has been suggested by his greatest historian that perhaps the hero is greater even than the poet.

Toward two in the morning the tide turned, and as the ships began to move down stream the signal was given and the boats were made ready. Soon the advance left the fleet behind and moved more swiftly under the north shore, the larger vessels following. Sentries hailed from the strand, but were deceived into a belief that the French supply-boats were passing. Soon the appointed bay was reached, but in the darkness the rowers grounded their prows a little below. Through the steep, pathless forest the vanguard climbed noiselessly, others following by the path, which had to be cleared of obstructions, and some even farther up the stream by ravines and water-courses. So precipitous was the hill that going was possible only on hands and knees. At length the top was reached. Quickly the weakened posts were seized, and as the firing of muskets gave the expected signal to the forces who were now waiting below on the narrow beach, the swarms of men began first to clamber and then more regularly to move up the path. The roads and outposts above having been seized by the volunteer adventurers, there was no resistance, and in the dawn Wolfe with his five thousand men stood safely on the long-expected field where the enemy must fight or surrender, within a mile of the prize to which he was pressing on.

[sidenote: Wolfe's Cove and the Heights of Abraham.]

The surprise was successful and complete, but the danger was immediate and great; on one side Quebec and Montcalm, on the other Bougainville and his troops. A hasty examination showed the most advantageous ground to be a narrow plateau, known as the Plains of Abraham, somewhat higher than the up-

[sidenote: Preparations for battle.]

THE PLAINS OF ABRAHAM 93

land on which they stand. It was really a portion of the level on which upper Quebec stood. To the north were the abrupt steeps falling to the meadows of the St. Charles, to the south the cliffs just scaled, the width was about a mile, and the English forces in proper array for fighting could not reach across when the right wing rested on the brow toward the St. Lawrence. At the other end, therefore, a flanking party was set perpendicular to the rest and facing the north. In the main line were about thirty-two hundred men, the remainder, some sixteen hundred in all, were divided between the left flank, the guard of the landing-place, and the reserve. Two field-pieces had been dragged up from the cove.

All night long the guns of Saunders's fleet had thundered while his boats had skirted the shore as if to land. Montcalm had been thoroughly deceived, and was not disabused until in the early dawn he heard the artillery of his southern outposts just before their capture. *The French unready.* After waiting in vain for an explanation, he set out on horseback to discover the cause. At the bridge of the St. Charles the close red ranks of the English became visible. An adjutant was quickly despatched for troops. The Guienne regiment had come up in the dawn, it was soon reinforced by other regulars as well trained as itself, but all told they numbered less than two thousand. Intermixed with them were about twenty-five hundred more, Indians and Canadian militia. Others were expected, but Vaudreuil retained them, still fearing an attack by the apparently watchful and busy fleet, and Ramesay, the commander of the garrison, refused both men and cannon on the plea of defending himself. At last three guns were extorted from him.

Capable, vigilant, and indefatigable as he had ever been, Montcalm was stunned. His subordinates, with criminal neglect, had virtually forfeited the natural

94 THE FRENCH WAR AND THE REVOLUTION

strength of their position in the desperate game. His well-considered plan of delay, long and carefully carried *Montcalm be-* out, was in a moment overthrown. Where *wildered.* he expected at the most "a small party come to burn a few houses and retire," stood an army of veterans. Corruption, selfishness, and incapacity environed him. For a time his auxiliaries harassed the English by the familiar tactics of bush fighting, and the cannon did serious execution. He might have postponed an action until the forces from Cape Rouge could make an attack in the rear. But he was overpowered by the unexpected crisis and emphasized the possibility of an English fortification which could repel Bougainville and cut off all the supplies of his army. Yielding to the passionate ardor of his men, he at last gave the fatal order toward ten o'clock of the cloudy, rainy morning.

The British had waited during these trying and seemingly interminable hours with the calmness and self-control to be expected of veterans. Wolfe was *The battle.* everywhere, encouraging, soothing, ordering. As the French came on, his little battery opened fire. Their evident aim was to flank and drive the columns back over the precipice. The onset was impetuous but irregular, and the English reserved their fire. The slow moments passed and but forty paces separated the lines. At the centre the quick order, the simultaneous volley thrice repeated, the groans of killed and wounded, the charge and rout, followed in the swift succession of but a few minutes. On the right the general himself led. Owing to fences and cornfields his ranks were broken and the charge less impetuous, but there, as all along the line, the rout of the French was complete.

Amid the awful clash death overtook the two conspicuous figures of the hour. Wolfe was wounded in the charge, twice as he pressed on and the third time fatally, when he fell and was carried by his own orders to the rear, anxious lest the forces should be discouraged by his fall. Knowing he would die surgical assistance was refused, but at the cry "They run; see how they run!" he rallied to ask "Who run?" Hearing the answer: "The enemy give way everywhere," he roused himself fully to the necessary decision. "Go, one of you, to Colonel Burton; tell him to march Webb's regiment down to Charles River and cut off their retreat from the bridge." Then in apparent resignation, and with his last breath, he murmured "Now, God be praised, I die happy." Montcalm, too, by a sad coincidence of fate, had been once struck by a musket-ball, but persisted in the duty of conducting his flying squadrons as they retreated toward the city gates. While rallying them to protect the other fugitives he received a mortal wound. Carried within the town, he survived to hold a council of war and write a letter to his conquerors, commending his brave men to their clemency. His last hours were spent in the consolations of religion, and he was buried the day he died, September 14th, in the chapel of the Ursuline Convent. It is believed that the grave was in large part a hollow formed by the bursting of a bomb. "Valor gave a united death, History a united fame, Posterity a united monument," runs the fit inscription on the monument in the governor's garden at Quebec, which bears on one side the name of Wolfe and on the other that of Montcalm.

Death of the two leaders.

On the eighteenth Quebec surrendered, and was occupied by a British garrison. In the mournful council over which the French general presided on the last day of his life, he gave it as his opinion that the forces must rally and fight again, or there would be an end of New France. But the governor was a poltroon as well as a backbiter and defamer. Conster-

Surrender of Quebec.

nation first, and chaos afterward, so utterly demoralized the conquered people that he lost the very semblance of braggadocio, and even Lévis when he arrived could produce no order.

That officer's tenacity was as great as his courage, and during the long and bitter winter, while England, both sides of the Atlantic, was ringing with the pious hallelujahs of the people and on one with the premature jubilations of the sinking aristocracy, he conceived and prepared a daring and yet reasonable design. From time to time rumors of attack reached the incredulous garrison, and they therefore established outposts at Ste. Foy in a forest five miles distant, and at Lorette. French grenadiers, Canadians, and Indians further appeared in considerable numbers, and it was found that strong posts had been established at inconvenient points in the neighborhood. Skirmishes, some of them serious, were not infrequent, and the commander of Quebec, Murray, a just and gallant man, became uneasy toward the spring, as he saw disease and death at work among troops not inured to such a severe climate. By April his able-bodied, serviceable men did not number three thousand, although there had been seven thousand in the autumn; seven hundred were dead, the rest were victims of a pestilence, scurvy, and dysentery.

Operations during the winter.

The same month found Lévis's preparations complete. Starting in boats from Montreal on the twentieth, with seven thousand men, new reinforcements were added at every town on the way, and he appeared, after a wild and stormy night, on the twenty-seventh, at Ste. Foy with a force of between eight and nine thousand. The youthful and undaunted Murray made a sortie and drew in his outposts. Next day he resolved to fight, disparate as the numbers were, and at

Ste. Foy.

the head of three thousand men, engaged the enemy on the very ground which had been drenched with blood in the previous September. His first onset was apparently successful, and the enemy withdrew to the shelter of the forest. But the French rallied, and two desperate struggles ensued at a windmill made famous as the Mill of Dumont. In the first the English prevailed, but were raked by a flanking fire ; in the second they were routed. After two hours of unsurpassed bravery, they were finally overpowered by numbers and forced to retreat behind the city walls. They lost one man in every three, and their opponents about eight hundred in all. The situation of Quebec was desperate. At once the French drew up their six war vessels in the river, and on shore began the lines for a siege. The fire from the town was so hot and incessant that they could with difficulty mount a gun. But undaunted to the last, their hope might not have been forlorn if vessels with munitions from France had reached them in season, as Lévis had prearranged.

The event was otherwise ; it was not a French, but an English fleet, which, in the third week of May sailed up the St. Lawrence. It promptly engaged the French ships. Their admiral fought obstinately to the end, but was captured and his fleet destroyed. Lévis awaited the decision and then retreated precipitately with his entire force, leaving sick, wounded, and all his guns to fall into Murray's hands. This was the real end of resistance, the gallant and ill-starred struggle of New France was over. All Canada below Three Rivers was lost, for the inhabitants had not repeated the conduct of the Acadians, but swore allegiance to Great Britain. There was nothing left but to concentrate farther away and make the final stand at Montreal.

Relief of Quebec by the English fleet.

Amherst at last began to show some mettle. Murray

was to advance up the river from Quebec. He himself, with his large force, was to make the long detour by Lake Ontario, and descend the river so as to cut off a retreat toward Detroit. Haviland was to force the passage by Isle-aux-Noix and the Richelieu River, from which Bourlamaque had retreated to consolidate his troops with those of Lévis, leaving seventeen hundred men under Bougainville. The last hope of the French was that the English expeditions might arrive separately, and in that event they hoped to defeat each one in turn. But the complicated plan of the commander-in-chief was perfectly executed, and by September 7th the city was surrounded. The next day it surrendered. By Amherst's leniency, honorable but decisive terms were made, and though the peace of Paris was not signed until three years later, that portion of the Seven Years' War fought in America, and known to us as one of the great turning points of our history, was over.

Canada conquered.

CHAPTER IX.

THE PEACE OF PARIS—1760-1763

Affairs in the Southern Colonies—Expedition against the Cherokees—New Territory Opened for Settlement—Indian Discontent—Revolt of Pontiac—Relief of Detroit and Suppression of the Rebellion—Naval Supremacy of England—The War Continued in Germany—Death of George II.—Accession of George III.—His Character and Policy—Pitt and Frederick the Great—Fall of the Ministry—Bute and the New Tories—Frederick and Russia—England and Spain—The Terms of Peace—Effect of the Seven Years' War on the Continent—Its Character in America and India—Determinative Results in the American Colonies—Its Relation to American Nationality and Independence.

NOTHING throws a more interesting light upon the relations of the colonies to each other at this time, than the utter indifference of the middle and southern ones to the struggle of those in the north. Men from all New England, from New York, and from New Jersey were found in every battle of the years 1759 and 1760. From Pennsylvania southward the interest was comparatively languid, and after the founding of Pittsburgh even Washington retired from the army to take up the pleasant duties of a country gentleman, and represent the Old Dominion in her legislature. The undisturbed quiet of the south was only threatened by the ever-arising disputes of the people with their governors, who sedulously labored for the maintenance of such supremacy as they conceived to be inherent in

Affairs in the southern colonies.

the crown and Parliament. To the same end they sometimes meddled with the petty disputes between the frontiersmen and the friendly Indians. In an access of zeal Lyttleton, of South Carolina, provoked a most ignoble quarrel with the Cherokees, who had so far been proud allies of England, and in 1757 had as volunteers protected the frontiers of Georgia and Carolina. The result was an embargo on all intercourse with them. They had become so dependent on the supplies obtained by barter that disaffection spread like a forest fire, and resulted in exasperating recriminations which finally led to bloodshed by the Indians, and violation of faith by the whites.

Expedition against the Cherokees.

Lyttleton set out with an expedition of which both Christopher Gadsden and Francis Marion were members, and awed them to temporary submission. But during the winter of 1759 and 1760, the tension became too strong, the savages broke their word, and frontier warfare of the most vindictive kind was waged from the early spring onward. Twelve hundred soldiers, highlanders and royal Americans, and seven hundred provincial rangers, Moultrie among the number, were united into an army to subdue the harassed and ill-treated Cherokees. They were outwardly at least a docile people; their settled homes and agricultural habits divided them by a wide interval from the Iroquois or the Delawares. At the first appearance of the white men they fled. Their farms and dwellings were devastated, and a summons issued for a council to settle terms of peace. But stunned and exasperated, they gave no response and retreated westward beyond the Appalachian Mountains into the upper valleys of the Tennessee. The army followed, fell into an ambush, but routed the undisciplined horde from their lurking places. Montgomery, the general, would, however, go no further, not even to Fort

Loudon, where the garrison was by this time perishing of hunger. He retreated in good order. Fort Loudon fell and the army was dispersed. The Cherokees were exultant and the colonies doubly depressed, their defencelessness being in their minds the corollary of the usurpations of their governors. The bitterness between the governor and army on one side, and the people, whose sympathies were with the frontiersmen, was destined to become one of the little rills which later united into the great stream of colonial discontent.

The invasion in itself considered was, however, a memorable fact, for it opened the way to the eventual seizure of the Creek and Cherokee lands and the extension of English-speaking colonization westward, from the southern as well as from the middle and northern colonies. *New territory opened for settlement.* It was an immediate consequence of the capitulation at Montreal that Rogers and his party of rangers penetrated the western wilderness around the great lakes, made a truce with Pontiac, the great Ottawa chieftain who had united under his nominal sway all the northwestern tribes, and then planted the English standard at Detroit, in token of the occupation of the whole lake country.

The regular warfare of Europeans was, of course, at an end. But the Indians were still to be reckoned with. In spite of the successful heroism of Christian Frederick Post under Forbes's direction, in spite of the diplomacy of Johnson, the good-will of the Algonquins was but temporary, and the allegiance of the Iroquois but partial. The western frontiers were occupied by the English and the posts garrisoned, but discontent was not allayed. The agents of the English in the fur trade were desperate and unprincipled men, who plundered and abused their savage clients. The wandering bands were no longer received at the stockades of *Indian discontent.*

the forts with smiles, and beguiled from their childish waywardness by indulgence. And above all, the various tribes saw their lands invaded by men who, unlike the French, had the fixed purpose of permanent settlement, and fiercely resented either intrusion or theft. The agents of the earlier traders were still numerous in the wilderness. They unceasingly circulated lying reports of French sympathy, and as the angry savages began to prepare for open rebellion, both encouragement and supplies in abundance were furnished by their former friends.

A leader for the red men is always at hand in times of excitement, because with superstitious awe they at-
Revolt of Pontiac. tribute a supernatural mission and powers to the first clever fanatic who claims them. Such a man was Pontiac, endowed in the highest degree with every quality of his race—courage, ambition, and eloquence; passion, inconsistency, and treachery. During the two years succeeding the surrender of Montreal was formed, by his address, a conspiracy of all the Algonquins, of some of the tribes on the lower Mississippi, and of two of the Six Nations. Its ramifications embraced the entire northern and western frontiers. The outbreak began on May 7, 1763, by an attempted seizure of Detroit; but the scheme had been betrayed to the English commander Gladwyn, and the treacherous plan of Pontiac was thwarted. A formal siege was opened two days later, and a fitful and murderous warfare began all along the line. Within a fortnight Fort Sandusky fell; ten days later Fort St. Joseph, near the head of Lake Michigan, was surprised; early in June Michilimackinac, on the upper lakes, was seized, and the garrison murdered. In quick succession Ouatanon, on the Wabash; Fort Miami, on the Maumee; Presqu' Isle, on the site of the city of Erie, with its outposts Venango and Lebœuf, making the

line to Fort Pitt, all fell into Indian hands, and the great fort at the head of the Ohio was itself besieged. In fact, of all the vast acquisitions west of the settlements, the posts of Detroit, Niagara, and Fort Pitt alone remained in English hands.

But savage fury soon consumes itself. The pioneers suffered intensely under repeated and furious onslaughts, but they fought with desperation, and where a fair field was given, as at Ligonier, Carlisle, and Bedford, their foes were frightened or beaten off. In July Bouquet, after a masterly march and a well-fought battle at Bushy Run, relieved Fort Pitt. Pontiac, with a constancy unprecedented in Indian annals, beleaguered Fort Detroit until September, when a vessel despatched from Niagara arrived with help. The conflicts under the walls of the fortification had been bloody and exhausting; the Indians, though on the whole victorious, now asked for peace, and in the late autumn Pontiac and his people withdrew. The rebellion was broken and virtually ended with the arrival of winter. The next two years were occupied with the pacification of the tribes. Pontiac made another rally to seize the Illinois country during 1765, but failed, and the English definitely occupied it. The whole episode is memorable for the sufferings and consequent exasperation of the frontiersmen. Too often they retaliated in the succeeding years by acts of barbarity and a policy of deceit. A century and a quarter has not diminished the intensity of hatred between English white men and the descendants of Pontiac's rebels.

Relief of Detroit and suppression of the rebellion.

In the perspective of history it appears as if England no longer had a reason for war; as if she should have urged and brought to a speedy conclusion the desultory negotiations for peace which began in 1759. She had conquered everything in America and the West Indies which France possessed, except a few islands and her claims to the shadowy land of Louisiana beyond the Mississippi. In the other hemisphere Clive had retaken Calcutta, overwhelmed Surajah Dowlah in the battle of Plassey and won Bengal; Coote had defeated Lally at Wandewash, and the possibility of French ascendency, or even equality, in India was forever ended by the occupancy of Madras. In all quarters of the globe the navy of Great Britain was again supreme. There was also a most urgent reason for peace in the situation of Frederick the Great. But the nation was ecstatic over its successes, and Pitt avowed that he desired not merely to humiliate but to exhaust the French. During the year 1760, therefore, nothing was done. The occupation of the quidnuncs was to discuss what England should keep and what she should surrender at the peace, a powerful party contending for retaining Guadaloupe, the more enlightened explaining that the West India trade was at a standstill, while the North Americans were doubling in numbers every twenty-five years; that, freed from fear of Canada, they would spread over the whole continent, confine themselves to agricultural pursuits, and furnish an unlimited market for the manufactures of the motherland. Colonial affairs being under the Board of Trade, the Lords in that body could unify their administration and indefinitely expand industrial prosperity at home.

In Germany the bloody and useless war went on. Ferdinand with his Anglo-German army kept the French, under Broglie, inactive throughout the year. In June the Austrians, under Laudon, defeated the Prussians, under Fouqué; in August they were beaten in turn at Liegnitz by Frederick, who prevented the union of the Austrians and Russians. But the latter surprised Berlin in October, and destroyed a large portion of it by fire. In November Frederick won another bloody and fruitless victory over the Austrians at Torgau, and from his camp at Bunzelwitz defied both Austrians and Russians. He was desperate and disheartened, gray-haired and wrinkled with premature old age, for an event of awful significance not only to him but to the world had taken place.

George II. died on October 25, 1760, and his grandson, George III., ascended the throne. During the long reign of thirty-three years which thus came to a close England had seen two brilliant phases of her history—a period of peaceful prosperity, a time of unequalled military success. The Crown as a political factor had been quiescent, the Whig aristocracy had done its work, and the people, under Pitt, had asserted itself in spite of constitutional limitations. Death of George II.

There had always been strong opposition to the German war on the part of those who disliked the attachment of the English kings for their Hanoverian possessions. It was heightened by the enormous cost to the taxpayers involved in Pitt's subsidies. The new king was a youth of twenty-two, with a fine figure and an engaging expression in his handsome face. He had been the pupil of his clever mother, and she had thoroughly engrafted into his slow, tenacious mind two lessons — to be an Englishman and to be a king. The former meant the abandonment of the Hanoverian policy, the latter the breaking down of aristocratic Whig rule by means of a cabinet and a responsible chief. Accordingly, the first words addressed to his subjects were such as his two predecessors could not have used : "Born and educated in this country, I glory in the name of Briton." And at once four changes were made in the cabinet. Newcastle was summoned as being the head, and Lord Bute, destined to be the royal Men- Accession of George III.

tor, was made Secretary of State, the others were not of importance. Pitt acquiesced, but he had not been consulted.

Superficially it appeared as if the accession of a "patriot king" had brought in an era of good feeling. The Jacobites came flocking back to court, and many of them were appointed to important offices. <small>His character and policy.</small> The king was neither licentious nor unprincipled, his personal character might even be called good. Though often compared with James II. for narrow-mindedness and obstinacy, yet it would be unsafe to describe him as mediocre. Conceited mediocrity often courts real greatness in others, and draws powerful minds into the sphere of its influence. But George III. had an instinctive abhorrence of ability either in life or letters. His education was so deficient as to be contemptible. He thought the masterpieces of English literature "stuff," and had a jealous aversion for every strong man. He described himself as a Whig of the Revolution, but he had been formed by the maxims of Bolingbroke and hated Pitt even when dead, for a proposal to erect a monument to the great man was felt to be a personal insult. Surrounded by the same cringing servility which the Stewart kings had exacted, obstinately determined to rule as well as reign, unmindful or ignorant of the development of the constitution since Sunderland's time, appreciating at its full value the power of appointment in the church and army, and to many important civil offices in the court and government, he soon surrounded himself by a faction. The "king's friends" were not a party, but bound only by the tie of royal favor they blindly did his bidding. Their power was the more pernicious because the Whigs were rent by internal dissension, and representation was so corrupt, jobbery in Parliament seats so.

rife, that the best sentiment of the country was against them. They could therefore fall an easy prey to the king and his men. Their policy, moreover, had always been nominally for peace, and now they were so exasperated by Pitt's constant demands for the support of the war that they might desert him at any moment. George understood the strength of the royal prerogative behind such intrenchments, in the face of such foes.

The resources of Prussia were apparently exhausted, and even with Pitt's munificent subsidy Frederick was hardly able to secure the absolute necessaries of warfare. The dogged persistency of his foes had the support of both numbers and wealth, so that they reappeared with undiminished strength after blows which would have prostrated an enemy of equal resources. And now the continuance of the subsidy was improbable. Nothing short of an intervention of Providence could tide Prussia over such a crisis. It is true that France also was exhausted. Choiseul was the minister of state, and with all his ability he could not be, and was not, the creature of Madame de Pompadour, who had once been the mistress of Lewis XV., but was now the pander to his senile lust and sought thereby to secure the mastery of the kingdom. Her bitterness toward Frederick was intense, and men long believed it was the continuation of her policy when peace was proposed if England would abandon his cause. The offer really sprang from Choiseul's insight that Prussia might one day rival France. It was indignantly rejected by Pitt. The peace party among the Whigs affected great displeasure. But Pitt, nothing daunted, assumed an attitude even more warlike. The conflict with France became hotter than before; Keppel and Hodgson seized Belleisle, off Brittany, in order that when driven to a peace France might gladly accept it as

<small>Pitt and Frederick the Great.</small>

an offset to Minorca. Dominica, in the West Indies, was likewise seized, and Pondicherry, the last important hold of the French in India, was captured. But such was the spite of his mistress against the Prussian king that still Choiseul could not yield.

At this juncture the notorious family compact was proposed by Charles III., of Spain, who regarded the French Bourbons as holding the leadership of the family. Spain was to support a peace if made. In return she expected the concession of Minorca from England. But there were also secret articles concluding an offensive and defensive alliance. The third Bourbon prince, the King of Naples, also adhered to both parts. The respective possessions of all the Bourbon powers were mutually guaranteed. Pitt haughtily rejected any indirect negotiation with France through Spain, and proposed the seizure of the Spanish treasure-fleet now on its way from the Indies, the occupation of Panama, and a general attack on the Spanish possessions in America. Such noble daring seemed madness to the jealous minds of his timid colleagues. He found but one supporter in the cabinet, his relative, Temple. On October 6th, 1761, the king received the resignation of that famous ministry which had carried England's fame to greater heights than it ever before had reached. Englishmen had permanently girdled the globe with English civilization, and opened boundless avenues to English enterprise. The Newcastle cabinet, of which Pitt was the soul, had been less than five years in existence.

The king had no small share in this fall. He had manipulated the elections so as to diminish Newcastle's influence, while urging Newcastle to what was really insubordination under the guise of self-assertion as the premier. He now turned on the patrician leader with direct insults and forced him to resign. Power was delegated to Bute on May 29th, 1762, and once again, after a century and three-quarters, the dominant influence in court and Parliament was Jacobite in every element except that it did not adhere to the extinct line. The Tories of 1762 were in reality a faction as unconstitutional in its methods and aims as the Royalists of the Restoration had been. The populace of London hailed Pitt with sincere and noisy enthusiasm as he drove through their streets; elsewhere, too, his support was stanch even in opposition. But the fickle element among the people felt the timidity of their early leaders, and the king, who was eager to begin his work of restoring the prerogative, earnestly desired peace. The subsidies to Frederick were at once withdrawn, and in the spring of 1762 the masterly inactivity of 1761 appeared merely to have postponed the inevitable ruin.

But deliverance came. The Empress Elizabeth died, and her nephew, Peter III., came to the throne. To this young and ardent enthusiast Frederick was a hero, and Russia became a friend. In less than half a year, however, the court intrigue of Petersburg cut short the career of the new Czar, and he was succeeded by his wife Catherine. She was a self-styled philosopher and reformer, in reality a woman of the highest intellectual and practical abilities, but a desperate wanton in her private life. She was no friend to the king of Prussia, and recalled from his army the troops her husband had furnished him; but she was willing to remain indifferent. Frederick's sharp tongue had made enough powerful foes. He bridled it and spoke her fair; Russia, though not an ally, was at least no longer an enemy. Two victories of importance were won in 1762. The preliminaries of the Treaty of Paris foreshadowed a withdrawal of the French armies. Peace with Russia, Sweden, and Austria followed ere long, and though the new English ministry had offered Silesia to Austria and East Prussia to Russia by the treaty of Hubertsburg, Prussia kept every inch of territory which she had gained.

Pitt's fall having been accomplished, the king, with a certain compensatory grace, offered him the choice be-

England and Spain.

tween the Duchy of Lancaster with five thousand pounds a year, and the governorship of Canada, without residence, and the same honorarium. The great commoner wisely refused anything for himself, but accepted for his wife the title of Baroness Chatham, with three thousand pounds a year for the lives of himself, his wife, and their oldest son. He may well have felt some complacency in the conditions of his opposition. He had still a strong following of the better Whigs, and his sagacity in what had been thought a chimerical scheme of war with Spain was soon proven. No sooner was the Spanish treasure-fleet safe in harbor, some three weeks after his resignation, than, in accordance with the secret terms of the family compact which he had divined, Charles took the initiative himself, and in 1762 declared war on England. Her retort was a counter-declaration and the speedy capture, according to Pitt's rejected plans, of Cuba, Manilla, and the Philippine Islands. Portugal at first remained neutral; but in the face of Spanish threats and actual invasion applied to England for assistance, which even Bute, who was now in power, could not refuse, at least temporarily. If the tide of success were to flow on it was certain that Pitt would return to power; the nation seemed not to care in the least that he had increased the public debt to one hundred and thirty-six million pounds by his lavish expenditures; their victories terrified the ministry more than defeats would have done, and they felt that peace must be made at every hazard.

Negotiations were opened with France, whose depleted treasury made her glad to treat. The old machinery of bribery and menace was set to work in the House of Commons to secure a majority, and when all was ready the surprisingly moderate terms of the Peace of Paris were announced. England was to leave France a share in the fisheries of Newfoundland and the St. Lawrence, with the islets of St. Pierre and Miquelon, to return Guadaloupe, Martinique, and St. Lucia. Cuba and the Manillas went to Spain. She was to keep Tobago, Dominica, St. Vincent, and Grenada ; Canada, Nova Scotia, Cape Breton, and all French possessions in America east of the Mississippi, except New Orleans, were surrendered to her. She was to exchange Belleisle for Minorca, and Spain was to cede Florida for Cuba and the Philippines. France, further abandoned all right to a military settlement in India, evacuated both the Hanoverian territory and Prussian forts which she held, and by a separate secret agreement compensated Spain for the loss of Florida in the gift to her of all Louisiana, which stretched away with indefinite boundaries to the Pacific. The stipulations were very favorable to England, but the annihilation of French prestige, to which Pitt had looked forward, and to which English victories had entitled the nation, was not secured. The nation as a whole was opposed to the terms, but Parliament had been secured for Bute and Grenville. The preliminaries were laid before both houses on December 9th, 1762. Pitt, suffering from gout and carried to his seat by attendants, made a somewhat theatrical appearance in the lower one to oppose the fisheries clause, and anything which looked to a possible restoration of French maritime power. But all opposition was vain, and the treaty was concluded at Paris on February 10th, 1763.

The terms of peace.

112 THE FRENCH WAR AND THE REVOLUTION

Effect of the Seven Years' War on the Continent.

The Seven Years' War had changed the face of European politics. Prussia, though spent and gasping, kept her acquisitions of territory, and the process of German aggrandizement which ended at Sedan had begun at Rossbach. The French monarchy having absorbed the religious, social, and industrial vitality of the land, had now exhausted it, and for the next twenty-five years it was to fight a losing struggle for life. The territorial expansion of England was enormous. Across one ocean America seemed secure, in the Orient the foundations were laid for the Indian Empire. And during the same period she had a second age of great inventions, which was illuminated by names like those of Watt, Wedgwood, Arkwright, and Brindley. The expenditure of energy had been commensurate, as far as the Continent was concerned, with the changes. Money had been poured out in floods. France, Prussia, and Austria were alike in the depths of poverty. Russia though not destitute, was ready for economy, and the national debt of England affrighted timid minds who were blind to the increase in her industries and the renovation of her social forces, which made it but a bagatelle. The waste of life had been appalling. Frederick the Great estimated that the total loss of all the contesting powers was not under eight hundred and thirty-five thousand men.

Its character in America and India.

In America and India, however, the case was far otherwise. Pitt boasted that not fifteen hundred Englishmen had fallen in America; Clive sustained a loss of twenty Europeans and fifty-two sepoys at Plassey; and Coote, at Wandewash, reported sixty-nine blacks and one hundred and ninety whites in his list of killed and wounded. There was this difference, however, between India and America. In the former the English gained an opportunity. They have since, to be sure, successfully and richly harvested the possible results. But in America their mastery was complete at the beginning of the peace.

Estimated in the light of subsequent events that portion of the war fought in North America was by far the most important. At the beginning of it the colonies rejected the Albany proposition for union, and were as exclusive in their notions of citizenship as the states of ancient Greece; at the close they were far from concordant, nor were they yet conscious of a common destiny, but they had recognized their strength in the great forces of money and men which they had raised and used; together they had felt the strong hand of a centralized military power, and the continued threats of parliamentary control alarmed them. There was, throughout, a vast disparity in the numbers engaged on one side and the other. But the physical geography of the continent which the French understood and used with consummate skill; their close, harsh centralization in government; their tact and unscrupulousness in dealing with the savages more than counterbalanced the superior numbers and wealth of the combined English and colonial power. The Indian allies of New France were in part missionary Indians, nominally converted to Christianity; but throughout the war it would have been impossible to distinguish the proselytes from the heathen, so cruel, savage, and untrustworthy were they all in the presence of an enemy. The Indian allies of England were comprised largely in the Six Nations, who were heathen, but had a certain nobility of character, a well-confederated government, and often in the hour of need were either lukewarm or neutral. But the sum of the whole matter was a well-defined feeling on the part of the English colonists that the red man and the white could not live together. At the beginning

Determinative results in the American colonies.

of the war free institutions had been under the constant menace of a French civilization, strong in refinement and centralized administration, but swayed by a government morally rotten, and the most despotic ever seen ; at its close the lower system of politics had disappeared, fear of the savages was removed, and the English in America were free both to consider their relations to the mother-country, and to study how their liberties and their prosperity were to find expression in their institutions.

It is customary in the United States to consider Wolfe's victory as the solstice in the ecliptic of modern history, since it secured America for English institutions, and American civilization is to dominate the world. Choiseul and Kant foresaw that the colonies, once freed from fear of France, would demand an independent development. Wolfe was a hero, Quebec was a glorious victory, and there is a sense in which the history of the United States began on that day. As an aid to memory and the imagination let it so stand. The demands of an incompetent cabinet for aid in the payment of the debt incurred in the war ; the development of party theory and spirit among all Englishmen, the colonists included ; the meddling mercantile temper of the time, all these may be thrown into the scale, yet one fact will outweigh them all — that in the unity and continuity of history the germ of distinction between England in Europe and England in America had been planted in the former long before, as early as the Reformation of the sixteenth century. Its growth had been continuous, first at home and then abroad, and the tree was already grown when Wolfe fell on the plains of Abraham. No doubt his victory cleared the forest around, and gave it light and air. But the battle of Quebec, glorious as it was, did but mark a

Its relation to American nationality and independence.

stage of growth and quicken vital forces which would have asserted themselves in any event. English institutions are not of one kind, and those to which America was secured were such as had been unfolded by the colonists and their friends at home. It is certain that the Whig aristocracy would not have tolerated the thought if they had understood that side of the war; even the sympathy of men like Wolfe and Pitt for the ideas of the English revolution, as the people in America understood and cherished them, was so slight as to be scarcely discernible.

CHAPTER X.

A NEW ISSUE IN CONSTITUTIONAL GOVERNMENT—1760-1762.

Disunion between America and England—Their respective Forms of Administration—Political Theories in Vogue—The Terms Provincial and Colonial—Theory of Grenville—Restrictions on American Trade—Practice of the Age—Royal Requisitions—The Plea of Gratitude—Legal Argument for the Taxing Power—Inconsistency of Claim and Conduct—Inadequacy of the English Constitution—The New Question—Writs of Assistance—James Otis and the Spirit of the Constitution—New York and the Appointment of Judges—The same Question Elsewhere.

THE years from 1760 to 1775 are among the most important in the history of constitutional government, because in them was tried the issue of how far under that system laws are binding on those who have no share in making them. They prepared the forces which led to civil war and tore apart two portions of the English-speaking people amid throes of violence like those in which most states are brought into existence. There are many points from which the events of those years may be viewed. The optimist who looks forward to a universal federation of all civilized nations feels that his millennium was so far postponed when parent and child separated, one of the two to dwell in the land of Canaan, while the other chose the plain of Jordan. But he must find consolation in the thought that millions have learned to live under free institutions in America who never could have done so

Disunion between America and England.

had the states remained colonies. He may regret that those of one speech should not present to the world an undivided force working for liberty and righteousness, but he will recall that the interchange of relations between the sister nations has awakened the public conscience of both, and wrought many a wholesome reform on each side of the Atlantic. If the breach was a revolution for America, it was the precursor of momentous development in England.

Twenty years of agitation, with seven years of fighting, left neither unchanged, and the change was a beneficent one in both society and politics. Two administrative devices to secure liberty have since divided Europe and America between them; but whether through constitutional monarchy with parliamentary government, or by the way of democratic republican forms with a strong elective executive and artificial checks on popular hurry, both have still a common end, and their use is destined to cover the earth with a family of free states sufficiently alike to check wrong and diminish bloodshed, different enough to prevent stagnation and keep the world on the way of progress. It is fortunate that the discovery of America as a separate nation was made when it was: we may cherish the fanciful regret that the separation was not as free from strife as that of Lot and Abraham. *Their respective forms of administration.*

The development of the English constitution was ever historical and not theoretical. Not but that theories were plenty; the middle of the eighteenth century was rife with them. Hobbes's Leviathan had sought to justify the Stewart claim of divine right; Locke's form of the contract theory had been the vindication of the Revolution. Bolingbroke was a clever theorist on the Tory side; the Whigs had a dozen defenders of their doctrine that Parliament was supreme *Political theories in vogue.*

both within and without the four seas which bounded Great Britain. These dogmas all had an influence in politics, but it had been slight when compared with the instinct of the people for the preservation of their property and liberty by any expedient logical or illogical. But now, almost for the first time, a theory was to play a decisive part in English history. For in direct opposition to the notion of parliamentary supremacy, it appeared to some men in England and to many in America, that their freedom and prosperity depended on the maintenance of sovereignty in the crown. Parliament was not a representative body, the ascendency seemed secure in the Whig aristocracy and the king evidently meant to assert his prerogative by becoming his own premier, not by the reassertion of the sovereign character of the crown as an estate of the nation, indivisible and supreme. George III. held the correct theory of the Whigs, that each member of Parliament represented all English interests; the new Liberals believed that he represented only the interest or borough which returned him, that there was no representation without a direct delegation of authority by a specific body of freemen.

Here lay the gist of the whole matter. Englishmen in America disliked the term Colonist more than that of Provincial, but they disliked both, for they seemed to imply that the royal charters had stripped them of rights and privileges which their kinsmen in England still possessed. In proof of their being freeborn Englishmen they could point to the language of the sovereigns who had established their local governments, and to the practice of the home administration which had thus far refrained from meddling, or raising money from them for imperial purposes except by requisitions on their assemblies which were directly representative of the property taxed. Grants had been

The terms provincial and colonial.

promptly and lavishly made, and in return the Americans cheerfully but inconsistently admitted the control by Parliament of all foreign trade and certain departments of domestic commerce as well. Their cheerfulness had been connected no doubt with the easy evasion of the Navigation Acts, which made profitable smuggling well-nigh universal among American merchants. It was clouded by the general military control, introduced nominally as a war measure, but really as part of a new policy.

Grenville, foreign secretary under Bute, and afterward premier, was less complaisant and more logical. He believed the English settlements in America to be colonies, and not royal dominions, subject to the crown but with independent parliaments; that they existed solely for the benefit of English trade under conditions expressed by the Navigation Acts, and that—irresistible argument—there was no distinction between custom-house dues which Parliament had always collected and internal taxes. The colonies had grown rich beyond the most visionary expectation, it was but right they should share the enormous burden which Parliament had incurred for their benefit. As the representative of a triumphant aristocracy, arrogant in the successes achieved by the nation, he therefore determined, with the king's approval, to devise a plan for general taxation and to execute the Navigation Acts. *Theory of Grenville.*

It will be remembered that under those enactments American trade was to be restricted in the following ways: By act of 1651, which was really aimed at the Dutch, goods could be exported only in English ships; by act of 1663 the same law was extended to imports; by act of 1672 the freedom of trade between the colonies was destroyed by laying imposts on commerce between them; by act of 1699 no wool, either in fleece, spun, or woven, could be exported *Restrictions on American trade.*

120 THE FRENCH WAR AND THE REVOLUTION

at all ; in 1719 the Commons declared American manufactures to be dangerous as conducive to independence ; in 1732 Parliament forbade the export of hats made in America ; in 1733 it laid a duty on the enormous imports of molasses except what came from the British West Indies ; and in 1750 it ordered the suppression, as a nuisance, of all rolling-mills, forges, and furnaces.

But legislative interference with trade was at that time universal. Every subject of the British crown in Practice of the England, Scotland, Ireland, and America, age. owed obedience to the same or similar laws, and every nation in Europe felt such enactments to be among the staples of legislation. The navigation statutes of the United States to-day are equally stringent on their regulative side, although in a different direction. Consider, moreover, that in the year 1760 the English in America were exuberantly loyal and intoxicated with the glory of English arms, to which they justly felt they had furnished no insignificant share. That loyalty continued as late as 1775, in almost undiminished measure. As for the right of Parliament to tax the American commonwealths, the Congress of 1774 " cheerfully " admitted it if confined to imperial matters, that is, to foreign trade. What then was the ground for discontent with the measures adopted in 1760 by the Board of Trade, through the cabinet and Parliament? [Not a farthing of the money to be raised by parliamentary taxation was to leave America, for all revenue was to be deposited in the colonial treasuries.] The accounts were to be kept in England, and appropriations made for two branches of colonial administration—the support of justice and the military budget.

Such specious pleading can only be met by the frank admission that there was inconsistency among the liberals from the beginning. It was partly logical and partly due to the distance between England and America, which made intercourse difficult and protracted. Moreover, the interests of the friends of liberty in England seemed to require one point of view, while the same class in America took quite a different one. They agreed only in a protest against the exercise of arbitrary power by either king or Parliament. Men like Jackson and Alderman Beckford, father of the famous writer, reasoned in Parliament that the colonies should have actual, as well as virtual representation, if that body were to lay internal taxes and control the revenues. But their friends in America knew that the plan was impracticable, and felt with Franklin that "when money is wanted of the colonies for any public service in which they ought to bear a part," they should be called on "by requisitorial letters from the crown (according to long established custom) to grant such aids as their loyalty shall dictate and their abilities permit." Royal requisitions.

Barre declared in the House of Commons that the colonies owed no gratitude to the mother-country for their prosperity and their emancipation from fear, because they had been planted by men who fled from tyranny to preserve the ancient spirit of English liberty, and that they had fought more for English advantage than for their own protection. And yet they were grateful, for the colonial assemblies sometimes made grants so liberal that Parliament returned a portion of them. [During the war they had enlisted and supported as many troops as England had sent.] The plea of gratitude.

The Whig argument for direct taxation was that the colonies were but corporations, their legislative power merely the making of by-laws. The king had granted the charters, but, Parliament being supreme, he could not grant legislative power, and they were therefore nothing but standing commissions, included under the general and supreme jurisdic- Legal argument for the taxing power.

tion of Parliament as similar concessions were in England. The liberals at home were hard pressed to meet this legal argument. Men of the type of Burke and Rockingham virtually accepted it, but claimed inexpediency; more radical minds, like Pitt and Camden, either plead that it was true only of Parliament with actual representation, or in more general terms that it was unconstitutional. The king's friends probably felt that ministers were responsible to the crown alone, and that the determination of the ministry was really a sovereign act of the crown, ratified by Parliament, but not initiated by it as a representative body. At least such a doctrine is implied in much of the language used during the wordy warfare of those years.

It may be well more concisely to recall the apparent contradictions thus indicated: An oligarchy in England pleading the supremacy of Parliament, Americans set on the sovereignty of the crown; the prerogative party in England determined to rule through parliamentary forms, with the king himself as prime minister, the cabinet to register his will, and so establish the monarch as absolute, the opposition pleading for actual representation and ministerial responsibility to the people; the Americans finding actual representation in Parliament inexpedient, demanding one form of taxation by their representative assemblies and cheerfully leaving another form to Parliament as it was; great English statesmen accepting the high Whig doctrine, but refusing to act on it; others, equally great, denying the doctrine, but from motives of loyalty refraining from possible resistance; lawyers on one side the sea spinning profound legal arguments from a given set of facts, men of equal eminence on the other side, but in the same profession, drawing political logic of incontrovertible force from the same premises.

Inconsistency of claim and conduct.

Amid such a maze we must again repeat to ourselves that the clew to history is not in logic or consistency, but in higher considerations of justice and right. Parliament was not representative, the American legislatures were. The old Whigs were *Inadequacy of the English constitution.* no longer progressive, the new Whigs had hardly living strength, and were an English, and not an American, party. The English in America had not yet read the book either of their past or their present, and behaved at one time like Englishmen, at another like Americans, according as they were looking backward or forward. The English constitution had never contemplated a problem like the present one; it could not develop harmoniously to include both peoples as it has since done without an experience by its supporters that institutions must adapt themselves to successive social states or disappear. In this alone lies the continuity of events from the beginning to the end of the Revolution.

The Americans were not the Englishmen known to the constitution; in fact they and their land could live, and do live, under its spirit, but not under the forms of 1760. They were already a na- *The new question.* tion of religious dissenters, being in the main Calvinists trained in the governmental methods of Presbyterianism or Independency; they had long been in an attitude of mild political dissent on various important matters, which had been postponed under the stress of war. These questions, which had existed from the beginning, were now to have full ventilation and be tried both in practice and theory. To the religious liberty long enjoyed was to be added a complementary political independence. Not all the facts nor all the deeds of the time conform to a single standard of perfect virtue on either side. Whether in the forum or on the battle-field the contest was between brothers; there was no nice line of separation on one side and on the other of either principles or conduct, for there were Tories in America and American sympathizers in England. But on the whole the movement was grand, because of its earnestness and sincerity; grander still because of its results in the purification of free institutions and their establishment on two continents in conformity to the needs of each. The step in the development of constitutional government which it represents was taken as illogically as any other, but it was as completely historical as any other before or since.

The shipping interests of New England were of the highest concern to all her people, and the prosperity of Boston in particular depended on them. While much of her trade was perfectly legitimate, much of it was in direct contravention of the Navigation Acts. Smuggling of all sorts was common, in particular the importation of molasses from the West Indies had assumed great dimensions; from the molasses was distilled rum, which was in turn shipped to Africa and exchanged for slaves, the slaves being brought out on return voyages and sold in the South. To prevent the evasions of owners and merchants the Lords of Trade instructed their agents to apply to the proper courts for authorization to search both stores and vessels. The Superior Court of the Province of Massachusetts had the powers of the English Court of Exchequer, and could therefore grant general warrants or writs of an entirely indefinite nature, controlling everybody and returnable to nobody, subjecting the domicile and property of anyone to search.

Writs of assistance.

The first application for a writ of assistance was made in 1761, and was vigorously resisted by the ablest men at the Boston bar, among whose names history has embalmed that of James Otis because he argued that the writ was dangerous in itself, and although backed by a statute of the reign of Charles II., was contrary to the spirit of the English constitution. General warrants were not yet declared invalid by the English courts, although they were soon to be so declared. His argument was therefore entirely political, and to reason that the courts could declare a statute unconstitutional and therefore void was a virtual denial of the supremacy of Parliament. The notion of the spirit of the constitution originated with the anti-prerogative party, its use by Otis was ingenious and daring, but while the court withheld its decision the writs were eventually granted. We have not, however, any recorded instance of their use. But thenceforward there were two parties in Massachusetts, the loyalists being led by Bernard the Governor, Thomas Hutchinson the Lieutenant-Governor, and the numerous minor office-holders with their friends and relatives. They were in constant communication with their superiors in England, and advocated with persistence measures which had already been suggested by royal officers—the maintenance of a standing army in America and the taxation of the colonies by Parliament.

James Otis and the spirit of the constitution.

One chief article of the Declaration of Rights in 1688 was that judges should be appointed during good behavior, and should not hold office at the king's pleasure. The principle stood as firm as ever in England, but for political reasons it was to be denied in the colonies, and formal instructions were issued in December, 1761, that the salary drawn by judges and their tenure of office should both be subject to control. When, therefore, shortly after Pitt's fall, the Chief-Justice of New York died, the new appointment was made as directed. It was a vital matter as to whether the court, if dependent, should depend on the people

New York and the appointment of judges.

or on the ministry, for it comprised in its jurisdiction the functions which in England pertained to the Courts of the King's Bench, of the Common Pleas, and of the Barons of the Exchequer. At once the legislature was roused to resistance, and declared that unless the instructions were withdrawn they would pay the judge no salary. Great bitterness of feeling came from the incident; the salary was paid by royal command from quit-rents, and the two parties, which were already inchoate, took actual form. As in Massachusetts, the officials were prominent among the loyalists, while the native lawyers, foremost among whom was William Livingston, led the party of liberty, and their watchword was the principles of the Revolution of 1688.

This matter of the colonial judiciary was made a test throughout the colonies. The Governor of New Jersey was deposed in 1762 for appointing a judge during good behavior. Maryland and Pennsylvania were made to feel their dependency in the same direction. The same year Bernard spent a sum of money to drive French privateersmen from the northern fisheries, and then demanded repayment. The legislature refused to yield the principle that the appropriation should have originated with them, and declined amid much excitement to grant the money.

CHAPTER XI.

THE STAMP ACT—1762–1766

The Ministries of Newcastle and Bute—Grenville and Townshend—Ministerial Responsibility—Wilkes and the *North Briton*—General Warrants and the Freedom of the Press—Proposition for a Stamp Act—Prosperity and Education in America—Colonial Unity and the Name American—Failure of Franklin's Protest—Enactment of the Stamp Act—Discussion of its Illegality—Its Reception in America—The Patriots and the Masses—Measures of Nullification—Taxation by Consent of the Governed—Call for a Congress—Significance of the Assembly—Inconsistency of its Memorials—Gadsden's Plea and the First Steps toward Union—Change in New England Opinion—The Rockingham Ministry—Attitude of English Factions—The Repeal and the Declaratory Act.

It does not appear that the majority of men, either in America or England, attached greater importance to these events than to the other squabbles of past years between the people and the office-holders. The voices which declared that with the conquest of New France there would be successful rebellion among the English colonies were not heard or not heeded. George III., at any rate, never faltered in his course. The instructions as to the judiciary and the enforcement of the Navigation Acts were issued by the cabinet in which Newcastle was premier, Egremont and Bute being the Secretaries of State, and George Grenville the leader of the House of Commons. In May, 1762, the duke finding himself contemptuously disregarded in the distribution of patronage, withdrew, and a ministry was

The ministries of Newcastle and Bute.

formed under the hated Lord Bute, with Grenville as Secretary of State. So contemptuous was their treatment of the Whigs, and so rash their haste to carry out the king's plans in creating a court party by the use of bribes and patronage, that the two Whig factions were quickly welded into a strong united opposition, supported by the mass of the people.

On April 8, 1763, Bute withdrew, Grenville became prime minister in his stead, and Charles Townshend, who had devoted himself to the study of the colonial question and held extreme views as to taxation, was retained as the First Lord of Trade, although Grenville did not entirely sympathize with his doctrines. The First Secretary of the Treasury was Jenkinson, reputed to have been the author of the Stamp Act. But Bute remained the back-stairs adviser of his friend and sovereign, and George, faithless to the notion of Bolingbroke's "patriot king," weakly gave his confidence to an "interior," or "kitchen, cabinet."

<small>Grenville and Townshend.</small>

"The public looked still," as Chesterfield said, "at Lord Bute through the curtain which indeed was a very transparent one." But Grenville was imperious and would be the creature of nobody. In the two years of his leadership the Whig oligarchy seemed to regain its old ascendency. Could Pitt and Burke have reformed its temper and its methods they might have given it an indefinite extension of power. As it was, Grenville adroitly offset the influence of the king by that of Pitt, neutralizing both. Parliament supported him. Bute was at his demand banished from favor and from court, and the responsibility for the misdeeds of his ministry rests with him. He was a statesman according to his light, but men of greater insight could influence and follow neither him nor the party. The liberal Whigs found a leader in the Marquis of Rock-

THE STAMP ACT 129

ingham, the extreme conservatives rallied about the Duke of Bedford.

Animosity and jealousy were rife. They were partly personal, but at bottom was the question of ministerial responsibility. The king's conception was suicidal, for under constitutional government a cabinet not answerable to the representative assembly, but to the crown alone, means that the king is responsible, and a free people must be able to change its servants at will. Otherwise the monarchy is absolute, and in defence of the doctrine that the sovereign might unite in his person the entire exercise of power one Stewart had lost his life and another his throne. The alternative, with such a view, is of course an elective executive, a discovery made later by the Americans. The other extreme view of ministerial responsibility was that the House of Commons, as sovereign, could alone make and dismiss cabinets. Unfortunately for the oligarchy, they forgot that the house was not a truly representative body, and that a committee of its members did not for that reason embody national power. The facts, too, were against them, because the king still chose or rejected ministers, and his confidence was necessary to their existence. The compromise view of double responsibility, now made possible by electoral reform, was then unknown. Where a ministry is primarily the public servant of a free country, and acts by principles and measures agreeable to a truly representative assembly, it can demand the confidence of the crown. The muddle was largely due to the entire absence of public discussion and the inability of the popular common-sense to express itself.

<small>Ministerial responsibility.</small>

The Revolution had secured the freedom of the press; but the press had actually languished in its emancipation because parliamentary debates were secret. For seventy years there had been no opposition to the ruling Whigs, and the nation had been so busy with war and religion as to neglect politics. But events *Wilkes and the North Briton.* had created a nascent interest in internal affairs. The Bute primacy in particular had roused the London populace, and John Wilkes, a keen editor, though an unscrupulous and scurrilous man, seized the opportunity to denounce him as a "royal favorite" in the pages of his journal, the *North Briton.* Soon afterward the king in his speech from the throne declared the peace of Paris to be "honorable to the crown and beneficial to the people." Wilkes, in No. 45 of his paper, made a direct attack on the language used. The engaging demagogue was also a member of Parliament.

He was arrested on a "general warrant," similar to the "writs of assistance" applied for in Boston, and *General warrants and the freedom of the press.* thrown into the Tower; but pleading his privilege as a member of the Commons he was released. In the course of the proceedings against him Grenville issued over two hundred writs against various papers, and thereby aroused a storm of indignation which compelled him to desist. Moreover, the legality of general warrants was submitted to the authorities. Two most important constitutional changes ensued. It was decided that warrants calling for the arrest of all persons guilty of a certain crime were unconstitutional because they assumed a guilt which might not exist; the freedom of the press was established by judicial decision, and the secrecy of parliamentary debate was destroyed. At a later time Wilkes also defended the rights of constituencies and opened the way for parliamentary reform.

While the exercise of arbitrary power in England was in these ways restrained, a sort of compensatory license for America was taken by the headstrong minister.

During 1763 the naval officers in America were invested with the rights of revenue officers for the better enforcement of the navigation laws, and efforts were made to commit the Board of Trade to a definite schedule of stamp duties. But Shelburne was the First Lord, and warily eluded the demand. It was Jenkinson who in September brought forth the full-fledged plan, having been in all probability the originator of it. The responsibility was, of course, Grenville's. In March, 1764, notice was given that it would be introduced at the next session, and when the solemn question of England's right to tax America was put, no one but Barre voted or spoke in the negative. Ample time was thus given for agitation in America. If newspapers, almanacs, marriage certificates, law documents, and other papers in constant use were to be stamped at the rates then current, the proceeds would be about one hundred thousand pounds a year, a substantial burden when added to the ordinary expenses of government for a population of some two million whites and five hundred thousand negroes.

<small>Proposition for a Stamp Act.</small>

So far the "Provincials" had been neither factious nor rebellious. They had a clear notion of their rights; experience had taught them that their rustic musters could fight always as well, and sometimes better, than the regulars; they feared the French and Indians no longer, and while as yet the lands beyond the Alleghenies were unsettled, yet the near future would prepare them for occupation. Burke could scarcely paint their unbounded prosperity and enviable lot. In sixty years they had quadrupled their exports, which had risen in value to forty-five million dollars. In mental training and intelligence they had kept equal step. The first printing-press had been set up at Cambridge in 1639; books and newspapers were

<small>Prosperity and education in America.</small>

abundant, and six prosperous colleges secured a learned ministry and liberal education for all professional men. Harvard was founded in 1638, William and Mary in 1692, Yale in 1700, Princeton in 1746, the University of Pennsylvania in 1749, and King's—now Columbia— in 1754.

While there was even yet a strong separatist feeling, yet at this distance it is clear that the work of unifica-

Colonial unity and the name American. tion had been constant and rapid. Their respective local governments had in common many important features, especially that of two houses for legislation, of which the lower was representative and laid the taxes. New Englanders and Virginians were now alike designated provincials, but the name Americans gradually superseded the other, and in 1768 the phrase American Whig was first used as the designation of the native party. Union against the French had left behind the instinct for union before any common danger. When, therefore, the subject of a Stamp Act was broached the colonies were united in opposition and on identical grounds. In reality there was an English constitution for America, of which the unwritten interpretation was universal among her people, that internal taxation without real representation was unthinkable, whatever views of personal royal sovereignty or parliamentary supremacy were held.

Benjamin Franklin was made the agent in London not only for Pennsylvania but for other leading col-

Failure of Franklin's protest. onies to remonstrate with the Government against the plan of a Stamp Act. They would listen neither to his protestations of inexpediency, to the humble petitions of the Americans which he wished to present against the act, nor to his fears of resistance. It does not even appear that he succeeded in awakening the public. Grenville had advanced with caution and taken a whole year to prepare his approaches.

On February 27th, 1765, the act which he had prepared passed the Commons, and on March 8th the Lords, the royal assent being given by commission on March 22d, for the king was then in a temporary condition of mental alienation. Barre protested in the house; but the vote was taken without even a languid interest, and at no stage was it seriously amended or debated. In the same session a modification of the Mutiny Act was passed, whereby requisitions might be made on the colonies to purchase rations or furnish the troops with other necessaries. By way of attempted alleviation, the rate of postage was reduced, in the hope that the revenue from that source would thereby be increased; bounties were granted for the export to England of certain kinds of lumber useful in ship-building; rice and such coffee as might be raised experimentally were freed from important restrictions; iron could be sent to England, and both iron and lumber to Southern Europe. The whale-fishery had already been opened to New England.

Enactment of the Stamp Act.

But the sop did not appease. The material advantages granted were really slight. Such petty but galling monopolies as made every household sensitive to the strong hand still remained. Not a copy of the Bible, for instance, could be printed in the colonies until after the War of Independence, and taxes on luxuries of every description increased the cost of living among the rich and influential. The slave-trade was guarded with vigilance, in spite of repeated protests from the South, and in the years from 1764 to 1779 fifteen thousand three hundred negroes were annually landed in West Indian and American ports. Accordingly, emphasis was laid on the newly rising con-

Discussion of its illegality.

ception, confined largely to the radicals, of the illegality of the stamp tax. To complete the picture, it was arranged that the courts of vice-admiralty, which under the trade laws adjudicated all causes and adjusted all claims, should consist each of a single judge without a jury, and that the salary of the judge should be paid from what he condemned.

Nevertheless the prevalent sentiment seemed at first to be one of sorrow. New England as a whole was even impassive. James Otis, while calling for a congress, counselled submission. But there were voices. Whitefield in New Hampshire, Dyer in Connecticut, and the newspapers of New York saw and said that persistence in such a policy would breed rebellion. Virginia was the first to apply the torch to public opinion. On May 30th her House of Burgesses, quickened by the oratory of Patrick Henry, resolved that taxation by themselves, or by persons chosen by themselves, was the first attribute of free Englishmen, as they were and had been from the first, their liberties being secured by inheritance and by royal charters; and that further, they would obey no law other than those passed by their own General Assembly, anyone asserting the contrary being an enemy. About the same time an unknown New Yorker, who wrote over the pen-name of "Freeman," published a since famous refutation of the plea of virtual representation which he closed with the words: "There never can be a disposition in the colonies to break off the connection with the mother-country so long as they are permitted to have the full enjoyment of those rights to which the English constitution entitles them. . . . They desire no more, nor can they be satisfied with less."

The more radical patriots formed an association known as the Sons of Liberty, and declared that having

Its reception in America.

the rights of Englishmen, they were to be ruled by their own laws and tried by men of their own condition. They were in the main artisans and laborers. Caring but little for the sentimental connection with England they cared everything for the principles of Magna Charta, and held with Coke that every act of Parliament contrary to them was void. Thenceforward the thoroughgoing minority of the colonists became more and more extreme, while the loyalists clung with greater devotion to the English affinity until they were scornfully denominated "Tories." A still larger number of people were the well-to-do, mildly patriotic townspeople and farmers, who with sturdy loyalty felt the home cause to be their own, but hoped to avoid any interruption to the practice of their comfortable trades and professions. It required a sharp crisis to open their purses and drive them to activity.

The patriots and the masses.

Such were the alarm and disaffection on every hand that, in general, threats sufficed to compel the stamp officers to resign. There were, however, serious mobs and riots in Boston. The stamps themselves were destroyed wherever found. The act was to go into effect on November 1st, but long before that time there were neither men nor means to enforce it. The merchants and people joined in milder but no less effectual measures, agreeing neither to import nor consume English wares until the act should be repealed. The lapse of but a short time gave a coherence to talk and writing which neither had yet attained. The best discussion of abstractions was that of New England, and of Samuel Adams in particular. He was a representative Calvinist, logical and fearless because under no bondage to the carefulness and self-indulgence of wealth. By him and Otis the American idea of the "true spirit of the constitution" was further interpreted. The interested

Measures of nullification.

motives of prospective office-holders were exposed, the natural rights of men were set above all tradition, and government shown to be founded in nature, not in force, as Hobbes believed, or in contract, as Locke would have it.

Colonists are men and citizens, and neither civil nor feudal law can limit their privilege. The imposition, therefore, of taxes, direct or indirect, without representation, is unjust and illegal. There was little which was new in all this, for "taxation only with their own consent" had been the ardent claim of the rebellious New York legislature in the previous September, when they disclaimed exemption as a privilege but "gloried in it as a right." The circumstances, however, added fresh importance to the principle, and the legislative committees of correspondence, already in existence, became a powerful engine in forging the ties of intercolonial union.

Taxation by consent of the governed.

Meanwhile the Massachusetts Assembly issued a circular letter calling for a colonial congress, the members to be selected by the popular house in each case. The invitation found a ready acceptance, and the congress met on October 7th, in New York. New Hampshire, though without a delegate, agreed to make the issue her own ; Georgia was sympathetic and arranged for early information of the result although she sent no representative. Virginia was thwarted in electing her members by the refusal of the Governor to summon the legislature, but her loyalty was only more conspicuous. North Carolina was not represented. The Stamp Act Congress was therefore composed of delegates formally elected by the legislatures of Massachusetts, Rhode Island, Connecticut, Pennsylvania, Maryland, and South Carolina; of the legislative committee of correspondence of New York, and of persons sent from New Jersey and Delaware with powers granted by formal

Call for a congress.

written injunction from the individuals composing respectively the legislatures of those colonies.

The Albany Conference of 1754 had been a practical failure, but it had at least displayed the conception of united action. The value of this meeting lay in an actual outline of real union. There was an authorized representation, but the step of binding enactment was not yet taken. In the deliberations New England held the narrow, legal, and separatist view that reliance must be placed on the charters. The sagacious Gadsden, of South Carolina, showed that they might plead their rights as Englishmen from charters, but that their specific claims were based on a broader ground which was common to them all. "There ought to be no New England man, no New Yorker known on the continent, but all of us Americans." His success was, however, not due to theory. The matter of colonial jurisdiction was probably in the mind of every member. Originally Massachusetts, Connecticut, Virginia, the Carolinas, and Georgia claimed the Pacific as their western boundary under the crown charters, which were based on the Cabots' discoveries. In 1763 a royal proclamation forbade land sales west of the Alleghenies, and so turned the whole Mississippi Valley into a crown domain. Colonization in regions so remote as to render allegiance precarious was discountenanced, and the two thousand or more white settlers already there were put under military rule. Gadsden's plea for the new concept of "America" prevailed.

Significance of the assembly.

In the end three memorials were drawn up, addressed respectively to the king, to the Lords, and to the Commons. Consistency is conspicuously absent from them. All plead the inherent right of trial by jury, aiming of course at the encroachments of admiralty jurisdiction, and the appointment of colonial judges during the king's pleasure. They

Inconsistency of its memorials.

likewise disclaimed the possibility of representation in the Commons, asserted that supplies to the crown were free gifts, and that taxes could be imposed only by representative colonial assemblies. But to the Commons they admitted a "due subordination to Parliament," and urged the old untenable position that while it might amend the common law and regulate trade throughout the whole empire, it could not tax the colonies for internal administration.

The fallacy of this was clear enough to the scholarly Gadsden, who opposed any petition to either house part- ly because they had already refused those presented during the preliminary stages of the Stamp Act, but chiefly because they held their rights from neither the Lords nor the Commons. But he yielded in the interest of unanimity. Toward the close of the session a vessel arrived with a new supply of stamps; party spirit ran very high, some delegates declaring that resistance to the Stamp Act was treason, and that anyhow each colony should act for itself. On October 25th, however, the majority finally signed the memorials, and the colonies became "a bundle of sticks which could neither be bent nor broken."

Gadsden's plea and the first step toward union.

The influence of the congress was immense. Under the guidance of Samuel Adams, and the leadership of Massachusetts, New England finally took the important step of supplementing her legal-charter plea by the broader one of liberty as an inherent right, and at last recognized America as a whole. The merchants renewed their old agreements, and resolved to renounce all trade if the act were not repealed. The first of November was signalized by general enthusiasm, with the cry of "Liberty, prosperity, and no stamps;" the newspapers appeared, as before, on un-

Change in New England opinion.

stamped paper, filled, too, with patriotic editorials and reminders to the authorities of the Porteous mob in Edinburgh. Colden, the Vice-Chancellor and executive of New York surrendered the stamps to the municipality, which speedily returned them to the hold of the ship in which they came. New Jersey disavowed Ogden, her lukewarm delegate, and Carolina praised Gadsden, her consistent and rebellious one. Throughout the land there reigned a strong enthusiasm, a fixed determination, and a most serious disaffection.

Four months before, the Grenville ministry had fallen. The arrogance of the oligarchy reached a foolish climax in the omission from the Regency Bill, which the king's recurrent attacks of insanity made necessary, of his mother's name. Distress among the working-classes created riots about the same time, and as a last resort a compromise ministry was formed under the protectorate of the Duke of Cumberland. Rockingham, the premier, was the leader of the liberal Whigs, a wealthy nobleman of mediocre capacity but good common-sense. He has, however, a lasting title to renown as the patron of Edmund Burke, the philosopher, orator, and statesman, whom he introduced to public life. Men, not measures, was his pledge on taking office, and his cabinet had no thought of repealing the Stamp Act, although its supporters in the main held parliamentary taxation of the colonies to be impolitic. Soon, however, a change of opinion appeared. As one fact after another was reported from America the Liberals began to think the internal taxation of the colonies not only impolitic, but unconstitutional.

The Rockingham ministry.

Pitt openly and vigorously advocated this view, and applauded the measures of defiance which had been taken. But Grenville with the majority stood fast.

140 THE FRENCH WAR AND THE REVOLUTION

They were willing to repeal the bill, but would admit no wrong in its principle. The petitions of Congress were not formally thrown out, but they were eluded. Finally, it was formally voted that Parliament held power as a trust, not as being a representative body, and had therefore a right to lay taxes on those not represented. After long discussion and tactical delay the opposition secured the use of the king's name, and declared that he was for modification rather than repeal, but for repeal rather than for enforcement. Rockingham, however, decided to stand or fall on the simple question of repeal. His followers were restive, commerce was declining to an appalling extent, the poor were without employment, and to raise a revenue the alternative was an increase of the land tax, a burden already odious to the landed aristocracy.

Attitude of English factions.

The vote was taken in the house of Commons on February 22d, 1766, and the majority for repeal was 108, the vote being 275 to 167. But before the final stage had been reached a concurrent resolution was taken asserting that Parliament had absolute power to tax, and that all declarations of the American assemblies to the contrary were vain. This step, moreover, was taken with full knowledge, because in an interval of debate Franklin had appeared before the house as a witness, and under a searching examination had not only declared the tax inexpedient, but had also explained that while his countrymen had never yet objected to external taxation, there were many who now began to reason that there was no intrinsic difference between that and internal taxation, adding sententiously that in time "the people may be convinced by these arguments."

The repeal and the Declaratory Act.

But with characteristic disregard this momentous reservation was temporarily overlooked on both sides the sea. English trade was to be revived, and there was little apprehension as to the Declaratory Act, because repeal seemed virtually to nullify it and concede the opposite principle, that representation is essential to internal taxation.

CHAPTER XII.

CONFLICT OF TWO THEORIES—1766-1768

Charles Townshend—The Chatham-Grafton Ministry—Consolidation of the New Toryism—Enforcement of its Policy—The Billeting Act in New York—A New Tariff—The King his own Prime Minister—The Constitutional Crisis—The Attitude of France—Change in Colonial Doctrine—The "Farmer's Letters"—America Indignant—The Colonial Officials—The Circular Letter from Massachusetts—Parliament Demands its Withdrawal—The other Colonies Support its Principle—Outbreak of Armed Resistance in North Carolina—New Orleans, St. Louis, and the New West.

THE repeal was, however, far from establishing a new constitutional principle. The Declaratory Act had been <small>Charles Townshend.</small> regarded merely as a sop to the new Tories, and their doctrine that Parliament laid taxes not as a representative body but in the plenitude of the power confided to it as a trust, had been regarded as a passing fancy. But Charles Townshend was a merciless logician as well as a brilliant rhetorician, and the warfare which he now began against the charters that supported America in its claims was waged on the basis of a definite parliamentary declaration. The compromise ministry of Rockingham had performed its task, and having explicitly taken its stand on "men," could not engage in a conflict over "measures," especially such weighty constitutional questions as were now involved.

Accordingly it fell, and the king, thwarted so far in his cherished ambitions by the aristocracy, now sent for Pitt. The great commoner was a feeble old man. His retirement had brought him neither health nor ease, and the haste in which he hurried to London was undignified and almost servile. So also were the appeals to a gratitude which was no longer an active sentiment, and to the authority of the king, by which he cajoled and threatened men into accepting positions in a new cabinet known as the Chatham-Grafton ministry. His first step was a false one, for he had been over-persuaded to admit to his cabinet council Townshend, unchanged in his opinions, and giving no guarantee as to his attitude regarding American questions. But his second step was fatal, for in creating himself the Earl of Chatham he seemed to the masses to have abandoned the people. He therefore lost his only support, the good-will of the nation, which had hitherto loved him for his scorn of parties, but now refused to condone the feeble-mindedness of broken health. Disheartened and suffering, he was unable from the first to hold the reins of power. The general disorganization left Townshend free to hasten disaster. {The Chatham-Grafton ministry.}

Shelburne had the colonial administration, but the king disliked him and was impatient of his leniency. The cabinet, therefore, took measures to enforce the rigor of the laws, and as the old Whig officers resigned their places one by one, the king's creatures were appointed to the important vacancies. At last, when the untiring and relentless orator, in open defiance of the cabinet of which he was a member, held up to scorn the distinction between internal and external taxation and declared the principle of the Stamp Act to be just, although the present crisis, precluded its enforcement, cheers rang out from both sides of the house, and official England was finally and irrevocably committed to the new Toryism. The reasons {Consolidation of the new Toryism.}

are patent. The aristocracy insisted on a reduction of the land tax, and, to the dismay of both Chatham and Shelburne, it was voted. The expenses of the present establishment in America must therefore be met by a revenue raised in the colonies. But public opinion supported Parliament, for the agitation of the Tories had now become incessant, and even the merchants were finally won over by the accounts of what had been passing.

The non-importation agreements of the colonists, their demands for the non-enforcement of the Navigation Acts, their determination to put all the expense of the late war on English shoulders, the vague and general sense of their ingratitude, the partial refusal of New York to billet troops, the defiance of Massachusetts, above all, the failure of the Americans to remit, all these themes were discussed in heated rhetoric which revelled in terms like folly, wickedness, and incendiary. When Chatham hastened, as fast as his acute suffering would permit, from Marlborough to London, in order to replace Townshend by Lord North, it was found that public sentiment would not tolerate the change. In the spring of 1767 the new policy was made operative.

Enforcements of its policy.

The legislature of New York had been deaf to the clause of the Billeting Act, whereby the requisitions of the commanding-general were made "agreeably to act of Parliament," and disdaining the absurdity which sought to secure the form of legislation and yet retain the rigidity of a parliamentary requisition, voted all necessaries as if of their own free will, granting only what an English legislature would have granted, and implicitly refusing some minor demands. The first measure of Parliament was, therefore, to enjoin it from any further independent action until it should comply with the letter of the Billeting Act. The

The Billeting Act in New York.

extreme gravity of this injunction, directed to the Governor, lay in its virtual declaration of parliamentary sovereignty; in reality it wiped out at a single stroke all the American charters. Such extreme courses, however, generally thwart themselves, and similar things had happened before in the mutual interrelations of the home and colonial governments.

The other enactments were more serious in reality, though less extreme in theory. A series of articles were selected on which direct duties were to be collected in American ports by officers who were to take a test expressly declaring their belief in parliamentary authority. There were enumerated wine, oil, and dried fruits as luxuries; paper, paints, and other necessaries. Finally, with insidious adroitness, the list was closed by the important article of tea, which by paying duty but once in the colonies would be cheaper for American than even for English consumers. The total revenue thus derived was at the king's disposal for the payment of governors, judges, and other crown officers. *A new tariff.*

It will be remembered that even the author of the Stamp Act had not shown such daring. The civil servants necessary for the execution of that act were to have been subject to the local legislatures, and the proceeds were to have been paid into American treasuries subject to the order of the Exchequer. Such rashness seemed therefore to the Whigs unparalleled, and they chose the moment and some trivial measure of procedure to attack the ministry. In the division there was a paltry majority of three for the latter, the king saw his chance to annihilate the Whigs and assert parliamentary supremacy in America by one stroke. With stubborn persistence, therefore, he withstood the natural impulse of Chatham to resign, put forward as a compromise Grafton to be nominal premier, *The king his own prime minister.*

and himself assumed the actual direction of affairs. The goal of his fatal ambition was reached. As a climax to the whole disastrous procedure the Board of Customs, charged to enforce the Navigation Acts and repress smuggling was established in Boston and writs of assistance were legalized.

Neither wing of the Whigs was blind to the constitutional crisis, and though Chatham was ere long entirely incapacitated for work, his friends were yet a force, and they, too, understood the impending danger. Meeting after meeting of the factions was held. But dull obstinacy presided over their councils, no agreement could be reached, and the delighted king saw himself the only support of a cabinet which was thus degraded to the same level with the so-called continental cabinets under the absolute monarchies which were his model. He had patronage worth six millions sterling a year; less than ten thousand voters chose the majority of the House of Commons, made supreme by the events of the last half century; and in the unstinted bribery which Walpole and Newcastle had made customary, he found the security of a majority sufficient to record his personal will as if it were true legislation. There could be but one ground for anxiety; it lay in the fact that returned Anglo-Indians, with their fabulous wealth, had raised the price of venal boroughs to three times that of twenty years before, and made such seats more difficult to control.

Was it wonderful that the spectacle of such degeneracy in England should awaken, as it did, the attention and sorrow of her friends and fill her enemies with hope. Choiseul, the great French minister for foreign affairs, was well informed concerning the unexampled development of the American colonies in population and wealth, and was watching with interest the incipient spirit of independence and sentiment for union. Surmising a possible renewal of his rival's fearless colonial policy on the return of Chatham to power, he had therefore by fine diplomacy forestalled him in the leading courts in case there should once again be war; France was ready and longed for the conflict which many thought could not long be postponed. Two remarkable changes could be cited in support of the opinion.

The first was a change in colonial doctrine. To the cry of, "no representation, no taxation," had succeeded a very different one—"no representation, no legislation." The origin of the new watchword is obscure. As early as 1766, and in the same year, Franklin before Parliament, and Hawley in the Massachusetts legislature, had forecast the possibility of the colonies assuming that ground as an English constitutional right. This was, of course, a new stage in the evolution of doctrine. James Otis had written a pamphlet to prove that there was no difference between internal and external taxation, if both were to be used to raise a revenue; that both were alike illegal when laid by Parliament for that end, and that the only legal action of the English legislature in regard to the colonies was the regulation of trade by external taxation, when necessary. *Change in colonial doctrine.*

But the event which marked its final adoption as an epoch in the constitutional struggle, was the appearance of the famous "Farmer's Letters" of John Dickinson, of Pennsylvania, which set forth the new theory of resistance to parliamentary aggression with such calmness and conclusiveness that it met with universal acceptance in America. Writing as an Englishman, thoroughly loyal to the crown, the author declared that to forbid certain manufactures in America, and then tax the manufactured articles by customs dues, *The "Farmer's Letters."*

was unprecedented in English legislation, and must be resisted as an oppressive innovation. The tone of all twelve letters is one of respectful remonstrance to a parent who has forgotten what is due to her children.

But the people of America were neither placid nor patient. The old agreements of non-importation were renewed; there was much violent talk in Boston about preventing the new and obnoxious officials from landing, and there rained down a pamphlet literature in which every aspect of the new principle was discussed. It was understood that, for the purpose of unifying the colonial governments, the charters were to be annulled on Mansfield's plea that they were void because of their extent; if the power of absolute legislation really existed by grant of the crown, the extravagant grant being void was to be withdrawn by Parliament. In response the position was taken that consent alone gives force to law. If this be not English right, said the Americans, why then should Ireland have a separate Parliament. Meantime, the action of Massachusetts was as cautious as the language of her citizens was heated, and Connecticut, whose most liberal charter was chiefly obnoxious, took care to give no overt ground for attack.

<small>America indignant.</small>

The second change which foreboded war was more illusive in its sources, but no less real and critical in its manifestations. Parliament was about to dissolve when Townshend died in 1767. No new legislation was therefore undertaken, but the cabinet was reconstructed. Shelburne was left without any real power by the subdivision of his department, Conway and the friends of America with him went out and six Bedford Whigs came in, among them Hillsborough as colonial secretary, and Lord North in the Exchequer, who were both the heirs and supporters of Townshend's policy. Early in 1768 the twelfth Parliament expired;

<small>The colonial officials.</small>

its successor was equally corrupt and servile, many of the seats having been purchased at prices ranging, it was said, from four to a hundred thousand pounds. There had been a revulsion of feeling among the English people against Townshend's revenue policy. A hundred and fifty new members sat in the house, but they were entirely heedless of public sentiment, and neither ministry nor policy had changed — so complete was the king's success in disorganizing the Whigs. The "King's Friends" were the germ of the new Tory party, and the Bedford Whigs were in reality identical with them in spirit. Chatham was displaying the temporary eclipse of his reason by an aimless and extravagant display in the rôle of king's confidant. Rockingham and his followers, the remnant of liberalism in Parliament, were in a minority too hopeless for organization, and under the unreformed parliamentary system the real liberals of the country, though numerous, were entirely unrepresented. Such was the explanation of a new attitude insensibly but firmly taken by the representatives of the crown in America, governors, judges, and officials generally. Magnifying into undue proportion every word and mood of the protesting colonists, they clamored for ships and troops, stirred up personal enmities, fomented faction, and deluged their superiors with accounts of "treason" and "rebellion," which existed only in their own timid and excited brains. More than any others they were responsible for what followed.

The time arrived for enforcing the new statutes, and the board of customs was duly organized in Boston. Soon after, in January, 1768, the Massachusetts legislature issued a remarkable circular to the other colonies, citing the original contracts between the crown and the colonies, the terrible consequences of James II.'s attempt to abrogate charters, *The circular letter from Massachusetts.*

and claiming as colonists their title by contract, by common, and by statute law to the privileges of Englishmen, among which were exemption from taxation except by their own representatives. But representation in Parliament being impossible, their own legislatures were alone competent. They therefore urged a united petition to the King as the umpire in their conflict with Parliament. Hillsborough had already issued a warrant on the Board to pay Hutchinson two hundred pounds. After the issue of the circular the Board set forth a memorial representing the impossibility of enforcing the laws except by intimidation.

But there was neither active resistance nor talk of it. Self-denial as to imported garments, tea, and any articles on which illegal revenues were raised, was the only weapon of the Americans. But the contentious governor prosecuted the newspapers, the crown officers pretended to be terrified by the state of public feeling and kept calling for troops. They were the more exasperated by the contemptuous defiance expressed by the citizens in a good order unwonted in such times of excitement as the celebration of the repeal of the Stamp Act. The strongest expressions of sympathy followed in other colonies, especially through Livingston in New York and Washington in Virginia. In April, Parliament demanded that the circular should be withdrawn and disavowed. Governor Bernard was instructed to dissolve the legislature as often as it should refuse, the commander-in-chief at New York was to maintain public order, and the first open act of armed hostility was committed by the despatch of a fleet and troops to menace Boston. But the public order was not endangered.

Parliament demands its withdrawal.

The Virginia House of Burgesses issued a second circular much bolder in tone than the first, calling now for

CONFLICT OF TWO THEORIES 151

union in defence of American rights and liberties. New Hampshire, Connecticut, New York, Maryland, and South Carolina supported Massachusetts in the refusal of her legislators to withdraw the document. Yet still the people, "versed in the crown law," as the English authorities admitted, carefully avoided any unconstitutional course or any seditious word. The conduct of their rulers was quite different. Without waiting for action in England, Bernard summoned a man-of-war from Halifax. Her captain began at once to impress seamen, and the sloop Liberty, a vessel belonging to John Hancock, was seized on a charge of false entry. That night there was a riot and the mob destroyed some property belonging to the officials. But when the troops despatched by Parliament arrived there was perfect order, in spite of the overbearing insolence of officers determined to illegally billet the troops on the town. Recourse was had to the courts, which firmly repelled the exasperating aggressions. The legal learning which every man seemed to possess in minute details was the efficacious weapon displayed against the attempts of officials to lay the responsibility of active resistance at the door of the Americans. *The other colonies support its principle.*

There were, however, both violence and bloodshed in North Carolina, where the sturdy farmers of the uplands, stung to desperation by the arbitrary exactions of officers responsible only to an absentee provost-marshal, at last organized armed bands for resistance. Justice at last became so uncertain, and litigation so extravagantly expensive, that these so-called "regulators" finally took action. Tryon, the governor, attacked them with fifteen hundred soldiers, and quelling the rebellion, proceeded to an inquisition. The extortionate and venal judge who had caused the outbreak was found guilty, and mulcted in a nominal fine of one *Outbreak of armed resistance in North Carolina.*

penny on each charge, while the leaders of the regulators were compelled to pay fifty pounds each, a sum enormous in that time and place. Spain had regarded the immense territory of Louisiana, acquired from France by the treaty of Paris, as a safeguard for Mexico, while England appeared to look on the Mississippi and the eastern half of its valley, as far as the Alleghenies, in much the same way as a safe, indefinite frontier against Spain. The wilderness was to remain unsettled, for colonies planted in it could neither be governed themselves, nor defended against others. Tryon's conduct indirectly thwarted the English policy, for the people of North Carolina, disaffected and undaunted, began to emigrate across the mountains to a land in which, though again to face the terrors of a ravaged frontier, they would at least be free.

Almost at the same time the inhabitants of New Orleans, determined to be either French or independent, rose against the sovereignty of Spain, and were free for a year. The remnants of the same population further north in Illinois, Indiana, and Michigan, turned their backs as far as possible on the English, and ignorant of the treaty of Paris, laid the foundations for the commercial prosperity of St. Louis, a city which they fondly believed to be still French. It had been founded in 1763 by Laclede. The existence of this population had made it difficult for Hillsborough to establish his line between savage dominion and English administration. Virginia claimed what is now Kentucky, and the entire territory northwest of the Ohio as far as the great lakes. New York claimed to Lake Erie. Maryland and Pennsylvania had settled bounds. At last, however, by two agreements, one made at Hardlabour, in South Carolina, one at Fort Stanwix, in New York, a line was definitely established from the junction in the latter colony of Wood Creek with Canada Creek, by the west fork of the Susquehanna to Kittanning on the Allegheny River, thence by that stream and the Ohio to the mouth of the Tennessee, which thus became the western boundary of Virginia. The idea was never adopted by the colonies and was futile from the outset, for the very next year Daniel Boone entered Kentucky.

CHAPTER XIII.

THE CONSTITUTIONAL REVOLUTION—1770-1774

Reply to the "Farmer's Letters"—The Colonies United in Purpose—Disorganization of Colonial Government—New York Suggests a Congress—New Opinions in Great Britain—Loyalty in America—The Boston Riots—The Battle on the Alamance—Burning of the Gaspee—Effects of Oppression—Failure of the non-Importation Agreements—Committees of Correspondence—Final Collapse of Colonial Administration—Constitutional Changes in England—Benjamin Franklin—The Hutchinson Letters—Franklin before the Council—His Conduct.

MEANTIME Parliament was again in session. Shelburne had been dismissed, and Chatham, having played to the end the ignoble part which George had assigned him, was permitted to retire. The ministry, with Lord North as premier, continued arrogant and determined for a time, although Burke, the orator of the Rockingham Whigs, inveighed against their inconsistency and fatuity. He showed that the Massachusetts Assembly had been neither treasonable nor even unconstitutional, and the authorities at last concluded that orders to deport men into England to be tried for treason, such as they had contemplated, must rest on actions of another sort, and find firmer legal support than the statute of Henry VIII. which Samuel Adams had scorned. But they determined to censure Boston, and still refused a repeal of the revenue laws. Parliament would yield nothing of its "sovereignty," though feeling the obnoxious acts of Townshend to be uncommercial.

THE CONSTITUTIONAL REVOLUTION 155

The plea of their illegality must, they felt, be abandoned before either modification or repeal. The ministry therefore issued an answer to the "Farmer's Letters," but feeling, no doubt, the force of the Whig position, and fearing the acute interpretation of constitutional law in which the colonies so excelled, they neither proposed the repeal of the charters nor any prosecution for treason. Their diplomatic isolation moreover was complete, and England's only possible friend was Spain, which was proceeding to recover New Orleans and Louisiana, but would be both a difficult and uncertain ally in a general war.

But their resolution found the colonies more united than ever. Virginia, in spite of the conciliatory measures of her new governor, Lord Botetourt, was accepting the guidance of her three famous patriots, Washington, Jefferson, and Henry. Her legislature decided that writs of assistance were illegal, the determination of Parliament wrong, that they themselves and they alone could impose taxes on the people who chose them, that union was lawful and expedient to preserve violated rights. Dissolved as a legal body, the members met as a convention, adopted Washington's scheme of non-importation, and issued for signature a covenant not to import slaves. Pennsylvania and Delaware fell into line. In Newport harbor a smuggling vessel was rescued from the revenue officers and their cutter destroyed. Conflicts like these were common throughout New England, and contributed to colonial impatience. In one of them James Otis received the blow on the head which led to the premature and deplorable loss of his faculties. A possible leader was lost in him.

<small>The colonies united in purpose.</small>

In Massachusetts the legislature was, after a long interval, convened by Bernard for the purpose of getting a grant of salary. They refused to act in the face of coercion with guards at their doors and regiments quartered near. Though adjourned by the governor to Cambridge, they still spent their time in discussing their violated liberties, passed resolutions asking for Bernard's recall, and refused appropriations either for his salary or for the supplies to the garrison. They were therefore prorogued. These two dissolutions are of the utmost importance, because they mark the beginning of a process which finally resulted in the entire disorganization of colonial government in America.

Disorganization of colonial government.

Scarcely less dangerous to England was the temporary success of her officials in securing by the most infamous acts the election of a legislature in New York, which after two successive refusals by its predecessors to provide for the garrison, surrendered at last everything the crown demanded. But the same body passed a resolution inviting the colonies to choose each two delegates who should assemble in a congress with power to legislate for the united colonies, in the hope of inaugurating American union without separation from England. Virginia actually chose her delegates, but the ministry forbade the meeting; they were right in their estimate of the scheme as dangerous and revolutionary. Parliament, wearied and confused by the tactics of the colonies, seized this opportunity to repeal all the obnoxious taxes except that on tea, which it stubbornly retained to display its sovereignty, or more probably, at the instance of the king, to display his supremacy. The Billeting Act had expired by limitation.

New York suggests a congress.

There thus remained, of all the exasperating measures which had led the colonies to the verge of open rebellion, the former tax on sugar, and a tax on tea light enough to be inconsiderable in regard to revenue, but burdened with a principle so obnoxious as to be destructive. The maladroit Tories had utterly failed in their programme for the taxation of the colonies, but had erected a principle destined to foster fatal animosities between brethren. At the same time the counter-revolution of opinion became manifest in Great Britain itself. Grattan entered on his glorious career of Irish agitation ; Chatham, recalling his former glories, suggested a process for the reform of the House of Commons, and for the first time in English history public meetings to demand popular rights were held. And the press, opening fire with the scurrilous and clever letters of "Junius," a pen-name which still shields an unknown writer, entered on a campaign fraught with the weightiest consequences for posterity. *[New opinions in Great Britain.]*

The three years from 1770 to 1774 may be said to open the third and final period of the constitutional revolution, the period which separated the colonies from the mother-country, and thus enabled them to lead by fifty years in establishing and realizing the principles of liberalism. They illustrate how unwillingly they entered on the extreme course of disruption, and how deliberate and long-suffering men of English blood can be in the face of oppression and irritation. Some Americans like Chief Justice Hutchinson, who was selected to succeed Bernard with the title of lieutenant-governor, and was then made governor, were more devoted to their English citizenship than to their private liberties. The number of such was large, and among them was for a time the greater part of the wealth, learning, and refinement. Franklin and Dickinson were long of this section. But the plain people like Samuel Adams were far more American than English in feeling, and the blunders of the ministry swelled their numbers by the addition of many rich, influential, and educated men. *[Loyalty in America.]*

The line of demarcation between the two classes became more definite in these years, although on either side were to be found, of course, both moderate and radical minds.

The process was hastened by two or three events of very unequal importance : the so-called Boston massacre, the battle of the Alamance, and the seizure of the Gaspee. The first occurred in 1770, almost simultaneously with the repeal of the odious taxes. The sons of Hutchinson were believed to be selling tea contrary to public policy and agreement, as the revenue figures proved that many other Boston merchants were doing, and riotous demonstrations were made before their door. The ubiquitous red-coats were drawn up within their barracks, ready for action. In the first general tumult a child was killed, though no shots were fired. There was an imposing but quiet funeral procession, and the citizens, under a calm exterior, gradually forged their anger to a white heat, until a fancied insult in the refusal to a soldier of work at the rope-walk exasperated the troops in equal measure. There were gatherings, insults, and alarms on both sides, until finally a soldier was struck and the ever-growing rumor came to the barracks in a false announcement that a sentinel had been killed. A corporal and six men with fixed bayonets sallied forth and fired. Three citizens were killed, two more mortally wounded, and six injured by the volley. The excitement was so intense that on the representations of Samuel Adams the governor yielded, the city was at last evacuated, and the regiments withdrawn to Castle William in the harbor. The commanding officer was tried and acquitted with due legal form, being actually defended at the instance of Samuel Adams by two young patriots, John Adams and Josiah Quincy ; two soldiers were convicted of man-

THE CONSTITUTIONAL REVOLUTION 159

slaughter, branded, and set free. Quiet was thus restored with suspicious promptness, but the name of "massacre," by which these events were designated throughout the colonies, is indicative of a sensation incommensurate with the facts. There were other conflicts between the populace and the military, especially those about the noted Liberty Tree in New York, but none so fatal as the one described.

There had been no reform in the government of North Carolina, and under Tryon the extortion of sheriffs, accompanied as of old the malfeasance of corrupt judges. Charges were framed on any trivial pretext against those farmers who had been connected with the old regulators, and representative men were seized and imprisoned without trial at New-Berne. At last the people rose again, and in a meeting numbering upwards of twelve hundred armed men formulated their grievances and demanded redress. Tryon, with disciplined troops of about equal number, marched to suppress the movement. He was met on May 16th, 1771, under a flag of truce, by the popular leaders—men like James Hunter and Benjamin Merrill—noted everywhere for moderation and integrity. But he refused to parley and demanded unconditional surrender. A battle ensued, in which the undisciplined backwoodsmen stubbornly and gallantly resisted for two hours, but the end was a rout. Twenty were killed and many were taken prisoners, while nine of the king's army were killed and twenty wounded. Of the prisoners one was hanged in chains as an outlaw, six after trial met the same fate. All the best lands were confiscated to the crown. As a consequence disloyalty spread apace; the counties of Orange and Mecklenburg were especially imbued with a patriotism never again quenched. Again bands of angry and disheartened frontiersmen crossed the mountains into

The battle on the Alamance.

Tennessee to prepare against the day of reckoning a commonwealth embittered against England as few others were.

The Gaspee was an armed English schooner which guarded the coast of Rhode Island, a region notorious for successful evasion of the revenue laws. Commanded by a bully, it committed while on its cruises many illegal acts of destruction to the property of the natives. Formal complaints to the authorities at Boston were answered by unqualified approval of these depredations. On June 9th, 1772, the clever skipper of the Providence packet, which the king's officer proposed to overhaul and search, drew the cutter, by an act of skilful daring, into shoal water where she stranded. The following night a large party of disguised men boarded her, and after a conflict in which the commander was wounded, seized and landed him and his crew, setting fire at the same time to the vessel. The officers of the law were powerless to discover the assailants.

Burning of the Gaspee.

Local pride has held up each of these events as the first important conflict in the struggle for liberty, but whether it was the Calvinistic Puritan of the North, or the Calvinistic Covenanter of the South whose blood was first shed matters little. The facts in each case show that the uprising was against oppression, not against England. The affair on the Alamance was as considerable as that at Lexington and of the same nature, although its consequences were not so immediate or momentous. Religious Calvinism, however, was rapidly undergoing a transformation into a political doctrine, which was destined to permeate the whole people as the dogmatic side never could nor did.

Effects of oppression.

In spite of these occurrences there was an outward appearance of reconciliation. The powerful mercantile

THE CONSTITUTIONAL REVOLUTION 161

society in the great towns was active and enterprising, but luxurious and socially ambitious. Means were found even in Boston to revive trade. New York, already the commercial metropolis, felt its social importance increased by the presence of the officers, and, knowing how the non-importation agreements were disregarded by New England, Pennsylvania, and Virginia, formally revoked them. The conduct of New York was open and honorable; but it was felt by many to be a serious concession and reprobated accordingly. When the news reached Princeton a body of patriot students forced the hangman to burn a copy of the resolutions. No means exist of determining exactly what youths stood about the fire. But the four classes then in college enrolled among their numbers names of men who afterward gained the highest distinction in American affairs, five who afterward sat in the convention which framed the Constitution, and one, James Madison, who became President of the United States. Philadelphia, like Boston, stood in awe of her radicals; but the period was one of outward calm and prosperity for her as well. Beneath the surface, however, the leaven of discontent was at work, and the disorganization of English administration went on to completion.

Failure of the non-importation agreements.

In Massachusetts Samuel Adams completed a perfect revolutionary system in the establishment of extra legal committees of correspondence between the towns, through which the remotest districts were instructed in the legal aspects of the conflict between legislature and governor, and united in harmonious support of his agitation. He put a new stone on the edifice of independence by his famous document, "Rights of the Colonies," issued in 1772, and read from north to south. The legislature of Virginia was the first to assemble after its appearance. In extension

Committees of correspondence.

11

of Adams's scheme it organized a committee of correspondence with the other colonial assemblies, and suggested the plan as worthy of adoption by all. One by one, as they were summoned by the governors, their first act was to follow the example of the Old Dominion. The consequences were doubly important, because the royal officials were now no longer the colonial representatives in the intervals between sessions, and the moral effect of proroguing the legislatures was neutralized, while at the same time the machinery for united action was not only erected but set in motion. The contagion of firmness and enthusiasm spread everywhere through the new channels.

Before long evidence began to appear that the old forms were in entire collapse. What order there was in Massachusetts resulted from the influence of the committee; in both North and South Carolina a dead-lock between governors and legislatures resulted in anarchy, and in the former there arose the self-constituted republic of Watauga, which was the only district of the State where justice was administered. In defiance of ministerial control, for though Hillsborough had given place to Lord Dartmouth there was no break in the former's colonial policy, the whole West was explored and many settlements made. Connecticut, with a charter for lands stretching away to the Pacific, seized the Wyoming Valley. The regions about Lakes George and Champlain, and the contiguous portions of the northern Connecticut Valley, threw off the government of New York entirely, and rendered obedience only to committees of their own people.

Final collapse of colonial administration.

During the years from 1770 to 1773 American affairs received but little attention in Parliament. Lord North was successful as premier in many directions, especially in keeping peace with Spain. Wilkes and the *North*

THE CONSTITUTIONAL REVOLUTION 163

Briton wrought, as has been said, a most important constitutional revolution as to the freedom of the press and the publicity of parliamentary debate, and quidnuncs were busy with the identity of "Junius." The colonial empire in India was daily winning ground, and the nation as a whole temporarily forgot the need for reform, the old methods being successful, the prime minister capable, and his majority secure.   *Constitutional changes in England.*

But in 1773 occurred an incident to which, more than any other, English historians persistently attribute the final rupture with the colonies. Benjamin Franklin was now a man in his seventieth year, and had long enjoyed a world-wide reputation as philosopher and sage. Kant called him the modern Prometheus. For nearly a quarter of a century he had been the advocate of good feeling between the English at home and their kinsfolk in America. He was loyal to the heart, and was resident in London as the agent of four colonies, Massachusetts, Pennsylvania, New Jersey, and Georgia, Edmund Burke holding a like office for New York. Franklin's efforts to mould English opinion were made, therefore, from the vantage-ground of both personal reputation and official dignity. Yet they were strangely abortive, and before long he came into possession of evidence that they were thwarted by influential persons at home.   *Benjamin Franklin.*

The fact was that Hutchinson, Oliver, and Paxton had long been in communication with Grenville through the intermediation of his private secretary, Whateley. Franklin obtained copies of this correspondence by means which he never divulged, communicated it to Lord Dartmouth, and by permission of the consignor forwarded it also to Samuel Adams, the Speaker of the Massachusetts Assembly, by whom it was   *The Hutchinson letters.*

read to the legislature. A tempest of popular feeling arose on both sides of the Atlantic. In America the immediate removal of both Hutchinson and Oliver was demanded, but "resentment against England was abated" when it was known who were the "authors of their grievances." In England Franklin was stigmatized as underhanded and dishonorable. He had uttered no word of complaint on the publication of the letters, he made no retort to the insults except to exculpate all others, and declare that he alone had obtained and forwarded the document. The rumor of the day asserted that Temple had purloined them from Whateley's brother, executor of his estate.

In January, 1774, Franklin was summoned before the Privy Council to be tried, nominally in regard to the petition he had presented for the removal of the men regarded in America as conspirators, but really to brand him with dishonor in securing the evidence of Hutchinson's double-dealing. Passions had been more and more inflamed, and the appearance of Franklin before the Council brought together the most famous men of the time. He was compared by the prosecutor to Sejanus, the tool of Tiberius, and insulted by charges that he was conspiring to secure Hutchinson's place by secret fraud. Franklin's counsel were overawed by the effrontery of attack and the applauding consent of the assemblage. Their replies were ineffective, and the impassiveness of the accused, conscious of his own rectitude, left on the public an impression that not having resented the intemperate language of his accusers he must have been guilty.

Even in the cold perspective of history he is still stigmatized in England as revengeful and base, as sharing in this dishonorable action with Grenville, Townshend, and North, the guilt of bringing on the English race the disaster of separation. It is unfortunately true that Poor Richard's philosophy is ruthlessly utilitarian, but it is neither incredible nor unlikely that the aged statesman, confident of the judgment which posterity would pronounce upon his life and work, simply despised the low violence of his assailants, and shielded in his own silence the more vulnerable character of some high-born and hasty friend who had in a weak moment, and with good motives, overstepped the bounds of social morality. His course when once in possession of the letters seemed clearer perhaps to him than it now does to us. It was a time pregnant with momentous issues; there were communications between officials on questions affecting the public welfare; if the Speaker of the Massachusetts house had used them in America without formal publicity the traditions of diplomacy could not have been violated and great good would have resulted. Let us waive the nice point of honor as a lapse due to human weakness, but resent as paltry and absurd the charge that a great man committed to a policy of conciliation, of which he was the ablest defender, shares in any degree the responsibilities of a blinded people led by an administration obstinate, haughty, and revolutionary in other matters as in this.

Franklin before the Council.

CHAPTER XIV.

RESISTANCE TO OPPRESSION—1773-1774

The Tea Tax—Resistance to Importation—Boston Resorts to Force—Lord North Retaliates—The Boston Port Act—Changes in the Massachusetts Charter—The Quebec Act—American Tories and Patriots—Respective Propositions of New York and New England—The "Continental" Movement—Passive Resistance of New England—Movement to Convene a Congress—Alexander Hamilton—Character of the Delegations—Royal Officials Menaced—The Savage to Fight against the Americans—The First Continental Congress—Dramatic Opening—Last Appeal for Justice—Two Assertions of Sovereignty—Significance of the Fight at Point Pleasant.

DURING the years 1768 and 1769 English trade with America had diminished by seven hundred thousand pounds, but the violation of the non-importation agreements had somewhat restored it in the following years, and a policy was now adopted in England which it was hoped would entirely destroy those agreements, restore trade by further lowering the price of tea, and leave untouched the principle of parliamentary supremacy which the king foolishly reiterated in a proclamation. The East India Company was to export its teas to America free of English tax and subject only to the old threepenny duty in the ports of entry. The principle thus saved they were to have a drawback of the tax collected.

The tea tax.

In 1773 cargoes were accordingly despatched to New York, Philadelphia, Charleston, and Boston, and consignees were designated to receive them. The agitation began in Philadelphia, where a mass meeting was held on October 18th, to denounce this new attempt in both principle and detail, and to demand the resignation of the company's agents. *Resistance to importation.* They promptly complied, and when the vessel arrived in the Delaware, on Christmas-day, it was stopped, and on the twenty-eighth the captain sailed back to England. In Charleston the tea was landed but was seized by the collector and stored in damp cellars, where it rotted. In New York the Sons of Liberty formed a vigilance committee, secured the resignation of the Commissioners, organized bands of "Mohawks" for resistance if necessary and ordered the harbor pilots not to bring the tea ship above Sandy Hook. It was promptly dispatched on its return journey as soon as it came within hail.

The measures taken in Boston were less immediately effective. Mass meetings were held and the Philadelphia resolutions adopted, but the consignees would not resign. Committees for resistance were organized and post-riders to communicate with neighboring towns were appointed. *Boston resorts to force.* When the first ship arrived, on November 28th, the owner consented to a short delay and a public meeting resolved that it must return. Both owner and master were willing, but the revenue officers and consignee insisted that she could not clear with the tea on board, and that, in accordance with custom, the owners must land it. Meantime two other vessels, each with a partial cargo of the same commodity, had threaded the tortuous and difficult channel of the harbor. Return was impossible in the face of the English guardships anchored below and all three lay beside the quays. Day and night a citizens' patrol prevented any discharge of cargo, and according to law the ships were liable to seizure within twenty days if not previously unloaded according to due form. On December 18th there was a meeting in the old South church of several thousand excited citizens, discussing the situation and waiting the event. The owner of the vessel which first arrived had vainly sought the governor's permission to withdraw his ship and returned after dark at a quarter to six with the announcement of his failure. A preconcerted signal was given, some forty or fifty men disguised as Mohawk Indians sprang from their ambush near by and, followed by the interested assemblage, set out for the wharves. In the presence of almost the whole populace the tea ships were boarded and all the tea, some three hundred chests, flung broadcast over the water. There was no rioting and no injury to any other property.

The spoken defiance of the other colonies had been quite as efficient as the combination of threats and force to which Boston was compelled to resort, but Lord North launched the first retaliatory and punitive measure against that city, which drew the opening bolts of wrath on itself as having in English eyes now reached a climax of which former instances of turbulence and rebellion had been but steps. English opinion, as far at least as it found expression in Parliament, supported Lord North in his measures. There was an opposition few in numbers but strong in brains, led by Fox and supported in the main by Burke. Tucker, Dean of Gloucester, and Cartwright, destined to carry great reforms in his own land, were foremost among the few in private life who understood the tendency of American affairs and favored it.

Lord North retaliates.

The first of Lord North's bills was the Boston Port Act, which closed the harbor until indemnity for the tea there destroyed should be paid and the king be satisfied that thereafter the city would obey the laws. The demand for indemnity was fair but the indefinite claim of

obedience was not only infamous in itself but, as Burke
said, punished the innocent with the guilty. After the
enactment of this law there was a temporary <small>The Boston
revulsion of feeling, for a bill to repeal the Port Act.</small>
tax on tea met with substantial support, although it
finally failed. Burke plead with impassioned oratory,
but in vain, that peace would be secure if England would,
by a return to her old and tried principles, permit
America to tax herself and to be bound in Parliament
only by laws of trade such as had always been passed
and obeyed.

North's second bill was a virtual abrogation of the
Massachusetts charter. The council of twenty-eight had
been hitherto elected every year in joint ses- <small>Changes in
sion of the assembly. The king might now the Massachusetts charter.</small>
appoint the whole body to any number, from
twelve to thirty-six, and remove them at pleasure. The
men so appointed were designated mandamus councillors. Thereafter town-meetings could be held only
by permission of the governor and for the sole purpose
of electing officers. Sheriffs were to return all juries,
and were to be named by the governor and hold office
during his pleasure. The third bill was really a device
of the king's, and it is said that the ministry was confused and shamefaced in presenting it. It ordained
that magistrates, revenue officers, or other officials in-
dicted in Massachusetts for capital offences were to be
tried either in Nova Scotia or Great Britain.

Another measure made legal the billeting of troops,
against which Boston had hitherto striven with success,
and a fifth, known as the Quebec Act, though <small>The Quebec
depriving that province of the right of ha- Act.</small>
beas corpus, restored the French customary law (*coutume
de Paris*), established Roman Catholicism as the state
religion, and by extending its boundaries to the Ohio

and Mississippi, shut off the Northern English Colonies from westward extension. This was intended as an arbitrary settlement of a vexed question. The Puritans, however, chose to draw little distinction between the prelacy of the Church of England and that of the Church of Rome, and exclaimed that the next step would be the establishment among them of English episcopacy. These laws were enacted by majorities varying between three to one and four to one, and to secure their enforcement Hutchinson was called to England and the two offices of civil governor of Massachusetts and commander-in chief of the king's forces in North America were united in the person of Gage, who was to garrison Boston with four new regiments. He was accordingly dispatched and entered the harbor in May, 1774. His first act was to prorogue the assembly, which was to meet again at Salem, the new provincial capital, after the enforcement of the Port Bill on June 7th.

Such a course could have but one effect in America. The moderate men were no longer united. Even in Boston there were some who remained submissive as well as loyal under the lash. They and their sympathizers elsewhere lost all influence, and under the designation of Loyalists or Tories suffered obloquy, and at times even ostracism, for their opinions. The radicals, at the other extreme, were triumphant. In New York the committee of correspondence had hitherto been despised by the upper classes. It was composed exclusively of "Sons of Liberty," most of whom were mechanics and shopkeepers belonging to the Church of Scotland. If North had hoped to isolate Boston for punishment and curry favor with the other seaport towns by overlooking their equally successful defiance he failed miserably. So universal was the sympathy for Boston in New York that the existing commit-

American tories and patriots.

tee, which the Royalists had stigmatized as the "Presbyterian Junto," resolved to take advantage of the rising tide to blend all classes for united action. With rare magnanimity they disbanded, their last official act being a proposal for a general congress, which they sent to Boston. Immediately there was formed a new committee, fifty in number, embracing all shades of feeling, and led by John Jay. The chairman was a graduate of King's College, which gave to the cause of American freedom not only that distinguished man, but one of even larger mind, Alexander Hamilton. At that time the former favored continued dependence if accompanied by liberty. The enlarged and influential committee carried with it the undivided approval of the colony in adopting as its own the proposition made by its predecessor for a general congress.

Hitherto New England had proposed nothing better to the country than an entire suspension of trade. For a time the two schemes were before the people in apparent conflict. The merchants of Philadelphia would not listen to the latter. With statesmanlike policy and rare tact the now famous Dickinson, known and respected for both the power and moderation of his writings, directed the uneasy and lukewarm disposition of his great province to the New York proposition. Connecticut, too, was hearty in her acceptance of it, while New Jersey adopted both plans, to suspend trade and send delegates to a congress. Baltimore merchants, tired of supplication, thought "something more suitable would suit their purpose," and Maryland fell into line. South Carolina resolved that "the whole great continent must be animated by one great soul, . . . and all Americans must resolve to stand by one another even unto death." *Respective propositions of New York and New England.*

As early as 1768 the English in the colonies who upheld the principles of the English revolution called themselves American Whigs. In time the title supplanted that of Englishmen, and ere long, from the constant use of the phrase "the whole continent" to express general action, came the fine adjective so long significant of union—continental.

The "Continental" movement.

The Virginia legislature on May 24th ordered the day on which the Port Act was to take effect to be observed as a fast-day, to pray for the intervention of God to avert "the dreadful calamity which threatened their civil rights and the evils of civil war." Complaisant as Lord Botetourt had been, even he had felt compelled in 1769 to dismiss the legislature; the imperious Dunmore, his successor, was no less prompt in 1774, but with a precedent before them, well known and admired, members met at once in a room near by, with their Speaker in the chair, and voted for a congress. The committee of correspondence was left in charge, and on May 29th it called a convention to elect delegates. Conventions, local self-government, war—such acts and thoughts showed how near was revolution. The influence of the Old Dominion was so great that her firmness put an end to indecision everywhere. North Carolina never wavered and followed the example.

It was the thirteenth of May when the Port Act reached Boston, on June 1st it was put into force; on the seventh the assembly met at Salem, with Samuel Adams as Speaker. The other colonies had observed the fatal day of tyranny as a solemn fast. In Philadelphia the bells were muffled and tolled, all shops except those of the Quakers being shut; in Virginia the churches were filled with mourning worshippers; in the middle and southern provinces the air was charged with a spirit of resistance. But in northern New England there seemed an inexplicable paralysis. Rhode Island

Passive resistance of New England.

was making ready, but had taken no irrevocable step. New Hampshire was reticent and cold, and the Boston committee merely drew up a covenant to cease intercourse with Great Britain after August 1st. When the legislature met, its opening resolutions were all for conciliation. Meantime there was no thought of active resistance, or any but legal measures, though the mandamus councillors had been appointed and were showing themselves active and subservient to the crown, though the number of the garrison was daily growing, and the leaders of patriot opinion were proscribed. Gage actually entered the harbor with an order in his possession to arrest Samuel Adams, Hancock, and others, but he had not dared to execute it.

At last, on June 15th, the first move in the second stage of organization was made. The Rhode Island Assembly had long been in close communication with that of Massachusetts to comfort and support them in the furnace of affliction which had been doubly heated for that perplexed but determined commonwealth. The decisive action of one followed close on that of the other in the active choice of delegates to a congress, Rhode Island voting on the 15th, Massachusetts on the 17th. Maryland, ignorant as yet of their work, and therefore with equal courage, followed on the 22d. The aristocratic committee of New York was drawn two ways. The Delanceys, whose sway had lasted four years, had recently been displaced by the Livingstons, who were Presbyterian and republican. Jay was a relative of the latter family by marriage though himself a Huguenot. The influence of the family connection secured a selection of delegates. The choice was made on July 4th, but three of the five members were distrusted as royalists by the radical patriots who were not represented at all.

Movement to convene a congress.

The latter therefore held a mass-meeting in the debates of which appeared for the first time the youth who was <small>Alexander Hamilton.</small> destined not only to lead the opinion of the great commonweath as an advocate of independence, but who later enhanced her glory by the support which he gave to the constitution. He was then a dark, frail-looking boy of fifteen, who had been born of Scotch parents in the West Indies and having been left an orphan had found his way to New York, where he was a student in King's College.

There was a certain half-heartedness in the New York delegation, and a hesitancy amounting almost to repulsion in that of Pennsylvania, where the <small>Character of the delega- tions.</small> Quakers longed for direct government by the Crown to free them from the yoke of the proprietors, and the Presbyterians, fearing an Episcopal establishment, were almost the only patriots. By a sad mishap, Dickinson, their leader, was at first left out of the delegation. He changed everything, however, when sent a little later to replace an original member who was not only lukewarm but was an ardent Tory and had been suspected of being a spy. The strongest ardor was shown in the selection of able and patriotic men by New Hampshire, New Jersey, the Carolinas, and Virginia. Many of the colonies, as Massachusetts, South Carolina, and Pennsylvania, appointed their representatives in legal form through the assembly. Others, as New Hampshire, New Jersey, and Virginia, preferred to send theirs from a voluntary convention. The instructions of the latter were generally more radical than those of the others, and Virginia seized the occasion to publish a scathing indictment against England in regard to the slave-trade. It denounced the Government as preferring "the immediate advantage of a few British corsairs to the lasting interest of the American states and to the rights of

RESISTANCE TO OPPRESSION 175

human nature, deeply wounded by this infamous practice."

Meantime provocation by the royal officials and recrimination by the populace went steadily forward in New England with equal step, and the condition of affairs grew most alarming. Mandamus councillors were compelled to resign, sometimes by moral, sometimes by physical force. The judges were not allowed to sit. Oliver, the chief justice, resigned under compulsion and there were threatening assemblies in many places which adopted noteworthy resolutions, calm in the recital of rights but definite in tone. The country militia began to arm and march for Boston. When the various local stores of powder were seized by the authorities and carried to the castle, Putnam in Connecticut heard a false report of collisions and some twenty thousand armed men in all were soon moving. *Royal officials menaced.*

Gage became as panic-stricken as his predecessors, begged for a larger force and shared with Oliver the opprobrium of successfully proposing that Canadians and Indians should be used as auxiliaries. Others had previously suggested it, but so far without success. In the ensuing conflict the administration in their desperation set loose the red cannibals, for such the Indian was, not against his own kind, as in the old French and Indian war, but against the frontiersman's defenceless cabin and the pioneer's camp. On September 5th the British began to fortify the neck which connects Boston with the main-land. *The savage to fight against the Americans.*

It is said that Cushing and Franklin had discussed the possibility of a general congress in 1773, and Hancock proposed one in March, 1774. The following May, meetings in Providence, Rhode Island, and in the city of New York voted for one; as we have seen, the Virginia House of Burgesses formally proposed *Dramatic opening.*

it and the initiative was taken by Rhode Island and Massachusetts. The first Continental congress met on Monday September 5th, 1774, in the Carpenters' Hall of Philadelphia. Eleven colonies were fully represented: Delaware partially, having three for the lower counties, and Newcastle. Georgia, weak and distant, sent none, but was in full sympathy. John Adams thought that of the fifty-five members a third were American Whigs, a third Tories, and the rest mongrel. The avowed object was "the union of Great Britain and the colonies on a constitutional foundation."

The voting was by the colonies, because the relative importance of each as to population could not be determined. On the motion of Samuel Adams, the extreme Calvinistic independent, an Episcopalian chaplain was chosen to open the meetings by prayer, and the proceedings were to be kept secret, although it was believed that Galloway divulged them during his membership. The opening was rendered dramatic by the receipt of an express from Putnam with the false news of a conflict. Muffled bells were tolled, dismay and sorrow reigned everywhere, and the clergyman, finding nothing adequate to the occasion in his liturgy, burst into extempore prayer. The deep impression thus made was not entirely dispelled when the facts became known.

The first Continental congress.

The ensuing debates displayed marked disagreement as to the essentials of united action. In general the opinion prevailed that extremes should be avoided, that a last appeal for justice should be made to England, and that there should be no assumption of sovereignty, although no member seems to have wavered in the determination to insist as an ultimatum that taxation and all legislation were the functions of American legislatures, and not of Parliament. Accord-

Last appeal for justice.

ingly their petition for redress was to the king, a very different course from that which the separate colonies had hitherto taken. Addresses were also issued, one to the people of the colonies, one to the inhabitants of Quebec, and one to the English nation.

Of the purely deliberative proceedings, however, by far the most important act was the famous declaration of the rights of the colonies. But despite the firmest resolution to keep within the avowed limits, two measures were adopted which presaged the future and sound to the reader of our time like the expression of a sovereign will. In the articles of the American Association, which were not only written but authoritatively sent out for signatures, is a prohibition of both importation and exportation in commerce with Great Britain until the repeal of the penal acts. The other was the expressed opinion that if the acts were to be executed by force all America ought to support the inhabitants of Massachusetts Bay in their opposition. The congress adjourned on October 26th, to meet again the following year if necessary, and the members returned to their homes feeling undoubtedly that war was not far distant. The utmost activity prevailed in the colonies throughout the autumn. Committees of correspondence turned into committees of safety or organized them, munitions were collected, the militia drilled, and every community instructed as far as possible in the art of warfare. A system of express riders was also created which proved of inestimable advantage in the dissemination of news.

Two assertions of sovereignty.

Far in the distant wilderness, as it then seemed, events were simultaneously transpiring, of trivial compass indeed, but pregnant with future union and independence. The Quebec Act had not only sought to re-establish under English protection a French empire in order to check the unruliness of the colonies, it had even made settlement in the north-west territory illegal. But there was already in existence one little independent commonwealth, destined never to come under English rule. On October 6, 1774, there was a skirmish between the frontiersmen and the Shawnee Indians at Point Pleasant, near the confluence of the Kanawha with the Ohio River. The victory of the former was a step toward the formation of other independent communities; thenceforward the backwoods were in rebellion and settlers must find an American title to their lands if they were to have any at all. Already the Ohio Valley and other attractive districts beyond the Alleghenies were dotted with rude hamlets and isolated cabins. The western claims of the colonies had in this way constantly been strengthened; now the intrepidity of their kinsfolk had openly defied the Quebec Act and welded the vanguard at least into indissoluble union for the enforcement of their one comprehensive claim, the right to settlement.

Significance of the fight at Point Pleasant.

THE NORTHERN COLONIES
ILLUSTRATING
THE FIRST-HALF OF THE REVOLUTION

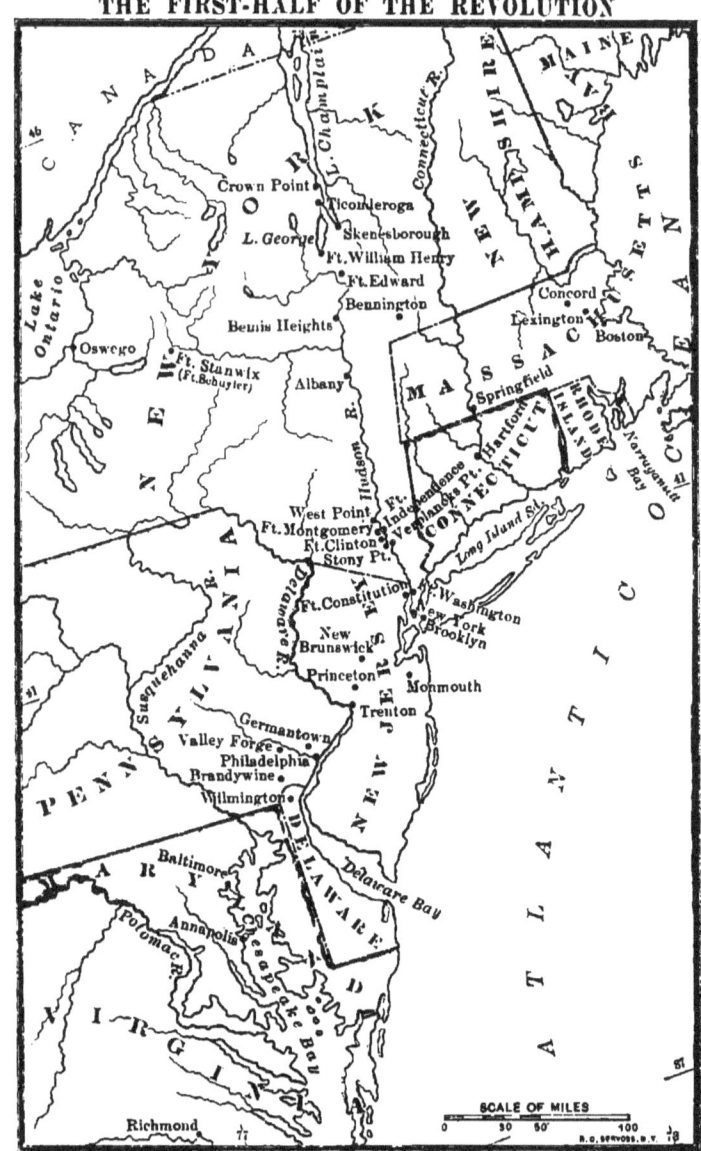

CHAPTER XV.

THE BEGINNING OF HOSTILITIES—1774-1775

Dissensions in Parliament and Cabinet—Chatham's Plan of Conciliation—Burke the Friend of America—Duplicity of the King—War Measures of the Administration—Return of Franklin—Burke on the Spirit of the Constitution—Effect of the News in America—Approach of the Crisis—The Gathering on Lexington Green—The Conflicts at Lexington and Concord—Retreat of the English—Boston Besieged by the American Farmers—The Colonies Organize for Armed Resistance—Overthrow of the Colonial Governments—Seizure of Ticonderoga—War Measures of Parliament and the King—Attitude of Europe.

ANOTHER general election in England returned to Parliament a still larger majority of the king's supporters. The enforcement of the penal acts was the distinct platform of the Tories. The remnant of the Whigs could not agree. There was a temporary restoration of Chatham's vigor, and Shelburne, his chief support, stood firm in the wise liberalism which he held but could not make popular. Rockingham shone in the reflection of Burke's splendid intellect, but such was the strength of factions that he was left without power to organize into compactness the opposition, which, however, was in another way quite as distant from the people as the Tories, and like its rivals firmly upheld the Declaratory Act. On the other hand, the king and North were often at variance. The latter continued to display his ingenuity and prevision. At

180   THE FRENCH WAR AND THE REVOLUTION

times he feebly resisted the diseased and excited activity of his sovereign, but he never failed to yield at the wrong moment.

The session stands unsurpassed in parliamentary annals for eloquence. Chatham was never greater as a statesman nor as an orator than when he unfolded his plan for conciliation—the obnoxious Acts to be repealed, the troops to be removed, the colonies to tax themselves, Parliament, as of old, to confine its imperial legislation strictly to the regulation of trade. It fell on enraptured ears but on hardened minds. Its echoes without renewed in many hearts the old English sympathy for liberty and its supporters.

Chatham's plan of reconciliation.

Once again also the merchants, compelled to inactivity by the suspension of trade, began to discuss the folly of measures which not only yielded no revenues to lighten their burdens but must be of doubtful constitutionality when men like Chatham advised their repeal. The habit of friendship for the colonies was strong upon Burke, his silvery voice and mellifluous sentences delivered such an eulogium on America as no man before or after him, no voice in or out of England, ever pronounced; but already the spell of Cassandra was working over him; nor could his moderation combat the insensate radicalism of the Tories. By overwhelming majorities Chatham's plan was rejected and a request from Franklin for a hearing refused.

Burke the friend of America.

On February 9th, 1755, Parliament addressed the king in support of the penal acts; he replied that he would enforce "obedience to the laws and the authority of the supreme legislature." Rockingham stigmatized the language as a declaration of war, and without the precincts of Westminster a stormy indignation soon arose over the extreme course of the ad-

Duplicity of the king.

THE BEGINNING OF HOSTILITIES 181

ministration. North devised and the king unwillingly consented to a seeming compromise, which the latter spoke of as an olive branch. They proposed that if any colony would promise a satisfactory contribution for the public defence, and the expenses of the administration, Parliament should refrain from taxing it. The dulness of the majority failed at first to apprehend the meaning of so specious a suggestion, and nearly overthrew the ministry. Nor did they, even when the excitement was allayed, quite grasp the fact that the new bill was intended to win New York and Pennsylvania, leaving the patriots of New England and Virginia without their powerful support, and thus destroying the force of united action.

Any possible temptation it might have held out to moderate and still loyal men like Jay and Dickinson was neutralized by declarations that no concession of principle would be made, and by simultaneous preparations for open hostility and coercion. Ten thousand troops were to be massed in Boston, and in place of the uncertain Gage, who was now pleading for moderation, Sir William Howe was to be commander-in-chief, with Henry Clinton and John Burgoyne as major-generals. Instructions were issued to intercept any munitions of war destined for the colonies. Public opinion in England was to be aroused against America by paid agents, among whom was Dr. Samuel Johnson. War measures of the administration.

It had seemed to Franklin that a climax was reached when the bill forbidding the New England colonies to fish on the Banks was seriously debated. It passed by a vote of 73 to 21. He knew that it was preliminary to other more terrible plans of coercion, to the organization of Indian ravages on the frontiers, and of servile insurrection against the Southern slave- Return of Franklin.

holders. Accordingly, while these final measures were being taken he was on his way to his native land. What had been sneeringly called an "embassy from all America," and was so in reality, thus came to a dismal end.

On March 22d, 1775, two days after his departure, Burke made another plea for reconciliation, declaring that the colonists were but living according to the spirit of the constitution, showing the same virtue as that of which Englishmen at home were so proud, and that magnanimity was expedient. For three hours Parliament heard his sane and eloquent words, but their argument was without response. The land for which he plead remained in ignorance of even the poor effort made a little later by Lord North, for the information received prior to Lexington contained nothing of it.

Burke on the spirit of the constitution.

News travelled so slowly that the course of parliamentary action had been imperfectly understood by the expectant colonists, but they readily grasped its general trend. Local and general conventions of a representative character were held to discuss the deeds of the Continental Congress, and to appoint delegates for another. Every possible measure for the accumulation of military stores and the training of militia was taken. Some of the almanacs which went to every farmer's house with information and amusement contained this year a recipe for making gunpowder. The occurrences of the time were merely a logical result of previous obduracy, strengthened now by the attitude of this latest Parliament. When a royalist sheriff from New York undertook to hold a court at Westminster, in what is now Vermont, the rangers of the district, known as Green Mountain Boys, resisted, and on March 13th blood was shed. There was a general uprising of the surrounding country, the royalists were

Effect of the news in America.

THE BEGINNING OF HOSTILITIES 183

captured and sent into Massachusetts for trial. Ethan Allen, the ranger captain, sent word that in case of need he was ready to seize Ticonderoga. In Virginia the governor seized the powder stores of Williamsburg and threatened to emancipate the slaves; the people stood firm on their famous Fairfax declaration and went on arming, collecting munitions, and organizing a revolutionary government. Among the substitute delegates to the next general congress appeared the name of Thomas Jefferson.

The minute men, or irregular Massachusetts militia, being now organized and equipped, Gage, in boyish bravado, sent a brigade to march out from Boston to Jamaica Plain and back as a challenge. <small>Approach of the crisis.</small> The grim farmers were not trapped, but their representatives in convention continued the series of sovereign acts to which necessity drove them. Dartmouth College had been established as a school for the youth of the Six Nations, missionaries were sent out by it into the northwest, to counteract, where danger was most imminent, the Canadian influences which were instigating the Indians to active hostilities against the Americans. The friendly Stockbridge Indians were also won to mediate with the Mohawks for their good-will.

Such events may be contemptuously dismissed as trivial acts of unruliness when viewed singly and objectively. In the mass they evince the triumph of a principle unwelcome to many, perhaps a majority of the English-speaking men in America. <small>The gathering on Lexington Green.</small> For nine long years the people waited, impatiently perhaps, but they endured, none the less loyally, employing in self-defence the weapons of peace, self-denial and legal shrewdness. Now the limit was reached. Already, in February, when the powder stored at Salem had been seized, a bloody collision was only prevented

184 THE FRENCH WAR AND THE REVOLUTION

by respect for the Sabbath, the day on which the English made their entrance. There was no later news from England than that of Parliament's vote of confidence in the king. Similar seizures of ammunition were being made north and south, no change of heart was anywhere visible. The crisis was reached in an attempt as petty in itself as any of those recorded. The momentous consequences had been prepared by the long and general agitation which produced the general congress. Armed resistance had been frequent enough, and was often successful; the next instance was to be determinative, because there was behind it the sentiment of a united people.

During the spring meeting of the Massachusetts convention, which, though a voluntary association without legal sanction, was both dignified and efficient, trifling stores of cannon, provisions, and powder had been gathered in various places, among others at the village of Concord, distant from Boston thirty miles, about six hours' march. The provincial assembly adjourned on April 15th, 1775. In the night of the eighteenth an expedition consisting of about eight hundred grenadiers and light infantry set out to seize the little arsenal. The country-side was carefully picketed, to intercept all communication, and the men were instructed to search for Samuel Adams and John Hancock, the newly appointed delegates to the next Continental congress, who, fearing arrest, were in hiding. But such precautions were rendered futile by the foresight of the patriots. A preconcerted signal was given from the most conspicuous belfry in Boston, and at once from across the water Revere and Dawes set out to alarm the adjacent towns. It was known that the British must march through Lexington. At two in the morning a hundred and thirty minute men were assem-

The conflicts at Lexington and Concord.

bled on the village green, determined to obstruct, and basing their action on the legal right to the king's highway. Being armed, stringent orders were given not to attack except in self-defence, and they dispersed for rest until summoned.

When at dawn on the nineteenth a drum-tap announced the approach of the regulars not more than sixty responded. They were greeted by a volley of abuse and orders to throw down their arms, and as they hesitated, the troops were commanded to fire. The melée lasted but a moment, and with an interchange of volleys the Americans retreated before the superior force of their enemy. Seven men of Lexington were killed, and nine wounded. Several English soldiers were slightly injured; but the column scarcely halted, and with cheers of exultation marched on its way to Concord, which they reached about seven. There had been two hundred militia in the town, but they had withdrawn across the river to the neighboring hill-tops to await reinforcements, taking with them the cannon and some of the stores. The British accordingly were unopposed, and destroyed what was left, scouring the valley for two miles, and setting fire to the village court-house. But by this time the express-riders had done their work, and men from every side poured in as the smoke ascended to guide their hurrying steps. Resistance was soon organized; at a little before noon firing began, the conflict being centred at the bridge. Isaac Davis, who had led the successful descent, and a few others about him had fallen. Two English soldiers were killed and several wounded. The English, outnumbered in turn, began their retreat.

The orderly march of the English soon became a rout, as the fire from the ever-growing numbers of minute men grew hotter and hotter from behind the fences, thickets, and trees which bordered the line of march. Like hunted animals the flying column halted now and then in brave defiance, but every sharp encounter only decimated them. Finally at two o'clock, the officers rallied the tired and discouraged soldiers into form, as Lord Percy with a force of twelve hundred men arrived to rescue them. But the ever-growing numbers of the farmers and their clever, desultory system of attack proved too much for even this reinforcement, the precipitate flight was hardly changed except in the matter of numbers. At sunset Bunker Hill, near Charlestown, was reached, and the exhausted soldiers were ferried over the bay to Boston, threatening, if they were molested, to burn the hamlet where they had taken refuge. The losses at Lexington and Concord had been very small, most disproportionate to the dignity which the affair afterward assumed; but on the afternoon of that portentous day the disasters were greater. Of the Americans forty-nine were killed, thirty-four wounded, and five missing; of the English, the total in the same categories was two hundred and seventy-three.

Retreat of the English.

Gage had always felt and expressed contempt for the feeble preparations of the colonies; Concord and Lexington were evidence of both the truth and falsity of his opinion. There was but little orderly efficiency among his adversaries on that day and they won by courage, numbers, and intelligent use of their chances. All that afternoon and night the stream of newcomers was steady, but they were without artillery, organization, equipment, or stores—they were nothing in short but a brave, undisciplined, and enthusiastic rabble. But nevertheless they were full of resources and amenable to reason. By the utmost exertion, a rude order was established before morning, and

Boston besieged by the American farmers.

THE BEGINNING OF HOSTILITIES 187

the dawn of April 20th saw Boston a beleaguered city. Within two days the siege was established. Putnam arrived with volunteers from Connecticut which also sent envoys to Gage, asking whether peace was now impossible. With the main body was a company from New Haven under Benedict Arnold. John Stark came from New Hampshire by forced marches with twelve hundred men, and Nathaniel Greene from Rhode Island with a thousand. Chelsea and Cambridge were occupied and the investment completed. The city was still in the same plight when Howe, Clinton, and Burgoyne arrived with reinforcements on May 25th. Within the town rage and disappointment paralyzed the English. In the scarcity of provisions, Gage determined to send the citizens to their friends without, and for a time a mournful procession poured across the isthmus, but he soon repented and withheld permission from the remainder. His hesitancy and inactivity were the best allies of his opponents.

The provisional assemblies of the New England colonies at once began to devise ways and means. The forces were organized by the appointment of superior officers, the subordinates being chosen for a time by the rank and file. The paper money of Connecticut, Rhode Island, and Massachusetts was made legally interchangeable, for, in the poverty of their resources, promises were a last resort. On the whole, delay and defence were aimed at in the provincial deliberations of these commonwealths, and a feeling prevailed that no decisive action could be taken before the approaching session of the general congress. But plans of the most important character were matured for securing the advantage of control over strategic points in the event of war. In something over a fortnight the news had spread throughout the united colonies. New York,

The colonies organize for armed resistance.

188   THE FRENCH WAR AND THE REVOLUTION

city and province, defied the remnants of royal government and seized all munitions of war. New Jersey, Pennsylvania, and Virginia disdained any overtures from the former authorities and adhered to the general plan of action. The governor of Georgia, farthest in distance of all her sisters, could only look on in impotence while the gunpowder and provisions of the Crown and the money of the people were forwarded to the scene of expected action. "A general rebellion throughout America is coming on swiftly," he wrote in despair.

In many places north and south the army officers threw up their royal commissions and accepted new ones from their colony conventions. Companies were organized and started for the seat of war. Delegates made ready and set out for the general congress while the popular provincial assemblies began to be designated as provincial congresses, and gradually assumed the functions of civil government. Some of the minor civil officials recognized their sovereignty and kept their places, but the greater officers of the Crown, whose united action in supporting parliamentary taxation and the establishment of a standing army had largely brought about the existing condition of affairs either fled to England or sought the protection of war-ships and garrisons. Dunmore actually fled before the menace of a public uprising. On receipt of the news from Lexington on May 2d, Patrick Henry put himself at the head of one of the numerous companies which had been organized by Washington, Lee, Jefferson, and himself as a committee of safety, and set out for Williamsburg. The governor declared him a traitor and threatened to burn the town. The whole country rose and would have joined the expedition, but Dunmore fled to a man-of-war. In Orange County, at the head of a patriotic association, was James Madison,

Overthrow of the colonial governments.

who had just graduated from Princeton, and fresh from the enthusiasm of President Witherspoon now called for reprisal, addressing to Henry a message of congratulation.

But of all the events between April 20th and May 10th, the one which stands pre-eminent was the seizure of Ticonderoga. The line of easy water communication between New York and Montreal had been of such transcendent importance in the French and Indian War that fabulous sums, estimated at millions, were spent on the fortress of Ticonderoga, which commanded the portage or watershed between the river systems of the Hudson and the St. Lawrence. In any conflict with England this same line would go far to determine the event, for by its control the British could isolate New England, prevent united action by land on the part of the insurgents, and secure communication with Canada to introduce troops and munitions from either end into the heart of the country. At this time the great fort was occupied by a very small garrison of some fifty men under Delaplace, but there were military stores of considerable quantity. The expedition to capture it was equipped in Connecticut, though by a sort of compromise it was commanded by Ethan Allen, with Arnold as associate. It was composed of men from the province which gave the funds, from Massachusetts, and from the New Hampshire grants. At dawn of the tenth the Vermont pioneer with eighty-three men appeared before the unguarded door of the fortress and rushing in, summoned the surprised and dismayed commander to surrender. "In whose name?" was the reply. "In the name of the great Jehovah and the Continental Congress!" came the all-significant and ready answer as Allen drew his sword. Quick compliance prevented even a single casualty. The comprehensive watchword

Seizure of Ticonderoga.

for every patriot was given. The glamour of the deed itself, the acquisition of the strategic key to the northeast, and, not least, possession of the much-needed stores gave a moral strength to the congress about to assemble which could have come from no other sources.

The accounts of American affairs which reached England late in May threw many into consternation. Civil war had broken out, veteran regulars had fled before untried militiamen and farmers. Such resistance was not easily to be subdued. Many of the middle and lower classes were to mourn for the dead strewn along the highway from Concord to Boston, and some cities virtually pronounced for the American cause. John Wesley, who had thus far employed his great talents to awaken opposition to colonial claims, now plead that force should not be used. Men like Keppel, Effingham, and the eldest son of Chatham refused service in an unjust and fratricidal war. Lord North was prostrated and would have resigned, but King, Cabinet, and Parliament were obdurate, and once again he weakly consented to remain. Large supplies of money were voted, and new arrangements were made for the energetic suppression of what was formally pronounced rebellion. But the masses were apathetic and men would not enlist. The king was as fertile in resource as ever, and determined both to purchase Hessian soldiers and borrow from Catherine of Russia her victorious legions.

War measures of Parliament and the king.

For the most part Europe failed to understand the situation and there was little intelligent interest. Her enemies had a groping hope that England was in serious difficulties, but that was all. Even in France, where there was every appearance of widespread enthusiasm, the feeling was largely a desire for revenge. The most far-seeing statesmen appreciated

Attitude of Europe.

the danger to European monarchy which lay in a spirit of revolt like this, but they determined to use it for their ends. The century had been rife with the most profound and brilliant political speculation. Philosophers hoped to see their cherished theories brought to the test. The court, the wits, and the people found a new topic of conversation in the political aspect of the question and reasoned with intelligent interest concerning obedience to law, the right of representation, and the overthrow of tyranny. Dangerous topics for the safety of the house of Bourbon!

CHAPTER XVI.

THE BATTLE OF BUNKER HILL—FEBRUARY-JULY, 1775

Self-reliance of the Americans—Their Attitude Toward England—
Conservative Elements—Patriotic Impulses—The Mecklenburg
Declaration—The Second Continental Congress—Its Apparent
Inconsistencies—Results of Moderation—The Virginia Burgesses and Lord North's Proposals—George Washington—Appointed Commander-in-Chief—Character of the New England
Army—Fortification of Bunker Hill—The Battle—The Result
Indecisive—Washington at Cambridge.

THE century or more during which the American colonies were left to shift for themselves had established in all a system of government nearly autonomous. During the nine years' constitutional battle just past they had denied the authority of Parliament, but they admitted the sovereignty of the Crown, and there had never been a break in the continuous expression of loyalty based upon the experiences of three generations in their relation to England. On the very eve of the collision declarations of unswerving fidelity were made by leading men. The colonists believed themselves to have surmounted the difficulties and hardships incident to the subjugation of a wilderness without considerable aid from home. They had even been the determining element in the last war, having furnished the brains, the money, and the men. The people of every faith and of all social classes had therefore a self-reliance which was felt to be justified by experience

<small>Self-reliance of the Americans.</small>

and an independence which sprang from both habit and tradition.

From the outset there had been representatives from nearly every dissenting and persecuted class in Europe, and from the outset, therefore, there had been men in America with no love for any existing European government. Neither Puritan nor Covenanter had cause to love the British constitution, which in its passage through the fires lighted by the Reformation, had been much purified, but was still monarchical, Erastian, and aristocratic. New England was altogether Puritan, the descendants of the Covenanters swarmed in Pennsylvania and the South. The claim which is made, but not substantiated, that the colonies aimed at independence from the first, has probably this basis of fact, that Calvinists and other dissenters, who had left home and friends for conscience sake, were always determined that their aim should not be shaken nor their destiny thwarted. Time and distance did much to soften hearts and remove bitterness, but there was always a steady stream of immigration from Great Britain, largely composed of grave and earnest men often called fanatics, in whose minds some wrong or grievance rankled. *Their attitude toward England.*

On the other hand, the unexampled prosperity of the colonies had softened the asperity of those who shared it, and there was in the Middle States and Virginia, a dominant population purely English in descent, loyal to Church and State, aristocratic in feeling, and disdainful of the uneasy reformers around them. They were largely supported by the peace-loving Quakers and the numerous Dutch, who, though Calvinists, had no longer any European connection, were content in their life of faith with its liturgical devotions, and with the ease and comfort which they enjoyed under English *Conservative elements.*

194 THE FRENCH WAR AND THE REVOLUTION

rule. Accordingly, even among patriots there were in all the colonies both radicals and conservatives. By this time the former were for defiance and independence by preference, the latter for conciliation if possible, but independence if necessary. The congress of 1774 was in the main an English convention, petitioning the crown and aiming at harmony. Only three of the eleven colonies, Virginia, South Carolina, and Massachusetts, were emphatic in their demand for redress. The articles of association and the determination to meet force by force were alternatives, hinting rebellion perhaps, but outrunning the temper of the majority.

Thus far every instance of armed resistance, from the battle on the Alamance to Lexington, had been the work *Patriotic* of radicals. Little by little their steady *impulses.* musing over theories of taxation and government had ripened them into logicians and statesmen. The youth of the country loved the men of action, the universities brought history and philosophy to the support of the patriots. The spirit of union was abroad in all classes and ages, to this was added among the rising generation, among the laborers, mechanics, and farmers, and among the entire population of the Alleghenies and the West, the spirit of self-reliance.

The westward immigration began among the misgoverned Presbyterians of Virginia and North Carolina, and *The Mecklenburg dec-* between the pioneers and their friends about *laration.* the head-waters of the Yadkin and Catawba; constant communication was maintained. The focus of their social life was the town of Mecklenburg, where the leading spirit was Ephraim Brevard, who had graduated at Princeton in the stirring days of 1768. The address offered to the crown in February, 1775, reached that village in May. At Charlotte was soon to sit a military committee of two delegates from each militia regiment, and Brevard was the clerk. During their sessions came the news of Lexington. Brevard offered, as tradition says, a series of resolutions relating to the facts, which were a virtual declaration of independence, suspending laws, vacating commissions, making provisional regulation, and acknowledging only the authority of the provincial congress. They were unanimously adopted on May 20th, and although no copy of them exists, there were adopted on May 31st another set amplifying the originals, which were recorded as in force until Great Britain should renounce her pretensions. No doubt has ever been expressed as to the authenticity of the latter, but that of the former has been repeatedly assailed. Against a strong local tradition that there were such resolutions is set the fact that the resolutions themselves were not preserved. The document in its final shape was printed; copies were scattered over Georgia and North Carolina, and one formally transmitted to the second Continental congress, which had assembled on May 10th.

Many important questions of federal interest could be answered if the nature of the second meeting between provincial delegates were clear. The first Continental congress had been composed in part of members regularly chosen by legal assemblies without the assent of the various governors, and in part of popular representatives irregularly appointed. That body had named its ultimatum, the collision had occurred, colonial governments had disintegrated, and now its successor was sitting, made up of nearly the same men commissioned and sent exclusively by voluntary assemblies without regard to council or royal governor, but also without regular or formal authorization by the people. Moreover, its acts will not endure the fierce light of logical analysis, although they

The second Continental congress.

are perfectly comprehensible by the aid of historic imagination. The world may move with scientific accuracy through the great phases of history, in the small ones there are times of contradiction and inconsistency, of courage and quickening, of doubt and darkness, of hope and assurance. Should New York oppose the landing of the English troops soon to arrive in her harbor? Congress desired her to act on the defensive and answered, No. Would the Continental assembly assume the charge of the forces about Boston? Could the provincial congress declare itself a constitutional assembly to establish legal government? The first of these two questions was referred to a committee which had not yet reported at the end of May. The answer to the latter was also postponed.

In order not to embarrass further negotiations for peace, Congress would gladly have gone so far as to arrest the works conducted by Allen to restore the strength of both Ticonderoga and Crown Point to their former impregnability. Jay moved and Dickinson seconded the humble petition to the king which was adopted and forwarded at the hands of Richard Penn, a descendant of the first proprietor. Neither one had a thought of abandoning Massachusetts. Duane proposed negotiations, but when the motion was carried there went with it a resolution to assume the defensive. Lord North's offers were received, but their insidious nature was exposed and the terms rejected. But on the twelfth of June a general fast was appointed on which they were to recognize "George III. as their rightful sovereign, and to look up to the great Governor of the world for the restoration of the invaded rights of America and a reconciliation with the parent state."

Its apparent inconsisten- cies.

Thus far the moderate party led by Dickinson had the control, and the Mecklenburg declaration of indepen-

THE BATTLE OF BUNKER HILL 197

dence must have been coldly received. . The delay did
honor to their hearts, and ultimately was the cause of that
unanimity with which New York and Penn- Results of
sylvania carried on the war. At the time it ap- moderation.
peared disastrous to the patriot party, which had no illusions concerning reconciliation, because in the interval
Carleton was concentrating his troops in Canada, Johnson was negotiating with the Six Nations, and a French
Canadian emissary was enlisting auxiliaries among the
Indians of the Great Lakes. The fugitive functionaries
of the crown had regained their courage to such an extent that Dunmore had hopes of committing Virginia
to favor Lord North's propositions, and summoned the
House of Burgesses to meet at Williamsburg early in
June.

Randolph and Jefferson left their seats in Congress to
obey the summons. On June 5th the debate began.
There was that in its tone which filled Dun- The Virginia
more with dismay, and pleading that he feared Burgesses and Lord North's
revenge might be taken on him for the out- proposals.
lawry of Hancock and Adams by Gage, he fled again to
take refuge on an English man-of-war. It was a most
merciless dissection which the North proposal underwent
at that meeting. To the final rejection was added an explanation that it should have been accompanied by a
repeal of all the penal acts, and an address, written by
Jefferson, was sent to the fugitive governor, declaring that
they would no long weary the king by petitions nor the
English nation by appeals. Soon afterward a provisional
convention met and assumed the reins of government,
raising troops and borrowing money to pay them.

George Washington was by common consent the representative Virginian. His family was both ancient and
gentle, and had, moreover, been resident in America for
generations; he himself reproduced, as far as possible,

the type of country gentleman from whom he was descended. His education, though largely self-acquired, was excellent, and being by profession a land-surveyor both his vocation and his pleasures had not only inured him to hardship but had developed his natural beauty into strength and grace. At this time he was forty-three years of age, six feet in stature, a daring horseman, and intrepid hunter. To his early experiences as a pioneer in the western wilds he had added that of five years' command of the Virginia militia in the eventful years from 1753–1758. From that date until the present juncture he had lived in happy wedlock on his estate of Mount Vernon, combining the duties of a planter, a justice of the peace, and a legislator in the House of Burgesses. In the latter capacity he had been silent but interested, conservative but determined, and though no agitator even the extremest radicals had learned to respect his judgment. At the same time he was most human in his sympathies and failings. Through frugality and a strictness of dealing which bordered on harshness he had accumulated wealth and lands, which in the later success of American independence acquired great value. His standards of social morality were on the whole higher than those of his class, and he lived in closer conformity to them than his fellows, but they would not perhaps meet the approval of the Puritan. He was altogether free from concealment or hypocrisy, although a certain haughty reserve was most useful to him as a commander.

The news from the army of New England grew more and more disquieting. Disorganization was thinning its ranks and the lukewarm acts of Congress had dimmed its enthusiasm. The New England patriots had come to prize the sympathy of their Virginia supporters, and with a wise unselfishness they named Washington to undertake the arduous task which could no longer be postponed. He was unanimously elected by ballot to be commander-in-chief of what was purposely designated not the national but the continental army. The action was lightly taken by many who did not appreciate, as Washington himself did, the toilsome labor and momentous consequences. Nevertheless with modest firmness he accepted, refusing, however, the proposed remuneration, and requesting only that Congress would reimburse his expenses, of which he would keep an accurate account. His commission was ample, giving him powers really dictatorial and directing him to take "special care" that the liberties of America should receive no detriment. He set out forthwith for Boston, where he assumed his office under the historic elm still standing on Cambridge Common.

But several days before his arrival, in fact on the very date of his commission, the volunteer farmers, half-armed, half-equipped, and not half-organized, had again shown their mettle in a conflict altogether different in character and proportion from the affairs at Lexington and Concord. *Character of the New England army.* Difficult as his task had been, the excellent but aged and now unwarlike Ward had brought some order out of chaos, organized a council of war, and evolved an excellent plan of operations. Every colony had its own militia laws, and long agitation had made the farmers readier to discuss than to obey. Obedience when rendered was to their own local officers, who in turn paraded swollen titles and followed their own devices rather than regular orders, as was seen in the preliminary movements before Bunker Hill.

Nevertheless there had been a beginning of works to fortify the heights in Charlestown, whither it would be easiest to make a sortie by water from Boston. These were known as Bunker Hill, from the name of a Scotch-

Irish settler. Near by was the eminence of Breed's Hill. The English looked on with anxiety at the progress of their opponents, slight as it was, and determined at last to move. On June 11th was issued a proclamation declaring that all persons found in arms against the sovereign would be hung as rebels and traitors, but offering amnesty to everybody except Adams and Hancock. The Americans were undismayed, and on June 15th about a thousand men under Prescott set out to continue the works. Before dawn on the 16th redoubts were begun and half-finished, but for some reason now unknown, on the lower heights of Breed's Hill; Putnam arrived during the day with a small reinforcement, but took position on Bunker Hill, following his instructions and justly deeming it the more important point, commanding as it did the only line of retreat open to the Americans. The English planted a park of artillery on Copp's Hill, and brought up two men of-war. Next day, the seventeenth, at three in the afternoon, under cover of the fire from battery and ships, a force of about twenty-five hundred was sent across the water and landed at the foot of Breed's Hill to attack the Americans.

Fortification of Bunker Hill.

The battle opened by a splendid but premature rush of the whole English force straight up the slope. The Americans, numbering about fifteen hundred, had been judiciously posted in two divisions of equal size, and met the advance by a carefully directed fire which drove the enemy back. After an interval of about fifteen minutes a second charge, more deliberate than the first, was repelled with equal skill and courage. There was a third and longer interval. The Americans were at the end of their ammunition, which had been gathered haphazard in such small quantities as could be found. The efforts of both the council of war and the

The battle.

committee of safety having been directed to the security of Cambridge, the combatants were left without resources of any kind. There must have been little straggling, for about eight hundred were left behind the works, while two hundred were in the temporary shelter of a fence. There was but enough powder for one more round. The English officers showed both courage and endurance. A second time the men were rallied, reformed, and encouraged ; a third time they moved upward with fixed bayonets, and aided by the enfilade of their battery successfully stormed the redoubt at last. In the ensuing mêlée the Americans passed almost unhurt through the broken lines, those who had powder using it with deadly effect, formed in good order, and slowly retreated over Bunker Hill to Prospect Hill, near Cambridge, where they threw up trenches and stood to await the British attack. But the English were too much exhausted to follow up their advantage, and the battle of Bunker Hill, as it has ever since been called, remained technically indecisive.

Morally and historically this conflict was a victory for the united colonies. Its glory belongs to no single name, for the command was divided and ineffective, the slender resources of the provincials were not husbanded, the battle took place where neither the council of war nor the committee of safety had intended, and among Washington's first stern duties was the holding of a court-martial. From the army of New England three hundred and four were wounded, a hundred and forty-five were either killed or missing. Many gallant leaders perished, among them Joseph Warren, whose fame calumny cannot dim. On the other hand, the men had fought bravely and behaved like veterans. The English losses were enormous, a thousand and fifty-four killed or wounded, of whom one in ten were officers.

The result indecisive.

The survivors, less than two-thirds of the total number, felt a respect for the courage of their adversaries which disheartened the commander. He wrote to the ministry that he could not bear his loss, that the Americans were not the despicable rabble he had supposed. Franklin in a letter to English friends tersely expressed the whole matter, "Americans will fight; England has lost her colonies forever."

Washington's journey to Cambridge had been like the progress of a conqueror, and awakened a most valuable enthusiasm in the towns through which he passed. He was authorized to establish an army of twenty thousand men in Massachusetts; but out of the materials at hand and with the money raised he could organize and train only fourteen thousand. Before long even they became discontented. Whole regiments marched away as their term of enlistment expired, and including in the total the five regiments of militia which had been called in from Massachusetts and New Hampshire, it was estimated that during the summer and autumn the force dwindled to ten thousand. They were ill-fed and badly armed, having not more than forty-five rounds of powder for each man. There were also ten thousand troops in Boston, English regulars, and the situation was precarious. The experience of Bunker Hill seemed, however, to have quenched their ardor, and their inactivity was the safety of their besiegers, giving time as it did for drill and the acquisition of military habits.

Washington at Cambridge.

CHAPTER XVII.

OVERTHROW OF ROYAL AUTHORITY—1775-1776

The Expedition against Canada—Siege of Quebec—Failure of the Campaign—Siege of Boston—The English Withdraw—Bombardment of Norfolk—Overthrow of Royal Government in the South and in New England—Anomalous Situation in the Middle Colonies—Beginnings of United and Independent Action—Paper Money—John Adams and the Conduct of Congress—The First American Flag—Trade Notions of Congress—The Petition to Parliament Rejected—The Americans Proclaimed Rebels—Purchase of Troops by George III.—Congress Petitions the King—Action of the Patriots—"Common-Sense"—Effect on Congress and the Country—Final Overthrow of Royal Authority.

SCHUYLER had been authorized to invade Canada, the governor of which proclaimed the Americans on the border as traitors and established martial law. The troops about Ticonderoga were found to be both undisciplined and insubordinate, but with the aid of his capable and amiable lieutenant, Montgomery, the new commander re-established discipline, and in September began his advance. The expedition was rash but brilliant, and met with temporary success. St. John was invested; but in a skirmish before Montreal, Ethan Allen was taken prisoner; he was afterward sent in irons to England. Carleton was then defeated and Montreal occupied. A reinforcement of eleven hundred men, under Arnold, had been sent by Washington. They started on September 19th, and penetrated the Maine wilderness, enduring the utmost

The expedition against Canada.

hardships of cold and hunger. Scores perished on the way.

When the forces of Montgomery and Arnold were united, on December 2d, there were but a thousand Americans in all, and two hundred Canadian auxiliaries, for at the end of their term of enlistment Montgomery's men had left for home in troops. Quebec was soon invested, however, and careful preparations made for a storm. Carleton held the citadel with sixteen hundred men. In it were also a large number of Americans who had been captured in various actions, many of them so daring that they verged on madness. On the last day of 1775 the lower town was attacked. There was a courageous and well-contested action, during which Montgomery fell and Arnold was wounded. With some eight hundred men, all that were left, the surviving officer sat down with stubborn courage before the walls of the city to continue the siege. Montreal was in American hands, and to all appearance two-thirds of Canada had been won.

Siege of Quebec.

In truth Carleton was master of the situation; well housed and well fed, his best ally against the little American army without in the snow was time. The following spring Wooster came up from Montreal in April with fifteen hundred men, and Thomas, appointed by Washington to the chief command, appeared on May 1st with eight regiments. But the besiegers were already reduced by disease to less than two thousand, of whom half were still down with small-pox, which had been raging in the American camp for months. A few days later arrived the English fleet with a large reinforcement of English and German soldiers. The order was given by Thomas to retreat, and a sortie from the city changed the retreat into a rout. The sick and disheartened Americans were further attacked from

Failure of the campaign.

an ambush near Montreal by a body composed of English, Canadians, and Indians, and lost four hundred men captured by the enemy. Several gallant attempts were made in June, under Sullivan, to arrest the demoralization of the American army of the north, but by this time there were ten thousand men in English pay on the soil of Canada—Germans under Riedesel, Irish under Burgoyne. They had arrived by way of the St. Lawrence and gave new strength to the resistance wherever made. Early in July the remnants of the American force were again at Crown Point. The campaign thus sorrowfully ended abounded in romantic and chivalrous incidents. Carleton showed clemency to his captives, and Montgomery was buried with the honors of war. Many ardent but unschooled Americans made ventures that are scarcely credible. While foiled and discredited they learned from failure lessons which were later of priceless value to them and their country. They came out of the fire of tribulation as undaunted as when they entered it.

It was possible for eight precious regiments—a whole brigade and a third, as the army was organized—to leave Boston and march for Canada, because the city had been finally evacuated. After serious delay ammunition began to arrive at the camp of Washington, and he felt assured by the prompt appearance of New England militia, when summoned, that he could maintain a proportionate force. On March 2d he began, most unexpectedly to the English in Boston, to bombard the city from the fortifications he had been constructing, hitherto useless by reason of his destitution in the matter of powder. For three days the fire on both sides continued; but while Howe was puzzling over the significance of the attack, his opponent, under cover of the noise and excitement, was busy with his spade. To the consternation of the beleaguered, it was learned that on the morn-

Siege of Boston.

ing of the fifth a strong redoubt on Dorchester Heights had been completed and occupied by the besiegers.

There were but two alternatives, evacuation or another attack like that of Bunker Hill. The former was chosen, and by the evening of the sixteenth the English fleet, with eight thousand troops on board, had sailed for Halifax. They left behind them in their haste precious spoils — twenty-five thousand bushels of wheat, two hundred and fifty cannon, and other material of war almost equally invaluable. The banished inhabitants hastened to their homes as the enemy departed. The victorious army made its formal entry on the twentieth, and, as a climax to their exultation, a few days later an English ship, loaded with guns and powder, entered the harbor in ignorance of the recent events and was captured.

The English withdraw.

These mingled successes and reverses in war were accompanied by similar ebbs and flows in the tide of legislation. In Virginia the provincial congress was sovereign except in and about Norfolk, in which for some time the royalists had assembled under the protection of a fleet. On December 14th, however, the town was captured by the popular forces. On the first of January, by Dunmore's orders, the English men-of-war drew up to the wharves, and for nine hours swept the place with shot from their guns. The sailors set fire to what the balls spared.

Bombardment of Norfolk.

Already chosen bodies of riflemen had been organized by the convention, and in an action against the ships, at Hampton, had held the enemy at bay ; now seven new regiments were raised and equipped — one of them was composed of Germans. In July, 1775, Georgia adopted the articles of the American Association, by a provisional assembly elected delegates to Congress, and committed sovereign

Overthrow of royal government in the South and in New England.

power for the time to the people. In North Carolina the patriots proscribed the numerous Tories—Scotch refugee Highlanders in great part—terrified Martin, the royal governor, into flight, and through an executive committee turned the militia into three regiments of regulars. South Carolina, under the lead of Laurens, succeeded in corresponding enterprises : the governor fled, the Tories promised neutrality, a regiment of artillery was raised, and the important fort which commanded Charleston harbor was seized and occupied. New Hampshire likewise drove off her governor, and was ruled by local committees and a provincial congress. Both Connecticut and Rhode Island already had charters which committed all power to the people, and their activity in prosecution of the war was in proportion to their freedom. Trumbull, governor of the former State, was one of the notable men of the Revolution, and Rhode Island would have been famous in her distinguished son, Nathaniel Greene, had her daring and self-sacrificing patriotism done nothing further.

But the constitutional situation was not so plain in the other colonies. The provincial congress of Massachusetts had petitioned for authority to organize a regular administration under the Congress at Philadelphia, but the answer was withheld, to the great discouragement of her people. In the two proprietary provinces of Pennsylvania and Maryland there was a nice balance of parties, and by its clever use the semblance of royal government was still maintained ; while at the same time and in a similar way, Tryon, of New York, and Franklin, in New Jersey, so evenly offset the moderates and radicals against each other as to preserve their own place and dignity all summer long. But, nevertheless, there was a divided authority in all these commonwealths. There was an executive commit-

Anomalous situation in the middle colonies.

tee in New York, and in Pennsylvania, New Jersey, and Maryland there were provincial congresses; all four, in spite of their anomalous position, were raising money, troops, and supplies for Washington and his army.

Such were the governments of the various communities which were now united in purpose, and were either *Beginnings of united and independent action.* seeking with greater or less zeal to secure redress from England for the restriction of their liberties, or else forcing themselves into the alternative of a declaration of independence. They had now an outward and visible union both in their army and in a deliberative assembly of uncertain character which had been already forced into acts of sovereignty, and had already been addressed as a sovereign by one of themselves. It adopted rules and articles of war for the army, assuming thereby the position and claiming the rights of an independent belligerent. It appointed four major-generals—Ward, Charles Lee, Schuyler, and Putnam—eight brigadiers, and an adjutant-general.

In response to Washington's representation of the destitution of his army Congress took the fatal step of issuing bills of credit, or continental currency. *Paper money.* This money was made a legal tender by threats of virtual outlawry from the committees of safety to any one refusing it, and every colony in proportion to its entire population, not including Indians, was to redeem this incontrovertible paper by a proportionate annuity beginning in 1779. Depreciation began, of course, at once, emissions became more and more frequent; although the army had a precarious support for a few years, and the beginnings of a navy were made by means of it, yet in the end the policy was nearly fatal to the succcessful conclusion of the war and to the construction of a federal government. When the answer to Massachusetts' request was finally given, she was directed to follow the usage of her charter and to choose a house of representatives by town meetings. Her people promptly accepted the plan; the house was elected, and in turn constituted an executive council of twenty-eight, assessed taxes, and otherwise performed the functions of complete independence.

The feeling of American self-reliance had grown in true Anglo-Saxon fashion as the result of action and in facing emergencies. There had always been dialecticians in plenty behind the agitation to weave an explanatory theory and spin subtle legalities. There were, however, a few minds in the English colonies trained in the broad discipline of history, understanding that development must be on lines of nature and habit. Such a mind was that of John Adams, hitherto an interested onlooker; but now, when assured of the true character of the movement, he strove as a participator to direct it and began to share its responsibilities. He would have had the continental congress take the throne of sovereignty, even at the risk of temporary usurpation, sanction the institution of limited governments in every colony, and so create a strong, central, taxing power able to defy the mother-country. But public opinion would not have supported such a radical course just at this juncture. With statesman-like wisdom he delayed making a formal proposition, and Congress still had to grope its way, offsetting one act of daring by another of timidity. There was no hope of union except in continued compromise, for without New York and Pennsylvania there could be no lasting structure.

Yet for a time acts which we now recognize as those of a sovereign were frequent. Armed vessels had been fitted out, first under Washington's authorization as commander-in-chief, and their prize cases had been adjudicated by a Massachusetts court of admiralty. Congress

John Adams and the conduct of Congress.

now assumed the task of creating a navy and chose a flag. The stripes in an early English merchant flag were *The first American flag.* increased to thirteen in number, one for each colony, in alternate red and white as they are to-day, with the crosses of St. George and St. Andrew on a blue ground in the corner. It was raised for the first time over Washington's head-quarters on New Year's Day, 1776. Franklin was commissioned to create a post-office. Congress continued, moreover, to seize supplies; it garrisoned fortresses on the Hudson, disarmed loyalists in the Mohawk Valley and Long Island, and ordered the arrest of Tryon, although he escaped.

At the close of its first session in July, with the humility becoming to British subjects and the determination of English remonstrants strangely combined, *Trade notions of Congress.* it resolved to export nothing directly to Great Britain, nor to the West Indian islands of the British and other powers. The English war vessels in the harbor of New York would no doubt have been ready to enforce this legislation for them! But fortunately, in spite of Isaac Sears's attempt to bring on hostilities, in which Alexander Hamilton, still a madcap student of Columbia College was a volunteer, moderate men like Livingston and Jay, assisted by the reasonable though radical Macdougall, managed to maintain a truce. Its duration was long enough to accumulate very considerable stores of powder through American ships trading with St. Eustatius.

The course of affairs was no more smooth nor consistent in England than in America. Richard Penn arrived in due season, but the news of Bunker Hill *The petition to Parliament rejected.* had preceded him and the administration would pay no attention to the humble petition of Congress. The country was even yet half-hearted; men were no easier to enlist now than before, although

OVERTHROW OF ROYAL AUTHORITY 211

the pliant Parliament would furnish even greater supplies to the king. Rockingham, Shelburne, and the other friends of America were helpless, and could only endure. Robertson supported the liberal cause, Hume's philosophy made him the bulwark of tyranny. Adam Smith, with his greater genius, spoke the enduring words which justified the attitude of the colonies. Later a great pamphlet on Liberty, the author of which was Richard Price, appeared, and most beneficently consolidated liberal feeling in its darkest hours. Its definition of liberty as a government of laws made by common consent was elaborated into a masterly plea for the colonists, and the author foretold that a conflict over the same principle would one day reform the House of Commons.

But the ministry recalled Gage, and refusing conciliation prepared a proclamation which was issued on August 23d, 1775, declaring the Americans to be rebels, and threatening with condign punishment both them and their abettors in England. In October the prosecution of the civil war was authorized in due constitutional form. The following May was to see the vacillating cabinet attempt to retrace its steps, but in the interval the king began to ransack Europe for the men which his own kingdom could not yield. For a time he cherished the illusory hope that Catherine II. of Russia would give him twenty thousand ; but she failed him in the crisis, and at last, probably through the influence of Vergennes, and with the license of feminine fickleness, advised him to yield the disputed points. The stubborn but inventive ruler then demanded of Holland the return of the Scotch Brigade, which, of course, survived only in name. In the seventeenth century its predecessor, among other British troops, had been sent to occupy certain fortresses in that

The Americans proclaimed rebels.

country as security for Elizabeth's loan of 1599. The Dutch now debated with characteristic delay, and gave the wily answer that he might have it as a loan if he would promise not to use it outside of Europe.

There remained the Germans as a last resource. The Peace of Westphalia had splintered that unhappy people, and left every princelet a complete license to dispose without control of land and subjects; almost every little court had become bankrupt in imitating the vices of Versailles. There was an awakened public conscience in the eighteenth century, and the feeble Diet had forbidden enlistment by foreign powers. But the presence of George's agents was ignored or winked at. His contracts were nominally with private persons. In Hanover, Waldeck, Brunswick, and Hesse Cassel the scandalous traffic was most successful at prices ranging from thirty to forty dollars, and even higher, for each man and life. The minor details of advanced pay and subsidies, of three wounded to count as one dead, and the like, seem incredible. First and last, upward of twenty-six thousand men were sold to the English king, and his treaties were calmly ratified in Parliament, but not without a warning given that the colonies too could appeal to foreign powers.

Purchase of troops by George III.

On August 1st, 1775, Congress had adjourned for five weeks. When the members reassembled they voted that a confederacy must be their last resort, and in the face of all the facts which now reveal their meaning so clearly but were to them of uncertain significance and only partially known, addressed a second petition to the king, asking for a restoration of the status antecedent to 1763 and disavowing the desire for independence. The truth is that Congress, for the remaining months of the year, stood awe-stricken

Congress petitions the king.

before its responsibilities. Severe restrictions were put on many of the delegates not to plan or contemplate, at least openly, a rupture with the mother country. Their compliance was seen in the second humble petition and the continued embargo on their own commerce. Both moderates and radicals, therefore, were thoroughly disheartened at the close of 1775, the former by the conduct of England, the latter by the continuous depression of trade and the shilly-shallying of Congress.

Such times make strange companionships. In these dark days had been formed a group of men representing the two extremes of then existing religious beliefs, but unanimous in the conviction that the time for radical political action had arrived. It was composed of Samuel Adams and Benjamin Franklin, Rittenhouse and Clymer, together with an acquaintance who had been for two years in America, Thomas Paine. The latter was the son of a Norfolk Quaker who had imbibed the extremest radicalism of the eighteenth century, and having been by turns a marine, an exciseman, a teacher of English, and a local politician, was now a professional agitator with the motto—where liberty is not there is my country. These friends knew that the common people of the colonies had far outrun their leaders in comprehending the situation ; that discontent with the present anarchy was rife ; that popular sagacity recognized independence as the only possible remedy for the evils into which they had drifted. They determined to make an appeal to the court of last resort, the general sentiment.

Action of the patriots.

Accordingly, on January 8th, 1776, appeared the famous pamphlet from the pen of Paine, to which Benjamin Rush had given the felicitous title, "Common Sense." It was a remarkable essay, masterly in its simple style, its lucidity, and its argument. Separation and the establishment of a republic were its plea, a plea which was soon enforced by the news of the king's attitude on the opening of Parliament. The effect was instantaneous. The subtle influence on the colonists of a complete and adequate expression of their sentiments made their blood course in a quicker flood. So overwhelming was the tide that the New York assembly appointed a committee to prepare an answer, but the committee decided that none could be given. Franklin and Adams agreed to agitate for confederation.

"Common Sense."

Washington was still watching before Boston, and such was the infection, that even Congress grew impatient for action. He could give no stronger proof of greatness than to risk his popularity as he did by quiet perseverance in his chosen rôle of the modern Fabius. They themselves determined that the provinces were at least free enough to guarantee their own welfare by contracting alliances if necessary. In spite of repeated and formal protestations from Pennsylvania of loyalty to the king, the work of raising men and funds went forward, A most important measure of retaliation against Parliament was taken in the authorization of privateering, and the king was charged with being the author of all their troubles because he had treated their petitions with scorn. Finally a decisive step was taken. In defiance of the Navigation Acts, American ports were opened to the commerce of the world, and the importation of slaves was forbidden. Samuel Adams thought in April that independence was virtually secured.

Effect on Congress and the country.

The great idea of his distinguished namesake was not diminished in importance by these events, and he now felt sure that "without the least convulsion or animosity" a legal government could be constituted within a month, deriving its authority and sanctions from the

OVERTHROW OF ROYAL AUTHORITY 215

people. In May, therefore, John Adams brought forward his proposition that "each one of the united colonies, where no government sufficient to the exigencies of their affairs had as yet been established, should adopt such government as would in the opinion of the representatives of the people best conduce to the happiness and safety of their constituents in particular and of America in general." For two days it was resisted. Pennsylvania clung to her proprietary government and her allegiance, while Duane felt that the New York delegation had no authorization for such action. On the tenth it passed. This was the culmination of the successive measures by which Congress had gradually overturned the authority of the crown and substituted that of the people. The colonies were never for a moment independent states. Separate declarations of independence there were, but they had reference merely to a provisional government under a union antecedently achieved in reality, if not formally. The loose, uncertain character of the continental congress does not alter the sovereign nature of its acts nor the sufficiency of its representative capacity. Its members were at least as regularly selected as those of the English Parliament then sitting, in accordance with precedents and traditions quite as valid in America as those which formed the English constitution were in England. And whatever the theory, the fact is that any measure of independence ever enjoyed by any one of the thirteen original colonies was gained by membership in a confederation which fought as a unit for external sovereignty, won it by united action, and was finally recognized by other nations not as a temporary league of independent states, but as the United States.

Final overthrow of royal authority.

CHAPTER XVIII.

THE MOVEMENT FOR INDEPENDENCE—JANUARY-JUNE, 1776

Parliament Declines Redress—The Ministry Proposes Pardon—Danger to English Institutions—The Colonies Temporize—French Agents in America—France Had Two Motives for Interference—Plan of Vergennes—English Strength in New York—Sears and Charles Lee—The City Fortified—North Carolina Tories Routed—The British before Charleston—Bombardment of the City—Success of the Defence—New Commonwealths—Virginia—Debates in Congress—New York Hesitates—Overthrow of the Proprietary Assembly in Pennsylvania.

GRAFTON, although himself a cabinet minister, had already warned the king that he was the victim of deceit. The answer was that Parliament was behind the war and would support it. Carleton had been made commander-in-chief of Canada and Howe in the colonies. Chatham introduced a bill in January, 1776, to repeal the late acts, to leave the charters secure, to recall the troops, and abandon taxation. A colonial congress was to determine what America should contribute to the payment of the public debt, and how the contribution should be raised. A similar bill was offered by Burke for the consideration of the House of Commons. Both were rejected with contempt and the king was apparently justified.

But the American news which arrived during the ensuing months was alarming, even to king and Parliament. On May 6th, North and his new Secretary for the Colo-

Parliament declines redress.

nies, Lord George Germain, made another futile attempt at conciliation. General Howe and his brother the admiral, were commissioned to pardon those who repented of disloyalty, and to abandon taxation; the charters, however, were to be revised. *The ministry proposes pardon.* It is difficult to believe in the sincerity of such half-way measures, which bear on their face the stamp of political chicane, and were intended partly to consolidate a parliamentary majority, partly to deceive the public by the appearance of magnanimity into the support of an unpopular cause.

And yet, critical as was the situation of English affairs, observers of European politics must have felt the empire founded on the old principles reasserted by the events of 1688 to be more solid than any other. *Danger to English institutions.* It is true that Hume, the arch-sceptic in an age of scepticism, had proved to his own satisfaction the unlawfulness of deposing tyrants, and foretold that the English constitution must therefore end in absolutism. Current events, too, seemed to justify him. But on the Continent sounder thinkers understood that an age of negations had long since undermined the foundations of existing institutions, by destroying that form of faith on which they had been built. The shell was hollow and would collapse, but somewhere new convictions of a positive moral quality would reconstruct a new system of government.

In the temporary eclipse of English understanding, the task which had been begun was to be taken up by the American colonies. Their faith in the right and their moral courage seemed strong enough, but their material resources were felt *The colonies temporize.* to be disproportionate to the task. It must be confessed, moreover, that in the ferment of opinions and discussion there had been a poor display of practical common sense.

Congress had craftily avoided the laying of direct taxes, and the last thing thought of by the uneasy provisional governments of the various colonies was to create a common treasury or do more than meet the present emergency by any shift, however impolitic. Aid came from a land which more than any other in Europe had suffered from the evils of absolutism.

France had a double interest in the development of American affairs. The old French and Indian war had been won by colonials, but she bore them no grudge. The greater efficacy of her centralized government had prolonged the struggle, but she had been overpowered by the same forces, now more evident in her old antagonist than ever, acting too in the same spasmodic way. King, courtiers, and an able ministry led by Vergennes, all knew alike that their country was financially debilitated and politically infirm. They were reaping a harvest they had not sown, and the spirit of independence rife in America might react on a monarchy so unstable in its equilibrium. But a successful revenge on their hereditary enemy might carry them over the crisis, and for a time the ministers dismissed their fears, equivocated with the English embassador, and sent agents to report on the state of the colonists. Each successive one—Bonvouloir, de Rayneval, and the rest—assumed more and more of a diplomatic quality, though nominally without any commission but the lowest. Beaumarchais, the brilliant man of letters but unsafe statesman, was at the same time present in England as an irregular and unattached envoy. The reports which reached Vergennes seemed to him incredible. He had long been aware of the prosperity of the American colonies, and of their increase in population. He was therefore ready to credit the accounts of their enthusiasm. But it is said that the folly of George and his ministers

French agents in America.

THE MOVEMENT FOR INDEPENDENCE 219

seemed to him impossible, and that his incredulity crippled for a moment his activity. Bonvouloir's statements about America were full and truthful, though not flattering, and explain the situation well. At his suggestion Congress refrained from appointing a plenipotentiary when they formed their committee to correspond with friends in foreign countries.

But there was another motive than revenge urging France to the support of the colonies, the genuine sympathy her people felt with the spirit of freedom abroad in the world. The quickenings of liberty were strong in French breasts, the foremost writers believed in and desired representative government. Turgot thought America might regenerate politics. It was feared that if England were the first to declare war, her colonies might recall their filial allegiance and return to the house of their fathers. Beaumarchais therefore urged a participation in their struggle before it was too late, while Turgot, who was more an economist than a philosopher, believed and said that such was the enthusiasm of the colonists for liberty, they could never be subdued; in view, however, of the exhausted resources of his native land, he felt that she should refrain from war. By various influences, the king was nevertheless won to the opposite policy. Silas Deane, the secret agent of Congress for purchasing supplies, was instructed to say that in the event of separation France was the power "whose friendship it would be fittest for us to obtain and cultivate." He was to ask for clothing and arms for twenty-five thousand men, for a hundred field-pieces and the necessary ammunition. The cabinet deliberated a month. The tide of public opinion was swelling into enthusiasm, and Vergennes finally proposed his plan.

He contemplated secret action by both France and Spain, in order that at least a year might pass before

England should learn the truth, and so force the Bourbon powers into open war. In spite of Turgot's warning the subsidies were granted, two hundred thousand dollars each by France and Spain. Before the end of the season, early in the summer, Beaumarchais was authorized to tell Arthur Lee that the colonies might rely on the king for a million dollars. This action was but the reflection of popular zeal, but in consequence Malesherbes and Turgot, the main-stays of the monarchy, left the cabinet. Such expenditures would destroy even the last vestige of permanency in the existing conditions of France.

<small>Plan of Vergennes.</small>

The English plan for the campaign of 1776 had been partly successful in the reconquest of Canada. But the all-important line of communication between Montreal and New York, through Lake Champlain and the Hudson, was held by the Americans, even if with a very precarious tenure. It was but a shattered, pest-stricken, and disheartened remnant which occupied Crown Point. The condition of affairs in the city of New York, at the other end, was anomalous: the moderate patriots in control and under a kind of truce making ready for war, the town itself to all outward appearance as loyal as ever, and the radical patriots divided between the temporary, uneasy acquiescence of Macdougall, and the fiery, mischievous zeal of Sears.

<small>English strength in New York.</small>

The latter had betaken himself in January to Washington's camp before Boston, and there won over Charles Lee to his schemes. This English adventurer had fought with more or less distinction during the Seven Years' War, had brought his laurels to Virginia, and from the outset paraded them so skilfully, that he was not only one of the four major-generals appointed by Congress, of equal honor with the intrepid Schuyler, the dignified and trustworthy Ward, the enthu-

<small>Sears and Charles Lee.</small>

siastic and dashing Putnam, but he even had it whispered that, should the reins grow slack in Washington's hands, he was the man to gather them up.

Sir Henry Clinton was at that moment leaving Boston with an expedition the destination of which was uncertain. Washington consented that Lee should adopt Sears's proposition, raise volunteers in Connecticut, make sure of New York, and destroy the Tory influence which was represented to be dominant. Suspicions were aroused in many minds by Lee's conduct, but he enlisted two regiments, made Sears his lieutenant-colonel, and by permission of the committee of safety entered New York on February 4th, the very day on which, to the angry surprise of the inhabitants, Clinton's ships came up the harbor. The fleet, however, soon passed on to its destination in North Carolina, and Lee began the erection of fortifications to command the East River and the Hudson. Such was his earnestness and success, so bitter the invective which he heaped on England and her ministers, so certain was he that the die was cast and independence assured, that he soon became the idol not only of the people, but of many among the ablest men in Congress, including Franklin and John Adams. On March 1st he was appointed to the command of the American forces south of the Potomac, and on May 7th he left for his post. *The city fortified.*

The second part of the plan for 1776 was to restore the king's authority in the Southern colonies. Seven regiments under Cornwallis were despatched from Cork in December, and these were to be conveyed by the fleet of Sir Peter Parker to the mouth of the Cape Fear River, to co-operate under Clinton, as commander-in-chief, with the North Carolina loyalists. But the rising of the settlers was premature and had been as unsuccessful as that of 1745, for partici- *North Carolina Tories routed.*

pating in which many of these very Scotch Highlanders were now in America. It was a strange turn that brought Allan Macdonald of Kingsborough, and Flora, his wife, famous for the rescue of Charles Edward·Stewart, under arms again, but this time in North Carolina and for the hated House of Hanover. Of such men there were seven hundred, and of their sympathizers five hundred, although five thousand were promised. But the Americans were not apathetic, and a second time the patriots of the South proved their courage. Being matched with their equals their success was complete. They made their stand under Caswell on Morris Creek, about twenty miles from Wilmington, and on January 27th engaged the enemy. The rout of the Tories was complete, some nine hundred prisoners being taken, and by April, when Clinton's arrival was expected, the whole colony was united against him.

Not until May, however, did the English fleet enter the Cape Fear. Learning that his allies were crushed, the commander-in-chief sailed away to attack Charleston before the American works on Sullivan's Island should be completed and the place thus rendered impregnable. The humor of South Carolina was well illustrated in the device which her convention had chosen in February, on the adoption of a constitution. It was the rattlesnake with thirteen rattles and the motto: "Don't tread on me." From the opening of the year, labor on their fortifications had been incessant. Rutledge, the president, was a man of the highest character, determined to assert the independence which the convention had declared, and about him were men of equal courage, perseverance, and resources— Gadsden, Moultrie, and the like. When Armstrong came at the command of Congress, to superintend the defence of Charleston, but little remained to be done. When

The British before Charleston.

THE MOVEMENT FOR INDEPENDENCE 223

Lee finally arrived, on June 4th, he, however, could find nothing as it should be, and his overbearing, querulous temper would have brought disaster but for the wisdom and firmness of Rutledge, which enabled Moultrie to complete his work on the all-important island. Six thousand men were assembled as a garrison.

On June 28th, the British, having spent nearly a month in preparation and reconnoitring, began the attack. The bombardment was fierce and skilful, but the soft palmetto logs and sand-banks of Moultrie's Fort were not seriously affected by either shell or cannon-ball. A manœuvre by which it was hoped to surround the fortifications and enfilade them was unsuccessful, for one of the three vessels grounded, and had to be burned to prevent her falling into the enemy's hands. The rest of the fleet suffered seriously from the American fire, which, though of necessity slow, was most skilful and effective. They had, moreover, fallen into a position from which an adverse wind and tide made it impossible to withdraw, and two vessels, being battered into wrecks, the men on the others grew anxious and disheartened. Finally, a body of seven regiments which had been landed on Long Island, and were to pass over to Sullivan's Island for an assault, found the strait between the two deeper than they supposed, and impassable. They spent their day, therefore, impotent witnesses of a disaster they could not help to avert. *Bombardment of the city.*

Toward nine at night the tide served, the vessels drew out, re-embarked the troops, and made sail for New York. There had been four hundred and thirty-five Americans in the fort; of these, eleven were killed and twenty-seven wounded. The English loss was seventy-three killed and a hundred and twenty-seven wounded. The day crowned the South *Success of the defence.*

with laurels. The daring and courage of the men dimmed the glories even of Bunker Hill. When the flag of the fortification, which has thenceforth been known as Fort Moultrie, was shot away, Sergeant Jasper leaped through an embrasure, and under the hottest fire caught up the standard and planted it on a bastion. "I am dying," exclaimed Macdonald, a common soldier, "but don't let the cause of liberty expire with me this day." Nearly three years elapsed before these heroes were called again to drive the British from their land. Within a short time the English troops from Charleston joined in New York the Boston force which had come down from Halifax, and excepting the island of Manhattan, the soil of the thirteen colonies was untrodden by English regulars.

The two Carolinas had thus not only declared, but in a sense established, their freedom from English control. Georgia was united with them in heart and action. Massachusetts and Rhode Island had together thrown off the trammels of English rule. New Hampshire was energetic in the work of independence. Connecticut, in the liberty she enjoyed as an English colony, had entered on the most complete participation in the activity of her New England sisters.

New common-wealths.

In May the constituent assembly of Virginia met to complete her separation from England, to establish a constitution, and to promote union. So far she had been the leader in organization and suggestion, if not in action. Could a community of aristocratic social character, with the English Church as an establishment, keep at the head of a movement so democratic? Mason had written in his fundamental and admirable declaration of rights the word "toleration." Madison, who was already influential, would not hear of the condescension implied in the word, and plead "that

Virginia.

THE MOVEMENT FOR INDEPENDENCE 225

all men are equally entitled to the free exercise of religion, according to the dictates of conscience." The word was stricken out—a small matter, perhaps, but conclusive as to the adaptability of that fine commonwealth for continued leadership. The convention completed its work on July 1st, and Virginia became a State. Could her political guides have transcended their age by two generations, and have granted equal rights, civil and political, to their slaves, the Old Dominion would still be united, and probably wield the sceptre of hegemony among the States which she did so much to create.

John Adams's resolution in Congress had virtually ended the Proprietary Government of Pennsylvania. The old Assembly, after long wrangling over instructions to their delegates against separation, finally sanctioned confederation and foreign alliances, but refused to hear of independence. The same day, June 8th, began the debate on the resolution introduced for Virginia by Richard Henry Lee, "that these united colonies are and of right ought to be free." Two days later the discussion was postponed for three weeks, that the delegates of the central colonies might consult their constituents. But committees were appointed to deliberate on the three crucial questions of the hour : The declaration of independence, the form of confederation, and treaties with foreign powers. *Debates in Congress.*

The flood which was thus let loose upon New York and Pennsylvania was irresistible. Delaware had promptly obeyed the call of Virginia in all these summonses. New Jersey gave full powers to her Assembly, which met on June 11th, and adopted a constitution inspired by Witherspoon, but written by Jacob Green, the Presbyterian minister of Hanover. The convention also voted for a government according to the recommendation of Congress, and for the support of *New York hesitates.*

15

the army. The overthrow of old institutions seemed a very serious step to New York, with her large and influential Tory population. Her borders, too, were menaced by savages, and thirty thousand English veterans were soon to occupy the capital. John Jay declared that until after the second petition to the king—written in 1775 by Dickinson—he heard no American express a desire for independence, and even yet many of the moderate patriots were making qualified, but unwavering, professions of loyalty. But now, at last, he could prove the hopelessness of redress by the reception of that petition, and on June 11th the electors were called on to give full powers for declaring independence to the newly chosen delegates. They refused.

The Pennsylvania Assembly, overwhelmed with disgrace and disowned in popular estimation, was dismissed by a great mass meeting from further duty. On June 18th a provincial conference of new men met, and without hesitancy usurped the powers of the body which had adjourned for two months, voting measures of defence and concurring in the resolution of Congress for independence. In Maryland the course of affairs was smoother. The governor withdrew, and a constitutional convention was called.

Overthrow of the Proprietary Assembly in Pennsylvania.

CHAPTER XIX.

INDEPENDENCE AND CONFEDERATION—JULY-AUGUST, 1776

Congress and the State Governments—Diversity of Opinion—Debate on the Declaration of Independence—Jefferson's Document Adopted—Adams and Witherspoon—Popular Enthusiasm—Character of the Paper—Real Nature of the Confederation—The Appearance of a Separatist Temper—Congress to be Stripped of Power—Conflict between Southern and Northern Opinion—Local Ideas of Independence Expressed in the Articles of Confederation—The Western Lands and True Union—Inefficiency of Congress—Fickleness of the Masses.

SUCH was the situation when the day arrived for renewing in Congress the debate on Lee's resolution for independence. A nice analysis of the constitutional conditions is impossible. Virtually all the colonies were in union with each other but sundered from Great Britain; virtually they all had local autonomy. The old charters of Connecticut and Rhode Island were sufficient for them, even in their separation from England. Four other colonies had adopted written constitutions before July 4th—New Hampshire on January 5th, South Carolina on March 6th, Virginia on July 1st, and New Jersey on July 2d. But the degrees of completeness and formal legality in their governments were widely different; virtually, too, there was a federal government above them all, conducting foreign affairs and the cognate department of war by the army and navy, imposing also certain principles and courses

Congress and the State governments.

of action upon the united provinces. But the central power was inchoate and unwilling to recognize its own existence.

And yet in human affairs, as in the sphere of the supernatural, the supremacy does not come by observation. The ideas of dependence, separatism, and tutelage were dominant still in thousands of minds, among them many commanding ones. The steps taken had been necessary to meet the demand of the moment in resistance to oppression, but were regarded as temporary and retraceable. Even among those who understood and accepted the logic of the position there were almost as many opinions concerning the degree and thoroughness, not only of what had been done but of the action still to be taken, as there were men capable of independent thought; in such a chaos order is, however, imminent, and the hour belongs to those who first discern its germs in the popular will. Such amplitude of discussion by the masses as that of these months and weeks was hitherto unknown, even in America. The glass was held up for all. Dickinson and his friends could not or would not see the brightening reflection of a new personality among nations, but the more thorough patriots beheld in it their justification, and never faltered in the course on which they had already entered.

The committee on the declaration of independence was composed of Jefferson, John Adams, Franklin, Sherman, and Robert Livingston. The draft of a document had been made by the first-named and submitted separately to Adams and Franklin, each of whom made a few unimportant verbal corrections. On June 28th it was submitted as amended to Congress. July 1st was the day appointed for considering the weighty question. Fifty delegates were in their places, every colony was represented, and every delegation but one had power to act. John Adams, who had already won his spurs as a debater, opened for the affirmative with power and passion. Dickinson replied at length, arguing that federation should precede separation. His colleague, Wilson, took the opposite view. Witherspoon followed, declaring that the country was ripe for independence and would be rotten without it.

When the vote was taken on Lee's motion, New York being still unable to act for lack of instruction, both South Carolina and a majority of the Pennsylvania delegates opposing, and Delaware being divided, it was adopted by the votes of the nine other colonies. Next day Jefferson's document was presented. The glowing passage it contained charging George III., as a criminal indictment, with having favored the slave-trade and slavery was stricken out by the desire of some Southern delegates ; so also was a severe censure on the people of England. It was otherwise slightly amended, and on the evening of July 4th, 1776, was adopted, in the form familiar to us, by the vote of twelve colonies. The date of its adoption is, by decision of the Supreme Court of the United States, that of our legal existence in questions of municipal law. *Jefferson's document adopted.*

There was an awe-stricken anxiety and little enthusiasm in Congress when they took this solemn step, there was even discord and angry passion. Adams had been, as Jefferson said, the Colossus of debate ; but we are told that toward the close of that momentous day, in a late hour, the fate of the paper was still in the balance. At such a time all but giant minds, and sometimes even they, feel an instinctive and uncontrollable shrinking. A trustworthy tradition declares that it was a solemn appeal to heaven, made by Witherspoon, and the force of his own courageous example, which turned the delicately poised scale at last. Even *Adams and Witherspoon.*

then there was a majority of but one, if the individuals composing the delegations be counted.

At first its reading made little impression on the army or on the people, who, feeling that the action was sim-
<small>Popular en-</small> ply essential and but in obedience to their
<small>thusiasm.</small> desires, thought of it as a matter of course and regarded neither the vigor nor the form of the language employed. Nevertheless there were exceptions; the populace of Philadelphia received it with acclamations and burned the emblems of royalty, while the old "liberty bell" of the state-house rang out its notes of joy. New Jersey with great military state formally published at Trenton the two together; her own constitution and the Declaration of Independence. The fourth provincial congress of New York, under the leadership of Jay, adopted it on July 9th, and sent the paper broadcast over the State; the joyous working-men in the city threw down the statue of George III. from its pedestal. In short, enthusiasm grew in the progress of the document throughout the land. When Lord Howe, in accordance with his instructions, sent conciliatory letters under a flag of truce to the leaders of Congress, the reply was an engrossed copy sent by that body, and the expression of a readiness for peace as between independent nations. The only result of the negotiation was an agreement honorable to both parties for the exchange of prisoners.

For many years large numbers in the United States regarded the Declaration of Independence as inspired
<small>Character of</small> and immortal, although there were always
<small>the paper.</small> voices to pronounce it perfervid, rhetorical, and radical. We have a calmer judgment now. On the one hand there is nothing new or original in the bill of rights it contains, and so far from its initiating a new government, the political existence of the United States, as distinct from the validity of its municipal law, dates

INDEPENDENCE AND CONFEDERATION 231

from the day of Lexington, when a united people, finding its ultimatum scorned, resisted force by force and began an organization which was neither independent nor sovereign until the successful issue of war made it so. It is, moreover, not self-evidently true that men are created "equal," as the word was used and understood by its writer; it is true that the sovereignty of George III. was renounced, not because he was a king, but because he was a tyrant; there is in those two clauses a curious inconsistency in the juxtaposition of ideas, at bottom irreconcilable with each other. On the other hand, there was in the language of Jefferson a cumulative statement of grievances, a directness of stinging censure, an avowal of irrevocable purpose, all carefully calculated to the attainment of a most important end and worthy of the highest admiration. In spite of the irreligious and extreme radicalism which underlies the implications of its language, it was adopted by the great popular majority as the best expression of its own will, a people who neither understood nor sympathized with Rousseauism, who were both pious and conservative to the core, and who had adopted democratic-republican institutions, without any reference to fine-spun political theories, solely because they were convenient, handy, and in accordance with their colonial history, with their habits both of religious and civil administration.

The years of the American revolution did not belong to an age of written constitutions and exact statement. The first continental congress was a more perfectly representative assemblage than any existing survivor, Parliament or Diet, of the early Teutonic custom. Under its auspices the colonies formed a union, imperfect but not ephemeral, and under that union they had separated themselves from England, six of them having adopted, before the Declaration of

Real nature of the confederation.

Independence, a satisfactory form of local government evolved from their experience, which was written down by four of them as their charters had been written. In the second continental congress that union was further completed in part by the recommendation to form governments not for separation but for union, and in part by adopting the phraseology of Jefferson—"we, the people"—which indicates the birth of a new nation. The feeling and language of the American leaders for the three years past is capable of no other meaning, and there is evidence that the people for some time so understood the position of affairs. The committee of Congress which reported a scheme for confederation recommended that each colony should keep "as much of its present laws, rights, and customs as it may think fit, and reserve to itself the sole and exclusive regulation and government of its internal police in all matters that shall not interfere with the articles of confederation." Neither they nor anyone at that moment appeared to doubt that the source of authority was in the people represented by a Congress which expressed their union—the continental American organization—as opposed to the colonial, separatist, and European connection which they were severing.

But the American people and their leaders had not then behind them a century of experience in harmonizing the spheres of local and general self-government. The energy and decision displayed since the springtime were spent; the distrust and timidity which the colonies as a whole had during the ten years past learned to feel toward England began to appear in reference to their untried experiment and to each other. Their determined colonial policy had been for each to retain control of its own troops and revenues, furnishing to the king whatever he required on his demand but by their own act. They

The appearance of a separatist temper.

could now think of no other relation to a federal government.

As to the question of large and small colonies, which had promptly arisen in the first Congress, there appeared three opinions: one vote for each without regard to size, representation according to population, and a combination of both plans. *Congress to be stripped of power.* What was to become of the western lands? Should Congress parcel out the vast domain northwest of the Ohio, or existing claims be satisfied? As to a standing army, the people remembered the principles of 1688, and Congress would only agree that each State should furnish militia—a citizen soldiery enlisted for short terms, and therefore unreliable and incapable of the highest discipline. In short, there appeared almost immediately a determination "to vest Congress," as Rutledge wrote, "with no more power than what is absolutely necessary." In August there was still no outcome to the wretched wrangle. Congress adjourned to April, 1777, the articles of confederation were not adopted until November of that year, and then in a form so different from that which the committee had reported as to be scarcely recognizable.

Requisitions for the support of the army were to be made on each State in proportion to its inhabitants, but in the Southern States there was a feeling that, as negroes were property, and as there was a disproportionate number of blacks in their borders, there was a certain injustice in this procedure. *Conflict between Southern and Northern opinion.* The federal relation began to gall immediately. In New England the purely democratic character of town government had not only created inequalities of representation in the colonial assemblies, which continue in measure to our own day, but had further emphasized the sovereign quality of the popular voice. The State legislatures had from the outset this stable basis, that they came annually direct from the people, and their sphere of activity embraced the whole circle of civil and political rights. Congress was a degree further removed from the people, and existed, moreover, as a war measure. It was not easy for the most adroit lawyers of that district, instinctively and firmly supporting federal supremacy, as most of them did, to make clear at the outset, to either themselves or others, the degree or the benefit of federal intervention in the sphere of legislation. In the Middle States both independence and federation had reached a distasteful importance, and particularism was none the less strenuous in that quarter, because every social rank and political sect found a different reason for it. The indisputable fact is, that there was no precedent in human experience for such a federal system as was needed, and the work of the patriots was near to destruction both in the irritation which this political novelty created and in the apathetic support which was given as a consequence to the fighting force, the army being the most palpable evidence of the federal relation.

It was not difficult, therefore, for the local legislatures to establish the practice of appointing and dismissing congressional delegates at their pleasure, and so to turn a revolutionary body with unlimited powers into a mere creature of the States. Before the articles of confederation were adopted they became, as Washington said, "a shade without substance," reposing on the theory that from the fourth of July, 1776, each colony was an independent State delegating at its pleasure, and according to its interest, a portion of its sovereignty for the regulation of foreign affairs, and retaining every other function not expressly so delegated. The article to which reference has been made now ran, " Each State retains its

Local ideas of independence expressed in the Articles of Confederation.

sovereignty, freedom, and independence, and every power, jurisdiction, and right which is not by this confederation expressly delegated to the United States in Congress assembled." The confederacy was "a firm league of friendship." There was to be a single house in Congress where each State had one vote. It might borrow money but not levy taxes, and all the security lenders were to have was the requisition of Congress on the States. It could declare war, make treaties, and lay imposts. It could not enforce enlistment nor compel the support of the army. It could pass laws, but not compel obedience; compose disputes between the States, but it had no power to secure their compliance with its judgment or with the foreign treaties it made. Even commerce was to be regulated by the States.

This particularist temper was further shown in the article declaring that "no State shall be deprived of territory for the benefit of the United States." New York still claimed by right of conquest the territory of the Six Nations, and the other larger States had claims of a similar nature. But New Jersey, Delaware, and Maryland could have no share in the boundless and fertile West except as members of the confederation. They therefore rejected the articles on account of this clause, although all the other States adopted them. New Jersey, however, held out but for one year, until November, 1778, and Delaware until May, 1779. Maryland alone remained firm until, in 1780, New York resigned to the union her claim to any lands beyond her present boundary. Virginia reserved her asserted ownership of the lands northwest of the Ohio until 1781, and then, first, the waiting State signed the articles, thus completing, by means of the West, what western settlement had already begun, a permanent and unchangeable union of the States in the face of theories

The Western lands and true union.

and articles like those to which she set her hand. The hope of Western settlers for prosperity and protection was in a federal state, not in a confederacy of sovereigns; the administration of that vast and splendid territory was as inexorable as fate in its requirement of a strong, indissoluble union.

As the war went on Congress, from the lack of real vitality, became more and more decrepit and inefficient. Its members were constantly absent, preferring the active political life of the separate States to the torpor of a discussion and legislation with no real power behind it. As foreign aid became more abundant and more certain, the entire nation at different times and at different places displayed an apathy in the performance of its duties which strangely contrasted with the magnitude of the struggle in which it had engaged. This was mirrored in Congress, which at last was but a mere tool of the States to borrow money and issue a paper currency, the shadow of a union whose reality was temporarily in Washington and the army. Its sessions were too often the scene of dispute between cliques representing the jealousies which arose from the ambition or spite of generals in the field. Gates, Charles Lee, and Conway found their adherents and fellow-schemers among its members. At times it lost all dignity, and in the absence of the general confidence and esteem of the country the only one who still spoke of it with respect was Washington, of all men the most sorely tried by its hostility and inefficiency. The pretenders and soldiers of fortune who plotted his overthrow seemed always to find sympathy in a body which notoriously failed in the continuous and hearty support of his authority, and in providing the supplies essential to the conduct of the war.

Inefficiency of Congress.

There was real greatness and true courage in the

American people and their leaders throughout the years and events antecedent to the Revolutionary War, and again in the days of constitutional recon- Fickleness struction subsequent to it. Throughout the of the masses. existence of the confederation, however, there was a display of littleness and meanness, of weakness and hesitancy, which narrows the number of great names for the period of hostilities to comparatively few. Such as there were, however, were truly great. Their owners tower superior to wrangling and ambition. Devoted to a principle and a cause they were unmoved by failure, by the fickleness of the mob, which often showed a short and dangerous zeal only to fall off like an autumn leaf, or by the too frequent selfishness of the mercantile classes. Without such loyal and true supporters even the superior greatness of Washington would have had no theatre on which to display itself; the great revolution in political principle accomplished by the fortitude and acumen of the last ten years, and culminating in the declaration of independence, would have been a dismal failure.

CHAPTER XX.

THE LOSS OF NEW YORK CITY—APRIL-DECEMBER, 1776

Three Divisions of the War—Importance of New York City—Arrival of Washington—The System of Defence—The Opposing Forces—The Battle of Long Island—Inefficiency of the American Militia—Evacuation of New York—Encampment on the Bronx River—The Battle of White Plains—Capture of Fort Washington by the British—The American Army in New Jersey—Retreat of Greene—Need of a Regular Army—Treachery of Charles Lee—Congress Authorizes Long Enlistments—Washington's Retreat across New Jersey—His Army Reinforced—His Successful Strategy—Lee Captured by the British—His True Character.

THE English had been foiled both at Boston and Charleston, but neither place was of the highest strategic importance in a war carried on according to the science as it was then understood. The brothers Howe, both the admiral and the general, were men of clearer understanding than the incapables to whom active operations in America had so far been intrusted by the English administration. After the opening scenes in the South and around Boston, the story of hostilities falls into three divisions—the conflict for possession of the Hudson, the campaigns on the Delaware, and the effort to regain the South.

Three divisions of the war.

In addition to the control of the interior, which the possession of the city of New York assured, the place had now become the largest storehouse of military supplies within American limits. It was the commercial centre of the country, although not yet as populous as Philadelphia, and many of its wealthy inhabitants remained loyal from both interest and conviction. It was therefore self-evident that after the evacuation of Boston an attempt to seize the town would be made by the English.

Importance of New York City.

The only place about the harbor available for a landing was Staten Island. American fortifications of more or less strength had been erected on the other shores, but Washington's numbers were too few to complete the investment. He had left three thousand men in Boston under Ward, and sent eight regiments under Thomas to Canada. It was therefore with a weakened and scanty force that he reached New York in April. Tryon was on an English ship in the harbor giving comfort and encouragement to the Tories, and fomenting plots of a most dastardly character against the persons and property of patriots. One of these was the seizure of Washington himself. The plotters were sometimes discovered, and, when they were, such was the exasperation of the New York patriots that they did not hesitate to cruelly maltreat them, a coat of tar and feathers being among the lightest penalties.

Arrival of Washington.

Lee had already planned and partially constructed a system of fortifications. Washington hastened the completion of the unfinished ones, and under the supervision of Greene and Putnam materially strengthened the fort on Brooklyn Heights. Additional earthworks were thrown up at Red Hook, Paulus Hook, and on the hills at Kingsbridge. On the north end of the island Fort Washington commanded the left bank of the Hudson; Fort Lee, opposite, in New Jersey, the right; and Fort George guarded the south end of the city. As a garrison there was an available force of between ten and eleven thousand men; nearly seven thou-

The system of defence.

sand being detached on furlough or sick. They had been hastily gathered in by order of Congress from Maryland, Delaware, Pennsylvania, and New Jersey, from New York itself, and from New England. Composed in part of militiamen, in part of regulars, this difference was further augmented by local prejudice and social peculiarities, which entirely destroyed any cohesion and made discipline impossible.

During the first fortnight in August there were landed from successive detachments of the English fleet forces which made the army nearly thirty-two thousand strong; about twenty-five thousand were effective, among them eight thousand and six hundred mercenaries. During the months just passed, independence had been declared at Philadelphia, Congress had declined North's perfunctory offers of conciliation, and arrangements for the interchange of prisoners of war had been concluded. The loyalists of Long Island were enrolled under the command of Tryon. Hostile movements at length began on August 22d, when fifteen thousand British troops were sent over near the Narrows to the eastern shore; on the twenty-fifth five thousand Hessians followed. There were eight thousand Continentals, under the immediate command of Greene and Putnam, to oppose them; the most notable corps of the American army was an artillery company, under command of Alexander Hamilton.

The opposing forces.

The attack was made on the twenty-seventh, and the consequence was further disorganization. Greene was ill, the advance forces under Putnam were overwhelmed and thrown back into Brooklyn with the loss of more than a thousand prisoners, among whom were two generals. The English, over-estimating the force opposed to them, came to a halt before the Brooklyn fort. Two days intervened.

The battle of Long Island.

The precious moments of delay gave Washington an opportunity to reconnoitre. Their strength was overpowering, and he decided for retreat. By a movement as masterly as any through which his victories were won, he drew off the remnants of his raw, undisciplined army, crossing the East River in fog and rain with all his stores. On the thirtieth the main body of his force was safely encamped on Manhattan Island and guards set to watch the movements of the enemy.

But the situation was disheartening. The English would not bombard the city of New York, for they intended to spare the property of Tories and capture the place for their own occupation. *Inefficiency of the American militia.* Washington momentarily took into consideration the destruction of the town as a military necessity, but Congress took the opposite view; the general had no confidence, however, in his militia and without them the place could not be held. A distressing incident which soon occurred justified the distrust. The English fleet was sent to threaten the front and western shore of the city, while a body of troops was landed from Astoria in Kip's Bay on the eastern shore. The militia fled before them in disgraceful confusion across the fields to Murray Hill. Two New England brigades were hastily despatched to arrest the flight, but they were no braver than the others and joined in the panic. Washington stood in the way with loaded pistols, but the hurrying men paid no heed to his commands or menaces. He is said to have discharged his side-arms over the vanishing soldiery, and to have flung his hat in angry despair on the ground as he exclaimed: "And are these the men with whom I have to defend America?"

The success of the English drove the army momentarily to entrench itself on Harlem Heights near Fort Washington; the commander's head-quarters were at Morrisania, on the mainland. The inevitable retreat from the city occurred on September 12th, and was conducted by Putnam with spirit and success; but the evacuation was so hasty that all the heavy artillery and stores had to be left behind, an irreparable loss to the Americans. A curious tradition relates that Howe's pursuit was hot and close until he reached the mansion of Mrs. Murray, mother of the once famous grammarian, which was noted for its hospitality and a cellar of old Madeira. The English general paused a moment for refreshment, and the patriotic mistress plied him so successfully with the precious liquor that some hours were gained for Putnam and his retreating soldiers. The English entered and occupied the city at once. Soon after, a fire destroyed old Trinity Church and the quarter in which it stood. The origin of the conflagration could never be determined, but the British falsely charged the Sons of Liberty with incendiarism and flung some of them into the flames.

Evacuation of New York.

In the meantime, September 11th, a conference had been held on Staten Island between Howe on one side and a committee of Congress, consisting of Franklin, John Adams, and Rutledge on the other, to consider the English offer of peace forwarded a second time to Philadelphia and by the hand of Sullivan, who had been captured by the British on Long Island. As the Americans insisted on the acknowledgment of their independence the result was nothing. Soon after, Nathan Hale, a gentleman by birth and a graduate of Yale College, entered the English lines as a spy. He was captured, brutally treated, and hung the day following, on September 22d. Both these incidents, especially the latter, embittered the popular feeling against the English.

The American fortifications at Harlem were too strong to be stormed, and on October 12th Howe sought to re-

THE LOSS OF NEW YORK CITY 243

peat the manœuvre which had been so successful, sending a body of troops by boats up the East River to outflank them. Washington and his generals determined, therefore, to move across the Harlem onto the mainland, leaving for the control of the Hudson a strong garrison in Fort Washington, which Greene considered impregnable. This was done, although with great hesitancy on the part of the commander-in-chief, and a fortified camp was established, extending thirteen miles along the Bronx River to the village of White Plains, which commanded the land routes into the interior. *Encampment on the Bronx River.*

Near this place the two armies met again on October 28th; their numbers were about equal, thirteen thousand more or less on each side. The Americans stood on the defensive, and on the twenty-ninth the English attacked. The first engagement was sharp but indecisive until Rall, with two German regiments, turned it to the British advantage. The latter, however, lost two hundred and thirty-one killed, wounded, and prisoners, the former one hundred and sixty. A severe thunder-storm supervened, and this, combined with the frowning appearance of the American breastworks, which were thrown up with the butts of corn-stalks, a material unknown to the enemy, discouraged them in a repetition of their charge, and they waited two days for reinforcements. On November 1st Washington retreated in good order, proceeding to New Castle which he entrenched, while Howe, by a sudden movement incomprehensible to his opponent, turned westward toward the river at Dobb's Ferry and then moved south. *The battle of White Plains.*

The American council of war was altogether misled, being convinced that the invaders were to cross the river and then march northward. Accordingly, a body of

244 THE FRENCH WAR AND THE REVOLUTION

troopers was sent over the river to reconnoitre, and four thousand men were stationed at Peekskill to guard the Highlands, so as to prevent, if possible, the junction of Howe's army with that of Carleton from the north.

<small>Capture of Fort Washington by the British.</small>

What was left of the main army followed to the west shore and turned south into New Jersey. The truth was that a traitor in Fort Washington had made plans of the fortress and its outworks, and fled with them to the enemy. Their present movement was directed against that post, which had been garrisoned with great loss of effective fighting troops to the American army, and against Washington's better judgment. It was assaulted on November 16th, from three different directions; the outlying forts were captured, the entire body of defenders driven into the narrow compass of the place itself, and no alternative left for them except surrender. The British lost three hundred and fifty Germans and five hundred English, killed and wounded in the storm. The American loss was twenty-seven hundred taken prisoners, a hundred and fifty killed and wounded, forty-three pieces of artillery, with small arms and stores. By this disaster Fort Lee was also rendered useless, as alone it could not command the wide river. It was therefore evacuated and in part dismantled.

Greene was left near by to guard the rear, as Washington turned toward the Delaware. Able, generous, and brave as the lieutenant was, his judgment had very recently been proven altogether incommensurate with that of the commander-in-chief, and he had now another bitter lesson to learn before he ripened into the maturity which afterward characterized him. Every action in this campaign had thus far been disastrous to Washington, and yet his opponent had been outgeneralled at every step. The river

<small>The American army in New Jersey.</small>

THE LOSS OF NEW YORK CITY 245

was not won, the struggle for its possession had been merely transferred to its upper waters, and the Highlands had been rendered substantially impregnable. The winter was near, and Howe's last move for the season was to cross into New Jersey with his Anglo-German army.

His objective point was Fort Lee, which he meant to fortify before withdrawing to the comforts and pleasures of New York for the inclement season and leaving to Cornwallis the task of securing the Delaware River. Accordingly, a reinforcement of five thousand men moved up the east side of the Hudson and crossed, with their artillery, about five miles north of the fort where Greene was stationed on the precipitous rock-walls known as the Palisades. Never dreaming that the English would really come that way and drag their cannon by main force up trails almost perpendicular, he was taken completely by surprise, and fled with his force of two thousand men, leaving cannon and tents behind. Fortunately he had presence of mind to send an express to Washington, who was thus enabled by a forced march to secure the bridge across the Hackensack River, to which the English were hastening, and thus cover Greene's retreat. *Retreat of Greene.*

This accumulation of successive disasters was producing in many honest but dull people a most painful impression concerning the commander-in-chief. The troops were utterly disheartened, and as their short terms expired they daily left the camp in considerable numbers. Congress had culpably neglected to authorize long enlistment, that is, for three years or the war, as Washington repeatedly urged ; the militia had in the crisis shown little endurance or courage, and the army was finally so decimated as to make the retreat across New Jersey appear like a flight of stragglers. *Need of a regular army.*

In this desperate plight Lee began to display his true character. Immediately after the march began orders were sent for him to close in and join the main column with his division. But he procrastinated and loitered aimlessly behind, apparently seeking a chance for some personal exploit whereby to distinguish himself and create a glaring contrast to the humiliation of his captain. A second time he was summoned, but with the same result, and Washington vainly waited five days at Newark before starting across the State for New Brunswick, Princeton, and Trenton, the line he had chosen for retreat. Lee's reputation had really reached alarming proportions; men remembered his long experience in Europe, they appreciated the excellence of his plan for defending New York, his success at Charleston had not been diminished as the news of it travelled on, and there was enthusiasm for him in all the country round about. His self-sufficiency grew with each succeeding day, he refused obedience for weeks, and no doubt dreamed either of an independent command or of the foremost place, should the general-in-chief meet with another reverse.

Treachery of Charles Lee.

Congress had at last roused itself to action. On the morrow of the reverses in New York, when it was just too late, they authorized long enlistments, and forwarded blank commissions to the head-quarters of the army. In December, three weeks later, when dismay and panic had overwhelmed the majority of the patriots, when Philadelphia seemed lost, and they were on the eve themselves of adjourning to Baltimore, they went further in the display of a supreme confidence in Washington, and temporarily invested him with the powers of a dictator.

Congress authorizes long enlistments.

THE LOSS OF NEW YORK CITY 247

In the interval the discredited and flying, but orderly, remnant of the troops reached New Brunswick on November 28th. They were marching through an unsympathetic country. After the close of the Staten Island conference Howe had issued a proclamation of amnesty, declaring that his Government was willing to repeal the whole series of odious acts; he now renewed it. *Washington's retreat across New Jersey.* Many in the neighborhood, unnerved by disaster, and feeling that resistance was hopeless, accepted his offers, even the officers of the State began to throw up their commissions and seek pardon. And in the very goal toward which the army was striving, there reigned an utter hopelessness. Pennsylvania had as yet no constitution, and her committee of safety was paralyzed. On November 30th the New Jersey and Maryland troops left for their homes, and the American effective force was reduced one-half. Lee still refused obedience.

There was here and there a ray of light in this darkness. In response to messages from Washington the New Jersey legislature began to take efficient measures, and Congress issued stirring appeals to the citizens in and near Philadelphia, which awakened a private enterprise nobly contrasted with the semi-official inefficiency. *His army reinforced.* Schuyler sent seven Continental regiments from the north which had yet a month to serve, and Washington left New Brunswick with a body of three thousand soldiers, just as Cornwallis was arriving from the north with a force of veteran troops twice as strong. Princeton was reached on the night of December 1st. Twelve hundred Continentals, under Stirling, were left there to check the enemy's advance, if possible, and Washington, with the remaining eighteen hundred, and his stores, pushed on to Trenton. After a week of uncertain repose for the weary men, broken at last by Cornwallis's advance from New Brunswick, the rear-guard followed. Their general, whose claim to a Scotch peerage gave him the courtesy title of Lord Stirling, by which he was always known in America, was of the Alexander family, and as enjoying the public confidence had been chosen long before—in 1775—by the New Jersey provincial congress to command one of the two battalions they had raised; but even he, on his own soil, was compelled to withdraw before Cornwallis's successful veterans, who entered the university town on December 7th, turning the handsome buildings into barracks and the stately old church into a storehouse and stable.

The American baggage and stores had, however, been safely transferred to the right bank of the Delaware, and Washington, after urging Congress to begin its preparations for the campaign of the following summer, turned back to rejoin Stirling. But he met his subordinate half-way, to learn that Howe had come out for his share of the expected laurels, and that no less than four thousand regulars were in pursuit, though a large force had been left in occupation of Princeton. The Americans, therefore, turned, crossed the Delaware, and proceeded to secure all the boats on the waters around for many miles, seventy, it is said. Howe had again lingered too long, this time a whole day, and reached Trenton just in time to see the last of his foes crossing the swollen wintry flood in safety. This retreat of ninety miles, in the depth of winter, leaving behind a country with bridges destroyed, and roads rendered so far impassable as to protract the enemy's march for eighteen days, during which such measures as could be were taken to avert threatened disaster and ruin, is second to no other of Washington's masterpieces as a general. Moreover, at the end, weak as his little army was, he occupied a position of great strength behind

His successful strategy.

THE LOSS OF NEW YORK CITY 249

an unfordable river, with control of all the boats on its waters.

These weeks saw the turn of Lee's fortunes. In consequence of the peremptory commands which finally impelled him to a partial activity, he reluctantly crossed the Hudson. But instead of following his commander he began to scheme with Gates, the adjutant-general, like himself a former English officer, for the independent command not only of his own division, but of all the American forces as far as the Highlands, that he might, if possible, secure to himself the glory of reconquering the Jerseys. Messengers were constantly coming and going with his secret correspondence. At last, on December 12th, he led his soldiers a few miles nearer the enemy, and himself pushed onward unattended to Baskingridge, expecting the arrival at that place of an agent from Gates. It was an inglorious fall which awaited him. He was surprised by a body of English riders when alone in a farm-house writing treacherous letters, and carried captive to New York, where he was ignominiously imprisoned, and held for trial as a deserter from the English army. *Lee captured by the British.*

His supposed importance gave great weight for a time to this capture, the patriots at large being still ignorant of his character and conduct. During his captivity he repeatedly declared that he was opposed to independence, and gave his captors all the information he possessed which might be of value. On December 8th, Howe had unwisely sent into Rhode Island a small expedition to occupy the important harbor of Newport. By an exploit of the Americans in July following, which was strangely analogous to that of Lee's capture, Prescott, the English general, was taken prisoner in his head-quarters, and the British were reluctantly compelled to an exchange of these officers of equal rank. *His true character.*

So strong were the suspicions of treachery that Lee's career for the remainder of the war was overcast. He was for a time restored to command, but his disgraceful conduct at the battle of Monmouth revealed his true character.

CHAPTER XXI.

TRENTON AND PRINCETON—DECEMBER, 1776

Congress Leaves Philadelphia—The Winter Quarters of the English on the Delaware—Washington's Plan for a Surprise—The Battle of Trenton—Courage and Activity Revived—Preparations to Assume the Offensive—The English March to Trenton—Camp on the Assanpink—Washington's Flank Movement—Battle of Princeton—The Americans at Morristown—The Delaware and Hudson Safe—Plans for Reorganizing the Army—Thwarted by Localism—Timidity of the States—American Success Justified the American Revolt.

THERE were delegates in Congress as undaunted as Washington himself. Samuel Adams and a few others, supported by good news of help from Europe, even opposed the proposed migration to Baltimore. Putnam was in command at Philadelphia, and compelled the co-operation in defensive measures of all except the Quakers, who refused "in person or by other assistance to join in carrying on the war," and were excused for their conscientious scruples. But the friends of the cause were, nevertheless, hard pressed to find good grounds for their determination to stand, and the now famous but then somewhat threadbare epithet of Fabius Cunctator, which they applied to sustain the waning reputation of Washington, was too often used in irony by his enemies. Accordingly the Government abandoned Philadelphia.

Congress leaves Philadelphia.

When Congress dispersed the outlook was certainly desperate; Canada lost, New York, as far as the Highlands, New Jersey, and Long Island—which held Connecticut in check—all in undisputed British possession; the fighting regulars under Washington would, on New-year's-day, be reduced in number to fifteen hundred, even when strengthened by the reinforcement under Gates and the division of Lee, now commanded by Sullivan. The English were ranging at will on the east bank of the Delaware, coming often within a few miles of Philadelphia. They were, moreover, in full possession of the facts, and feeling their best policy to be delay, made ready for the winter in comfortable quarters at New Brunswick, Princeton, Trenton, and Bordentown. Howe returned to New York. Cornwallis was to sail for England. Grant commanded the British at New Brunswick, the Hessians at Trenton were under Rall, those at Bordentown under Count Donop. These Germans had been assured they would find their fortune in America, and they left no chance for gain untried in the plunder of the inhabitants, while they gratified their passions in scandalous license. Their name was for years a synonymn for brutality. Nevertheless the natives, believing the war a failure, surrounded the American camp as spies, and sullenly refused to commit themselves to a lost cause. Washington's lines stretched along the right bank of the Delaware from Coryell's Ferry to Bristol, and were commanded at various points by Stirling, Mercer, Stephen, Fermoy, Ewing, and Cadwalader.

The winter quarters of the English on the Delaware.

The river was swollen and full of running ice. According to the reports of English spies Washington's men had neither shoes, stockings, nor blankets, and were dying of cold and starvation. Grant informed Donop that the American general knew how weak both Princeton and Trenton were, adding that he must be on his guard against an attack, although

Washington's plan for a surprise.

it was improbable that one would be attempted. The division generals on both sides thought such a plan impracticable ; Rall and Donop virtually dismissed the thought from their minds. Gates declared that the British would build boats, make a flank movement on the American right, and take Philadelphia. Under this pretext he set out nominally to assist Putnam in his defence of that town. In reality he passed on to intrigue in Congress at Baltimore. It was therefore on his own responsibility that Washington fixed a date for the enterprise considered by others so desperate, but which he determined to try. It had to be conducted also by his own enfeebled men, for Putnam would not weaken his garrison.

On the afternoon of Christmas-day the available force, two thousand four hundred in number, set out for Mackonkey's Ferry, nine miles up the river from Trenton, where the boats were all in readiness. At twilight the boats were manned, chiefly by sailors from Marblehead, and the troops began to embark. The night was cold and clear, with bright moonlight until eleven o'clock when snow began to fall. The sky was soon overcast, and toward the end the dangerous crossing was made more horrid by utter darkness. As the march toward Trenton proceeded, sleet and rain began to fall in place of snow, so that the heavy soil of the roads was turned to sticky mud, making the advance difficult and adding further danger to the adventure. The Hessians had once been alarmed during the night, but when the city was reached and the attack commenced they were in the heavy sleep of the early morning. The general and his men were taken unawares, and roused themselves with difficulty from the effects of a holiday merriment which was probably far from innocent. The action was short and decisive. So quickly was the town

The battle of Trenton.

invested that only one hundred and sixty-two of the garrison escaped. Of the rest, seventeen were killed and nine hundred and forty-six were made prisoners, of whom seventy-eight were wounded. Among the captured stores were twelve hundred small arms and six field-pieces. There were two Americans killed, four wounded, and—awful witness to the severity of the night—two frozen to death.

Thus in a few days the whole aspect of affairs was changed. The flying, disheartened Continentals were now transformed into an enthusiastic, well-appointed, and offensive force. Good news spreads rapidly; the scattered and waiting bands in the northern part of the State began to collect at Hackensack and Morristown, while reinforcements came up from Philadelphia. Courage was restored, and Congress felt that if there were still a fighting chance in the face of so powerful a foe their treaties with foreign powers were more than paper, and their promises at home could be kept. The autocratic powers hastily given to Washington from Philadelphia were defined and renewed for six months from Baltimore. But a dictatorship without men or money was a maimed dignity. The air was full of promises—ten millions to be borrowed in France at six per cent., five millions more of Continental paper to be forced on the people—but in the meanwhile there was a desperate emergency and not a penny wherewith to meet it. In these straits the commander actually gave a pledge of his own fortune, and others, among them John Stark, of New Hampshire, followed the heroic example. But the most successful ally of Washington in this extremity was Robert Morris, who first collected among his friends five hundred dollars in coin, and a few days later, after a house-to-house inquest, was able to put fifty thousand dollars in cash at

Courage and activity revived.

the disposal of the general-in-chief, a sum more precious at that moment than ten times the money in some less urgent hour.

As quickly as possible the English and Hessian forces were collected at Princeton, until seven—some accounts say eight—thousand troops, the flower of the army, were there assembled. Cornwallis in dismay hastened from New York to take command, leaving his mails aboard the ship on which he had taken passage for London. *Preparations to assume the offensive.* Cadwalader crossed from Bristol and occupied Burlington for the Americans. The New Jersey legislature convened to promote officers and encourage enlistments, and the Eastern regiments, whose terms expired on December 31st, were induced to remain for six weeks longer. On New-year's-day, therefore, Washington was again on the left bank of the Delaware. As before, he had dauntless courage and a well-matured plan, but he was now equipped as never before. There was hope in all hearts; two thousand of his men who had seen hard fighting and privation were in a sense veterans, and the three thousand volunteers who had come in from the neighborhood and from Philadelphia, were willing and strong. Unfortunately many of his soldiers had learned the Hessian vices, and it required stringent restriction to prevent the pillage of farms, under pretext that the owners were Tories. Such was the fickleness of the populace that, after the turn of affairs, scarcely a farmer would avow any sympathy for the invading army, and many gave proof by actions of the sincere patriotism they now felt, whether it had been unbroken or intermittent.

The next day the British army, with the exception of three regiments, set out for Trenton. Their advance was checked half-way by skirmishers at Maidenhead, now Lawrenceville, where a brigade was left on guard, and for the remaining six miles they could march but slowly under the irregular but galling fire of riflemen and light artillery concealed behind fences, trees, or other ambush. It was four in the afternoon when they confronted the American rear-guard, which Washington himself commanded. The Assanpink Creek is a considerable tributary of the Delaware, and the intervening time had sufficed to throw up between the two streams and on the bank of the former a fortified camp. Into this the Continentals withdrew, slowly and in good order, with an apparent self-confidence which seemed to inform Cornwallis that they merely declined battle now to await a later and more favorable instant; this impression was strengthened by unbroken labor in the trenches, as if the morning would be the chosen hour. The Germans and English accordingly encamped for the night, and messengers were sent to call in two of the three regiments at Princeton, and the brigade from Maidenhead.

The English march to Trenton.

Camp on the Assanpink.

With the advancing night the camp-fires lighted by both sides shone clearer in the thickening gloom, those of the Americans burned with a brightness which failed to arouse suspicion. By midnight there was perfect quiet. Among Cornwallis's men it was the stillness of confident repose, in Washington's camp all were wakeful and alert. The mild weather of the preceding day had been followed by a sharp, hard frost, which changed the roads from mud to stony hummocks. In the small hours a guard was told off to continue the ruse by keeping the watch-fires clear. The entire remainder, artillery included, set silently forth by a roundabout road behind the Assanpink for an eighteen-mile march to Princeton, which they saw in the early morning on its hill-top, distant about a mile.

Washington's flank movement.

The two English regiments were only then on their way by the main road or king's highway to Trenton. One had just passed the bridge over Stony Brook when Mercer with a detachment advanced and blew it up. The English waited to reunite and then charged, driving with their bayonets the weary Americans up onto higher ground, the vantage being useless to Mercer because his men had not that weapon. On either side were two field-pieces, which being well handled kept up a constant fire. The cannonading recalled Washington, who had passed on to the south, and also informed Cornwallis, ten miles away, of the success with which his left· had been completely turned. He therefore hastened with his main column to the scene of conflict, but long before his arrival the reinforcements from the American line had turned the tide against the fearless but scattered foe. Two English regiments reformed in the town itself, but were dispersed by the fire of cannon planted and served by the townspeople. At last all three regiments were demoralized and ran, leaving two hundred dead and two hundred and thirty of their number captive. *Battle of Princeton.*

Washington in this affair showed a personal courage and carelessness of danger never afterward forgotten—it was simply a miracle that, standing as he did, not thirty yards from the ranks of the volleying foe, he escaped unhurt; the other American officers emulated his example, and many gallant gentlemen, among them Hugh Mercer, remained on the field. The losses from the ranks were slight. Cornwallis, with his habitual dilatoriness, reached one end of the village street as his triumphant enemy was leaving the other to destroy the English stores at New Brunswick. But the American troops were too battle-worn for the task, and accordingly Washington turned northward *The Americans at Morristown.*

to the high ground near Morristown, where he established his head-quarters. The English saved their stores, and seemed happy to secure even New Brunswick as an outpost. Their jubilant foe established lines from Amboy around by the south and west to Morristown: slight and flimsy as it was, the front was brave enough to accomplish the end in view.

The affair at Princeton changed the hope awakened by that of Trenton into fruition. The Jerseys were retaken; both Hudson and Delaware were safe. The total result of the first campaign by a well-equipped and numerous Anglo-German army was to hold Newport, in Rhode Island, and the city of New York, with outposts at Kingsbridge on the north and New Brunswick on the south. Elsewhere on American soil there was not an armed enemy. New England, the Middle, the Southern States were free again. The American forces were animated and encouraged, Washington's worth was at last fully appreciated by the troops, while in civil life distrust, alas! gave place to jealousy. On January 5th the New Jersey militia attacked and defeated a force of Waldeckers at Springfield, killed nine and took thirty-nine prisoners. The same day George Clinton moved over the Hudson River from Peekskill with an American detachment, and without a blow the English fled from Hackensack and abandoned Newark. Elizabethtown was also surprised by a command under Maxwell, and a hundred prisoners were taken. It seems well-nigh incredible that simultaneously with these events, during debates in Congress concerning reinforcements to the army, a spirit so small and contemptible should have arisen as to encourage the introduction of a resolution instructing Washington not only to curb the enemy but to annihilate him before he could be strengthened. The insult was actually passed by a majority of one.

In September of this year a committee of Congress had visited the American camp on the Harlem, to further confer with Washington about the organization and equipment of a respectable force fitted to carry on so important a war. They agreed, after a consultation protracted by clashing local interests, that the States should furnish eighty-three battalions of seven hundred and fifty men each, in number according to population and wealth; Massachusetts and Virginia each fifteen, Pennsylvania twelve, North Carolina nine, Connecticut eight, South Carolina six, provincial New York (the city was in English hands) and New Jersey each four, New Hampshire and Maryland each three, Rhode Island two, Delaware and Georgia each one. Every State was to enlist and equip its own troops at the cost of the general treasury, although they might offer for themselves any bounty necessary to secure the quota. All officers under the grade of lieutenant-colonel were to be local appointments; but they, like the rest, were to hold commissions from Congress, and both classes, along with the privates enlisted for the war, were to receive land bounties and pay from the confederation. *Plans for re-organizing the army.*

But the States had been so occupied with questions of their rights and sovereignty, and in the main so indifferent to the hard labor of securing their liberties, that enlistments were as slack as the public temper. *Thwarted by localism.* It was believed that many were holding back in the hope of increased bounties from State, county, or townships, as the case might be, and, contrary both to Washington's desires and the public policy, some of the States did increase their offers and thus put a premium on selfishness and calculation. In December Congress had authorized the commander-in-chief to raise a special levy which should be under his own direction: sixteen infantry battalions, three artillery regiments, three thousand light horse, and an engineer corps. For six months all promotions under the rank of brigadier were to be in his hands. In spite of all hindrances the enlistments made some advance, old officers received encouragement by promotion, and new ones were appointed. Stirling, Mifflin, St. Clair, Stephen, and Lincoln were made major-generals, though Benedict Arnold was passed by ; a number received commissions as brigadiers, but the name of Stark was omitted from the list.

For a time the English refused an equitable interchange of prisoners, claiming that their enemies were rebels. They, however, had some five thousand captives, many of whom they maltreated shamefully, and the Americans had three thousand, so that circumstances compelled an unwilling compliance by Lord Howe with the ordinary rules then in vogue for civilized war. Congress had the best will to create a navy, and a committee drew up a pompous scheme for twenty men-of-war to protect American commerce. But their plan outran their means, and it was by privateersmen that three hundred and fifty English vessels, valued with their cargoes, at about $5,000,000, were captured during the first year of the war. The pernicious work of the times was the continuous issue of paper money, not only by the representatives of the union but by the States as well. Busy with drawing up written constitutions which declared virtual independence of the union by assuming the monopoly of taxation, they yet feared, in the uncertain loyalty of so many of their inhabitants, to jeopardize their very existence by actually exercising the power of the purse.

Timidity of the States.

A dispassionate review of the year 1776 seems to justify two generalizations : first, that in spite of inconsistency, feebleness, and jealousy as to the details of finance and administration, both union and independence in some form were rendered more secure by the very vacillations of public opinion, and that in the uncertainty of military operations they might have been jeopardized by a higher hand in Congress. Second, that the matchless strategy of Washington, aided by excellent generals, could, with the more permanent army and growing confidence which another year would have supplied, have in the end overmatched any land force England was able to transport to America. If these conclusions be true, the American cause was indebted to the outside aid, which appears in the next phase of the war, not for ultimate but for speedier success than it would otherwise have attained. Posterity must express a profound and hearty gratitude for the good-will and the assistance of foreign nations and individuals, but impartial history repudiates the claim, so often made in recent years, that the United States owes its independence entirely to the intervention of strangers.

American success justified the American revolt.

CHAPTER XXII.

BENNINGTON AND THE BRANDYWINE—JANUARY-SEPTEMBER, 1777

Secret Assistance from France—Franklin in Paris—French Volunteers—Lafayette and De Kalb—Success of Franklin's Negotiations—England and the Coming Campaign—Expedition of the Howes against Philadelphia—Preliminary Movements in New Jersey—Schuyler and Gates in the North—Danbury and Sag Harbor—Burgoyne Takes Ticonderoga—Indian Barbarities—Increase of Schuyler's Force—Fort Stanwix—The Fight at Oriskany—Stark at Bennington—The English Defeated—General Howe at Elkton—Washington's Army—The Battle on the Brandywine—Loss of Philadelphia—The English at Germantown.

THE politics of the Family Compact between France and Spain had made essential the delay of a year before the former could actively participate against England in the American war. The subsidies had been given and arrangements made for supplying munitions from the government arsenals of France through concealed channels. Congress had requested Arthur Lee, a Virginian resident in London, to collect information, and early in 1776 it sent out Silas Deane as an agent. The former had become intimate with Beaumarchais, who was also in London as an irregular agent of France, and by his intermediation the first subsidy of two million livres reached America. The great comedian traded under the fictitious style of Rodrigues, Hortales & Co., and expecting payment in colonial wares, sent to the United States one hundred

Secret assistance from France.

cannon, four thousand tents, clothing for thirty thousand men, and arms of all kinds. Another alias was Durand, that by which he was known at Havre in December of the same year, while rehearsing in the town theatre his own comedies. Deane, with the best intentions, involved his country in endless difficulty, while securing also the most precious assistance. Putting the largest interpretation on his powers he entered upon the most extravagant negotiations, granted commissions of the highest rank to volunteer officers, and when finally Lee reached France the two together, aided by Beaumarchais, seriously endangered the good name of Congress by their rashness.

The secret preparations of the cabinet for war were steadily progressing, but the nation was becoming impatient. The ardent youth saw under the text of the Declaration the principles of the predominant French philosophy, and were only the more enthusiastic as they heard the news of successive American defeats. Toward the end of September Congress had commissioned Franklin and Adams to act with Lee in securing from Lewis XVI. the recognition of independence. Franklin sailed on the Reprisal, the first American national fighting-ship, and after an eventful voyage, during which several English merchantmen were captured, arrived in Paris on December 21st, just in time to avail himself of the current of popular sentiment then setting so strongly against the apparent procrastination of the authorities. He was already known by reason of his scientific research as " le grand Franklin ; " his diplomatic success soon paralleled his personal reputation, for he became immediately and literally the most popular man in France. Republican comfort and simplicity, combined with benevolence and intellect, as exemplified in the quiet house at Passy where he lived, became a fashionable rage. Vergennes at once received the commissioners, but in secret, and granted a new subsidy of two million francs, payable quarterly.

Among other volunteers, the Duke Charles-Francis de Broglie presented to Deane's notice, on November 5th, the Baron de Kalb, who though a Prussian by birth had long been in the French service, having fought at Rossbach and Bergen and acted as agent for Choiseul in a voyage of inquiry to America in 1769. Next day De Kalb appeared at Deane's house with three friends—the young Lafayette, his brother-in-law, and his cousin—who had secretly banded to enlist themselves and their fortunes for America. The two latter fell away before the discouragements of their noble friends, De Kalb and Lafayette persisted and entered into a definite engagement in February, 1777.

French volunteers.

It was at the charge of the latter that the secret expedition which bore them to America was fitted out. Both were unknown to Congress, and their reception was clouded by the remembrance of recent annoyances from Deane's impossible promises to indifferent adventurers. But Lafayette soon won the confidence he deserved, and became a member of the general staff. His name was destined to shine in American history with a lustre greater even than that which attaches either to the devoted Poles, Kosciusko and Pulaski, both of whom were passionate in their love of freedom and lavish of their precious services, or to the calm, judicious Steuben, who in the hour of despair pointed the way to a restoration of hope and strength. De Kalb was at first the agent of De Broglie in his chimerical scheme to supplant Washington and become a William of Orange for the United States. Later he abandoned any hope of success, but to the last the American officers distrusted him. His correspondence was so large and

Lafayette and De Kalb.

continuous that they felt it must have some secret end.

Three other vessels put to sea with stores, and two of them arrived safely; the third was captured, for by this time England was roused and scoured the seas with her cruisers. But American trading vessels were protected in French ports, as far as the French policy of delay would permit, and privateers were also permitted to refit. Franklin and his fellow-commissioners began their labor of negotiation immediately, and while the tripartite diplomacy of France, Spain, and the United States seemed to move slowly, yet it appeared certain that war with England would be declared by the two continental powers not later than 1778. Thirteen years had elapsed since the humiliating treaty of 1763, and, if they were to secure their revenge, longer postponement was impossible. *Success of Franklin's negotiations.*

English preparations for the next campaign were quite as active; nearly four thousand new troops were bought in Germany, and three thousand men were enlisted from the Tories and recent immigrants in America. Savage bands were organized for work on the frontier, particularly to the north. Parliament suspended the writ of habeas corpus as to prisoners taken on the high seas, impressed American seamen, and commissioned privateers. The nation seemed to have returned to the Toryism of James II., and endured the heavy taxes laid by the ministry for the conduct of the war without a murmur. Burke sought authority to negotiate with Franklin for conciliation; Chatham, foreseeing the French alliance, demanded unconditional redress of American grievances. Parliament would listen to neither. Howe had asked for fifteen thousand men to end the war the coming summer; Lord George Germain refused, and sent the reinforcements to *England and the coming campaign.*

Carleton, that Burgoyne and he might have better success with an expedition from the north than the Howes had had in the previous year at Boston and New York.

The indignant brothers recalled the troops from Newport, in Rhode Island, determined to combine their sea and land forces, evacuate New Jersey, and proceed by sea against Philadelphia, whither Congress had returned in March, 1777. They opened the campaign in June by a feint, massing all their force of seventeen thousand men at New Brunswick as if about to cut off Sullivan's division at Princeton and set out once more across the Delaware. Sir Henry Clinton was to remain in New York and hold the attention of Washington until the two moves were made by Burgoyne and Howe.

<small>Expedition of the Howes against Philadelphia.</small>

Washington's effective force in March was three thousand strong. The enlistments had been so slow that the average number in the battalions was two hundred and fifty, instead of seven hundred and fifty. In Massachusetts and elsewhere resort was had to a forced levy which included many negroes, and before the campaign opened he had four thousand more—raw troops for the most part. The army was divided into forty-three regiments, ten brigades, five divisions. With this force he moved from Morristown to Middlebrook, nine miles from New Brunswick. Howe vainly strove to turn his left, or bring him to battle on the lowlands, and on July 5th embarked for Philadelphia. Putnam was appointed to defend the Highland posts, where it was not only possible but probable that the English forces of Burgoyne and Howe would seek to join, and thus at last secure the Hudson. He was to have eight of the fifteen Massachusetts battalions.

<small>Preliminary movements in New Jersey.</small>

The department of the North, comprising Stanwix, Ticonderoga, and Albany, had so far remained under the command of Schuyler, who for various reasons felt himself justified in a severe arraignment of Congress. In April, Gates, who knew how to win the favor of the legislators, was sent to replace him. After a thorough examination of the circumstances, Congress, by a majority of one, reinstated Schuyler for his splendid services to the cause. Good work had been done in the interval. Ticonderoga was reinforced by militia and new levies from Massachusetts. The two men were left, however, in an indefinite relation to each other, which bred a serious quarrel, and thus fermented at last a peevish local jealousy between democratic New England and aristocratic New York. After the necessary evacuation of Ticonderoga and the withdrawal of the forces under Schuyler to Fort Edward, the public was a second time moved to unjustifiable censure of his conduct, and on August 1st he was formally superseded by the arch-schemer, Horatio Gates.

<small>Schuyler and Gates in the North.</small>

While these precautions were carefully taken, two minor successes gave a cheerful opening to the year. Tryon had debarked two thousand of his Long Island royalists at Danbury, in Connecticut, and destroyed the American stores collected there. Arnold avenged the loss by a successful attack in which the English lost two hundred men. Still further reparation was obtained in May by the feat of Colonel Meigs, who destroyed at Sag Harbor, on Long Island, a large magazine of English supplies, took ninety prisoners, and burned eleven ships. The latter officer received a sword from Congress in recognition of his daring, and the former was at last rewarded by the tardy honor of promotion to the rank of major-general.

<small>Danbury and Sag Harbor.</small>

Burgoyne reached Canada early in May, and in virtue

of his commission assumed the chief command. By the middle of June his force was fully equipped and the march began. Conferences were held on the way with the Indians, and proclamations compounded of threats and exhortations were issued to the Americans. On the first of July he reached Ticonderoga, and by the erection of a battery at Fort Defiance, on the neighboring hill, dislodged St. Clair and the garrison of some three thousand men, destroying all the boats and stores. To secure his communications he left in the famous fort a body of troops so large that it weakened his invading army unnecessarily. The Americans wisely withdrew from one post to another, until a stand could reasonably be made south of the wilderness, with the help of the militia which Schuyler was gathering in from the immediate neighborhood and the other reinforcements which were sent mainly by New England for Lincoln's command, and by George Clinton, now governor of the State. Some of these, Morgan's band of five hundred rangers, for instance, were even sent by Washington.

Burgoyne takes Ticonderoga.

The Indian allies of Burgoyne gave free play to their native brutality, murdered the helpless, and committed nameless barbarities. Outrages like that which made the innocent and trustful Jane McCrea, who, though affianced to a lieutenant in the English army, was the sister of an Albany Whig, the heroine of tradition, were of far-reaching consequence in rousing the surrounding farmers to action, and feeding the fires of patriotism. Burgoyne's own feelings of humanity were outraged, but he dared not punish the assassin. When, however, he enjoined his allies from gratifying their savage instincts they lost heart and fell away from him in numbers.

Indian barbarities.

There could have been no finer strategy than Schuyler's. The English army, encumbered with great baggage-trains, was three weeks in traversing the wild, tangled, and nearly trackless forest between Skenesborough and the Hudson. Every day weakened its force, while that of the Americans was hourly strengthened by the arrival of new men and the growth of an irresistible enthusiasm. In fact it was the very size of Schuyler's hitherto retreating and idle army which led to invidious comparisons with the scanty numbers on which the people relied for the defence of the rich country south of New York and of the seat of government. But Washington showed his disdain of the public jealousy by sending both Arnold and Lincoln to comfort Schuyler and help him in the coming crisis. [Increase of Schuyler's force.]

To insure Burgoyne's success beyond a peradventure an auxiliary expedition, which had been for some time under consideration, was at length organized under the leadership of St. Leger, and despatched according to Germain's orders. It was to proceed by way of Lake Ontario, Oswego, and the Mohawk valley, to strike the Americans on their flank and rear. On the divide between the water-sheds of the Mohawk and the Great Lakes stood Fort Stanwix, a small frontier post held by seven hundred Americans under Colonel Gansevoort. As the enemy in superior numbers approached, the danger became so imminent and manifest that the militia of Tryon County, German settlers for the most part, were summoned, and under the command of a gallant old man, General Herkimer, they set out to relieve and reinforce the garrison. The British expedition was composed in large part of Indians, under Johnson and Brant. St. Leger arrived on August 3d, and beleaguered the fort before the militia could come in. An ambuscade of savages was then laid to surprise Herkimer. [Fort Stanwix.]

On the sixth, at Oriskany, within a short march of Stanwix, the Americans fell into the snare. A terrific slaughter, lasting an hour and a half, ensued, as the Indians fell on both flanks from their lurking-places in the forest, and the white men stopped the advance. Herkimer was severely wounded, but supported against a tree in a sitting posture calmly encouraged his men until the end. A sally from the fort was made, but without results. The total loss on both sides has been computed at nearly four hundred. The victory remained to the Indians. St. Leger was, however, so weakened that he could not even attempt to carry the place by assault. Meantime two messengers had reached Schuyler. Arnold with a relief corps was promptly despatched to repel the besiegers. By an industrious use of emissaries, exaggerated rumors were disseminated in St. Leger's camp and the dimensions of the coming army so magnified that the Indians, overwhelmed with panic, seized from their allies what plunder they could snatch and fled. The few English, Hessians, and Canadians which composed the remnant of the expedition, began their retreat on August 22d. Dismayed and aghast at the unreliability of the Indians the panic spread and soon converted their movements into a flight.

The fight at Oriskany.

To give St. Leger every chance, Burgoyne himself had planned a diversion against Bennington, on his other wing, where there was supposed to be an American depot. Near by the redoubtable Stark was in command of a few hundred militia-men from the Hampshire grants. When news of the intended attack was received, active preparations to strengthen his force began immediately. Warner, of Vermont, brought the strongest reinforcement, but the first to come was a militia regiment from Berkshire, Massachusetts, under

Stark at Bennington.

the fighting parson, Allen, who reminded Stark that Berkshire men, though summoned before, never had yet been given a chance for glory, and would not come again if disappointed now. This remark and Stark's first declaration next morning, "Ours before night, or Molly Stark's a widow," foreshadowed a hand-to-hand and desperate conflict. The British force at first detailed by Burgoyne was composed of Hessians, loyalists, and Indians, some seven hundred in all, and was commanded by Baum. But to insure success Breyman, with nearly as many Brunswick yagers was despatched the next day.

On August 16th the battle was joined. The ensuing struggle was one of the most stubborn in the war. Here again the Indians proved utterly unreliable, and exclaiming that the woods were full of Yankees, fled almost at the first onset. Baum was killed, and his white troops surrendered. Breyman arrived soon afterward and fought bravely for a time, but he too was routed. On the English side only sixty were killed, but nearly seven hundred men and four cannon were captured, Baum's force being simply annihilated. The Americans lost forty wounded and thirty killed. The battle of Bennington has been justly regarded as a decisive engagement. It left Burgoyne with both flanks exposed, demoralized his centre, caused large numbers of Indians and Canadians to fly in hopeless terror to their homes, and gave additional moral strength to Washington, who heard the news while awaiting near Wilmington, Delaware, the arrival of the Howes. The northern army had secured a strategic advantage, and was strong in both numbers and courage when Gates arrived to supersede Schuyler on August 19th.

The English defeated.

It was a fleet of three hundred ships in which the English had sailed from New York for Philadelphia. Howe had been baffled in his attempt to cross New Jersey the previous year, the sea-voyage was scarcely more successful; for when he arrived off the capes of the Delaware it was found that obstructions had been so placed as to make the ascent of that river impracticable. Accordingly he determined to go further south, sail up Chesapeake Bay, and march from Elkton at its head across to Philadelphia, a distance of fifty-four miles! The long voyage brought him scarcely nearer his goal than he had been at Perth Amboy. The English were thirty-three days on shipboard, and when they landed, their force of some seventeen thousand men found themselves once more confronted by Washington, who had interposed his army between them and their goal.

<small>General Howe at Elkton.</small>

The American commander had been vainly struggling to secure a national army. State feeling had grown steadily more unreasonable and violent, the dangers to liberty of a standing army being constantly displayed as a bugbear against a definite policy and concerted action. Congress, moreover, had but little opportunity for legitimate work, however urgent, for their time was monopolized in the wrangles of office-seekers, both native and foreign. A call was issued, however, for the militia of Maryland, Delaware, Pennsylvania, and New Jersey. The Jersey men were already occupied in the Highlands; none of them and but few of the others obeyed the summons. In the total of between fourteen and fifteen thousand under his command there was but a small body of reliable veteran troops. In point of numbers also, there was, of course, marked superiority on the English side.

<small>Washington's army.</small>

The opposing armies meet on September 10th, at Chad's Ford of the Brandywine Creek, which flows into the Delaware near Wilmington. There was very little organized action on either side, and the engagement was

BENNINGTON AND THE BRANDYWINE 273

a series of distinct conflicts. Knyphausen engaged Washington in the centre, while Cornwallis ascending the stream easily routed the right wing under Sullivan. Great gallantry was displayed on both sides; many of the French officers, among them Lafayette, fought with spirit and daring, while Pulaski, the Pole, displayed the qualities which have made his name renowned. The American loss in killed, wounded, and prisoners was upward of a thousand; that of the English about six hundred, not inconsiderable as Sir William Howe said in generously emphasizing the bravery of the Americans. But the victory was with the English and decided the fate of Philadelphia. *The battle on the Brandywine.*

Washington drew off his shattered army in tolerable order, and as the English were detained in the transfer of their wounded to Wilmington, took a position near Germantown, carefully guarding the approaches to prevent his being shut in between the Delaware and the Schuylkill. Congress fled first to Lancaster, and later to York. On the sixteenth the two armies were within striking distance, but a storm intervened and the Americans withdrew behind the Schuylkill. Wayne was left to turn the English, if possible; but on the twentieth he was betrayed by a Tory, overpowered by a force of regulars under Grey, and the city was open to the conquerors. *Loss of Philadelphia.*

But Washington, though defeated, was still a dangerous foe and near at hand. He had reinforcements from Putnam and Smallwood of Maryland, in addition to Wayne's detachment, which had rejoined the army. Howe moved down the west side of the Schuylkill, but finding the Swedes' Ford entrenched he turned and crossed higher up, reaching Germantown on the twenty-fifth, where he encamped with his line at right angles to the long village street, *The English at Germantown.*

18

about the middle. Washington withdrew to Metuchen Hills, some miles distant. On the twenty-sixth Cornwallis with three thousand men occupied Philadelphia. All the patriots had fled, and of the five thousand inhabitants or less who remained, even the Quakers and loyalists gave little evidence of pleasure. Moreover, there was no communication between the army and the fleet, for the Americans still held the forts, named respectively Mifflin and Mercer, which commanded the confluence of the Schuylkill and Delaware below the city.

CHAPTER XXIII.

SARATOGA AND THE FRENCH ALLIANCE—SEPTEMBER-DECEMBER, 1777

The Army of the North—Its Position near Stillwater—The First Day's Battle at Bemis's Heights—The English Pass the Highlands—The Battle of Freeman's Farm—Retreat of Burgoyne—Surrender at Saratoga—The Battle of Germantown—Affairs near Philadelphia—Summary of the Year's Campaign—Congress and the Cabal—Continental Money and Valley Forge—Prosperity of the People—Success of the State Governments—Weakness of the Confederation—The Public Finances—The News of Saratoga in France—The Compact of Friendship.

THE army of which Gates took command was the most efficient so far organized by the Americans. It was somewhat larger than that of Burgoyne, and through the generosity of France supplementing the grants of New York, was well equipped. *The army of the North.* On the right bank of the Hudson, north of the Mohawk, were about ten thousand men, including the militia from the neighborhood. Some of them, like Morgan's rangers and the New York regulars, were tried and veteran. Among the leaders were Livingston and Peter Van Cortlandt. The right wing across the river was composed of New England militia, resplendent with the success at Bennington, and commanded by Lincoln, who had not only the affection of his men, but could ever arouse in them an intense and patriotic enthusiasm. Arnold was returning on the left with the laurels of Stanwix, eager for glory and consumed with ambition. Schuyler received Gates politely, and with admirable self-control gave all the information at his command for the use of a rival who had schemed for his humiliation. But being treated with discourtesy he withdrew to his home, leaving his successor to reap where he had sowed.

On the eighth of September the advance began, and on the twelfth the Americans were encamped near the village of Stillwater, on Bemis's Heights, a line of hills perpendicular to the course of the Hudson and reaching eastward almost to its banks. Gates commanded the right near the river, Arnold the left at Freeman's farm. Burgoyne's advance through the wilderness had been unaccountably slow ; both his Canadian and Indian allies had shown themselves untrustworthy, and, worse than all, Ticonderoga, with a garrison of two hundred and ninety-three regulars, its arms and stores, had been recaptured by a party of American light horse which also burnt the flotilla of boats. Retreat was thus entirely cut off, and a somewhat disheartened force of about six thousand men advanced with lagging steps toward the well-chosen position of their opponents.

Its position near Stillwater.

Finally, on the nineteenth, Burgoyne attacked in three columns, his centre charging up a ravine to turn the American left, which consisted of three thousand troops, largely the farmer militia. Arnold's chance had come and the battle raged literally with fury, hot and direct, with little or no attempt at tactics or manœuvre, until nightfall, some three hours or more. It was utterly indecisive and victory was won by neither side. The American loss was three hundred and twenty, while that of the English was over six hundred. The latter, however, held the lower slope, which had been lost and won a dozen times in the surging charges of the day, but their advance was

The first day's battle at Bemis's Heights.

checked, and that in a conflict of regulars with militia. The unstinted use of Canadian bushrangers and Indians to harass the Americans failed entirely, and the regular forces were not even entrenched in the new position they had won. Arnold naturally felt that the day was his, and would have continued the conflict next morning while the enemy were weak. But Gates asserted his technical authority against Arnold's moral right, and refused. The latter, fretted by a delay which extended not to hours but to days, and in the self-importance of sensitive pride, hastily and rashly resigned.

On the twenty-first a message from Sir Henry Clinton in New York reached Burgoyne's camp at Freeman's farm. A diversion was to be made against the militia force under Putnam, which Washington had set to watch the Highlands. How long could the invaders from the north hold out? The answer, taking careful account of stores and the endurance of the troops, was, until October 12th. Meantime Putnam was drawn off behind the Peekskill hills by a feint, and two thousand English and Germans were landed to storm Fort Clinton. But George Clinton, now governor, had foreseen the scheme, and thrown himself with a few hastily gathered men into the works, while his brother James was sent to Fort Montgomery for its defence. There was therefore a gallant resistance on the west shore, but the battle of Stony Point was a defeat for the Americans, and both posts were stormed on the same day, October 6th. The Continental vessels sent to guard the great iron chain and boom stretching from Fort Montgomery to the mountain known as Anthony's Nose proved inefficient, and the obstacles were captured. The coveted water-way was thus opened to Albany, and the English scouts plundered

The English pass the Highlands.

the mansion-houses with which the river was even then lined, as far north as Kingston.

But the success was worthless, for Burgoyne's calculation had been illusive. He had taken advantage of Gates's supineness to entrench himself at Freeman's farm, but forage and supplies were cut off by American scouts on every side. The Tories, Canadians, and Indians, who had served thus far as auxiliaries, became more disheartened as the patriots of the surrounding country grew more bold, and deserted in ever-increasing numbers. On the other hand, the American forces were ever growing by the accession of volunteer farmers, for the harvest was now past. Lincoln also came across with two thousand militia and took command of the right wing. The situation of the English was becoming desperate, and on October 7th, Burgoyne threw out a reconnoisance of fifteen hundred men in line of battle to test the American strength, and at the same time to cover a foraging party. His artillery, well served and efficient, was posted about half a mile from the American camp. Gates sent a detachment to thwart the movement. The English left and right were easily turned, but the Germans in the centre fought bravely, and Arnold, though without a command, impetuously put himself at the head of his old forces, and with conspicuous valor led the assault. The courage of the English was splendid, but the Americans came in on their rear, captured the artillery, and compelled them to withdraw into their entrenchments. Even then Burgoyne was so exposed that, but for the failing light at nightfall, his camp might have been captured.

This second action at Bemis's Heights, though Gates again was not in the field, was the decisive battle of the campaign. The Americans lost fifty killed and a hundred and fifty wounded, among the latter was Arnold.

The battle of Freeman's farm.

But the total English loss in killed, wounded, and prisoners was six hundred and twenty-five. Their entrenchments, moreover, were so weak that the same night, the seventh, they began to retreat. On the tenth they were in position beyond the Fishkill, a tributary of the Hudson near Saratoga. The horrors of the march are better known from the memoirs of Riedesel than almost any scene of the war. The rain fell in torrents; sick, wounded, and baggage were left behind, a scant three days' provision remained, and it was a forlorn and dispirited army which hastily entrenched itself at Saratoga. Their case was even worse than they knew, for Stark, with fresh militia from New Hampshire, and several other American detachments were closing in on the rear, while Gates was content to spend two idle days in the abandoned camp of his enemy. *Retreat of Burgoyne.*

Negotiations were opened by Burgoyne on the fourteenth. A convention between the two commanders was finally completed. Its terms were absurdly lenient, for the English were at the mercy of a superior force; but Gates is said to have been informed of the events at Stony Point, although Burgoyne remained in ignorance until the sixteenth, the very day when, under the new banner of the stars and stripes, the formalities of surrender were accomplished. This was the end of the season's campaign for the possession of the Hudson. From May to September the English had lost in killed, disabled, and captives, nearly ten thousand men, among whom were personages of the highest distinction. The river, except at its mouth, was in virtual possession of the Americans, although the victorious army melted away as rapidly as it had gathered. The militia returned to their homes and vocations; the little nucleus of enlisted Continentals was all that remained to recall its existence. *Surrender at Saratoga.*

It does not appear that Washington ever intended to leave Philadelphia in English hands without another blow. He had to remove the serious hindrance to action caused by the conduct of the rump Congress sitting at Lancaster and York through a skilful use of the ever better news from the north, explaining to his soldiers that he too might lead them to victory because of Howe's supineness and incapacity to command. The army moved from its position at Metuchen Hills in the evening of October 3d, and reached Chestnut Hills in the early morning of the fourth. A dense mist enveloped the whole country, concealing its movement from the English, who were still encamped across the street of Germantown. Washington knew that they were weakened by detachments sent to convey provision trains from Chester, and hoped by a successful surprise to throw the diminished, but still superior, force of his enemy into panic. At early dawn the division under Sullivan attacked, and for a time success seemed assured, for the English were momentarily dismayed. But Greene's column, the main force destined to turn the enemy's left, had been misled in the darkness and arrived in breathless disorder to meet troops which had regained their confidence and were drawn up in strong formation. The day was really lost by nine in the morning, but the retreat of the Americans was bravely and successfully covered by Wayne. The defeat was serious in the loss by Sullivan and Greene of more than a thousand men, while the British casualties were but half the number.

The battle of Germantown.

The first news to reach Washington on his retreat was that of Stony Point, but soon came the inspiring accounts of Saratoga. New regiments came in and he was able to resume for a time his menacing position before Germantown. The country at large felt the encourage-

SARATOGA AND THE FRENCH ALLIANCE 281

ment not alone of victory on the Hudson, but of the vigor which neutralized the defeat on the Brandywine by the speedily renewed attack on the Schuyl- Affairs near kill, and the overthrow at Germantown by so Philadelphia. prompt a renewal of ability to continue fighting. Such, in fact, was the respect felt by the British for American arms, that Howe withdrew to Philadelphia and began operations to remove the obstructions between the city and the fleet below. Donop and his Hessians first strove to storm the works at Red Bank, commanded by Christopher Greene, but they were repulsed. The Americans fought with courage and skill unsurpassed in the war. The ships sent up from the English fleet ran aground and were fired by a cannonade from galleys and floating batteries. There were many minor movements, however, in the neighborhood, resulting in conflicts favorable on the whole to the British. In one of them Lafayette distinguished himself against the Hessians.

It was November before, at last, the longed-for communication was established. Howe was so disheartened by the stubbornness of a resistance which robbed him of the fruits of victory, that he the year's asked leave to resign, and filling the air with campaign. complaints of Germain, declared that without great reinforcements not even another campaign would end the war. He might well feel as he did, for while the English spent the winter in riotous gayety in Philadelphia, losing all benefits from its capture, the Americans beset every approach, and the close of the year 1777 found the entire country, excepting only Long Island, Staten Island, and the three cities of Philadelphia, New York, and Newport, again in the possession of its defenders. Washington and his army went into winter quarters at Valley Forge. It is useless to speculate concerning undeveloped possibilities ; but the events of the war down to the French alliance and the declaration of war by the French administration, did not portend defeat to the Americans even if unassisted. Such was the condition of English politics that, inadequate as her efforts now seem in the light of her subsequent greatness, they were in that day and in the temper of her people, the utmost she could possibly exert. The real strength of the American people had, on the other hand, not yet appeared; what most strikes us in our present cohesion and power is the sorry tale of those public weaknesses and that disorganization which were both, in large measure, due to the possibility of attaining the end through European complications, by foreign aid and without serious self-sacrifice.

It has been justly remarked that the Continental money and the Continental Congress were together at their lowest in Lancaster and York. The really great and strong delegates were for the most part absent. Franklin, John Adams, Jefferson, John Rutledge, and Jay, were either in Europe on diplomatic missions or doing necessary work in States where public opinion needed strength and guidance. Of all the rest there were sometimes present but nine members, rarely more than seventeen. There was much talk of how unfavorably Washington's failures contrasted with Gates's successes. The enemies of the commander-in-chief were not only heard and harbored, but during the winter was formed an infamous cabal to destroy his influence. Its members were Gates, Lee, Mifflin, and Conway. Their scheme was to despatch a midwinter expedition to capture Canada and win Lafayette to their side by offering him the independent command. For a time their machinations seemed to prosper, for they had the sympathy of many individual delegates in their jealousy of Washington. Even Samuel Adams and Richard Henry

Congress and the cabal.

Lee thought him lacking in energy, and charged him with favoritism in his appointments.

Meantime the proper work of Congress was neglected. Their credit was destroyed in part by the reverses of the army, but mainly by their tentative and feeble tone in dealing with the States, and their failure to assert and exercise the right of taxation. Many of the States had, in their early zeal, exceeded their requisitions both of men and money, and now began a thrifty retrenchment; Continental paper, with nothing behind it but a timid Congress with uncertain powers, was not worth half its face value. For a time, therefore, there was lacking both the will and the way even to support, much less strengthen, the army. The rigors of that winter were excessive; the soldiers at Valley Forge had neither food nor clothing nor fuel, and the fortitude of Washington, his officers, and his men in the endurance of want, misery, and even starvation, is on one hand the evidence of their greatness, on the other a stigma on the good name of the confederation.

<small>Continental money and Valley Forge.</small>

For the country was prosperous, and that in a sense not ordinarily connected with the notion of war. The masterly strategy and tactics of Washington had snatched moral victory from the jaws of actual defeat, and confined the theatre of operations to a comparatively small territory. Throughout the South the rich crops of that favored climate had year by year been safely gathered; in Pennsylvania and New England the harvests were abundant. For three years past the population of the country was not only increasing, but pioneers were steadily winning new empires in the valleys of the Ohio and its tributaries. The commerce of Massachusetts was restored to its former dimensions and activity, bidding defiance to the repressive measures taken by England, while at the same time five hundred

<small>Prosperity of the people.</small>

and fifty British ships, valued at twelve millions of dollars, had been captured.

In addition to this, the new State governments were working well. While in themselves and as now constituted they were revolutionary, they nevertheless inherited an administrative system adapted to the wants and traditions of the people, moulded in the main on the immemorial customs of Englishmen on both sides of the sea, but now adapted in important particulars to the circumstances of American independence. Congress at the outset was an extra-legal body, created and sustained by popular Continental opinion. These governments were its children, dependent for any sovereignty they might ever acquire on the success of a rebellion formerly proclaimed, organized, and sustained by Congress. In the event of success the traditions of the individual colonies and the habitual obedience of their respective populations to the common law, moulded and interpreted by the statutory enactment of each legislature, would, of course, secure a partial internal sovereignty; but they never had, and by reason of the necessity for confederation to conduct foreign affairs and support the army, never could have an independent external sovereignty, however low might be the terms in which they were willing to express national existence and union.

Success of the State governments.

The nice distinctions of logic often disappear in the alarums of war and the tumult of revolution, sometimes waiting long to take an awful revenge for their disregard. Congress had neglected its opportunity to exercise the power of the purse, and such was the obstinacy of Delaware and Maryland that the flimsy confederacy existed only in fact and not *de jure*. The cry of 1688 had been Liberty and Property, and the heart of the American people, full of zeal

Weakness of the confederation.

for the lessons of that epoch, was naturally also where its treasure was. From behind the barred doors of a wrangling and divided Congress came no appeal directly to their ears, and as time went on their patriotic energies and affections centred in the State legislatures, which first mirrored popular opinion by treating Congress as a convenient intermediary for the conduct of the war, and in turn reflected the congressional temper by avoiding taxation through the issue of paper money. The reflex action upon Congress was disastrous, and the resources of the nation were never completely shown for lack of prompt and direct action in its administrative machinery.

At the opening of 1778 there was in circulation a paper currency with a face value of about sixty millions, thirty-four of these Continental and growing worthless, partly because of the ever vaguer powers of Congress, and partly because of the better security behind the twenty-five millions issued in various sums by the individual States in imitation of, but in direct rivalry with, the others. There was a further debt of about five millions contracted by Congress, and so low had the national credit sunk that even Americans accepted the paper with reluctance at half its par value. The real support of the army thus far had come from requisitions on the States, which had steadily furnished provisions, equipments, and men, according to the formal terms of confederation, whether ratified or not. And the army, with its commander-in-chief, was now almost the only expression of union, even though removed from the people by the intermediaries of their separate legislatures and Congress. The troops had suffered a serious mortality, not on the field of battle as much as in the slower but equally sure processes of sickness induced by the various degrees of nakedness, starvation, and general

The public finances.

privation which were entailed by the absence of an efficient commissary department. And now requisitions were uncertain, because some States were beginning to husband their resources for a long struggle, while Congress was cherishing illusory hopes of immediate, or at least speedy, peace, as a result of the coming French alliance.

Throughout the year now drawing to its close Franklin had been steadily and successfully moulding French opinion to the support of the American cause. Vergennes was on one side striving to convince Charles III. and the Spanish court that the hour had come to strike a blow in concert against their mutual rivals by the open support of her revolted colonies, while on the other excusing the delay of France to her people and to the American commissioners by the plea of existing treaties and a general unreadiness. At last, in the early winter, it became evident that Spain would not move, such was the stolid repugnance of both Charles and his minister, Florida Blanca, to support a successful rebellion. The news of Saratoga aroused the French nation to an impatient enthusiasm, and even the careful and unimpassioned minister himself believed that Howe would be defeated and surrender, thus virtually closing the war before France could share in the benefits of victory.

The news of Saratoga in France.

Two days after the arrival of a courier announcing Burgoyne's surrender, the formal negotiations for open alliance were begun. On December 17th, a week later, Franklin was informed that the king, moved by the interests of France and sympathy for the American cause, was ready to recognize the independence of the United States. He was immediately to furnish three million livres, and Spain had promised a like sum. The treaty was not, however, completed and

The compact of friendship.

signed until February 6th, 1778, Vergennes having been notified two days before of Spain's final and definite refusal to become a party. According to its terms there was an immediate compact of friendship, to be made public, and an eventual treaty of alliance, to be kept secret for the present. By the former was assured a complete commercial reciprocity between the two countries, and the United States might grant like conditions, if they so desired, to other favored nations. The treaty of alliance was to come into force only in the event of a declaration by England of war against France. By it the king guaranteed independence to the United States with sovereignty and whatever territory they held at the end of the war. The latter guaranteed to France her possessions in America. Neither of the contracting parties was to conclude a peace without the assent of the other. The following month England recalled her ambassador, which was an informal declaration of war. Actual hostilities began three months later. The following year Spain permitted the interest of the Bourbon compact to outweigh her distaste for American freedom and joined France in the alliance.

CHAPTER XXIV.

RECOGNITION OF AMERICAN INDEPENDENCE—JANUARY-JULY, 1778

National Sentiment in England—The Rockingham Whigs—British Supremacy Endangered—Conciliation as a Political Expedient—Proposal to Yield Independence—Public Reception of Franklin at the French Court—Congress Ratifies the Treaty—Collapse of the Cabal—Reorganization of the Army—Conciliation Offered—Failure of the Mission—The English Abandon Philadelphia—Their March Impeded—The Battle of Monmouth—Incidents of the Fight—The Massacre of Wyoming.

National sentiment in England. THE news of Burgoyne's surrender had produced a positive and immediate effect in England. The king's friends and the mass of the people aroused themselves for a more effective resistance, and the enlistment of Englishmen became for the moment so much less difficult that various cities were able to raise each a regiment and to put additional native forces at the disposal of the Government. The previous year but four thousand men could be raised, now there were as many from Glasgow, Edinburgh, Manchester, and Liverpool alone, and besides there were others from the Highlands and from various English shires. The American Tories had proved a sorry resource, less than twelve hundred having been enrolled by Tryon and Delancey, while the untrustworthiness of Indians had been conclusively proven in the northern campaign. Moreover, the attention of the world had been finally drawn to the infamy of the traffic in German troops, as the meanness and greed of the sellers were revealed in their manipulation of the market. Mirabeau finally began an agitation so spirited that the Landgrave of Hesse felt it necessary to make a reply. It was needful, therefore, for the continuance of the struggle that a truly national sentiment should be aroused, and Saratoga had that effect.

The Rockingham Whigs had lost their hold in politics largely because of their open sympathy with the Americans, believing as they did that the cause of liberty in England was identified with the success of their struggle. Fox and Burke, Richmond and Chatham, wielded the weapons of rhetoric, sarcasm, and downright attack as they have seldom been used in Parliament. Subscriptions for the ill-treated Americans held by the English as prisoners of war were opened and numerously signed. The liberals in general felt that Burgoyne's defeat should mean their triumph. In spite of the national uprising they would probably have won in the end, for North, and with him many who were not Whigs, was convinced of the necessity for peace. *The Rockingham Whigs.*

But the French alliance determined the complete separation of America from England. As yet the contract of friendship and commerce was the only part known. George III., firm in his purpose to reduce the colonies at any cost of men and money, stifled for a time the convictions of his devoted and too complacent minister by appeals to personal devotion and a sense of honor, dreaming still of an alliance with Catherine II., who cared nothing for western affairs and was reserving all her force to found a Christian empire on the Bosporus. The news of the French attitude suddenly and completely changed the aspect of English politics. A general European war was not only possible but actually looming on the horizon. The Whigs saw *British supremacy endangered.*

their opportunity, for the old alliance of England with the Protestant powers of Germany against the Bourbons could alone secure her against the loss of the position she had so proudly asserted in the Seven Years' War. Chatham had already explained again and again that the united colonies could never be conquered, had inveighed against the use of "the horrible hell-hounds of savage war," and in one splendid burst had declared, "If I were an American, as I am an Englishman, while a foreign troop was landed in my country I never would lay down my arms: never, never, never." He had long contemplated a change of ministry and the conciliation of America, now the rupture of diplomatic relations and probable war with France might secure both and restore the union of the English empire. The national sentiment against America was infinitely weaker than the immemorial and traditional hatred of the Bourbons. Conciliation forthwith became the national policy, and no ministry could withstand the demand for it.

It was therefore as a political expedient and from no sense of justice that the king permitted North to follow at last what he declared had always been his convictions, and pass through Parliament a series of conciliatory bills granting everything which the States had at first demanded, abolishing the tax on tea, and repealing the bill for governing Massachusetts. Plenipotentiaries were to be sent for the conduct of negotiations. When in April these steps were completed, North, feeling perhaps the inconsistencies of his career, would have gladly made way for the Whigs, who were clearly entitled to carry out their own policy. But George III. would listen to no such proposition, and the heterogeneous ministry was continued in power by the support of the crown and by a majority of members representing no principle except parliamentary

Conciliation as a political expedient.

supremacy, which they had virtually confessed to be a tyranny when applied to unrepresented people. The very principle which had established English liberties must undermine those of America when, as now, the crown was able to create a parliamentary majority by patronage, and by political chicane use it as a tool.

Languor, doubt, and irresolution were shown to such an extent in the execution of the conciliatory measures that if the king and cabinet had intended to thwart the popular will they could not well have acted otherwise than they did. Their language, unlike that of the bills, was harsh and often opprobrious, while the choice of members for the diplomatic commission was little less than an insult. The second portion of the treaty between America and France could not, of course, be long concealed. Rockingham would have broken the alliance by conceding independence, but Chatham made his last and most sadly dramatic appearance in Parliament, on April 7th, to denounce it and to rouse his country to the horrors of dismemberment. He died the next month, and George was finally emancipated from the restraint he always felt under the eye of his greatest subject. *Proposal to yield Independence.*

Such was the urgency of the crisis that in spite of pride, in the face of consistency, and without the popular warrant, an emissary was sent by the ministry to open negotiations with the American commission in Paris, on the basis of a virtual independence, limited only by commercial preference over other lands for the mother-country. It was too late. Franklin and his colleagues had been publicly received in formal audience on March 20th, amid the plaudits of the nation. Malesherbes had remarked that Franklin was a printer and the son of a tallow-chandler. The throne, the aristocracy, the burgesses, and the laboring *Public reception of Franklin at the French court.*

classes all knew it, but for various reasons he was the idol of all except the first. The moral effect of such a deification on the conditions of French society, with its revolutionary theories and its ideals of individual worth and personal liberty, was incalculable. The king himself did not deeply disguise his distaste for the policy forced upon him ; but the queen's sympathy, though perhaps shallow, was nevertheless hearty, and the cause was not only popular but fashionable.

This sufficient recognition of sovereignty exhilarated the advocates of independence in America. On April 22d Congress, using language almost identical with that of the previous November, resolved not to treat with English commissioners "unless they shall either withdraw their fleets and armies or in positive and express terms acknowledge the independence of the States." France had already fitted out two fleets, one at Brest, to engage the English fleet in European waters, the other at Toulon, which sailed for America under D'Estaing on April 17th, but owing to adverse winds and accidents did not reach Delaware Bay until the beginning of July, two weeks after Howe's fleet had left it. On May 4th Congress ratified both portions of the French treaty, and addressed the country as if independence were already secured. The people grew in turn as enthusiastic for France as the French were for them, and in much the same passionate sentimental way. Lafayette became, and has remained, the idol of the United States. The international sympathy, though tried by time, by differences of interest, and the widest divergence in religious and political institutions, continues firm and strong, the more so that the French Revolution, consequent to the success of our own, and measurably produced by it, has finally, purged of all distasteful excesses, resulted in a firm and tolerant republic.

Congress ratifies the treaty.

The cabal formed in the early winter against Washington collapsed almost as soon as its schemes became public. The people became stronger in his support as they learned how dark and ruinous had been the conspiracy against him. Congress, too, repented, and, yielding to the force of public opinion, roused itself to energetic though spasmodic action. Conway was made commander in the North, but complained of his exile and resigned. He had been accused by Cadwalader of cowardice in the battle on the Brandywine. Wounded in a duel with that officer, he wrote a servile apology to Washington and sailed for France, whence he never returned. Mifflin and Gates were compelled to silence, and remained to display, the former his better side, the latter his true character, in the subsequent stages of the war. Lee was soon to be utterly discredited.

Collapse of the cabal.

A congressional committee, moreover, set out for Valley Forge, where the remnant of Washington's army had spent the awful winter, and had sometimes under the lash of dreadful suffering had recourse, for the barest support of life, to marauding and other doubtful courses. Steuben, once aide-de-camp to Frederick the Great, joined the army toward the end of February, and in May was appointed inspector-general in place of Conway. His fine system of tactics and drill was at once introduced, new troops were called in, and the new spirit of organization restored courage and efficiency in the army. Most of the French officers, chilled by the coolness with which their extravagant expectations were met, had returned home at the expense of Congress, but Lafayette and a few of the choicest, some ten in all, remained. They were given rank and employment. Pulaski also was put in a cavalry command, and Kosciusko was appointed to fortify West

Reorganization of the Army.

Point. Greene was most efficient as head of the commissary department. The terrible blunder of retaliation in barbarity was made by the enlistment in Virginia and the Carolinas of two hundred Indians to serve under Nathaniel Gist.

The first knowledge of North's conciliatory measures had come to America through New York. The fragments which reached Congress caused some anxiety lest the people might be recalled to their old allegiance by such sweeping and unexpected concession. But nothing definite or authoritative was known until after the ratification of the French treaty. On June 6th Sir Henry Clinton, who had been appointed to succeed Howe as commander-in-chief, formally communicated to Congress the official text of the bills. The same day the three commissioners arrived. Of the three —Carlisle, Eden, and Johnstone—not one was a friend of the American cause, and two at least had been its most abusive enemies. But such was the character of their embassy that they never doubted of success, forgetting how delay, tyranny, and opprobrium had settled the conviction of the American leaders that English liberties could only find their full development this side the sea under a new government with perfect sovereignty.

On June 17th Congress formally refused conciliation unless accompanied by the acknowledgment of independence and the cessation of the war. The commissioners replied in two letters of July 2d and 18th. These were purposely relegated to the limbo of a routine which made no answer to their unauthorized proffer of independence in everything except foreign affairs, and did not even directly communicate to the writers a resolution declaring their mission of no effect. The offers were three years behind the time; they might be nothing but a move in the game which the king and his ministers were playing to deceive the House of Commons. The Articles of Confederation were signed by ten States in the interval. In August Reed informed Congress of an attempt by Johnstone to bribe him, and finally the resolution was taken to break off all communications with an embassy which counted Johnstone as one of its members. It appears to be a fact that the patriotic leaders, fearing the effect of these efforts on a people tired of the sacrifices entailed by war and encouraged by the suggestions of Gerard de Rayneval, the first French minister to the United States, adopted a course deliberately intended to turn the whole affair into ridicule. Their success was due to the unfortunate antecedents of the commissioners and the personal character of one of them. Gates was the only American officer willing to meet them in conference. Washington and the active patriots of the country were with Congress. The real temper of the commissioners was shown in a proclamation issued just before their departure in October, declaring the alliance of Protestant colonies with Romish France to be monstrous; that the real interest of America was sacrificed to the ambitions of a few; that if the colonies did not submit within forty days the sole object of the war would be to devastate the country.

Germain was aware of D'Estaing's departure and of his destination. He therefore ordered a concentration of the English forces in New York, and Philadelphia was evacuated on June 17, 1778. Clinton's plan was to cross New Jersey to Sandy Hook, where the fleet was to meet him and assure the easy transport of his forces by water to the city. The effective force with which he crossed the Delaware has been variously estimated at from twelve to seventeen

The English abandon Philadelphia.

thousand. Three thousand loyalists had been embarked to proceed with the fleet by sea, but there was, nevertheless, an army of camp-followers flying before the expected vengeance of the Americans when they should return, and a baggage-train some twelve miles long.

Washington at once moved from Valley Forge, entered New Jersey sixteen miles above Trenton with nearly ten thousand men, and pressed on to Hopewell. Lee had noisily asserted throughout the winter that whatever the English did they would not abandon Pennsylvania; he was now quite as confident that the Continental forces should not risk a pitched battle but harass the enemy on his march. Washington, supported by Greene, Wayne, Cadwalader, and Lafayette, was determined to the contrary, and sent out a body of fifteen hundred to act in union with the New Jersey militia, who were working wonders in creating obstacles to Clinton's advance. The bridges were burned, the wells choked, and a harassing skirmish constantly maintained on the enemy's left.

Their march impeded.

The English baggage-train was so cumbersome that they could not hope to cross the Raritan unmolested, and the army, therefore, swerved eastward, arriving at Freehold, the chief town of Monmouth County, on June 26th. The Americans reached Cranberry on the same day, and the order was issued to Lee, three miles in advance, to prepare a plan of attack, but he refused. The heat was excessive, and the next day being rainy as well, both armies rested; but Washington peremptorily ordered Lee to throw out six to eight hundred skirmishers. The morning of the twenty-eighth was clear, though the heat was still intense. The English moved, but the commander's order to Lee was so reluctantly and slowly obeyed as to be ineffective. The attack was begun by Dickinson, of New Jersey, with

The battle of Monmouth.

his militia, Lee being absent on the right, striving, as he claimed, to draw off the rear-guard of the enemy, entangle it in ravines, and so destroy it. But his strategy was futile and his men were disheartened, for Clinton sent Knyphausen forward with the baggage and reinforced his rear. It was an inexplicable obstinacy with which Lee refused to attack and continued his marchings and crossings; finally he began to retreat with his two brigades, explaining to Lafayette that he could not stand against forces so superior. Lafayette sent for the commander-in-chief, who arrived to find the retreat in full progress. With a few sharp and awful words Washington changed the direction of the troops. Wayne's regiments were quickly formed in a ravine under the hot fire of the British, and their advance was successfully checked until the remaining American force could be drawn up on high ground. The English fell back, but reformed in a strong defensible position; the Americans encamped on the battle-field.

The battle of Monmouth was the last general engagement on northern soil, but it was one of the most terrible. The thermometer registered 96° Fahr. in the shade, and under the relentless rays of *Incidents of the fight.* the sun many men on both sides fell dead from their exertions without a wound. The Americans lost in killed and wounded two hundred and thirty, the English four hundred. The desperate determination in the fighting was illustrated in the conduct of Moll Pitcher, wife of a Continental artilleryman, who aided her husband in the thickest of the fight, and when he fell promptly took his place in serving the gun. Seven hundred negroes fought with their white fellow-citizens on that memorable day. The result was a victory for neither side, but Clinton withdrew at midnight and Washington did not follow but marched away to his old position of advantage behind the Hudson River. He earned anew the affections and respect of the country by the sturdy blow, and Wayne's conduct was so splendid that he became a popular hero. Lee was court-martialed for his behavior, found guilty of insubordination, and suspended for a year. He was afterward dismissed for an impertinent letter to Congress, and retired to private life in Philadelphia, where he died in 1782. The depth of his faithlessness was unknown until 1857, when the publication of the Howe papers proved him to have been an arch-traitor.

A week after the battle of Monmouth, on July 3d, occurred the massacre of Wyoming, the name by which the upper valley of the Susquehanna, in Pennsylvania, was and still is known for some twenty miles. Under the charter granted by Charles II., Connecticut had claimed the district, and it had been settled by a colony of her thrifty inhabitants. The great tribe of Seneca Indians were still smarting under a sense of the wrongs which they believed themselves to have suffered at the hands of the French, who were now allies of the Americans, and it was not difficult for an English emissary to induce them to take revenge on the defenceless settlers who were, moreover, invading the wilderness. An expedition for the purpose was organized. There were about seven hundred men, the large majority Indians, but a considerable minority rangers. The settlement was taken by surprise, the villages and stockades burnt, two hundred and fifty persons scalped, and the remainder put to flight or shot. The leaders of the murderous band reported to Germain a loss of two whites and eight Indians, stating that they had burned all the mills and a thousand buildings. The community of Wyoming was thus annihilated: the ministry not only commended the exploit, but

The massacre of Wyoming.

proposed others of a similar nature. There were humane men in England to stigmatize such barbarity as it deserved, but the policy which led to it was not abandoned, and it is easy to conceive how strong became the American determination to be rid of such savagery.

CHAPTER XXV.

EVIL EFFECTS OF THE FOREIGN ALLIANCE—1778-1779

Arnold at Philadelphia—The Government Returns—D'Estaing's Failures—The Expedition Against Newport—Situation at the North—Humiliation of the Confederacy—Straits of the English Ministry—Ambitions and Fears of Spain—Spain Joins the Alliance—Western Settlement—Clark's Expedition—Louisiana and Florida Lost to England—France Expects Peace—Movements of Clinton—Stony Point—Sullivan's Campaign Against the Iroquois—The Fiasco of Castine—The Exploits of Paul Jones.

NEWPORT and the island on which it stands, New York, Ogdensburgh, Niagara, and Detroit were the only points now held by the English. Arnold was sent to command the recovered city of Philadelphia. The traditions of English occupation, with its luxury and riot, combined with his own inclination, led him to assume an extravagant style in living. His manners were marked by a childish air of self-importance, and before long it was rumored that his money transactions were irregular. It must be confessed that the conduct of many among the returning Whigs was far from admirable. In a spirit of retaliation several Tories were seized in New Jersey, tried, and sentenced to be hung. But Livingston, the Governor, pardoned them all. In Philadelphia, however, two were hung.

Arnold at Philadelphia.

The supreme executive council of Congress promptly returned to that city and resumed its sittings, while other members followed in little groups and slowly.

There was a plan to secure for the Government the deserted property of the loyalists, but it was utterly thwarted by private scheming and greed. In the depreciation of the Continental currency speculation ran wild, the sober supporters of Congress could make no headway against the wild gayeties of the commander and his set. Finally, there were two passionate factions, Arnold was court-martialled, convicted of serious indiscretion, and sentenced to a reprimand. His proud temper could ill brook such humiliation, and the circumstances probably made him receptive to the suggestion of treason.

The government returns.

D'Estaing's career seemed doomed to futility from the outset. Had he reached the Delaware earlier he might have beaten Howe, and consequently, Clinton, finding no transports at Sandy Hook, would probably have been compelled to capitulate. There was to be another fiasco. Finding the English gone, the French admiral promptly sailed for New York, where he was to co-operate with Washington, who had moved to White Plains, for a combined attack by land and sea, but he could find no pilots to carry his ships into the bay and bring them to a position suitable for attack. Washington then proposed an expedition against Newport. Sullivan, with two divisions under Lafayette and Greene, was to lead a force of regular Continentals and as many militia as he could get together from the neighborhood into the island and attack by land, simultaneously with a bombardment from D'Estaing's ships. It was hoped that the entire garrison of six thousand would be compelled to surrender.

D'Estaing's failures.

The land force was promptly organized and ready in due season, but again, as in crossing the ocean, there were unnecessary delays in the movement of the French fleet. It was August 8th when D'Estaing forced an entrance to Newport harbor. But this time the English had shown capacity and speed. Clinton was marching rapidly with four thousand troops to the relief of the city, and Howe's fleet had followed so promptly as to be already in sight of the tardy French; D'Estaing turned and sought the open sea for a decisive engagement. But a violent storm arose and scattered both fleets. It even disabled the Americans on shore, who were under canvas, but left the English in the town unharmed. Sullivan was able, however, to retreat from the island without serious loss. The French admiral gathered his ships to refit in Boston, but he was coldly received, and his name was unjustly execrated throughout New England. Howe returned to New York and relinquished his command to Admiral Byron.

The expedition against Newport.

The situation in the North, as it then was, remained substantially unchanged to the end of the war. It is perfectly expressed in words written at the time by Washington: "After two years' manœuvring and the strangest vicissitudes both armies are brought back to the very point they set out from, and the offending party at the beginning is reduced to the use of the spade and pickaxe for defence. The hand of Providence has been so conspicuous in all this that he must be worse than an infidel that lacks faith, and more than wicked that has not gratitude to acknowledge his obligations." The real weakness of America was in her own folly, or rather mania, concerning taxation, and in the preference by her leaders of local interests to the Continental welfare.

Situation at the North.

The campaign of 1778 came to a premature close for lack of money. Congress had neither the inclination nor the courage to ask or assume authority to lay taxes; the States were busy with their own promis-

EVIL EFFECTS OF THE FOREIGN ALLIANCE 303

sory notes, the country was flooded with English counterfeits of Continental currency, and the obligations of the union were growing more and more worthless. Throughout the summer the operations of agriculture had been unchecked by the presence of an enemy, and by the end of October the country had garnered another rich harvest without molestation. But such was the moral imbecility produced by a now rampant separatism that Congress confessed to France that their only hope was in foreign loans, and with words which in the perspective of history sound pusillanimous asked for the "protection" of the king. They also addressed the country in language which showed a disintegration of force, using "inhabitants" where they had previously used "people." It was about this time that common usage began to substitute for the term United States the significant one of Confederated States. Even at Valley Forge, Washington, in the height of his restored influence and once again in possession of extraordinary powers which made him a virtual dictator for four months, had pleaded in vain for long enlistments. Congress displayed the bugbear of a standing army and persisted in the plan of annual drafts. *Humiliation of the confederacy.*

Germain hoped that the American cause would eventually fail by financial mismanagement; but meanwhile the ministry was desperate. There were thirty-three thousand English and German troops in the rebellious colonies, supported by an expensive fleet, and there was virtually nothing to show for all these exertions except New York and Newport. The temporary enthusiasm of the nation had subsided and enlistments had come to a stop, the Germans in America deserted with alacrity, and the national debt was increasing with alarming and startling rapidity. The really great public men of the nation were *Straits of the English ministry.*

304 THE FRENCH WAR AND THE REVOLUTION

constantly expressing regret at the continuance of the war, their admiration for the American leaders was not concealed, and a readiness to yield American independence began to permeate all classes. Burke denounced the latest manifesto of the parliamentary commissioners to the Americans as a "dreadful menace," and Rockingham pronounced it "accursed," for since the coming of Christ war had not been conducted on such inhuman ideas.

Spain found herself in a serious crisis. The secondary rôle she was playing under the Family Compact was humiliating; but worse than that, her colonial system in South and North America was jeopardized. This was due to three causes - first, the slackness of administration at Madrid; second, the enmity of the Jesuits, to whose missionary zeal so much was due; and third, to the temper of the age. Her vast possessions included the greater portion of the western hemisphere, for even in North America she claimed and hoped to secure a share of the great territory east of the Mississippi as far as the Alleghenies, while everything west of that river belonged to her; the great mercantile nations were thirsting for the beneficent settlement of territories so rich, but closed as yet to commerce and the use of man. If the English colonies should secure their independence, the infection of liberty would certainly spread in the northern continent. Florida Blanca, therefore, would have made the erection of a Chinese wall of separation by a sharp delimitation of boundaries a condition of the Bourbon alliance against Great Britain.

Ambitions and fears of Spain.

An indecisive engagement in July, 1778, between the Channel fleets of France and England opened hostilities, further delay was impossible. Spain twice offered mediation and a settlement of boundaries, but the English ministry declined with amused disdain. At this juncture Congress took the wise step

Spain joins the alliance.

EVIL EFFECTS OF THE FOREIGN ALLIANCE 305

of dissolving her diplomatic commission in Paris and appointing Franklin sole plenipotentiary. Vergennes had confidence in him, but using the incertitude and slowness of the American government as an argument that they never could be an aggressive power, he convinced both himself and the Spanish minister that the western frontier of the United States would in any event be the Alleghenies. At last, by an agreement to restore Gibraltar, Minorca, and Pensacola, with the Florida coast, likewise to expel the English from Honduras and Campeachy, the end which seemed so essential to Vergennes was gained. Spain signed the treaty on April 12th, 1779, and declared war in June. On the twenty-fifth a fleet sailed from Cadiz to join that of the French.

This new alliance, according to international law, released Congress from its promise not to make peace without France. But events were happening in the Western wilderness destined in the end to prevent the disintegration of the union, and at the same time to thwart the plans of the Bourbon powers. The possession of the Mississippi Valley in its integrity has been from the beginning the assurance and the cement of union. The men who won it and occupied it have been in a high sense the makers of the United States. As early as 1776 the pioneers in and about Harrodsburgh had chosen delegates to the Virginia Assembly, and after the declaration of independence the district was recognized as the County of Kentucky. One of the first representatives was Clark, who, after consultation with Thomas Jefferson, Patrick Henry, and others, spent the year in securing authorization and supplies for an expedition into the interior. His plans were at length perfected, and with a sufficient sum of money he returned home in January, 1778, to begin the organization and outfitting of his men. By June 26th all was in readiness;

Western settlement.

20

306 THE FRENCH WAR AND THE REVOLUTION

five companies of about forty each were embarked on the river, and on July 4th they reached their goal, the ancient settlement of Kaskaskia, not far from the Mississippi, on a tributary of the same name.

The place had been an English post, but in 1775 Carleton withdrew the garrison to strengthen that of Detroit, Clark's expedition. relying on the soldiers at Vincennes and the Indian parties which were constantly moving backward and forward to hold the frontier. The Americans took possession without a blow, the French inhabitants willingly swore allegiance to the United States, and established the County of Illinois in the State of Virginia. Kahokia submitted in the same way, and a priest named Gibault undertook a conciliatory embassy to Vincennes, which, with its garrison, likewise renounced English supremacy. But a party of British from Detroit recaptured it in December. During the same season another expedition, under Willing, of Philadelphia, captured the English forts on the lower Mississippi, of which Natchez was the most important. Throughout the winter of 1778-79 the Indians were on the war-path in the English interest. They sought scalps and took no prisoners, for Hamilton, their employer, gave bounties only for the former. In February, however, Clark, after a hard fight, recaptured Vincennes, both town and fort, cutting off the supply trains from Detroit, and taking prisoners the convoy of forty men.

In April was gathered a force of some fifteen hundred men. They were commanded by Evan Shelby and Louisiana and Florida lost to England. equipped by Isaac, his son. Encountering the hostile Indians at Chickamauga they nearly annihilated the power of the savages, and rendered the scheme of an attack on the South from that quarter impossible. The channels of immigration toward the fertile plains were thus cleared, and before

the plans of Spain were completed they were already
thwarted, for the whole bank of the Mississippi from
Kaskaskia southward to Natchez was already in American hands. Galvez, the Spanish governor of Louisiana,
acted with promptness after the declaration of war,
raised a motley force, consisting in part of the regulars
at his disposal, but chiefly of American volunteers and
negroes, and wrested from the English all western Florida except Pensacola.

The long paralysis of English activity was largely due
to a remarkable natural phenomenon, the terrific frost
of eighty days in the previous winter, which France expects peace.
suspended all energy in public life for that
time and for many weeks subsequent. The French
alliance did nothing to arouse Congress. They fondly
expected a speedy peace, and arrangements were actually
made for its negotiation. Vergennes succeeded first in
neutralizing the freedom of negotiation they had secured
by the accession of Spain, and binding them not to conclude a treaty without the formal consent of France.
The question of boundary was to be conceded; Canada
and Nova Scotia on the north, the Atlantic on the east,
Florida on the south, and the Mississippi on the west,
provided America would not insist on the exclusive right
to navigate it. The north and south boundaries were
those declared by England in 1713. Bitter discussion
arose over the fisheries question, resulting in a decision
to insist on their enjoyment as before the war. Finally
a formal appeal was made to the States for help in
money matters, but no response was expected or made,
for there was a general reliance on further subsidies
from France and Spain. Fifty millions more of Continental currency were issued during January, and an
equal sum from time to time throughout the year. By
June the market value of a Continental dollar was one-

twentieth of its face; by the end of the year, when the sum total in circulation was two hundred millions, it was worth less than a thirtieth. The financial collapse was complete.

Gates had three thousand men in New England, with head-quarters at Providence; there were six thousand in the Highlands under McDougall and Putnam, and Washington had seven thousand between Middlebrook, in New Jersey, and Newburgh, on the Hudson, where his head-quarters were. The English had eleven thousand men in New York and five thousand at Newport. And yet the summer of 1779 was a season of general inactivity at the original seat of war, though there was desultory fighting of considerable importance both North and South, as well as that among the pioneers already mentioned. Clinton became restless under the fire of hostile criticism as he lay shut up in New York, and in May despatched an expedition with two thousand men to the Chesapeake. In pursuance of the ministerial policy of devastation the prosperous Virginia shores were ravaged, a hundred vessels burnt, and the English ships returned to New York with a rich booty—seventeen prizes and three thousand hogsheads of tobacco. The Virginia government retaliated by the seizure of property belonging to British subjects. Early in June Clinton himself led a sally forty miles up the Hudson, and occupied Stony Point on one side and Verplanck's on the other. The Americans were thus deprived of all communication between the opposite shores south of the Highlands.

A similar foray wrought serious havoc on the Connecticut shore at Norwalk, Fairfield, and New Haven. These depredations could not be permitted to continue. Washington and Wayne elaborated a plan which the latter carried to successful execution. With the utmost care and secrecy twelve hundred men were led in detached columns by the mountain passes of the Highlands to a rendezvous within two miles of Stony Point. After a brief reconnoissance by Wayne the attack began in the early morning of June 16th. The works were stormed at the point of the bayonet, and five hundred and forty-three prisoners, officers and men, were captured. Cannon and stores were removed and the fortifications razed. The American loss was about twenty, and they had regained the all-important King's Ferry. Another brilliant exploit was that of Henry Lee, of Virginia, who with a small party surprised the fort at Paulus Hook, now Jersey City, and almost without a casualty captured the garrison of one hundred and fifty-nine men.

The Indians, moreover, and their Tory allies, were punished for the continued and bloody excesses which were the fitting sequels to the massacres of Wyoming and of Cherry Valley. Congress had in February consented to an expedition against the Iroquois; and in August, after inexplicable delays, a force of about three thousand men under Sullivan entered the Susquehanna Valley. Before their arrival the patriots had commenced a series of desultory movements against the enemy. These were now strengthened and continued until the Onondagas, Senecas, and Mohawks were thoroughly cowed. A pitched battle was fought at Newtown, near Elmira. The mixed force of some six hundred Indians and English was led by Brant, Johnson, and the Butlers. The whites fled, and the red men finding their allies could not protect them, begged for permission to remain neutral. The early season had been unexampled for horrid excesses, at its close the perpetrators had lost their own homes and crops. No sooner, however, did Sullivan proceed than the allied Tories and savages rallied again, and in one long revel of

Sullivan's campaign against the Iroquois.

destruction spread desolation along the frontier. For lack of money and provisions the little Continental army could proceed no farther than the Genesee Valley.

During the same month an attempt against the English post of Castine, established in June at the mouth of the Penobscot, in the Maine wilderness, was also thwarted. In July Massachusetts, with an access of natural but ill-considered resentment at what was an inexplicable act of bravado, fitted out two frigates, twenty-four transports, and nearly twenty privateersmen to meet daring with daring and destroy Castine. A thousand men were embarked. In due time, on July 28th, these arrived before the place and disembarked. The strong fortifications defied their efforts and protracted the siege. The expedition had been followed by five English frigates and a sixty-four-gun ship, which arrived from New York the second week in August, to find the Americans again embarked and offering resistance. The very same day the English attacked and overpowered the adventurers. Soldiers and sailors alike landed to escape capture, and set fire to many of their own ships. The brave but Quixotic party then set out on their weary retreat of three hundred miles through the forest wilderness. Saltonstall, the Continental commander, was court-martialled and degraded. Lovell, the local officer, was acquitted. The cost in money had been enormous; those who incurred it would not pay, and as the blame had been fixed on the Continental authority, eventually, but most reluctantly, it was assumed by Congress.

The net result in the North, therefore, was a slight gain for the Americans, especially as they held King's Ferry and as Newport was now abandoned, owing to a determination to strengthen New York against a possible attack by the French fleet and American army in conjunction. Moreover, there was great encouragement on the ocean. A Scotch adventurer of remarkable character, named Paul Jones, had two years previously taken service with the United States as a naval officer. In 1778 he surprised Whitehaven, and in July of this year had sailed from L'Orient with a squadron of five small vessels—two American and two French men-of-war, with one privateer—to cruise on the coasts of Ireland and Scotland. In September he descried off Flamborough Head a merchant fleet from the Baltic, under the convoy of two war-ships, the Serapis and the Countess of Scarborough. An hour after sunset, on the twenty-third, Jones, in the Poor Richard, of forty guns, engaged the Serapis, of forty-four. The battle lasted at short range for an hour and an half, and the American ship was sadly battered. Her commander bore down and grappled his antagonist. Two hours more of a desperate hand-to-hand conflict ensued in the long twilight and dusk of those latitudes, and at length the Serapis struck her colors. Next morning the American commander had just time to transfer his men and stores to the prize before his own vessel sank. The French frigate Pallas, after another gallant action captured the Scarborough, and the fleet bore away for Holland, entering the Texel, October 4th, 1779.

CHAPTER XXVI.

CAMDEN AND KING'S MOUNTAIN—1779-1780

Hostilities in Georgia—English Authority Re-established—Lincoln and D'Estaing Fail before Savannah—Proposition to Arm Slaves—Fall of Charleston—English Policy in the South—Measures Taken by Cornwallis—The Reign of Terror in South Carolina—The Patriots Prepare for Resistance—Gates Defeated at Camden—The Frontiersmen Meet the Crisis—Battle of King's Mountain—Moral Effect and Character of the Victory—Greene Relieves Gates—Bankruptcy and Mutiny in the North—Failure of Plans for Co-operation between Washington and D'Estaing—Arrival of Rochambeau.

THE year 1779 is not memorable in the annals of the Revolution for these successes and reverses, but for an entire change in the seat of war. The plan for a Southern campaign had been matured by Germain in the previous year, but had for a time remained in abeyance owing to a lack of new troops. An effort was made to enlist men in America, but only a few could be secured, and these were for the most part Irish Roman Catholics, who hated France because she had expelled the Jesuits. The arrival of the French fleet also made it more difficult to land such soldiers as were available. Two expeditions of refugees entered Georgia from Florida and ravaged certain districts, but their career was short. Lincoln, who had been wounded in his Northern service was now convalescent, and had received the appointment of commander-in-chief for the South. Early in January, 1779, Prevost, who was the English military governor of Florida, marched with a small con-

Hostilities in Georgia.

THE SOUTHERN COLONIES
ILLUSTRATING
THE SECOND-HALF OF THE REVOLUTION

tingent to Savannah, outwitted Robert Howe, the naval commander, and took the city. Campbell advanced and occupied Augusta. Both he and Prevost feeling secure in their positions, began almost immediately the devastation of the surrounding country, and the soldiery plundered at will.

The salient features of the curious resistance which similar conditions had made necessary in the North were to be repeated with little variation in the South, the chief difference being in the activity and violence of the numerous Tories who dwelt in the midlands. With a small nucleus of Continental regulars Lincoln soon collected a considerable body of militia, and North Carolina sent a second force of two thousand under Ashe, the arms for whom were furnished by South Carolina, which also provided supplies and raised a regiment of dragoons. The entire army numbered about thirty-five hundred. Some minor actions between the marauding British and the militia turned to the American advantage; but Ashe, who had been detailed with a separate command of fifteen hundred men was defeated on March 3d, at Brier Creek. Georgia was now nearly lost and the royal government temporarily re-established.

Proposition to arm slaves.

During the latter part of 1778 and the first half-year of 1779 the fleets of Byron and D'Estaing had been in the West Indies carrying on an intermittent warfare with checkered successes. The French took Dominica, and the English seized St. Lucia. For six months D'Estaing was blockaded at Port Royal, but when, in June, 1779, Byron sailed for England in a convoy, the French admiral took both St. Vincent and Grenada. He then avoided the general engagement which the English sought, and in response to a letter from the French consul at Charleston, appeared early in September off Savannah. Men and am-

English authority re-established.

munition were landed to assist in a siege of the city, which by this time Prevost had strongly fortified. But owing to uncertainty and lack of concerted action week after week passed before the first lines of approach were thrown up. The stormy season was at hand, and the fleet might easily be driven off the coast. It was, therefore, determined to try an assault on October 9th. D'Estaing landed with his men, and led one column composed in part of North Carolina militia to the attack. The other, under Lincoln, moved simultaneously. The onset was desperate, but it was met by a fire no less so. For a moment the American flag appeared on the rampart, but it disappeared as the two South Carolina lieutenants who bore it were shot down. The French standard-bearer also planted his banner on a conspicuous spot, but only for an instant. The result was an utter discomfiture of the assailants. Six hundred Frenchmen fell slain or wounded, among the latter D'Estaing himself. The Americans lost about two hundred. Pulaski, the gallant Pole, was struck by a ball, and died soon afterward. The English loss was trifling.

The failure was attributed to the information given by a deserter to the English. But in every case, so far, disaster seemed to wait on enterprises undertaken conjointly by the allies. The fleet sailed back to the Antilles. Nevertheless its presence on the coast had delayed the movements of the English, and it was December before three thousand troops from New York, under Campbell, finally landed. Clinton's flotilla of transports had been scattered by adverse winds, and it was not until January, 1780, that he himself, with six thousand men, reached the mouth of the Tybee River.

Lincoln and D'Estaing fail before Savannah.

The English forces were at once directed against Charleston, which both opponents held to be the key of the Southern States. Washington counselled Lincoln to keep in the open country where his strength lay; but yielding probably to an over-strong public impulse, the American leader threw himself into the city, secured supplies for a siege, and fortified the neck. Seven hundred Virginia regulars had been sent from the North as a reinforcement to Lincoln, and Cornwallis came in April with three thousand men from New York to complete the overwhelming superiority of Clinton. At this juncture Laurens arrived from Washington with a proposition to arm the negroes. Men of color had bravely fought at Monmouth. The capture of slaves by the English was a source of profit so immense that they never dreamed of emancipating the blacks. It was very likely that negroes would fight for American liberty in the South as bravely as they had already done in the North, especially if they might hope to secure their own freedom at that price. The plan was debated and angrily rejected.

English policy in the South.

Meantime the surrounding country had been invested by Cornwallis and the siege was successfully progressing. Arbuthnot with an English squadron safely crossed the bar under the guns of Fort Moultrie. Georgia was already lost, and thoughts of a surrender were entertained and discussed. Finally Clinton was asked for terms by the dispirited civilians, who would have agreed either to neutrality or to capitulation. He refused to treat except with the military authorities. There was disaffection of the most serious kind in the city, and languor marked both the siege operations and the defence. Finally, after the third parallel of approach had been completed, Lincoln yielded to terms of a very stringent nature, and on May 12th surrendered. The number of combatants included in the articles embraced all inhabitants who had ever par-

Fall of Charleston.

ticipated in resistance on the American side, and was nearly five thousand. There were also valuable cannon and other munitions in the place. And so rich was the little town of fifteen thousand people that the booty was worth about three hundred thousand pounds sterling.

The loss of Charleston was morally an awful blow. The State government was utterly disorganized and its members fled northward. South Carolina was open to the enemy and was soon overrun by parties sent in all directions to plunder and terrorize. For a time the population seemed stunned and no resistance was made. Tarleton and his troopers became a scourge. In a single skirmish with the militia he killed over a hundred men, wounded a hundred and fifty of the fugitives, and himself lost but eighteen men. Menacing proclamations were spread broadcast, and his name became a word of horror. By June Clinton felt himself justified in proclaiming the re-establishment of royal government. The act was most ill advised. Tories and plunderers had done their worst, and the English officers were enrolling company after company of royalists. A desperate people roused itself to retaliate ; many even of the trimmers and indifferent were stung to activity. But the step was taken in order to lend one ray of glory to his American career, the active part of which was now nearly over. Dispirited by the lukewarm support of the ministry, and irritated by the evident favor which Cornwallis enjoyed, he chose this juncture to resign the command into the hands of his subordinate and departed for New York, cherishing the belief that two Southern States were subdued ; that there were few, as he wrote, in South Carolina who were not either prisoners or enlisted in the English ranks. He felt assured also of his reputation in that the rich supplies of cotton, rice, and indigo, which were as

Measures taken by Cornwallis.

CAMDEN AND KING'S MOUNTAIN 317

current as gold, would now be cut off and the crippled States compelled to yield.

Cornwallis found himself with an effective force of about seven thousand men. With these and the new regiments which he hoped to raise among the abounding Tories of North Carolina, who were only waiting for his arrival, as he believed, to rise and deliver the State into his hands, he intended to march victoriously to the Chesapeake, leaving behind him a land subdued and reorganized under colonial governments. The devastation of the country remained unchecked, and as the ruthless leaders still further alienated minds hitherto undecided, the patriots began to gather head. The configuration of the State made Camden on the Wateree an important gateway to the northern interior. It was occupied by Lord Rawdon with a small garrison of English regulars, and Cornwallis advanced from Charleston to make it secure. *The reign of terror in South Carolina.*

The highlands to the northwest were the safest rallying-point for the Americans, because there, as in the lowlands, the people were ardent supporters of the cause. Thither under Sumter repaired the determined band of volunteers, and they were soon strengthened by a regiment composed of their brethren. These men had seemingly yielded to the English requisition that all male inhabitants should be enrolled as militia, but having received their arms and equipments had then deserted in a body. Virginia and North Carolina both sent contingents of volunteers. Washington, too, had detached for the relief of Charleston the largest number he dared to send away from his diminished army, but the difficulties of transportation had been insuperable, and it was June before they approached. Kalb was the general in command, Williams his capable adjutant. The men were poorly clad and *The patriots prepare for resistance.*

badly fed, the heats of summer had induced disease, and they were totally unfit for a campaign. But Gates had been chosen by Congress to replace the captured Lincoln as commander in the South, although Washington had recommended Greene. In spite of Kalb's strong protest and a memorial from the officers, marching orders were given the very day of Gates's arrival. After a slow and disastrous march, during which serious mutinies were threatened, the relieving force arrived before Camden simultaneously with Cornwallis. On August 14th, 1780, the two forces were within striking distance.

Gates's utter incapacity was soon proven. By an ill-advised night-march of his army the battle was joined at half-past two in the morning of the sixteenth, when for the first time Cornwallis's presence became known. At the very outset the American cavalry broke and fled, the untrained militia of North Carolina and Virginia followed in panic without an effort at resistance. The English formed in a strong position between two swamps, and the American attack on the front was successfully repulsed. The Continentals from Maryland and Delaware resisted long and desperately under the leadership of Kalb, who fought with stubborn courage until his horse was killed under him and he himself pierced by no less than eleven bullets. Overwhelmed by superior numbers he and his command were compelled to yield, and shortly after the brave leader died. The monument ordered by a grateful Congress to be erected at Annapolis to his memory was long delayed, but has finally been built: his life was mysterious, but his good fame has grown with years. The defeat was soon a disorderly rout; Gates, neither knowing nor caring for the fate of his men, fled on his charger, riding through Charlotte to Hillsborough, two hundred miles in three and a half days. The English losses were very se-

Gates defeated at Camden.

CAMDEN AND KING'S MOUNTAIN 319

vere, about five hundred picked troops ; those of their opponents are unknown, but they must have been heavier. The American officers with what soldiers could be collected rallied under Sumter, but retreating carelessly they were surprised and routed by Tarleton.

The victory at Camden seemed to intoxicate Cornwallis. Confident of support by the ministry he instituted a second reign of terror in South Carolina, hanging militia-men who had gone over to the Americans and despatching cruel agents *The frontiersmen met the crisis.* to further devastate uncertain districts in order that he might leave no foe behind him on his northern march. But the swamps of the Pedee and Santee were inaccessible to strangers, while their intricate passes and island glades soon swarmed with patriot refugees. The undaunted Williams gathered and armed a force in the district around the village of Ninety-Six to encourage the people and undo the sorry work of the English. Francis Marion, a famous partisan, justly called the Bayard of the South, gathered a band of devoted followers, and with sleepless vigilance patrolled the lowlands to the very doors of Charleston. Sumter, undismayed, began a similar career in the mountains. Cornwallis was ignorant of the dangers which beset him in spite of his triumph, when, on September 2d, he began his march, opening his line until the left wing under Ferguson reached westward into the hill country at the base of the Appalachians. The centre under his own command advanced to Charlotte, and easily repelling a spirited attack made by a few skirmishers occupied the town.

This was the darkest hour of the struggle for independence. The confederation was bankrupt, the people in the Northern and Middle States apathetic, Congress hopelessly feeble, Washington without support and crippled by poverty, French aid unavailing, treason in high places, victorious invaders marching irresistibly and leaving desolation behind. To many the end seemed near, but aid rose in a most unexpected quarter from a land unknown to the English and unfamiliar to nearly all Americans. The backwoodsmen of the Alleghenies were destined not only to make American union essential, but to turn the beam at the very crisis when independence hung wavering in the scale. Already the hardy settlers of the mountain districts, Presbyterian Calvinists for the most part, no lovers of the parent which had been but a stepmother to so many of her unprivileged children, had heard of the invasion, its successes, and its outrages. Their trusted leaders were men in whom conviction and conduct were closely related in religion, politics, and warfare. From distant settlements and remote valleys, from Watauga and the Virginia mountains came companies and regiments, to which organization for the emergencies of a frontier life was a second nature. They were commanded by men whose names are now familiar to every school-boy studying the geography of those parts, Shelby, Sevier and Cleveland, Campbell, McDowell, and Williams.

Battle of King's Mountain.

Thus was formed a true army of the West, as it was designated, about seventeen hundred strong and commanded by its own officers. The commander-in-chief was Williams. Ferguson had posted a force consisting of eleven hundred and twenty-five men in a position of great strength on King's Mountain, the last summit of the range stretching eastward on the border between North and South Carolina. There, on October 7th, the encounter took place. It was long and severe, an unbroken fight lasting for hours. At the end both Ferguson and Williams were dead. The Americans had lost about one hundred men,

Moral effect and character of the victory.

but the British division was annihilated, four hundred and fifty-six being killed, six hundred taken prisoners. The effect of the victory was electric. Cornwallis was stunned, and turning on his steps began to retreat to Winnsborough. The spirit of the people was revived and the whole country-side rose to harass his march, Sumter seriously annoying him on his flanks. The weather, too, was inclement, and the fever miasm claimed many victims among the unacclimatized English; Cornwallis himself was among the afflicted. Tarleton was attacked, defeated, and driven in, and the year which had promised so well at its opening for English success ended in overwhelming disaster.

It is customary to compare the battle of King's Mountain with the affairs at Lexington and Bennington. This is not unnatural, for they were all the work of "embattled farmers." But the earlier was a defeat, and merely showed that the Americans would fight; the second was a victory gallantly and desperately won, but the men were well equipped, were within reach of a military depot, and had the moral support of a strong organized army near by. King's Mountain was the unassisted work of men who met a disciplined force of white soldiers for the first time, at a moment when the American army had disappeared in inglorious defeat, and all hope of success had vanished from the hearts of any but the most sanguine. In its character and its effect the fight at King's Mountain is the most typical of any revolutionary conflict, exhibiting as it does the unsuspected resources of the insurgents who had unwittingly created behind their older settlements a rear-guard which now claimed a new empire outside the original colonies, and was the nucleus of a nation, displaying a possibility and a promise of ultimate success at the moment when the older colonies were displaying their separatism and lassitude in ways and for reasons which posterity can understand but not admire. The disappearance of the force which fought it was as curious and phenomenal as their appearance. The army melted away insensibly, as company after company marched back to their frontier homes.

In the interval gained by the battle of King's Mountain, Gates re-established his head-quarters, collected fifteen hundred of his scattered army, and returned to Charlotte. But he was now known in his true colors; Congress recalled him, and finally chose the energetic and clever Greene to replace him. The wholesome change took place in December, 1780.

Greene relieves Gates.

"These are the times which try men's souls:" thus opened one of the eighteen essays of the "Crisis," written at intervals between 1776 and 1783 by Paine, to revive from time to time the ever-drooping spirits of Washington's neglected army. The phrase was never more true than in the months of 1779 and 1780, during which the Northern army sat watching the English in New York, who were inert but fairly comfortable, while they themselves were face to face with conditions scarcely better than those of Valley Forge. The confederation was buried under mountains of worthless paper; Continental obligations, State obligations, Congressional drafts on European agents, quartermaster's obligations given in form for requisitions, counterfeits of some or all of these. Bankrupt in funds and credit as the country was, the army was no longer paid, the spirit of mutiny was rampant, desertions were constant, and the men who from a sense of fear or honor remained either sustained themselves by marauding or suffered want. In December, 1779, Congress made an attempt to secure some further requisitions from the States; Virginia replied with a dangerous assertion of independence, and expressed alarm at the substitution of demands for

Bankruptcy and mutiny in the North.

recommendations as an unjustifiable usurpation. In January, 1780, there was neither bread nor meat at West Point for over a fortnight ; during the absence of Clinton the few thousand English left at New York under Knyphausen thought famine was at their doors because the surrounding waters were frozen. The fleet could, of course, bring no provisions to them, but they were able to offer hard cash, ringing coin, for the rich products of the neighborhood, and the temptation overpowered the patriotism of the farmers.

A subtile poison had instilled itself into the popular blood, even the patriots of radical stamp were under its influence and seemed to have forgotten the days of energetic manhood. This venom was a selfish conviction that France and Spain would deal with England, and in the hour of victory Congress as a committee, with slight but sufficient delegated power, would gather the fruit of independence. To the superficial observer it appeared as if disintegration were complete, the battle fought but lost by apathy. Amid such moral and financial disaster Washington's foresight was unavailing. He had cherished and matured a great design for the co-operation of the French fleet with his own land force in the capture of New York. D'Estaing had permitted himself to be drawn into the Southern campaign in the hope of a trivial advantage which he did not gain, and the opportunity was lost. This was but an example of the cross purposes which had so far nullified any possible benefit from the alliance. The despatches of the French ministers and the journals of the French officers in America unite in proving how thoroughly they misunderstood the men with whom they had to deal. There is a tone of sarcastic superiority, of good-humored ridicule, of minute and carping criticism which is entertaining and in-

Failure of plans for co-operation between Washington and D'Estaing.

structive, but of friendly sympathy either with a raw and unformed people, or with the great cause in which they were engaged, imperfectly understood even by themselves, the only representative was Lafayette.

Early in 1779 this serious and now matured youth, the confidential friend of Washington, departed for France. He received an impressive and hearty welcome at court, his representations were heard and weighed; the ministry determined on measures more effective than any they had yet taken. In May, 1780, he returned with the news of his success, and on July 12th a squadron of fifty transports, with their convoy, reached Newport. Washington by a skilful demonstration kept the English in New York, as he had the year before prevented their advance beyond the Highlands of the Hudson. Six thousand men, under Count Rochambeau, were safely landed, and when Rodney with his fleet appeared they were so entrenched that he passed by. Reinforcements were to follow, but they never arrived, as the English blockaded the harbor of Brest, from which the next instalment was to sail. The French army was well supplied, paid the farmers for its requisitions with coin, and for the long months of its expectant inactivity brought great local prosperity to the neighborhood. Winter at last came on, and it was not until late in the campaign of 1781 that they saw any service. Washington was for the moment encouraged, but he could not be content. In order to end the war there must be co-operation in some decisive stroke between a strong land force and a fleet powerful enough to nullify temporarily, at least, the naval superiority of the English, and thereby prevent the enemy from either receiving assistance by water or securing its retreat on the same element. In September he visited the French camp to enforce his views, and preconcert measures with his allies.

Arrival of Rochambeau.

CHAPTER XXVII.

THE SOUTHERN INVASION REPELLED—1780-1781

Washington Reprimands Arnold—Arrest of André—His Character and Guilt—Insubordination in the Army—Robert Morris and the Finances of the Confederation—Arnold in Virginia—Lafayette and Steuben—Greene Creates a Southern Army—Morgan at Cowpens—Greene's Retreat—The Forces at Guilford—Cornwallis Victorious but Thwarted—Groton Heights—Effect of Rawdon's Cruelties—Greene Marches Southward—Defeat at Hobkirk's Hill—Sumter and Marion—Battle of Eutaw Springs.

THE treason of Arnold, which disclosed itself during Washington's temporary absence, was a serious discouragement, not symptomatic, however, of prevailing and hidden disaffection, as might have been feared, seeing how insubordinate and unruly the unpaid officers and men occasionally were. In accordance with the verdict rendered in Philadelphia by Arnold's judges, Washington administered the reprimand, but in a letter both gentle and considerate. The culprit had been recklessly brave during the early years of the war, and to the fertility of his genius some most important prefatory movements were probably due. Hoping that the prodigal would return, the rebuke was further broken by his appointment to the important command of the Highlands.

<small>Washington reprimands Arnold.</small>

But Arnold's moral and financial ruin had gone hand in hand. Almost immediately he opened negotiations with Clinton for the betrayal of his trust. The chosen agent of the British commander was a young officer of engaging presence, excellent parts, and good family, Major André. His success in reaching Arnold's quarters and concluding the negotiations was complete. The journey to West Point was by water, but unforeseen circumstances compelled his return by land. Documents concerning the nefarious transaction were concealed on the young officer's person. Disguised as a traveller and provided by Arnold with a passport through the American lines he set out on horseback for New York. Near Tarrytown, on the east shore, which he reached on September 23d, he was stopped by a party of three Americans, who were neither regulars nor militia, but volunteer patriots watching the movements of suspected Tories in that troubled region between the English and American zones of influence. The appearance and conduct of André were suspicious, and losing his head he forgot to show Arnold's passport. His captors accordingly searched him, and discovering both the character of their prisoner and the evidence of Arnold's treachery, promptly carried the papers and their bearer to the American head-quarters.

Arrest of André.

Washington had just returned by Hartford from his eastern journey. In spite of sentimental pleas of youth, station, obedience to superiors, and the like, coming with bad grace after the fact, André was tried by a military court in due form on the charge of being a spy. He was convicted and sentenced to be hung, his judges being convinced by the most conclusive considerations; to wit, his disguise, the nature of his errand, and the information he had obtained, which would have been used whether the plot failed or not. The execution took place on October 2d. In the heats of passion which then arose and lasted for many years after the war was over, aspersions were constantly cast on Washington's character because he would not at least

His character and guilt.

THE SOUTHERN INVASION REPELLED 327

commute the sentence to military execution by shooting, and spare André the shameful death of the gallows. Americans were not slow to retort by citing the case of Nathan Hale, and producing cumulative evidence as to the ill-treatment of their captured countrymen when not a shadow of doubt could be cast on their character as prisoners of war. The wordy discussion was perhaps necessary, but it introduced many irrelevant considerations. The question of André's character and guilt was one of military law, and the finding of the court is no longer disputed. In the condition of the country at that juncture executive clemency would have been criminal, and it is a doubtful hypothesis that it could ever have been justified by any considerations or under any circumstances.

Unfortunately the felon himself escaped, reaching New York in safety on September 24th, to claim and receive, in the chilling atmosphere of social aversion, the price of his treason, thirty-two thousand dollars in money and an office on Clinton's staff. *Insubordination in the army.* His character was further blackened by a proclamation which he issued offering similar rewards to those who would follow his example. There was no response, but the critical condition of the army was shown by two serious mutinies in January, 1781; one by Pennsylvania troops no fewer in number than thirteen hundred, who successfully claimed to be dismissed on the ground that having enlisted for three years or the war their time had expired. They themselves, however, seized the British agents who sought to tamper with their dubious patriotism, and the prisoners, tried by authority of Congress, were convicted and hung as spies. The second instance of insubordination was that of the New Jersey regulars, who were encouraged by the example and success of their neighbors. In the former case Washington had felt leniency to be necessary and had so advised Congress, but the spreading contagion had to be sternly checked. Two of the new ringleaders being seized and shot, the unruly battalions quickly returned to duty and complete subordination.

Such were the results of timidity and incapacity in the administration of financial politics. Throughout 1780 the only contributions obtained from the States were raised in kind and chiefly by the commissaries of the army. To meet what was ignorantly but naturally conceived to be the wilful and artificial depreciation of the currency, a plan of refunding was broached which would meet artful speculators on their own ground—the redemption of two hundred millions outstanding by a new issue of ten millions, bearing interest at five per cent., and redeemable in natural produce at the end of six years. Four parts were to be directly at the disposal of Congress, six were to go to the States according to the proportion of old notes presented by their authorities for redemption. The expenses of 1780 were three millions in specie, the loans which Jay had negotiated in the interval at Madrid and Franklin at Paris, together with the new credit of Congress, would cover the immediate claims. The scheme was partially successful, and so far a helpful support. But the new era of solvency dawned when Robert Morris was appointed, in February, 1781, to devote himself to the theory and detail of further financial administration. It was found that the holders of paper obligations were in great measure willing to forego whatever trifling value their bills might have, the great majority refusing to present them for such partial payments as they would have received, especially when, as the course of exchange soon determined, forty dollars of the old emissions had to be given for one of the new,

Robert Morris and the finances of the confederation.

and a real dollar in coin became successively worth various sums up to five hundred nominal dollars of the old Continental paper.

Although the Old Dominion had given way to a temporary outburst of passion when a feeble and somewhat discredited Congress used strong language incompatible with the false position it occupied, her true and tried temper reappeared when real danger menaced not only the common cause but the very territory of the South. The efforts she put forth to furnish troops, first to Gates and afterward to Greene, for the defence of the Carolinas, left her own valleys and shores unprotected, and Clinton took advantage of the fact to find employment for Arnold. English soldiers would neither serve under him nor with him, and he was therefore put in command of a Tory troop and landed on the Virginia shores to ravage at will. He was soon strengthened by the arrival of Phillips from New York with a body of regulars. Among other dishonorable exploits the renegade general burned Richmond, which had recently been made the capital city of the State, and on January 20, 1781, he had established himself at Portsmouth, some distance from the mouth of the Chesapeake.

Arnold in Virginia.

Steuben, with a small corps of observation, was immediately despatched to watch his movements. Washington got together a force of twelve hundred from New England, which were equipped in measure by the expenditure of two thousand guineas borrowed on Lafayette's private credit, and put under the command of the young general to follow and support Steuben, using as best he could the information obtained by the clever German. Jefferson importuned the aid of a French squadron from Newport, for the American strength was insufficient. The French ships were driven back to Rhode Island by an English detach-

Lafayette and Steuben.

ment from the fleet at New York, and Clinton put Phillips, who had two thousand men, in command at Portsmouth, where Arnold's force of a thousand men remained for the time. For a moment it appeared as if Cornwallis would be at liberty to direct his main army against Lafayette, who had retreated as far as Annapolis with his little company of shoeless and shelterless men, but having received important and imperative orders had halted there to share in the later developments of that determinative year.

Greene was not only a true-hearted and capable man but he had learned valuable lessons in the school of experience under a master since recognized by military experts of all lands as one of the great generals of all time. Gates's removal had been rendered more bitter by family bereavement, and Washington, in a spirit of genuine forgiveness, sought to temper his affliction by a letter of friendly consolation for both sorrows. Whether or not the discredited man could have redeemed his character is uncertain ; the reorganization, or rather the creation of a Southern army at Charlotte was the work of Greene, who arrived in December, 1780, and awakened a spirit of co-operation throughout the entire section. Virginia, under the impulse of Jefferson and by a splendid effort, raised eight hundred regulars and seventeen hundred militia. This feat saved the Southern States, for these troops, with the remnants which Gates had reassembled and volunteers who with the revival of hope were ready to fight again, gave him eventually upward of thirty-six hundred men. But his early operations were conducted with a feeble, dispirited force.

Greene creates a Southern army.

Cornwallis had meantime called in three thousand soldiers from Portsmouth, where they lay ready to invade Virginia, having come, under Leslie, from New York by

THE SOUTHERN INVASION REPELLED 331

way of Charleston, and again he set out for Camden, anxious to carry out the old plan and forced therefore to repeat in a measure old manœuvres. Once again he threw out his left wing, under Tarleton, to a position nearly identical with that of the previous year, and once again a like disaster befell it, but the scene was Cowpens, at no great distance from King's Mountain. The American commander was Morgan, the adventurous Virginia free-lance, who with personal followers and some other companies entrusted to him by Gates, had marched by several remote valleys toward the border of North Carolina. But he had now closed up his line with the idea of rejoining the centre, and with about nine hundred men in well ordered array, met Tarleton on January 17th. The English force of eleven hundred was annihilated, while that of the Americans suffered but few casualties. Tarleton and a few troopers managed to escape. Morgan, so exhausted by the rude campaigning of the wilderness that he never again could participate in the war, nevertheless proceeded, with scarcely a check, to unite with Greene, and on February 9th reached the camp at Guilford Court House.

<small>Morgan at Cowpens.</small>

But Cornwallis, reinforced by Leslie, had destroyed all his heavy baggage, and, though harassed at the fords by American attacks or checked in his advance by swollen currents, was pushing forward in light marching order. So few in number was Greene's army that he had withdrawn across the Roanoke into Virginia, where the strong and welcome contingent of that State came in and for the first time gave him a fighting chance. The English plan of leaving no enemies in the rear was carried out as far as possible, Wilmington and New Berne being occupied by soldiers from Charleston. North Carolina thus restored to royal domination,

<small>Greene's retreat.</small>

Cornwallis had intended to effect a junction with Arnold's force in Virginia to complete the conquest of the South.

But Greene was at last strong enough to dispute the field, and accordingly recrossed the border into North Carolina to meet Morgan, reaching Guilford Court House, now Greensboro, on February 10th. Cornwallis, knowing the wretched condition of the Americans in the lack of accoutrements and supplies, was anxious for an immediate engagement. But his opponent was not to be surprised. By a series of clever retreats, lasting four days, and by successive feints during the ensuing week, he effectually thwarted the English general and postponed the battle. At length, several important bodies of militia having come in from the neighborhood, on the fourteenth of March Greene returned to Guilford and, carefully choosing his ground, awaited the attack. In the disposition of his troops he threw the militia forward, carrying out a favorite but untried theory that they were more valuable in the attack than as a reserve. There were upward of sixteen hundred veterans with two thousand militia in the three American lines, while Cornwallis had less than two thousand regulars; but the Americans were destitute and worn out, while the English were fresh and well supplied with all necessaries. The attack began in the morning of March 15th.

The first onset of the British was made in mass and the American van of eleven hundred untried local militia fled in terror, many of them without having fired a shot. The second line, composed of Continentals from Virginia and Maryland, resisted gallantly for a time but retreated before the bayonet charge of the English regulars. Perhaps a third of the Americans were in the last reserve, and still stood where they had been placed, but Greene, believing the day irre-

THE SOUTHERN INVASION REPELLED 333

trievable, determined to withdraw, and did so, conducting his retreat in good order. He lost his artillery and upward of four hundred men, while he was further weakened by the departure for their homes of nine hundred militia whose time was almost, but not quite, completed. On the other hand, five hundred and seventy of the British were killed or wounded, so desperate had been their valor. The affair was a victory for Cornwallis, but the surrounding population was patriotic, the loyalists had been harried into flight or inaction; Greene was chagrined and anxious to fight again. The enemy's numbers were now too small for a further stand and there was nothing left for the conqueror but temporarily to accept the rôle of defeat. The retreat began, and with the remainder of his army he reached Wilmington on April 7th. North Carolina was never again under English control.

The plan to leave no enemies in the rear was of necessity abandoned, but the northward march was to be continued. By previous arrangement a portion of the Charleston garrison had reached Wilmington and the reorganized force set out to join at Petersburg the army which Clinton had sent from New York to the Chesapeake under Arnold and Phillips. It met with little resistance on the march and arrived on May 20th. Phillips was dead, and Arnold was promptly dismissed to New York. He was, however, not yet relegated to obscurity. In the following September he was sent with a force of English soldiers to capture the important seaport of New London, in Connecticut. The place was sacked, but the native militia made a heroic though desperate resistance in Fort Griswold, on Groton Heights. When compelled at last to capitulate, quarter was refused by their captors who were frenzied by their own losses, and the commander was run through with his own sword by the English major to

Groton Heights.

whom he had just delivered it. The Americans lost but twelve men in repelling the attack, but after the surrender upward of seventy were killed and thirty wounded. The English lost forty-eight who were killed and double the number who were disabled and wounded. In his report to Clinton, Arnold represented the action as honorable warfare. He was never again employed in the public service, the rest of his life being spent in obscurity and embittered by remorse.

The successor of Cornwallis in the Carolinas was Lord Rawdon, who faithfully carried on the policy of his predecessor in dealing with the patriots whenever they fell into his power. There were many men of limited capacity who wavered in such extremities and turned first this way and then that, in the hope of quiet and protection. Some were thorough loyalists, many, perhaps a small majority, were at heart in sympathy with the American revolt. Such men were treated with uniform cruelty, even when the impossibility of protecting them gave the English no right to demand even a show of loyalty. The consequence was a smothered but bitter disaffection, which grew in extent with every day; but the people were overawed and cautious, so that a timid inertia continued to lame the local militia. It was therefore with a force reduced to eighteen hundred men that Greene marched into South Carolina to cut off the communication of Charleston with Camden and Ninety-Six.

Effect of Rawdon's cruelties.

Greene's real courage and ability were fully displayed in the subsequent events. His force was insufficient to guard Virginia, and with the trust in others which characterizes great minds in a crisis he left it unprotected to march into the interior of a doubtful territory, without the possibility of securing communications in his rear or establishing a base of

Greene marches southward.

THE SOUTHERN INVASION REPELLED 335

supplies. Lee and Marion with the light cavalry were to manœuvre in the low country against the line from Charleston to Camden, Sumter with a few State troops was to keep the district between Ninety-Six and Camden, Pickens with the mountain volunteers was to capture supplies destined for Augusta and Ninety-Six, while the commander himself was to move directly against the controlling point.

The march to Camden occupied thirteen days. Greene did not find the enemy exactly where he expected and encamped at Hobkirk's Hill near by. After some unimportant movements he returned to the same place and on April 28th was surprised by Rawdon with a force somewhat inferior to his own, but not before he had been able to array his troops. The battle was as stubborn and bitter as any of the war, but Greene was again defeated, with a loss of three hundred men. Again, however, he drew off in good order, his loss was no greater than Rawdon's, and although the latter was soon reinforced by five hundred men, he could not again baffle Greene's strategy and force the Americans to an immediate engagement. *Defeat at Hobkirk's Hill.*

Meantime, on April 26th, Lee and Marion had captured a British post on the Santee, and his communication being thus broken, Rawdon set fire to Camden and withdrew. Throughout May both Sumter and Marion carried on a ceaseless and successful warfare; Orangeburg, Fort Motte, Fort Granby, Fort Cornwallis, and Georgetown fell into their hands, and by the middle of the month the State as far as Augusta and Ninety-Six was again under American control. Early in June Pickens captured Augusta, and Greene had already besieged Ninety-Six. The latter fortress, however, was soon relieved by Rawdon and the garrison withdrew in safety. *Sumter and Marion.*

336 THE FRENCH WAR AND THE REVOLUTION

The remainder of the summer passed without any great activity. The Americans encamped in the hills near Camden, while the English reoccupied Orangeburg. Rawdon went back to Charleston, where he hanged Isaac Hayne, a native planter who had deserted from the British and had been recaptured. He then sailed for England, but the ship was taken by the French and he himself made a prisoner. The execution of Hayne was justly regarded as murder, and the name of its perpetrator was execrated. Such was the effect on the public temper that the native militia now fought like veterans. At the opening of September Greene set his force in motion to drive the enemy from his position. The English, now under the command of Stuart, retreated. Their first halt was at Eutaw Springs. On the morning of September 8th they were overtaken at that place and in the fighting which followed Marion and Pickens with their militia bore the burden of the onset. The Americans were victorious and the British fled. The pursuers were hot and rash; there was a temporary and serious check to their course, in which many brave men were captured and carried by the flying English to Charleston. The American loss was five hundred and fifty-four, that of their enemy nearly a thousand. Colonel Stuart with the remnant of his force withdrew to Charleston, Greene to his position on the heights of Santee. Defeated in almost every important encounter, the American general and his capable lieutenants had nevertheless gained their end. The three cities of Charleston, Wilmington, and Savannah remained temporarily in English hands, but Georgia and the Carolinas were freed from invasion or the fear of it.

[margin: Battle of Eutaw Springs.]

CHAPTER XXVIII.

YORKTOWN—1781

Plans of Cornwallis—His Advance against Lafayette—The Pursuit and Retreat—Steuben Creates an Army—Disagreement between Clinton and Cornwallis—Position of the Latter at Yorktown—Arrival of the French Fleet under De Grasse—Washington's Plans—Sectional Feeling among the States—Events in the North during 1780—Conferences of Washington and Rochambeau—Clinton Expects an Attack on New York—The Combined Armies March Southward—The Threatened Mutiny at Philadelphia—Defeat of the English Fleet in the Chesapeake—Investment of Yorktown—Cornwallis Surrenders—Disposition of the American and French Forces—Closing Events of the War.

IN the early spring, Lafayette had received orders from the North of the utmost importance, a general statement, namely, that Virginia was soon to be the centre of operations, and that to this end he must defend it temporarily as best he could. Scarcely more than a boy in years, he was now displaying the qualities of a veteran in the difficult part assigned to him, which he filled entirely on his own responsibility, though nominally under the command of Greene. There had been a curious analogy between the determination of Greene to abandon Virginia, and that of Cornwallis to desert the Carolinas. The former had used the geography of the disputed territory with skill, and won by strategy. The earl, however, had counted on English ascendency at sea, and was indifferent to the topography of the low lands which were his goal. He

Plans of Cornwallis.

knew, but disregarded, the great streams which flowing southeastward divide the State into long peninsulas, which open to receive an army from the landward, but, being enclosed on three sides by the waters, are a trap to one unsupported by a fleet.

Richmond was the central depot for military stores in Virginia, and thither, by a forced march of two hundred miles, Lafayette, with a thousand men, had betaken himself from Annapolis, to join Steuben, who had raised a few hundred militia, and await the coming of Wayne from the North with a thousand Pennsylvanians. For nearly a month he held in check the superior force of Phillips and Arnold, at Petersburg. When Cornwallis arrived, on May 20th, and dismissed Arnold, he found himself at the head of seven thousand men, but realizing the insufficiency of this number for his great plans, at once appealed to Clinton for reinforcements from New York. There was no delay, however, in moving against Lafayette.

His advance against Lafayette.

Washington and Greene had learned the tactics of retreat before superior forces, and Lafayette was scarcely their inferior in the art. Withdrawing step by step in the direction of Fredericksburg before the English, he occupied the strongest positions, and finally, without risking a battle, met Wayne on June 7th. Tarleton was despatched on raids to Charlottesville and Albemarle, in order to disperse the legislature and seize stores. On his return the conclusion was reached that Lafayette's force being now equal to a defensive campaign, caution required a return to the base of supplies and a temporary cessation of operations. Accordingly, the English marched back first to Richmond, and then across the Chickahominy to Williamsburg, marauding as they went. The arsenal stores destroyed at Albemarle, the excellent cavalry horses and

The pursuit and retreat.

other captured supplies, together with the booty taken from the Virginians in the course of the month, were worth sums estimated by millions.

When for the first time Steuben had reached the goal of his ambition by obtaining an independent command in Virginia, he had displayed his genius in raising and equipping troops for Greene. So now he steadily increased the force of Lafayette. There were upward of five thousand men in the army which, following on the flanks of Cornwallis, did what was possible to restrain his pillaging. On July 6th Wayne rashly brought on a partial engagement at Greene Springs in which serious loss was inflicted on both sides, but the Americans were defeated. Cornwallis, in accordance with orders from Clinton to seek a defensive position, continued his march to Yorktown, called in the garrison from Portsmouth, which increased his army to nearly eight thousand men, occupied Gloucester on the opposite shore of the York River, and proceeded to throw up intrenchments while his active and well-equipped riders ravaged the country for miles around. Lafayette remained in camp at Malvern Hill.

<small>Steuben creates an army.</small>

The movements of the English in Virginia had been in partial accord with orders received from Clinton. Between him and Cornwallis there was now a hearty dislike, engendered by mutual jealousy and distrust. Sir Henry knew how hopeless would be any attempt to reduce Virginia, which was a focus of American patriotism, and realized the strategic importance of New York, which he felt to be threatened by the armies of Washington and Rochambeau in possible co-operation with a French fleet. The earl, assured of ministerial favor and scheming to supplant the general, blindly desired to evacuate New York, transfer the seat of war to Virginia, and with the help of Rodney's

<small>Disagreement between Clinton and Cornwallis.</small>

fleet reduce the South to subjection. He was angered by repeated messages from Clinton, received on the march through Williamsburg and afterward at intervals, demanding the return of three thousand troops to New York, and would gladly have withdrawn to Charleston.

The situation was indeed a disappointing one for Cornwallis. In abandoning Portsmouth he had left no avenue of retreat toward the South. Greene had checkmated his movement to secure the Carolinas and narrowed his chances for victory to a combined operation in which success, if obtained, must be shared with the fleet. Lafayette was within attacking distance, ready to thwart any movement inland. As yet the English were masters of the Chesapeake, but the few weak vessels could make no resistance in case a French squadron should arrive before the English, and there was already a French naval force at Newport. All this he knew. What he could not know was that a powerful armament under De Grasse had left Brest in March, 1781, for the Antilles, to continue the naval war with England in the West Indies, and that the commander's orders were to sail in July for North America, there to co-operate with the allied armies of the United States and France.

Position of the latter at Yorktown.

It was August when the French admiral, with twenty-eight vessels, containing, besides sailors and marines, four thousand soldiers under Saint Simon, sighted the Virginia shores. No opposing force of adequate strength was in the Chesapeake. Rodney, instead of following his adversary, had gone to England on private business and left Hood, a subordinate, with an inadequate force to meet and co-operate with the expected fleet from New York under Graves. The latter lingered until the French squadron from Newport had sailed to join De Grasse. The landing of Saint

Arrival of the French fleet under De Grasse.

Simon's army, therefore, was accomplished without difficulty. Before the first of September, Lafayette, whose ambitions were now realized in the important station he had reached, found himself in command not only of his own forces at Malvern Hill but of the auxiliaries furnished by his native land, who encamped near by in a place of great strength and raised his effective force to about eight thousand men.

From the beginning it had been clear that the American cause was dependent for success on the union of the colonies. For that reason it was essential that New England should not be cut off from the others by the loss of New York and the Hudson River. With a single eye to that end Washington, disregarding personal appeals from his Southern friends, undeceived by every feint and stratagem, in the face of apathy and opposition, with a decimated army lacking equipments and often the barest necessaries of life, had persistently held the long line of investment from Middlebrook in New Jersey around by the north to the Highlands of the Hudson, whence he had unbroken communication with the Eastern States. *Washington's plans.*

From the earliest times it had been the colonial habit to throw the burden of defence on the localities most in danger. Throughout the French war there had been a development of the same spirit, each colonial group furnishing men and supplies for the conflict in its immediate neighborhood. The same disposition lingered in the Eastern States. There had for a long time been no fighting of importance on or near their lands. Their mercantile instincts had reasserted themselves with mastery, and the commerce of New England was again most flourishing. They were now secure, for after July, 1780, Rochambeau and the French fleet were at Newport, and there are indications *Sectional feeling among the States.*

that the people were not anxious for his departure. Washington was no longer supplied with men, as in the sacrifice of local Southern interests to those of the once fiery patriotism of the North and East he had reason to expect he would be.

Such was the destitution of the American army that they could not use the opportunity of an attack on New York which the formation of solid ice in the waters round about during the severe winter of 1779–80 had afforded. The English, however, were kept in constant dread of such a movement. The ensuing summer was barren of substantial results. There were deeds of daring like Wayne's unsuccessful attack on Bull's Ferry in July, and the fruitless expedition to Staten Island in October. There were conventions at Boston and Hartford, and much talk about "the vigorous prosecution of the war and the reception of our French allies," about giving more power to Congress, about raising troops and providing the munitions of war. The only real gain was in the ever-improving system for military organization, devised and slowly introduced by Steuben. The plan for co-operation against New York, concerted between Rochambeau and Washington at Hartford, had been frustrated by Arnold's treason and other less prominent events. The opening of another year was not more promising. The Southern and Central States were indifferent, the troops mutinous, and Clinton was still striving to foment treason.

Events in the North during 1780.

Finally, in May, another conference between Washington and Rochambeau was held at Weathersfield, in Connecticut, and in accordance with their agreement the French army at once set out for the Hudson. Clinton was fully informed of all these movements, and expected, as Washington desired that he should, a combined movement against New York.

Conferences of Washington and Rochambeau.

As if in execution of such a design an attack was made in July on the English posts, but with no results except that Clinton called for Cornwallis's troops and sent his subordinate to Yorktown. The summer passed with the army in a defensive attitude, the commanders establishing communication with the French admiral and arranging for a decisive blow. On August 14th the news came that De Grasse was to enter the Chesapeake.

There had been two courses open to Washington— consistent adherence to his policy of warfare on the Hudson or an entire change of plan. In the former he would have displayed a certain discordance with the French movement, in the latter he must practise self-denial and reverse a settled judgment. In addition to other considerations was the determining one that no offensive operations could be successful with neither a French fleet in New York waters nor any of the longed-for reinforcements which New England should have furnished. With true greatness he combined the elements into a single problem and solved it by a compromise. The American forts were garrisoned for defence, the base of operations secured for the future by northward outposts against Canada, and measures taken to confirm in Clinton's mind the belief that New York was in danger. Some days were thus consumed. The army began to cross the river, but Clinton, in spite of warnings from his Hessian lieutenant at Kingsbridge, held his conviction more stubbornly than ever and believed the movement was against Staten Island. By the twenty-fourth the march toward the south began. Philadelphia was reached on September 2d.

Clinton expects an attack on New York.

The combined armies march southward.

The New England troops, their pay now long in arrears, were worn out by the long march and, being ignorant of their destination, began to follow the pernicious example previously given by those of the Middle States. Mutiny was feared. Morris had no available funds, and Rochambeau magnanimously gave twenty thousand dollars from his own store. Most opportunely John Laurens arrived at that moment from France with supplies of all kinds and five hundred thousand dollars in cash. The just demands of the soldiery were satisfied in part, and their loyalty grew strong as their spirits rose. On the fifth came the news of De Grasse's arrival, the army heard it on the sixth, and two days later the movement was consummated by the assemblage of the whole force at the head of the Elk River, whence they proceeded in French vessels and without molestation to the York River. Washington himself, with his friends Rochambeau and Chastellux, rode in the saddle to Williamsburg, by way of Mount Vernon, revisiting his home for the first time in six years. The union with Lafayette occurred on the fourteenth, and the troops from the North were all safely landed by the twenty-sixth. Two days later the entire force, numbering about sixteen thousand, was before Yorktown.

The threatened mutiny at Philadelphia.

But meantime a naval manœuvre of the utmost importance had been consummated. Graves and Hood having at length joined forces, arrived off the Chesapeake on September 5th, when De Grasse was daily and hourly expecting the squadron from Newport under De Barras. They made preparations for attack, and the French fleet drew out in line of battle to defeat their purpose. There was a sharp conflict of some hours, in which the English suffered serious loss, but no general engagement. For five days the fleets were within fighting distance, but the intention of the French admiral was to keep open the mouth of the bay for the entrance of the Newport squadron. He

Defeat of the English fleet in the Chesapeake.

was successful. The opposing commanders returned to New York, and the united French fleets were free to beset Yorktown with no less than thirty-five vessels of the line. De Grasse, however, would have gone to sea with nearly all his ships, for he learned that there were reinforcements for his enemy at New York, and feared both the approach of autumnal storms in a landlocked bay and a blockade. Washington and Lafayette prevailed on him to remain.

Cornwallis was holding a fortified camp some distance in advance of his lines. The French would have stormed his position, but he voluntarily abandoned it. On September 29th, the investment of Yorktown was complete. On the night before October 6th the Americans and French simultaneously began the trenches of the first parallel, and on the ninth they were completed. With unusual promptness the second parallel was begun three days later, on the twelfth. Two British redoubts impeded its progress. The American batteries began on the fourteenth to bombard them, and continued some hours until breaches were made. At a preconcerted signal two columns, French and American respectively, advanced, one against each. The American assault on the right was led by Alexander Hamilton. His success was instant and complete, so gallant were his lieutenants and so daring his men. The American loss was very slight and only eight of the enemy were injured. The French, on the left, were prematurely discovered, their struggle was long and bitter, and a hundred brave men fell before the works were taken. The same night the besiegers' trenches included the two outposts.

There was but a single desperate chance left to Cornwallis. Gloucester Point, on the opposite shore, was beleaguered by a force comparatively small. His hope

Investment of Yorktown.

was to transport the garrison thither and break through the French dragoons and marines who, with the Virginia militia, had been sent to invest his fortifications at that place. Early on the sixteenth he ordered a sortie against the narrowing lines of his besiegers, but a momentary success was soon checked by the stronger force of his enemy. At dusk on the same day he began to ferry over the soldiers, but a storm arose and prevented the accomplishment of his purpose. Thwarted in his last resource, with famine impending, he yielded to necessity, and on the seventeenth asked for terms. The following day a commission of four members, two from the British army and one each from the American and French, drew up in form the details of surrender. They were identical as far as possible with those exacted by Clinton from Lincoln at Charleston, severe but just: public property to be surrendered, private property respected, and the Tories left to the mercy of their fellow-citizens. The ceremonies took place on the afternoon of the nineteenth, Lincoln representing Washington as commander-in-chief of the allied victors, O'Hara acting for Cornwallis, who pleaded illness and remained in his tent. The Americans and French stood in line as the English marched by and stacked their arms, their standards furled and their drums rolling a quaint measure known as the "World turned upside down."

The prisoners of war numbered eight thousand and eighty-seven, of whom eight hundred and forty were sailors; in addition to the small arms of the captured there were two hundred and forty-four cannon included in the surrender. Thirty-five ships and seven thousand men were the French contribution to the victory, nine thousand soldiers that of the Americans. The same day Clinton sailed from New York with seven thousand soldiers and the refitted fleet for the relief of Cornwallis, but he was met off Cape Henry by the packet containing Cornwallis's despatches and returned to New York, where he remained until the final evacuation of the city. The Americans would gladly have seen De Grasse depart to recapture Charleston, but he had remained longer than he wished, and sailed away for the calm waters of the West Indies; Washington and his army returned to their position before New York, Rochambeau and the French troops encamped at Williamsburg, Wayne departed with the Pennsylvania Continentals to reinforce the army in South Carolina.

In November Greene assumed the offensive once more, but he had to contend with mutinous disaffection among his new forces, and the situation remained unchanged about Charleston. Wayne marched into Georgia the following spring, and after two successful skirmishes, one with English troops, one with Indians under an English officer, compelled the British to take refuge in Savannah. In general the country at large was heartily sick of the war. The rejoicings over the surrender at Yorktown were general and hearty, but they were not followed by any preparations for the active continuance of operations. There was a universal reliance on some hoped-for turn of affairs in English politics, a settled determination to raise no further funds nor men, and a stolid persistence in sectional self-assertion with no care for the public interests except among the patriotic few.

Closing events of the war.

CHAPTER XXIX.

THE PEACE OF VERSAILLES—1782-1783

American Independence and European Politics—England and the Bourbon Powers—International Law—Blockade and Contraband—The Continental Neutrals—The Armed Neutrality—William Lee and the Amsterdam Proposal—Position of the Netherlands—The News of Yorktown—Fall of the North Ministry—State of English Parties—The Rockingham Ministry—American Peace Commissioners—The Terms proposed by Congress—Oswald and Franklin—Grenville and Vergennes—Cross Purposes in the Negotiation—The Shelburne Ministry—Position of Jay and Adams—Franklin's Attitude—The Wishes of Vergennes—Secret Mission of Rayneval—Jay's Proposals—Final Negotiations—Character of the Treaty—The General Pacification—Fall of Shelburne's Ministry—The Coalition Ministry—Final Ratification of the Treaty.

THE war was over, but Americans could not know it as a certitude, while in fact the revolution was far from being accomplished. The rest of the struggle was to be fought in the English Parliament. The truth, unpalatable perhaps, to the self-sufficient, but comforting to the patriot, is that the stars in their courses had been fighting for American independence. A Providence in history can nowhere be more clearly seen than in the study of our own origins. If the so-called doctrinaire requires a text from which to prove the unity of history, he will choose the connection of the American revolution with contemporary European politics as his theme. As this is not our

American Independence and European politics.

subject we must be content with a short glance at the facts.

In the state system of Europe equilibrium had so far been maintained in some degree by a careful regard to that doctrine known as the balance of power, according to which no one state was to secure an undue preponderance in any way whatsoever. *England and the Bourbon powers.* Local interests were always working in the opposite direction, and England had gradually secured not only vast colonial possessions, but a virtual mastery of the seas. The present struggle was one phase of an effort by the Bourbon powers to deprive her in part of both. Incidentally there would be opened to all the European powers channels of trade hitherto reserved to Great Britain. To that extent, therefore, all Europe would look on with complacency and see England so far humiliated. This was true as a matter of course in the case of Austria, which not only belonged to the sisterhood of Roman Catholic powers, but was also now in open alliance with France and Spain. It was also true of Russia, Prussia, and even of the Dutch Republic, the ally of England for a hundred and six years, but her rival in the carrying trade of the world's commerce.

The peace relations of the modern European nations were comparatively easy to regulate. But for the very reason that they were sisters, and had all sprung from the same womb, that of the *International law.* Holy Roman Empire which died as they were born, their relations in time of war were most complicated and difficult. Among other doctrines held with reference to these was that of contraband, that certain articles, namely, could be seized wherever found, as an act of self-defence, because without them an enemy was weaker as a belligerent. Under this theory there could be no question about guns, powder, and other munitions, but many, especially the jurists of maritime powers, held that clothing, food, and similar supplies were quite as essential to successful warfare as weapons with which men actually fought or might fight.

A further extension of the same claim was that almost any harbor of an enemy might be regarded as under *Blockade and contraband.* blockade if a display of force, natural or artificial, was made before it. England in particular regarded all goods belonging to an enemy as contraband, no difference under what flag they were found, and asserted that by reason of her insular position any enemy's harbor opposite her shores, or before which her flag floated from a vessel, was both really and technically blockaded. In accordance with this contention her ships scoured the high seas, searching any vessel whatsoever, as containing possibly contraband goods, and policed the territorial waters by the shores of hostile powers on the plea that their ports were blockaded. The neutral states foresaw that such a policy would ultimately trample all their rights under foot.

The reasons why Great Britain sought the alliance of Russia have been explained. When Paul Jones brought *The continental neutrals.* his prizes into the Texel they were safe because of the national Dutch temper, for no nation had suffered like the Dutch since the outbreak of the war. Their carrying trade had been nearly ruined by British privateers, and their traders were at the enormous expense of armed convoys. The first thought of Russia, Prussia, Denmark, and Sweden was to drive by force all privateers, including the English, from their immediate neighborhood. But England could desire nothing better, for her commerce with Russia would thereby be protected against the American privateers which were endangering it. Holland was the home of international law, and France in her maritime inferiority had always contended for neutral rights such as were secured by the peace of Utrecht. It gradually became clear that the general welfare of neutral powers required a further extension of an inchoate principle, and the lesser states of the north naturally looked to Russia as a leader.

Spain had joined the Franco-American alliance for various reasons, among others to regain Gibraltar. In 1779 a Dutch fleet convoying a number of Dutch vessels loaded with naval supplies had been captured by the English, and almost simultaneously Spain had seized two Russian ships laden with provisions, on the plea that their cargoes might be destined for the revictualling of Gibraltar. This brought matters to a crisis, and the armed neutrality of the northern powers was the consequence. According to its terms, set forth by Russia in February, 1780, no goods are contraband, except arms and ammunition, no port is blockaded except when a sufficient number of war-vessels make entrance or exit dangerous, and a neutral flag protects all goods except contraband, not only on the high seas but from port to port. Spain, France, and the United States all saw their account in such an agreement, for its tendency was to weaken England and compel a peace advantageous to them. The neutral powers of the continent one by one adopted its provisions, and assured thereby a permanent development of international law. *The armed neutrality.*

During these negotiations William Lee, an American agent in London, who was at the same time a British merchant, had concerted with an irregular commissioner from the city of Amsterdam an outline for a commercial treaty between the Netherlands and the United States. When, in 1780, Henry Laurens, the American commissioner to negotiate a Dutch loan, was captured by the English while travelling to his post, a draft of this document was found *William Lee and the Amsterdam proposal.*

among his papers. The Dutch claimed that it was purely a personal matter between two individuals, the English that the paper was semi-official, and implicated the whole republic in an act hostile to its ally. Accordingly the states of Holland formally repudiated the act of Amsterdam. At the same time it was clear that for the protection of their commerce against England they were about to join the league of northern powers.

The republic was still rich, very rich, but it had been enfeebled by a monstrous development of the commer- Position of the cial spirit in exclusive devotion to gain, and Netherlands. by internal dissensions under a bad constitution. England therefore determined to prevent its adhesion to the new league by a declaration of war, and to that end demanded that the Amsterdam authorities should be punished. The nature of the demand is clear in the fact that Laurens, the second party, and a prisoner in their hands, was neither tried nor even specially punished, except in the severity of his imprisonment. The Dutch republic accepted the terms of the armed neutrality on December 24th. To forestall any possible advantage to the Netherlands of the formal declaration of war, which was to be made on the thirtieth, hostilities began early in the month by the seizure of some two hundred Dutch merchantmen, and the despatch of orders to capture St. Eustatius, in the West Indies, the free port whence America had during the early stages of the war obtained such important supplies. The place was seized in February, but was shortly recaptured by the French, and throughout the year England's fortunes in the West Indies were at the lowest ebb. They did not turn until April 12th in the following year, when Rodney's great and bloody victory off Dominica restored the naval position of Great Britain, and by soothing the national pride paved the way for peace.

Such then was the situation of European affairs when the news of Cornwallis's surrender reached London on November 25, 1781, two days before the open- *The news of* ing of Parliament. Lord North, aware since *Yorktown.* 1779 of the uselessness of further bloodshed, but over-persuaded by his master and acting contrary to his convictions, might well give way to a dramatic despair and pace the room with wild gesticulations exclaiming, "It is all over." His country was in active warfare with the United States, France, Spain, and Holland, in passive but disastrous hostility with the armed neutrality which already had the sympathy of those powers of importance that had not yet joined it. At home the Whigs were as bitter in their opposition as the long contempt for liberal principles shown by the king and government could make them. All Europe longed for peace, and both to that end and for the better security of the balance of power every nation except Spain desired the independence of the United States. Spain, for obvious reasons, feared the extinction of her rights in North America if a great power were established east of the Mississippi.

Nevertheless when a motion calling for the cessation of hostilities against the colonies was put on November 25th, it was lost by a majority, ominous be- *Fall of the* cause of its wasted number, but nevertheless *North minis-* a substantial one. The king, under the spe- *try.* cious plea for the integrity of the empire, reasserted his persistent determination to carry on the war. Another attempt made by the liberals, on February 22, 1782, to coerce the administration also failed, but the adverse majority was only one. At last, on March 4th, the rising tide of popular feeling found expression in the house, and by a majority of nineteen it was declared that those attempting to prosecute the war in America "for the purpose of reducing the revolted colonies to submission" would be considered enemies to king and country. On March 20th the ministry resigned.

George III. was for the moment overpowered and stunned as he saw the ruin of his cherished hopes of ex-
State of ercising supreme power by the assertion of
English par- the prerogative. But he soon regained his
ties. composure, and with it his adroitness. The Whigs were of three opinions concerning the essential questions of constitutional development—one small faction was soon to merge with the new Tories, another, with Rockingham at its head, was true to the party tradition, and a third, represented by Shelburne their leader, were the real liberals. In the hope probably that an equilibrium of only the most unstable character would exist in the new cabinet, Shelburne was chosen to form a ministry. But the representative of Chatham's ideas refused to be caught in the trap, insisted that Rockingham be called, and prevailed.

The task was delicate, but it was performed. Thurston, the chancellor, was held over from the North ad-
The Rock- ministration; besides the premier there were
ingham minis- Fox, Cavendish, Keppel, and Richmond of the
try. old line; Grafton, Shelburne, Camden, Ashburton, and Conway of the new. The balance of interests was too nice to be permanent, the members being hopelessly divided as to the burning question of parliamentary reform. Fox, as Secretary for Foreign Affairs, was to negotiate a peace with the European powers; Shelburne, as Secretary for the Colonies, was to treat with the United States, not yet recognized officially as independent. From the outset Fox wished to monopolize the entire negotiation and drove Shelburne to shifts which subjected both him and the Americans to criticism.

When two years previously Kaunitz was organizing a peace convention in Vienna, with the idea that Russia and

Austria were to mediate between England and the Bourbons, and thereby obtain great concessions in the Orient and Italy, the American Congress had been asked by the French minister at Philadelphia to prepare its terms and appoint its commissioners. Accordingly five negotiators were elected in order that every sectional interest might be represented. The men chosen were John Adams, Jay, Franklin, Jefferson, and the elder Laurens. An ill-conceived dislike for the French made Adams unwelcome at Versailles, and he departed for Holland to secure, if possible, a loan from the Netherlands. After Laurens's capture he was accredited as minister, and though not yet received as such was still at The Hague. Jay was in Spain, vainly striving to open negotiations with that jealous power. Laurens was a paroled prisoner in London, and Jefferson, occupied with his duties as Governor of Virginia in repelling the invasion of Arnold and Cornwallis, had never left America. Although the latter was especially appointed plenipotentiary in 1782 to treat for peace, he had scarcely received his commission when news came that the negotiation was virtually completed, the preliminaries having been concluded by Franklin, with the aid of Adams in Holland, and of Jay, who had been summoned from Madrid.

American Peace Commissioners.

The terms on which mediation would be accepted were not definitively formulated in 1780, but left in the vaguest shape because of the general lassitude in the North, and the earnest desire on the part of the South to be rid of the scourge under which its people were now writhing after the war had been transferred to the Carolinas. Expressing a desire for the cession of Canada and Nova Scotia, the instructions said their acquisition was nevertheless not an ultimatum. Under the circumstances,

The terms proposed by Congress.

therefore, it was unavoidable that the opening stages of negotiation should be irregular. In the sequel it proved that the closing stages must be equally so.

As early as March 22, 1782, Franklin wrote a letter to his old friend Shelburne, expressing satisfaction with the turn affairs were taking. Almost immediately, on April 6th, a reply was despatched by the hand of a Scotch merchant, Oswald, who owned large estates in America and was a friend of Adam Smith. The letter was merely an introduction of the bearer as an accredited agent to express the personal views of his principal. Laurens was meantime released and went at once to his post, where he and Adams remained awaiting events, the latter being formally received in the same month as minister to the States-General of the United Provinces. On the arrival of Oswald, Franklin, by a letter written on the twenty-second, called Jay from Madrid. Parliament had not as yet raised its interdict against negotiating with the colonies, and the introductory communications between Franklin and Shelburne were merely tentative. The former suggested the cession of Canada as indemnity partly for the losses of the successful patriots, partly to provide the American Tories with estates in place of those they had lost by confiscation. The English minister replied that such a proposition could not for a moment be entertained; on the contrary, England should receive an indemnity for the evacuation of Savannah, Charleston, and New York, which she still held; to that end the Penobscot River might be made the eastern boundary of the United States.

Oswald and Franklin.

The plenipotentiary of the English Foreign Office was Thomas Grenville, who was ordered to open negotiations with Vergennes on the basis of yielding the independence of the United States as part of the consideration for which the Bourbons had been fighting. They indignantly repelled the proposal, asserting that they had found the United States independent. It had been a sufficiently amusing turn in affairs that Franklin should, as he did, introduce to the French Minister of State the agent of Great Britain, who was a Grenville at that and son of a sire who had proposed the Stamp Act, but he had no share in the absurd offer thus made. On the contrary, both he and Shelburne desired that the negotiations between England and her former colonies should not be hampered more than good faith required by the complications of continental diplomacy. On receipt of the news from Rodney the cabinet, feeling that the national self-respect was thereby regained, formally agreed that in treating with France and Spain they would "propose the independency of America, and not make it a condition of a general treaty."

Grenville and Vergennes.

In dealing with Franklin and Jay, Fox would gladly have made the same arrangement, in order to transfer the conduct of affairs to his own department. A like spirit was shown by Grenville, who, although accredited only to France, busied himself in trying to learn from Franklin the American proposals, but failed, and turning to Oswald extorted a half knowledge of the facts. In a letter to Fox he communicated his misleading information, aspersing the character of Shelburne's agent, and the minister, failing to comprehend the real truth, became more persistent in his purpose to force a recognition of independence. It was a curious web of cross-purposes that Shelburne, a friend of America, should delay the acknowledgment of independence that he might in the end propose the best terms, while Fox, with no real difference in policy, should strive to hasten it that he might serve his own ambition without regard to ultimate terms; that Vergennes, who

Cross-purposes in the negotiation.

had the interests of France in mind, should insist on it as a preliminary while cherishing as his dearest purpose a limitation of the American territory to the narrowest possible bounds; that Franklin, because of his loyalty to France, should deprecate hasty action in separating from Vergennes, while Jay, with the keen vision of a newcomer, saw that he must be urgent to forestall the scheme of the French minister, which, when he reached Paris on June 23d, he almost instantly detected. The English cabinet, however, refused to sustain Fox, and as a consequence he resigned on June 30th. The disintegration of the ministry was completed by the sudden death of the prime minister on the day after. During the few months of its existence the Rockingham government had done a wondrous work; giving legislative independence to Ireland, now rapidly following the American example of rebellion; striking the shackles off Irish trade, carrying through a bill for the economic reform of government; making prominent the distasteful question of parliamentary reform, and opening an avenue to the ultimate triumph in England itself of the liberal principles for which her colonies had so successfully striven.

Persistent in his old policy of dividing parties and forming cabinets as weak as possible, the king summoned Shelburne, although the Duke of Portland was the heir to Rockingham's position as leader of the old Whigs. Of this faction the majority now adhered to the Tories, although a considerable number came over to the rising liberalism represented by Shelburne under the leadership of the Duke of Richmond, who was retained along with Keppel. William Pitt succeeded Cavendish as Chancellor of the Exchequer, Shelburne himself was First Lord of the Treasury, and Thomas Townshend was appointed to the post of Secretary for the Colonies, while Lord Grantham be-

The Shelburne ministry.

came Minister for Foreign Affairs. The composition of the ministry was in some measure the work of the king, and Shelburne, though a sincere and consistent believer in reform, was at the time suspected by many of having been dazzled by royal favor because he upheld the rights of the crown and people against the assumptions of the aristocracy. There was no truth in the insinuation, and now that he was assured of control, Parliament proceeded to pass an act enabling the government to treat with the United States not as thirteen separate colonies, which they had hitherto been in the letter of English law, but as a single power, under the style of the Thirteen United States. Grenville had, of course, resigned, and the powers of Oswald were modified according to the new formula.

The only obstacle to completing the treaty was Jay's feeling that independence ought to be recognized by a proclamation, which should at the same time order the evacuation of the harbor cities of America still held by English forces. *Position of Jay and Adams.* This gave rise to dangerous delay. A compromise was finally proposed, but not immediately accepted, by which the preamble to the treaty should definitely and emphatically recognize independence without reference to the adoption or rejection of other portions. Negotiations were thus prolonged until September, 1782, when Townshend yielded, explaining, however, that the formal authorization must await an act of Parliament. Jay stood firm in his demand, even at the risk of the indefinite delay whereby success was jeopardized. Meantime the question arose of how far the American commissioners must be bound by their instructions from Congress to act in concert with France and keep equal step with Vergennes in the negotiations. Though indifferent to the complications of English politics, Jay and Adams clearly understood the situation in France. The latter, negotiating with the Netherlands for the recognition of American independence, was still resident at The Hague, although chief of the commission to treat with England; but he shared as far as possible in the councils of his colleagues. Both he and Jay were concerned for the end, without regard to their instructions, which being virtually dictated by Luzerne, the French minister at Philadelphia, were sufficiently timorous. They had been passed by Congress on June 15th, 1781, and, directing the American agents to be confidential with the French Government, instructed them "ultimately" to be governed by its advice and opinion. They were repeated by formal vote in October, 1782, too late to reach the commissioners, who had gladly forgotten them.

Franklin felt that the end could better be secured by obeying the instructions and yielding in matters of detail to hasten the conclusion of business before a new cabinet crisis in England could possibly endanger it. He seems to have thought sufficient Oswald's first indefinite commission "to treat with the colonies and with any or either of them, with any description of men in them, of and concerning peace," and with stalwart good faith insisted on keeping Vergennes informed not of confidential detail but of the fact of negotiation; his colleagues were of another mind and determined to disregard the French interest for the sake of what they thought the highest principle, the independence and dignity of America, without regard to her treaty engagement, which many, moreover, considered cancelled in international law by the French alliance with Spain.

Franklin's attitude.

Vergennes had informed Grenville that the English demand for restitution of conquests could not be considered; that in 1756 his country fought for boundaries on the Ohio and in Maine, but by the peace of 1763 had kept all of New France; that while in the present war France had primarily fought for American independence, she had in the course of events contracted other obligations and would keep all she had gained; that consequently the question of independence was confined to England and the United States. But this was antecedent to Rodney's victory over De Grasse, and on September 13th, 1783, the famous three years' siege of Gibraltar by France and Spain, conducted against Eliott by D'Arcon, whose floating batteries could "neither be burnt, sunk, nor taken," ended in disaster to the Bourbon cause. The moral effect of these reverses changed Vergennes's attitude radically. Liberal England was now in power and well disposed toward liberalism in America. To reknit the questions of American independence and co-operation in negotiation with his own interest would be a great gain, and if at the same time he could appease Spain by limiting the territories ceded to the United States, he would score a diplomatic triumph. His position was, that by the treaty of 1778 his country sought the independence of the United States within their colonial limits, but he would be willing to divide the great Western lands between the United States, England, and Spain. The fisheries on the Banks he maintained belonged to England and France; independent America must renounce her colonial share in that source of wealth and training-school of seamen. The attitude was exactly that of an adroit craftsman who regarded, as many French writers still do, the American Revolution as but a phase of the perennial struggle of England and France for supremacy in the West. It was distinctly hostile to the interests of a groping but conscious democracy, with a manifest destiny for united action to secure the Western hemisphere for free institutions.

The wishes of Vergennes.

Franklin had informed Oswald in July what the conditions of peace would be: first, the acknowledgment of independence; second, the frontier on the Canadian side to be as it was before the passage of the Quebec act, and on the west to the Mississippi; third, participation in the fisheries. On the change of ministry Shelburne sent Vaughan, a friend of Franklin's, to assure him that there would be no change of policy. Oswald's new commission came on July 17th, and Franklin certainly thought this one "would do," as Vergennes did also. Jay's position has been stated. At this juncture the French minister entered on a course of double dealing. The motives are uncertain, but the facts are clear and seem capable of but one interpretation. During the late summer Marbois, secretary of the French legation in Philadelphia, wrote a letter which was intercepted by the English and communicated to Jay. It proved to be a plea against America sharing in the fisheries. On September 15th Rayneval, a former agent of the French Government in America, received from Vergennes formal instructions to proceed secretly to London and demand for Spain either Gibraltar or a compensation for it, but to refuse if questioned to engage in conversation concerning American affairs. Jay suspected what is now known, that there was something behind this, and Rayneval, in 1795, confessed that he was also to learn the truth concerning certain overtures made to De Grasse. It is also known that he "expressed a strong opinion," in his interview with Shelburne and Grantham, "against the American claims to the fisheries and to the valleys of the Ohio and Mississippi."

Secret mission of Rayneval.

By this time Vaughan had become the confidential friend of Jay. Without the knowledge or concurrence of Franklin he was prevailed on to accept a mission to Shelburne, and convey to him the considerations which should influence Great Britain in treating with America. She could not conquer and ought therefore to conciliate; the United States would not treat except on an equal footing, and it might be to the interest of France, but was not to that of England, to postpone independence until a general peace. America would not make peace without the fisheries, and would be so irritated by exclusion from navigating the Mississippi that the peace if made would be little more than a truce. Jay also thought that there should be reciprocity in trade and commerce. West Florida should not be left in Spanish hands, as endangering the trade of both countries. England was to share the free navigation of the inland waters and the great river, "which," wrote Jay, "would in future be no less important to Great Britain than to us."

Jay's proposals.

Shelburne had once before determined to divide the Americans from their allies. Then it was to gain a tactical advantage over Fox, now the opportunity would give him a tactical advantage over France and was irresistible. Vaughan returned to Paris on September 27th with a new commission for Oswald on the lines suggested, authorizing him to treat with the ministers of the United States. Franklin and Jay proceeded at once, and in perfect harmony, to further negotiations, but without consulting Vergennes. On October 5th Jay completed his draft of preliminaries, which Oswald at once forwarded to London. Adams, having concluded a treaty with the Netherlands, arrived in Paris on October 25th, and disregarding diplomatic formalities made no visit to the king's minister until some days had elapsed, permitting the public prints to announce his presence. He believed that Luzerne was plotting in Congress for his removal, and felt even less love for Frenchmen and things French than he had

Final negotiations.

done before. Almost simultaneously came the results of Shelburne's deliberation. They were at variance in some important respects with the draft, and Strachey, the Under-Secretary of State, was sent to enforce the particulars of the English contention.

The negotiations which ensued lasted until the end of November. They turned chiefly on the point of whether or not American merchants must pay for the goods they had purchased before the war, and on the question of compensation to the American Tories for the confiscation of their estates. Franklin felt that as the British armies had in great part destroyed the goods for which pay was demanded, England should indemnify her own citizens. The king of England thought that the honor of his throne was concerned in securing reimbursement to the loyalists for their losses. The British negotiators gained the first demand entirely, in answer to the second they obtained merely a promise that Congress would recommend the policy to the States. The main points as to independence and the boundaries were freely conceded, but while Adams secured a fairly definite line for the northeast border, that of the west was left, unfortunately, vague and general. At a future time it was found that deficient geographical knowledge had made necessary a survey and readjustment of the entire boundary. The Americans were to enjoy the same rights in the fisheries which they had had as English colonists; but while they might dry their fish on other unsettled shores they might not do so on those of Newfoundland; at the same time they secured the exclusive right of fishing on their own coasts. Jay's proposition for reciprocity in commerce and trade was rejected, but England retained the equal privilege with the United States of navigating the Mississippi, which separated them from the Spanish possessions, and had no natural geographical connection with those of Great Britain. There were two blots on the pages of the remarkable document thus outlined : one, the suggestion implied in the enumeration by name of the Thirteen States, that the United States were not a nation ; the other, a virtual recognition of slavery. Laurens had been exchanged for Cornwallis, and appeared at the last moment to insist on a provision that, when the English evacuated American soil they should not carry away "any negroes or other property of the inhabitants." There was one secret clause determining the southern boundary in case England should recover West Florida by her treaty with Spain. The commissioners affixed their signatures to these preliminary articles on November 30th, 1782, but with the understanding that the treaty was not to be concluded until after the general pacification, in which Spain, France, and Holland were also concerned.

It is customary to look upon the work thus accomplished as a triumph of American diplomacy. Since the Staten Island conference in 1776, America had insisted on the recognition of her independence as preliminary to any negotiation. *The general pacification.* Adams and Jay were the successful agents in securing that concession. France and Spain earnestly desired to limit American territory on the west by the Alleghenies. The violation of instructions from Congress, in which the same two commissioners were chiefly concerned, thwarted Vergennes and prevented such a disaster. Secrecy would nevertheless have availed little but for the good-will of England, which though defeated in America was triumphant over the Bourbon powers in the successes of Rodney and Eliott, and now meant to use American independence for the purpose of diminishing the claims sure to be made by Spain. The intermediate stages of the negotiation were incontestably the work of Jay and Adams.

What they might have resulted in except for the beginning and end, both which were the work of Franklin, cannot be estimated. His colleagues were the statesmen and politicians, standing out for American claims and detecting the schemes of Vergennes; he was the statesman and diplomatist, opening the way by his first exorbitant demand for acquiring the territories actually secured, turning the position of England in regard to the restitution of estates by gravely suggesting a commission to estimate the value of American property destroyed in what the English Whigs always described as a wanton and unjust war, and finally appearing before Vergennes with a copy of the preliminaries to forestall his accusations of ingratitude and bad faith by the plain, truthful, and convincing statement that he and his colleagues were guilty of neither, but only of diplomatic discourtesy. With no disparagement to the merits of all three, who were great and able each in his way, the fact in the last analysis appears to be that the terms obtained were due directly both to Yorktown and to diplomatic craft, but indirectly and mainly to the flood-tide of the liberal and just views held by most Americans and many influential Englishmen. Shelburne and Franklin were men representative of a public virtue which was rising higher and higher at the close of the eighteenth century, and was eventually to submerge the wrecks and derelicts of both mediæval aristocracy and modern absolutism.

That this was largely true was proven by subsequent events. Savannah and Charleston were evacuated in 1782, the former in July, the latter in December. The formal cessation of hostilities between England and America occurred in January, 1783, and was officially proclaimed by Congress on April 19th, eight years after Concord. The prelim-

Fall of Shelburne's ministry.

inaries of peace, between Great Britain on the one hand and the continental allies on the other, were signed on the twentieth of the same month, in the presence of Franklin and Adams, and the American preliminaries now became a treaty in fact. Simultaneously Holland and England concluded a truce. But the final and formal termination of the war was not reached until the following September, when the plenipotentiaries of the powers concerned met at Versailles and signed what is known as the treaty of Versailles and Paris. According to its terms France received Tobago and Senegal; Spain was compelled to relinquish all hope of Gibraltar, obtaining only the retrocession of Minorca and Florida. The clauses arranged between England and the United States in the previous November were of course incorporated.

The reason for this long delay was not in one sense a resurgence of conservative influence. Vergennes, if indeed he were really grieved, was easily pacified, for a few days after Franklin's interview communicating the conclusion of negotiations on the part of England and the United States, France acceded to the request of Congress and granted a new loan of six millions of francs, to cover the expenditures of 1783. When the question of ratifying the American treaty was brought before Parliament, in December, it was selected by the Conservatives and the malcontent Whigs as a means of overthrowing Shelburne. Many thought the concessions too great, the king could not dismiss his feeling of bitterness that the empire was dismembered and no certain provision made for the loyalists. Lord North wanted a monopoly of lake navigation and an independent Indian state, Burke showered invective on the ministry and their measures. The only defender of the treaty in the Commons was William Pitt. Similar considerations were advanced in the upper house, and Shelburne could not withstand the torrent. The ministry resigned on December 24th, and the fate of the treaty was in the balance. By what seemed a disgraceful coalition between the Tories and old Whigs the notorious ministry of North and Fox was formed, but only after days of struggle and under the displeasure of the king, who looked on North as a traitorous deserter and on Fox as an enemy.

The much-abused coalition was not a mere accident of party government. It stood for something. By a curious subversion and rearrangement Shelburne's opinions favored in part a return to the old order and an active participation of the crown in government. Fox, on the other hand, held to the notion of a continuous historical development of parliamentary supremacy, and the gradual extinction of the crown even as a regulative force. No one had more reason to support this position than North. Shelburne's remedy for the existing conditions was what has since been known as parliamentary reform by the extension of the suffrage, so as to secure a real representation of the people and thus counterbalance the power of the crown. The remedy of Burke and Fox was the system of so-called economic reform, whereby privilege was to be maintained in the aristocracy, lawyers, and merchants, while the evils of place and patronage were to be abolished and a retrenchment in the public finances thereby secured.

The coalition ministry.

The practical result of Fox's temporary victory was unfortunate for the United States. The old Whigs stood firm on the Navigation Acts in order to secure the world's carrying trade for England, and were, of course, supported by the mercantile classes. For this end a commission was promptly despatched to Paris in order to negotiate a commercial

Final ratification of the treaty.

treaty with the American ministers, which would retain for England, by the same interference with freedom of trade which had so far been her policy, the monstrous monopoly she was losing. The skill, insight, and true greatness of the three American commissioners foiled the plan. They were not overawed by the dangers of delay nor by a menace of failure, and the treaty ratified at Versailles in December was the same they had made. But in the long months which had elapsed between Oswald's first mission and the final authoritative adoption of the preliminaries, most serious harm was nevertheless done. The old bad elements of English conservatism had reasserted themselves as a power, the seeds of ill-will between the two English nations were prematurely sown, and the harvest, which the newer people reaped in the first twenty-five years of national existence made necessary a second war for independence before they were strong enough to fight it.

CHAPTER XXX.

WEAKNESS AND STRENGTH

American Independence and European Politics—The Former and Later Generations—The American Navy—Its Achievement—Its Gradual Diminution—Privateering—Morris and the Finances—Expense of the War—Congress and the Army—Washington Allays the Discontent—The Army Disbanded—The Cincinnati—Washington's Political Insight—The Southern States—The Middle States—Their Occupations and Educational Institutions—New England—Massachusetts and Virginia—Character of the Revolution—Effect on Ecclesiastical Movements—Slavery—Tendencies toward Union in State Administrations—Importance of the New Forces—Literature of the Revolution—Signs of a National Spirit—Political Writers—The New Society.

IN speculating as to what might have been, it seems likely that as European politics were in these years so *American Independence and European politics.* complicated and arranged as to throw all the continent in the scale against England, and as English politics were so developing as to create a true liberal party which was steadily a friend to American liberalism, we could by the vigorous use of our resources have won our independence without foreign assistance. In the beginning we proved our capacity and displayed our resources. But in fact it was to the French, our faithful and loyal allies to the end, that we owed ultimate success in the actual conflict, and it was through the adroit use of European diplomacy and party politics that we obtained the favorable terms of peace which gave us a national territory in spite of sectional prejudices.

The contemplation of weakness, vacillation, and lukewarmness displayed at one time or another in every district and by all classes except the one which was composed of a few steadfast leaders with their devoted followers, should overthrow that view of our history which refers everything good to the forefathers and everything bad to their successors. Estimating the men of that day in the light of their times we may well be proud of them, but we should also remember that what they began in imperfection has been preserved by at least equal wisdom and equal fortitude both in war and peace; that the stability of the small beginning has been secured in a structure large beyond their visions, built by architects at least as capable as they and perhaps as creative, for the federal state as we have it was probably not in their minds at all. The Constitution even was in part the work of a generation which did not begin the Revolution, and has by the interpretation of still later ones been steadily adapted to conditions not foreseen. *The former and later generations.*

Throughout the struggle thus brought to a close there had been naval warfare, both regular and irregular, which was in some ways of very great importance. Reprisals for the depredations of English revenue cutters and warships began in Narragansett Bay and were continuous thenceforward. Washington gave the broadest interpretation to his first commission, and sent authorized vessels to prey on English shipping. Massachusetts soon had a little fleet of six ships afloat. The example thus set was quickly followed by private enterprise in nearly every State. Vessels were overhauled, prisoners taken, and stores captured. By the middle and end of 1776 Congress had a navy of its own numbering thirteen ships; five of thirty-two guns, five of twenty-eight, and three of twenty-four. *The American navy.*

The officers of the new naval power were men of energy and skill in their profession. But they had a difficult task, and sometimes by the complications of international law fell into strange plights in their attempts to dispose of their prizes before the French alliance was consummated. But in spite of all discouragements the services of men like Jones, Biddle, and Wickes were invaluable both in encouraging their compatriots and in the actual gains they made. English merchants were first stunned and then terrified by deeds like the sally of Conyngham from Dunkirk, in which he captured the Harwich packet, irregular as his act may have been. In two years, eight hundred English vessels were seized.

<small>Its achievement.</small>

By 1778 eight of the fleet of Congress were either taken or destroyed, and four new ships were commissioned to supply their places. By that time, however, a powerful French fleet was in American waters. Jones's exploits have elsewhere been referred to. Simultaneously one English store-ship after another was captured this side the sea, and not without hard fighting, by such American officers as Manly, Hopkins, Hallett, and Williams. The disastrous failure of the Massachusetts enterprise against Castine brought the American navy to the verge of ruin. Thenceforward the regular warfare against England by sea was virtually carried on by the French. Two American frigates, however, the Congress and Alliance, won laurels until the end of the war.

<small>Its gradual diminution.</small>

But privateering assumed dimensions which are now difficult correctly to estimate, so untrustworthy are local records and so absurd the notions of different writers. The official records at the national capital are, however, certainly accurate as far as they go, and they probably cover most of the facts. From them

<small>Privateering.</small>

it appears that about fifteen hundred and sixty-eight public and private armed vessels were fitted out in the United States between 1776 and 1783. Of these more than half were from New England. In the list of States Massachusetts leads with five hundred and eight, Pennsylvania follows with four hundred and seventy-nine. Then come in order Maryland, Connecticut, each with less than two hundred, New Hampshire with nearly a hundred. The list then runs—Virginia, Rhode Island, New York, South Carolina, New Jersey, and North Carolina, with from five to twenty-five each. The successes of the privateersmen were enormous, and such were the profits of adventurers and owners that New England was never more prosperous in its entire history than during the last years of the Revolution, while some Philadelphia merchants amassed fortunes. It is estimated that as high as seventy thousand American sailors were afloat at one time engaged in the struggle with England, either as regulars or privateersmen. There was probably one year, 1776, in which at various times ninety thousand Continental soldiers and militia were in service or at least enrolled, but in general the numbers of the American land force did not reach fifty thousand.

When Congress, in 1781, determined to substitute a single head for each of its most important committees, Robert Morris was made the financial agent of the confederation. He committed the uncertain and timid body of which he was a member to a temporary policy of strong union by securing the charter of a national bank with four hundred thousand dollars capital. Massachusetts alone resisted. By adroit manipulations and powerful energy the plan succeeded, at least while it had the support of Congress, and its author was emboldened to suggest federal taxation in the shape of contributions from excise imports and land. *Morris and the finances.*

Momentarily there was a prospect that the United States, with their wealth and prosperity scarcely checked by the war, would be completely solvent and meet all their obligations. The Middle States were brought in some degree to terms, but neither the East nor South could overcome their original repugnance to pay.

The total cost of the war made an average annual expenditure of twenty millions of hard dollars. First and last the country received from France, Spain, and Holland about twelve millions, of which nearly two and a half were gifts from France and Spain. At the peace there was a public debt of between nine and ten millions, of which seven were owing to France, two to Holland, and the rest to Spain. The remainder of the immense expenditure for the war, a proportion of nearly five-sixths, was really borne by the people, though in the most irregular way, the losses by the utter extinction of value in continental paper generally falling upon the patriots and the poor. Congress disbursed about two-thirds, the separate States about a third of the total. As to the public debt, Franklin made an arrangement by which the arrearages of interest were forgiven by our generous ally, and the principal was to be repaid in yearly instalments, to begin three years after the peace.

Expenses of the war.

In spite of its great services, Congress at the close of the war was held in no esteem whatever. Its career had been one of compromises to such an extent that the people at large, with a too common inconsistency, despised them for pursuing a course initiated rather by the delegates than by public opinion, but supported at a later time by a general resurrection of local jealousy. The situation was made acute by the fact that promises of pay to the army had not been kept. The American seafarers during the war seem to have been satisfied with their own self-help, and well they

Congress and the army.

might be if half of what was told about captures were true. The case was far different with the army, which from first to last was but wretchedly supported, and was often regarded even with jealousy, by communities who recalled their own sufferings and those of their forefathers at the hands of a trained and centralized soldiery. The troops were, therefore, outraged by the apparent indifference of Congress in filling its empty treasury in order to fulfil its broken promises to them. They would not have been indisposed to exert a forcible pressure on the civil power to compel the levying and collecting of continental taxes. Some strong advocates of a true federal union, and many of the creditors of Congress, were willing to try the experiment. The movement was partly organized and was actually initiated at the army headquarters in Newburgh by well-written addresses to the soldiers, which bore the name of Armstrong.

But Washington was averse to such extreme measures, and by his commanding personal influence succeeded in averting the calamity of a civil war between the respective advocates of loose and strong federation. A mutinous handful of exasperated soldiers did, however, actually threaten Congress, and its members fled in panic from Philadelphia to Princeton, where they summoned Washington and consulted in regard to the size and organization of the small standing army which was to be maintained for the defence of the frontier. The establishment of a militia for the regulation of internal order, of the military school, and other matters of a like nature were considered. The immediate demands of both officers and men were met by partially funding the sums due into the general debt, giving paper obligations for three months' pay to the men, bearing interest at six per cent., and by voting to

Washington allays the discontent.

the officers certificates for five years' pay, also bearing interest at six per cent., commuting the half-pay for life promised at Valley Forge into full pay for that period. Both sorts of paper were really irredeemable, but necessity compelled their acceptance. Public meetings in many parts of New England displayed a bitter opposition to the Commutation Act for promising even the little it did. Greene's army in the South was literally starving, the proverbial ingratitude of States having been shown by South Carolina.

Both North and South, individuals and troops of men were hastening to their homes to resume their labors and support their families. The army melted insensibly away until but a few companies were left. Finally, on receipt of news that peace was concluded, the few remaining forces were successfully disbanded by formal proclamation, November 2d, 1783. Some years elapsed before even partial justice was done to the brave veterans who had been temporarily the dupes of that misguided and narrow sentiment of local prejudice, which sprang from overstrained devotion to abstract principles.

The army disbanded.

Just before their final separation the officers, at the instigation of Knox, formed a society to perpetuate the memory of their participation in great deeds. As Cincinnatus had left the plough and returned to it, the members were to be known as Cincinnati, and membership was to be hereditary. The country felt that wherever soldiers met there would be advocates of "a hoop to the barrel," as they themselves were wont to phrase their devotion to strong union among the States. Many professed alarm at the establishment of an hereditary aristocracy. The society was never popular, but it abolished the hereditary feature and still exists, its vacancies being filled by election.

The Cincinnati.

The last English soldiers remaining in America sailed from New York on November 25th. It was estimated that twenty thousand loyalists left their homes to settle in Nova Scotia, Canada, the Bermudas, or the Antilles. Washington and Clinton, governor of the State, entered the city at the head of the few remaining companies of the army on the day the British departed. On December 4th, a farewell meeting of the officers was held, and a few days afterward the commander-in-chief set out for Annapolis, whither Congress had then removed. On the twenty-third he delivered "to the United States in Congress assembled," a memorable short address of resignation and retired, as he supposed, to private life. In eight years he had expended from his private purse sixty-four thousand dollars. For this, as by agreement, he asked reimbursement, but demanded nothing for his own arduous labors. During the weary days of waiting and fighting he had pondered the questions of the time, and with almost superhuman insight reached their solution. In the previous June he had, therefore, written a letter to the State governors, which contained the essential policy from which his country has never departed, except to its hurt: "First, an indissoluble union of the States under one federal head; second, a sacred regard to public justice; third, the adoption of a proper peace establishment; and fourth, the prevalence of that pacific and friendly disposition among the people of the United States which will induce them to forget their local prejudices and policies, to make those mutual concessions which are requisite to the general prosperity, and, in some instances, to sacrifice their individual advantages to the interest of the community. These are the pillars on which the glorious fabric of our independence and character must rest." These remarkable words presaged

Washington's political insight.

a new rôle for their author. He had organized and conducted the struggle for independence, he alone could organize and conduct the impending struggle for true federation.

The modelling of a great picture is said to require the use of deep shadows and strong light. A panoramic view of the United States at the close of the Revolution will disclose both. Their population had increased from 1775 to 1783 by about five hundred thousand souls, the total being estimated at three and a quarter millions, but of these there were now six hundred thousand slaves. This negro host was largely in the five Southern States—Virginia, Georgia, the Carolinas, and Maryland—giving them nearly half of the whole. Society in this section was aristocratic, even the poor whites being for the most part attached to some rich family, and living without influence in a semi-patriarchal relation. Although the Anglican Church had fallen into decadence for several reasons, the chief one being its loyalty to England, yet its essential characteristics were dear to many, and by a complete regeneration it became a strong American Church almost immediately after the war. Methodism had its American beginning in New York, but during the years of the conflict its adherents grew in numbers and influence, and when organized as an American Church it spread with rapidity and contested with the calvinistic Baptists the supremacy among the masses of the Southern States. The occupation of all classes in the South, merchants and planters, poor whites, free negroes, and slaves, were all directly and indirectly connected with agriculture. The college of William and Mary, though crippled by poverty and closed during the war, had exerted a strong influence in training the minds of the upper stratum of society, but the education of the people in general was sadly neglected.

The Middle States contained less than a third of the total number of inhabitants, Pennsylvania being the second State of the Union, following Virginia, and New York ranking fifth, that is, after Massachusetts. As in certain parts of the South, the Presbyterians were very numerous throughout this section. There were other strong denominations affiliated by calvinistic belief, like the Baptists and Dutch Reformed. The orthodox Quakers were numerous and wealthy. There were also, of course, many belonging to the churches already mentioned. Philadelphia, with thirty-two thousand inhabitants, was the first city of the Union, wealthy, public spirited, and gay, though in the latter particular Baltimore was considered to outstrip it, for there alone existed a theatre. Neither Quakers nor Presbyterians would tolerate one in their town of brotherly love. New York, which in 1775 had but twenty-three thousand inhabitants, had been nearly ruined by the careless occupation of English and tories during the war, but its broad waterway into the interior, and the affiliations between its Dutch citizens and those of Albany, together with its splendid and accessible harbor, were destined to quickly restore its prosperity and influence. The Dutch of New York, like the Germans of Pennsylvania, were an invaluable element in the creation of public confidence and the restoration of regularity in the occupations of the people.

The agriculture of the Middle States was utterly unlike that of the South. Small holdings were the rule, and farms were tilled by their owners or by hired help. The staples were those of home consumption, and commanded a good market at the doors of those who raised them. There was a beginning of manufactures, and an extensive commerce. There were four colleges: King's, now Columbia, in New York; Princeton and Queen's, now Rutgers, in New Jersey; in Philadelphia the University of Pennsylvania. Three of them were well equipped for the time and very influential. The first and last, although Jay and Hamilton were graduates of Columbia, were nevertheless chiefly important in the cities which contained them, while Princeton, which was a child of Yale, through its relation, on one hand, to New England, and its religious connection with Presbyterians, Quakers, and Dutch, on the other, had a clientage from all three sections of the country, and exerted a national influence. Witherspoon, its president, although a Scotchman by birth, was an active and ardent patriot, and of the youth trained by him no less than nine sat in the convention which framed the Constitution. The influence of the universities was very strong in that body. It had fifty-five members; thirty-two of them were men of academic training. London, Oxford, Glasgow, Edinburgh, and Aberdeen had shared in forming the minds of five, about the same number had been connected with the checkered fortunes of William and Mary, one was a graduate of Pennsylvania, two of Columbia, three of Harvard, four of Yale, and nine of Princeton.

Harvard and Yale were both the offspring of that orthodox calvinistic Puritanism or theocratic Congregationalism, which was the prevalent faith of New England. Ancient and dignified in their origin, influential and pronounced in their teachings, their tremendous power was exerted both before and during the Revolution in a community fit to be swayed by philosophy and learning. Brown and Dartmouth were still in their infancy. There were fifty-six names appended to the Declaration of Independence. Of these eight were graduates of Harvard, four of Yale, three of Princeton, two of Pennsylvania, two of William and Mary, three of Cambridge, two of Edinburgh, and one of St. Omer's. The population of New England, although comprising Quakers, Baptists, and even Scotch Presbyterians, was nevertheless the most homogeneous in any section. Whatever its later modifications, the division of the Reformation known as calvinism laid hold of a distinct type of man, and while the other States were largely calvinistic New England was predominantly so. The people were shrewd, reticent, undemonstrative, and laborious. They were in the main well educated, and self-reliant in both opinion and conduct, having a curious mixture of traditional reverence combined with the courage of their convictions in a high degree. The jealousy of charter rights, which they had felt more keenly than most, was the key-note of the Revolution, the lukewarmness which they displayed in the later years of the war was begotten of their local devotion and the intensity with which they applied themselves to their well-developed commerce and agriculture. There was no leisure class, in fact neither classes nor masses, their institutions in Church and State being purely democratic, even to the verge of disorganization. Massachusetts was the fourth State in the Union in point of population, having about three hundred and eighty thousand, and thus coming after Virginia, Pennsylvania, and North Carolina. There were about a million people in all New England. Boston was a little city of some twenty-three thousand persons, covering three hills and overlooking a good harbor.

But from the beginning of the struggle for the charter liberties of Englishmen there was a close connection between Massachusetts and Virginia, in both of which the fires of patriotism burned brighter than elsewhere. The outbreak was largely the work of the radicals in these commonwealths, although there were warm and courageous patriots in

Massachusetts and Virginia.

great numbers everywhere. The continuous prosecution of the war was in the main the work of moderate liberals, who had acted slowly in the beginning, but having reached conviction were self-sacrificing and tenacious in moments of trial.

Character of the Revolution.

The entire movement was a development rather than a revolution in constitutional ideas, though revolutionary in the severance of political connection with England. Men of all classes and of all religious denominations and of all the civilized races settled on the continent were contributors to the final result. While the seeds of religious, social, and political difference germinated a second time in the years of warfare and produced the disheartening results observable at the close of the struggle, both in regard to public credit and State separatism, yet there were also conditions favorable to preserving for united advantage what had been won by united exertion.

The gains of the Revolution were at first observable mainly in excellent State institutions emancipated from royal or Parliamentary control and but slightly changed to meet necessary emergencies. The change in other directions was equally deliberate and conservative. The movement for the disestablishment of the English Church and entire religious liberty began in Virginia before the war and was carried to successful completion shortly after. It was simply a question of time when the other States would take identical ground regarding any religious establishment. The Puritans of New England had always been advocates of a certain connection between Church and State by imposing religious tests for the exercise of political rights. The Presbyterians of America, although often confused with the former because of the slight difference in doctrine, differed widely from them in race and political theory. They took a radically opposite view. It was

Effect on ecclesiastical movements.

their influence which carried Virginia, and in the end prevailed everywhere. By the power of men either indifferent or hostile to religion working on a general feeling that ecclesiastical and dogmatic tests should be utterly eliminated, an appearance of absolute neutrality and even hostility in regard to Christianity on the part of the Federal Government was conveyed through the omission of any religious reference, even to the Almighty, in the Constitution when finally adopted.

Slavery also was a burning question. It existed in all the States. Some among them, like Virginia, took immediate measures either to check the slave trade or stop it altogether. This feeling of the Old Dominion was but temporary, and on the introduction of the cotton-gin the entire South became ardent advocates of slave labor. In Massachusetts, where its abuses had in early colonial days received a recognition in law, an enlightened sentiment had arisen and prevailed in securing complete emancipation. It gradually disappeared in the other Northern States, either legally and from public disapprobation or because it was not profitable.

<small>Slavery.</small>

In nearly all the States there was a limitation of the suffrage by a property qualification of some sort. In all of them, except those of New England, the old English notions of primogeniture and entails found expression in the laws, and in New York there were manorial privileges like those of feudalism. But all these were abolished within a few years. In every State, without exception, the common law of England was the law of the land, except when abrogated or modified by statute. The statutes of England and of the colonies enacted before the Revolution retained validity. There was the same general form of government in all thirteen, working smoothly with a governor and two houses, the upper one formed by remodelling the

<small>Tendencies toward union in State administrations.</small>

former council and the lower one directly representing the people as it had always done. The judiciary practised the same English forms and kept their seats on appointment either for a long term or *quamdiu se bene gesserint*, that is, for life or good behaviour. The lawyers cited English decisions then, as now. In short, there is a very perplexing resemblance in the institutions of the new States to the English Constitution as it was then understood, or rather misunderstood. But the resemblance was due rather to a natural historical development than to intentional imitation.

These considerations prove how active and strong was the principle and fact of union among these commonwealths, whose conduct in the jealous assertion of their autonomy jeopardized not only the success of the war, but the ultimate success of the very principles for which they had fought. But it is given only to the most acute minds to understand the tendencies of their own times. An impartial judge of the circumstances must remember the narrow horizon, not merely of Americans but of most Europeans, at the close of the eighteenth century. He must recall that the wisest men in Europe and the most profound students of history had seen free institutions working successfully only in small countries, that they distrusted any attempt to unite large numbers under republican institutions, and that no one really understood experimentally the principle of representation in the double and indirect sense America has given to it within a century. The notion of union was sentimental rather than practical, the State governments seemed to include the regulation of nearly all the most important relations of life as to civil and religious liberty, property, and the administration of justice; the nature and functions of federal government were neither studied nor understood, and the existence of any strong central sovereignty, however constructed, would naturally appear a menace to freedom in the nearer interests which affect the daily, hourly life of every man. Add to this that the difficulties of intercommunication between the various communities were enormous, travelling being for the most part still on horseback or by rare and slow mail coaches. Slight differences had thereby been accentuated into local jealousies and suspicions like those which still survive between Europeans and Americans, so that, taking all considerations into account, it must appear marvellous that the difficulties in the way of federation were no greater than they were. The period immediately after the peace was perhaps critical, but it is creditable to the time that the obstacles were surmounted at all.

The literature of the Revolution showed no abrupt change in the character and temper of the people which had been so conservative in other directions. The literary fashion of America was and remained with slight modifications identical with that of the mother-country. *Literature of the Revolution.* The principal events of both the French war and the Revolution produced a quantity of ballads and songs. The death of Howe, the victory of Wolfe, Burgoyne's surrender, and the battle of Trenton represent one class of subjects, while abstract themes like American independence or liberty in general represent another. They are all equally stilted and are written in the manner of Butler, Pope, Gay, or Shenstone. One only has survived, "Yankee Doodle," or the "trifling provincial," as the title may be literally rendered. The words are a satire on the American militia by the English regulars, and the tune dates from the days of Charles I., being an English adaptation of a Dutch melody.

About the middle of the eighteenth century was born

a group of men, connected for the most part in one way or another with Connecticut and New Jersey, though Brackenridge was born in Scotland and Hopkinson in Pennsylvania, who were destined to occupy a well-defined position in literature. Their names are familiar, Trumbull, Dwight, Lemuel Hopkins, Humphreys and Barlow, Brackenridge, Francis Hopkinson, and Freneau. The "MacFingal," of Trumbull, the "Columbiad," of Barlow, the "Modern Chivalry," of Brackenridge, the "Battle of the Kegs," by Hopkinson, and the poems of Freneau are the best known among their productions. It is customary to trace in these works the influences of Puritan and Presbyterian provincialism and to dismiss them with a patronizing smile. It may at once be admitted that, judged by the so-called absolute standard of fine art, or in comparison with the few immortal monuments of pure literature, they shrink into small dimensions, if not into insignificance. But their authors did a great work for their times. Dwight, Brackenridge, and Barlow were chaplains in the army, and encouraged the troops by both sermons and songs; Freneau was an agitator, a prisoner of war, and an influential patriot. The others were equally active in other spheres. But, taken together, these men mark the faint beginnings and bring to light the promise of a national spirit. Though the history of literature may pass them rapidly by, the historian must note them as a company of remarkable men, understanding and cherishing the social and political transition of which they were a part.

Signs of a national spirit.

This age of our history has been designated that of the Titans: Edwards, Franklin, Otis, Henry, Paine, Witherspoon, Madison, Fisher Ames, Jay, John Adams, Marshall, Hamilton, Jefferson, and Washington himself. These men were all, in a greater or less degree, literary men. Their writings are for the

Political writers.

most part strong and terse, sometimes they are elegant. But with them all the English language, whether written or spoken, was but the means to an end. Edwards was the representative of the religious and philosophical life of his time, as Franklin was of the practical and secular. The traditions of that glowing eloquence which flowed from the lips of Otis, Fisher Ames, and Henry are still distinct, but all three were primarily legists and patriots. Paine was a clever and successful pamphleteer, Witherspoon was the scholar in politics, the "councillor of Morris, correspondent of Washington, rival of Franklin in sagacity and resolution." Marshall was primarily the jurisconsult and really belongs to the coming constructive age. John Adams and Madison, Jay and Hamilton, Jefferson and Washington; we think of statesmanship, of political wisdom, of the highest military capacity in mentioning their names. And justly so, for while their writings are probably equal to any similar body of political literature, their capacity in the conduct of affairs has put them in the foremost rank among, not the writers, but the makers, of history. If Jefferson embodied whatever was revolutionary in the movement of his times, and Franklin stood for the historic continuity of his country's life, Washington's was a seraphic spear which turned in both directions to guard the new people from the extremes of either radicalism or conservatism. The evidence is in their writings as well as in their actions, and the three may stand as types of all the manly forces which united in the final result.

We are often told that the peace was but the beginning of the most critical epoch in American history. This is true if our eyes are fixed on slavery, on separatism, on local jealousies, on personal selfishness or ambition, on the hesitation of a newly liberated people with a form of government undeveloped

The new society.

and almost untried. But there is no essential in the organism which was not in the embryo, and if we pass over the vanishing factors we shall discern, half-hidden, perhaps, but strong, the increasing forces ; vigorous nationality in common institutions and destiny, strong leaders versed in the history of their forefathers and appreciating the problem of progress along traditional lines, a people passing through a difficult transition but conscious of their identity and their duty. History is both a succession of states in society and at the same time a record of great names. The latter are already discernible at the close of the war ; the new state of society among English-speaking men which these names evince is likewise already in being. While its qualities manifest themselves later and more slowly, while its development is accompanied by friction and anxiety, its existence is, nevertheless, assured.

APPENDIX

I.

CHRONOLOGICAL TABLE

	A.D.
Peace of Aix-la-Chapelle..............................	1748
French incite Indians to hostility.	1750
French attack Ohio pioneers...........................	1752
Building of Fort Duquesne............................	1753
Washington at Fort Necessity....................July 4,	1754
William Johnson commissary for the Iroquois............	1755
Battle of Braddock's Fields......................July 9,	1755
Battle of Lake George......................September 8,	1755
War declared between England and France........May 18,	1756
Fall of Oswego...............................August 14,	1756
Armstrong captures Kittanning..............September 7,	1756
Alliance of England and Prussia..................January,	1757
Coalition ministry of Newcastle and Pitt............June,	1757
Massacre of Fort William Henry................August 9,	1757
Battle of Rossbach..........................November 5,	1757
Defeat of Abercrombie at Ticonderoga.............July 8,	1758
Capture of Louisburg...........................July 26,	1758
Capture of Frontenac.........................August 26,	1758
Capture of Fort Duquesne by Forbes........November 25,	1758
Capture of Fort Niagara by Johnson..............July 24,	1759
Capture of Ticonderoga by Amherst..............July 26,	1759
Battle of Meriden ....August 1,	1759
Battle of the Plains of Abraham.............September 13,	1759
Surrender of Quebec......................,........September 18,	1759
Battle of Ste. Foy ....April 28,	1760
Surrender of Montreal and Canada............September 8,	1760
Death of George II. and Accession of George III. October 25,	1760
Writs of assistance in Massachusetts.....................	1761

APPENDIX

	A.D.
Bourbon Family Compact....................August 15,	1761
Resignation of the Newcastle-Pitt ministry......October 6,	1761
War between England and Spain................January,	1762
Bute Prime Minister.........................May 29,	1762
Peace of Paris..........................February 10,	1762
Grenville Prime Minister.....................April 8,	1763
Pontiac's conspiracy............................May 7,	1763
Revenue Act for the Colonies passed.............March,	1764
Passage of the Stamp Act.....................March 22,	1765
Rockingham Prime Minister.................... July,	1765
Stamp Act Congress in New York.............October 7,	1765
Brown University founded..............................	1765
Repeal of the Stamp Act...................February 22,	1766
Duty imposed on tea and other commodities..............	1767
New York enjoined from independent action.............	1767
Customs officers appointed.............................	1767
"Farmer's Letters" written by Dickinson...............	1767
Chatham Prime Minister.......................August,	1767
Queen's (Rutgers) College founded......................	1767
Grafton Prime Minister......................December,	1767
Massachusetts issues circular letter..............January,	1768
Bernard dissolves Massachusetts Assembly..... .....April,	1768
Riots in Boston occasioned by seizure of sloop Liberty. June,	1768
British troops in Boston........................October,	1768
Organized resistance in North Carolina..................	1768
Settlements in Tennessee.............................	1768
Botetourt dissolves Virginia House of Burgesses..........	1769
Dartmouth College founded.............................	1769
Repeal of all duties except that on tea.............March,	1770
Lord North Prime Minister.	1770
Boston "Massacre"........................March 5,	1770
Battle on the Alamance ....May 16,	1771
Burning of the Gaspee......................... June 9,	1772
Virginia appoints Intercolonial Committee of Correspondence...	1773
Hutchinson letters divulged by Franklin.................	1773
Boston Tea-party......................December 16,	1773
Franklin before the Privy Council..............January,	1774
Passage of the Penal Acts........................March,	1774
Enforcement of the Boston Port Bill..............June 1,	1774
First Continental Congress ....September 5,	1774

APPENDIX 391

	A.D.
Indian fight, Point Pleasant	October 6, 1774
The American Association	October 20, 1774
Chatham and Burke plead for reconciliation	1775
The conflicts at Lexington and Concord	April 19, 1775
Capture of Ticonderoga	May 10, 1775
Second Continental Congress	May 10, 1775
Mecklinburg Resolutions of Independence	May 20, 1775
Washington commander of the American forces	June 15, 1775
Battle of Bunker Hill	June 17, 1775
Siege of Boston	July, 1775
Capture of Montreal	November 12, 1775
Siege of Quebec	December, 1775
"Common Sense" published	January 8, 1776
Boston taken by Washington	March 17, 1776
Congress directs colonies to organize their own governments	May 15, 1776
British driven from Charleston	June 28, 1776
Declaration of Independence	July 4, 1776
Battle of Long Island	August 27, 1776
British occupy New York	September 15, 1776
Battle of White Plains	October 28, 1776
Battle of Trenton	December 26, 1776
Battle of Princeton	January 3, 1777
Adoption of the American Flag	June 14, 1777
Battle of Oriskany	August 6, 1777
Battle of Bennington	August 16, 1777
Battle of the Brandywine	September 11, 1777
Battle of Bemis's Heights	September 19, 1777
Battle of Germantown	October 4, 1777
Battle of Freeman's Farm	October 7, 1777
Burgoyne's surrender at Saratoga	October 17, 1777
The confederation of the States	November 15, 1777
The French Alliance	February 6, 1778
Parliament's offers of conciliation	February, 1778
Battle of Monmouth	June 28, 1778
Massacre at Wyoming	July 4, 1778
American retreat from Newport	August 29, 1778
British capture Savannah	December 29, 1778
British victory at Brier Creek	March 3, 1779
The Spanish Alliance	April 12, 1779
Capture of Stony Point	July 16, 1779

APPENDIX

A.D.
Naval victory of Paul Jones ....September 23, 1779
Lincoln and d'Estaing repulsed at Savannah.....October 9, 1779
Clinton captures Charleston ....May 12, 1780
Battle of Camden ....August 16, 1780
Capture of André ....September 23, 1780
Battle of King's Mountain.....................October 7, 1780
Battle of the Cowpens........................January 17, 1781
Battle of Guilford.............................March 15, 1781
Battle of Hobkirk's Hill........................April 25, 1781
Battle of Eutaw Springs....................September 8, 1781
Surrender at Yorktown......................October 19, 1781
Cessation of hostilities......................January 20, 1782
Rockingham Prime Minister....................March 20, 1782
Completion of peace negotiations...........November 30, 1782
Treaty of Paris and Versailles...............September 3, 1783
Evacuation of New York..................November 25, 1783

II.

BIBLIOGRAPHY

The works of Francis Parkman form a complete and exhaustive history of the French in America. The two portions, entitled respectively Montcalm and Wolfe, and The Conspiracy of Pontiac, cover the period of the Seven Years' War in America. They are admirable in respect to thoroughness, reliability, and style.

The general histories of Bancroft, Hildreth, Lord Mahon, and Lecky are accessible to all. Bancroft's is a monumental work of the first importance, philosophical, yet minute and painstaking. Its faults are those of style and sometimes of bias, which, however, is never sufficiently concealed to be dangerous. No one has so conscientiously used the original sources, nor had access to so many and important ones as he. The student must use the original as well as the revised or centennial edition. Lord Mahon is the contemporary representative of the English view, and is quite as polemic as the American statesman. The portion of Lecky's great work relating to American affairs is concise and has the appearance of impartiality, though written with a tinge of Tory feeling.

The huge volumes of Justin Winsor's Narrative and Critical History of America are very valuable to the student for their full references to books and sources. The plan is confusing to the general reader, and while many of the monographs are fine, there is a necessary diversity in treatment and style which shows the dangers of historical dissection. The Reader's Handbook of the American Revolution by the same editor is an excellent bibliography and indispensable both to the investigator and the reader. Its use will obviate the necessity of any other, except for works published since 1879.

The three volumes of John Fiske, two on the Revolution and one on the Critical Period of American History, can be recommended almost without a reservation. The style savors a little of the popular lecture, but the facts are clearly given and the judgments are excellent.

Much interest has been manifested in France under the republic concerning American history and the United States. The extensive work of Doniol, Histoire de la participation de la France à l'établissement des États-Unis d'Amérique, Correspondance diplomatiques et documents, views our struggle as an episode of French history, but makes accessible much hitherto unavailable material. So also does the interesting volume, Documents on the American Revolution, edited by John Durand. Circourt published, as an appendix to the French translation of Volume X. of Bancroft, a volume of hitherto unused original documents from the French archives. Moireau's Histoire des États-Unis is an intelligent and sympathetic attempt to use the newest materials. The earlier history by Laboulaye has permanent value, and that by Botta, an Italian, though published nearly a century ago, is not yet antiquated.

The standard collections of contemporary records are the Journals of Congress and the Secret Journals of Congress, the Diplomatic Correspondence of the American Revolution, the Life and Writings of Washington, and the Correspondence of the American Revolution. The three last are edited by Sparks, and his method of correcting "errors of grammar and obvious blunders, the result of hasty composition," has given rise to some controversy. Besides these there are Force's American Archives, Niles's Principles and Acts of the Revolution, Moore's Diary of the American Revolution, and many others of less importance. There are many other interesting collections of private correspondence, of pulpit and forensic orations, of ballads and songs, of editorial writing—in short, of everything which sheds light on the times of the Revolution. Their titles are given in Winsor's Handbook. Bancroft, in the prefaces to his original Volumes VI., IX., and X., gives an account of his manuscript sources. The fac-simile of manuscripts in European archives relating to America and the catalogue of all original documents in European archives which illustrate American history, edited by B. F. Stevens, are of the utmost value.

The following is a list of other works, all valuable in their way, which may be useful to those who have no extended book-list at hand. It is given simply as a selection.

For the French War: Mante's History of the Late War in North America; Rogers, Journal of the French War; Barnaby,

APPENDIX 395

Travels through the Middle Settlements of North America ; Grant, Memoirs of an American Lady (Mrs. Schuyler).

For the Constitutional Revolution : Hutchinson, History of Massachusetts, also Diary and Letters ; Pitkin, Political and Civil History of the United States ; Frothingham, Rise of the Republic and History of the Siege of Boston ; Greene, Historical View of the American Revolution ; Thompson, The United States as a Nation ; Almon, Charters of the British Colonies ; Stokes's Constitutions of the British Colonies ; Poore, Collection of the Federal and State Constitutions, Colonial Charters, and other Organic Laws of the United States ; Massey, History of England ; Adolphus, History of England ; Donne, Correspondence of George III. ; May, Constitutional History of England ; Alexander Johnston, his articles in Lalor's Political Cyclopedia ; Grahame, History of the United States ; Doyle, The American Colonies ; Wells, Life of Samuel Adams ; Works of James Otis, Patrick Henry, John Adams, and Benjamin Franklin.

For the War of the Revolution : Bryant and Gay, History of the United States ; Hart, Formation of the Union (Epochs of American History); Baker, Itinerary of General Washington ; Gordon, History of the Rise, Progress, and Establishment of the Independence of the United States ; Ludlow, The War of American Independence ; Carrington, Battles of the Revolution ; Lossing, Field Book of the Revolution ; Mrs. Mercy Warren, American Revolution ; Ramsay, History of the American Revolution ; Lee, Memoirs of the War in the Southern Department ; Thatcher, Military Journal from 1775 to 1783 ; Smith, American War from 1775 to 1783 ; Trescot, Diplomacy of the American Revolution ; Lyman, Diplomacy of the United States ; Elliot, American Diplomatic Code ; Curwen, Journal and Letters of an American Refugee in England ; Stedman, History of the American War ; Sabine, Loyalists of the American Revolution ; Ryerson, Loyalists of America ; Jones, History of New York during the Revolutionary War ; Frau von Riedesel, Letters and Memoirs relative to Burgoyne's Expedition ; Stevens, Campaign of Virginia, Cornwallis-Clinton Controversy ; Neilson, An Original of Burgoyne's Campaign ; Garden, Anecdotes of the Revolutionary War ; Mrs. Ellet, Women of the Revolution ; Johnston (H. P.), The Yorktown Campaign.

The Biographical Literature of the times is extensive, and the works of nearly every man of distinction have been collected and edited. The most important are the following : Appleton's Cyclopedia of American Biography ; American Statesmen Series ; Flanders, Lives of the Chief-Justices ; Sparks, Library of American Biography ; Lives of Washington, by Sparks, Washington Irving, Aaron Bancroft, Marshall, Everett, Upham, and Cornelis de Witt ; Sparks, Works of Benjamin Franklin ; Bigelow, Life of Benjamin Franklin, written by himself and edited from original manuscripts ; Hale, Franklin in France, from original documents ; McMaster, Benjamin Franklin as a Man of Letters ; Lives of Franklin, by Parton and Bigelow. Other notable biographies are : Patrick Henry, by Wirt and by William Wirt Henry ; Samuel Adams, by Wells and by Hosmer ; John Adams, by Adams ; James Otis, by Tudor ; Thomas Jefferson, by De Witt, Tucker, Smucker, Randall, Parton, and Morse ; Alexander Hamilton, by Hamilton, Marshall, and Morse ; James Madison, by Rives and Gilman ; John Jay, by Jay, Flanders, and Whitelocke ; Nathaniel Greene, by Greene ; Marshall, by Magruder; Gouverneur Morris, by Roosevelt ; Shelburne, by Fitzmaurice ; Robert Morris in Finances of the Revolution, by Sumner ; Joseph Reed, by Reed ; Charles Read, by Read ; Richard Henry Lee, by Lee ; Arthur Lee, by Lee ; Stark, by Stark and Everett ; Trumbull, by Stuart ; Putnam, by Humphreys and Tarbox ; Schuyler, by Lossing.

The best naval histories are: Cooper, Naval History of the United States ; Clark, Naval History of the United States ; Emmons, Navy of the United States ; Hall, Naval History of the Revolution, in Vol. VI. of Winsor.

The State histories are numerous, and the collections of the various State Historical Societies grow larger and more valuable every year. The most important details of various events will be found in the following: Maine, by Williamson ; New Hampshire, by Belknap ; Vermont, by Allen, Hall, and Williams ; Massachusetts, by Barry, Bradford, Minot, and Holland ; Connecticut, by Hollister, Peters, and Hinman ; Rhode Island, by Arnold ; New York, by Dunlap and Jones ; Pennsylvania, by Gordon ; New Jersey, by Mulford ; Maryland, by McSherry ; Virginia, by Campbell, Howison, Burk, Girardin, and Jefferson ; North Carolina, by Cooke, Jones, and Martin ; South Carolina, by Ramsay, Moultrie, Gibbs, Simms, and Drayton ; Georgia, by Stevens ; Roosevelt, Winning of the West.

INDEX

ABERCROMBIE, General, 5, 51; before Ticonderoga, 65, 67, 69
Aborigines. *See* Indians
Abraham, Heights of, Wolfe's plan to scale, 88; battle on the, 93, 94, 95
Absolutism, work of, 1
Acadia, boundaries of, 46; treatment of, by English, 46. Winslow in, 48; dispersion of the natives of, 48
Act of Settlement, 2
Adams, John, counsel for English soldiers, 158; his broad views of government, 209; proposes in Congress the independent government of the colonies, 215; his resolution ended the proprietary government of Pennsylvania, 225; argues in Congress for the declaration of independence, 229; peace commissioner at The Hague, 335
Adams, Samuel, on the Stamp Act, 135; pleads for liberty, 138; his patriotism, 157; after the "Boston Massacre," 158; organizes committees of correspondence, 161; his "Rights of the Colonies," 161; reads Hutchinson letters to Massachusetts Assembly, 163; in the first Continental Congress, 176, 184; excepted from amnesty, 200, 213
Aix-la-Chapelle, Peace of, 2, 38
Alamance, battle on the, 159
Albany, troops billeted in, 52
Alexandria, Congress at, 41
Allen, Ethan, his readiness to seize Ticonderoga, 183; and Arnold seize Ticonderoga, 189; captured and sent to England, 203
America, geography of, 24
American, the name, 132, 172

American Association, 206
American Colonies. *See* Colonies.
Americans, the, proclaimed rebels, 211
Amherst, character of, 61; at Louisburg, 64; loiters at Crown Point, 81; captures Montreal, 98
Amsterdam, commercial treaty proposed by, 351
André, Major, capture of, 326
Anglican Church, the, in the United States, 378
Anglo-Indians, their influence in parliamentary corruption, 146
Armstrong, John, at Kittanning, 54; at Fort Duquesne, 73
Army, American, weakness of, 245; plans for organizing, 259; disbanded, 376
Army of the North opposed to Burgoyne, 275
Arnold, Benedict, at Boston, 187; expedition of, to Canada, 203; makes a successful attack on the English army in Connecticut, 267; resigns his command after Bemis's Heights, 276; leads the assault at Freeman's farm as a volunteer, 278; in command of Philadelphia, 300; courtmartialed, 301; reprimanded by Washington, 325; his treason, 325 *et seq.*; in Virginia, 329; at Groton Heights, 333
Austria, alliance of, with Russia, 38; alliance with France, 39

BAPTIST Church, the, in the United States, 378
Barlow, Joel, 386
Barré replies to the plea of gratitude, 121; opposes Stamp Act, 131, 133

398 INDEX

Beaumarchais in England, 218, 220; secures a subsidy for America, 262
Bedford, leader of the old Whigs, 129; his followers predominant in the Chatham-Grafton ministry, 148; his followers and the new Tories, 149
Bemis's Heights, battle of, 276, the second action at, 278
Bennington, battle of, 271
Bernard, governor of Massachusetts, 125; demands money from Massachusetts Legislature, 126; summons man-of-war from Halifax, 151; his recall demanded, 155; recalled, 157
Bigot, knavery of, 59; peculations of, 75
Bill of Rights, 3
Billeting Act, 51, 52; consequences of, 54; resisted in New York, 144, 145
Blockade and contraband, England's position as to, 350
Board of customs, established at Boston, 146, 149; finds it impossible to enforce the law, 150
Bolingbroke, his theories, 117, 128
Boone, Daniel, in Kentucky, 153
Boscawen, in the St. Lawrence, 41
Boston, Stamp Act riots in, 135; Board of Customs established in, 146, 149; threatens the revenue officers, 148; revenue riots in, 151; "Massacre," 158; the "tea-party" in, 167, 168; North's retaliatory measures against, 168; Port Act, idem; union of colonies, to support, 170; fortified by the English, 175; invested by the Americans, 187; besieged by Washington, 205; evacuated by the British, 206; population of, 381
Botetourt dissolves Virginia Legislature, 155, 172
Bougainville arrives, 53; at Isle-aux-Noix, 98
Bouquet at Bedford and Grant's Hill, 72
Bourlamarque at Isle-aux-Noix, 81; at Montreal, 98
Brackenridge, Hugh H., 386
Braddock, character of, 40; convenes Alexandria Congress, 41; march to Fort Duquesne, 43; defeat of, 44; death of, 45
Brandywine, battle of the, 273
Bribery in English politics, 4, 146
Brunswickers and other Germans sold to George III., 212
Bunker Hill, 199; battle of, 200 et seq.
Burgesses, House of, at Williamsburg reject North's proposal, 197
Burgoyne, John, 181; in Canada, 267; takes Ticonderoga, 268; advances from the north, 276; retreats after the engagements at Bemis's Heights, 279; surrenders at Saratoga, 279; effect of his surrender in England, 288
Burke, relation of, to the Whigs, 128; to Rockingham, 139; supports position of Massachusetts, 154; colonial agent for New York, 163; opposes the penal acts, 168, 169; his eloquent eulogium on America in Parliament, 180; his ineffectual plea for reconciliation, 182
Bute's ministry, 109, 127; fall of, 128
Byng, Admiral, 5

CABINET, the English, 3, 122; responsibility of ministers in, 129
Calvinism in America, 160, 378
Camden, defeat of Gates at, 318
Canada, 26; expedition of Schuyler against, 203; Burgoyne in, 267
Cannibalism of Indians, 57
Cape Fear River, Clinton enters, 222
Carleton defeated by Schuyler, 203; made commander-in-chief of Canada, 216
Castine, failure of the expedition against, 310
Cartwright, opposes North's penal acts, 168
Catherine of Russia, 13
Charles III. of Spain, 108; declares war on England, 110
Charleston bombarded by Clinton, 223; captured by the British, 315; evacuation of, 366
Charters, character of colonial, 122
Chatham (see Pitt), his coalition with Grafton, 143; dares not remove Townshend, 144; reconstructs the ministry on Townshend's death,

148; his humiliation as king's confidant, 149; resigns power, 154; suggests parliamentary reform, 157; eloquence of his plea for conciliation, 180; last appearance in Parliament, 291
Cherokees quarrel with Lyttleton, 100; capture Fort Loudon, 101; settlement of their lands, 101
Choiseul, French minister, 107, 108; foresees American independence, 114; his interest in American colonies, 147
Churches, the different denominations, in the United States, at the close of the Revolution, 378
Cincinnati, the Order of the, 376
Clark, expedition of, into the interior, 305 et seq.; recaptures Vincennes, 306
Clinton, George, defends Fort Clinton, 277
Clinton, Sir Henry, 181; leaves Boston for Cape Fear River, 231; attacks Charleston, 223; returns to New York, 223; passes the Highlands, 277; replaces Howe, 294; despatches an expedition to the Chesapeake, 308; desires to hold New York and abandon Virginia, 339
Colden surrenders stamps, 139
Colleges in America, 132, 380
Colonies (see American colonies), character of, 7, 37; and the French War, 79; strength of their forces, 79; relation to each other, 99; discontent of, 101, 120; institutions of, 110, 115; separation from England, 116; charter rights of, 118, 122; theory of, 120, 122, 147, 157; wealth and education, 131; colleges in, 132, 380; union against Stamp Act, 132, 138; jurisdiction over western lands, 137; English grievances against, 144; Choiseul's interest in, 147; their governments to be unified, 143; dissolution of their royal governments, 155, 156; their loyalty, 157; effects of oppressing the, 160; social and commercial state of, 161; collapse of their administration, 162; united to support Boston, 170; their reception of Boston Port Act, 172; organization of, after Concord and Lexington, 187; destitution of their troops, 343
Colonists, loyalty and self-reliance of, 192; character of the, 193; their prosperity, 193; large conservative element among, 194; the spirit of union among, 194
Columbia or King's College, 132, 379; Jay a graduate of, 171; Hamilton a graduate of, 171
Commerce, English, captured in the first year of the war, 260; American, regulation of, by Congress, 210
Commissioners arrive with the conciliatory offers of Parliament, 294
Committees of correspondence, 161, 162
Concord, the conflict at, 184 et seq.; losses at, 186
Confederated States, use of the term, 303
Confederation, weakness of, 284: the creation of the States, 234; its powers and lack of executive, 235; articles of, signed by the States, 295
Congress, meeting and composition of the Stamp Act, 136; memorials drawn by, 137; influence of, 138, 139; its petitions disregarded, 140; new, suggested by New York, 156, 171; other colonies accept proposition for, 171; character of delegations to first continental, 174; the idea of a general, 175 (see Continental Congress); the first proceedings in, 176 et seq.; declaration of rights by, 177; acts of, discussed throughout the country, 182: an English convention, 194; questions before, 196; petition of, to the king, 196; moderation of, 197; appoints generals, 208; issues bills of credit, 208; regulation of American commerce by, 210; petitions George III. for a restoration of the old government, 212; authorizes independent government by the colonies, 215; avoids the laying of direct taxes, 218; the debate in, on Lee's resolution for independence, 227; committee of, on the declaration

of independence, 228; adopts Jefferson's document, 229; a perfectly representative assemblage, 231; completes the federal union, 232; a disposition to limit its powers to the minimum, 233; its inefficiency during the war, 236; finally authorizes long enlistments, 246; leaves Philadelphia, 251; at a low ebb, 282; ratifies the treaty with France, 292; refuses conciliation, 294; appoints Franklin sole plenipotentiary in Paris, 305; terms of peace proposed by, 355; held in low esteem after the war, 374

Connecticut, Stamp Act in, 134; cautious in regard to her charter, 148; seizes Wyoming Valley, 162; supports idea of general congress, 171

Constitution, "spirit of," 132, 139; the American, in part the work of a later generation, 371

Constitutional government, new issue in, 116, 118, 123, 132

Constitutional revolution in America, first stage of, 6; second stage of, 147; third stage of, 157

Continental, the name, 172

Continental congress, suggested, 175; composition of the first, 176; the second, 195

Continental currency, issued, 208; depreciation of, 283, 322; amount and value of, 285

Conway, General, leaves for France, 293

Cornwallis sent to the South, 321; treatment of South Carolina by, 317; retreat of, after King's Mountain, 321; in Virginia, 331 et seq.; defeats Wayne at Greene Springs, 339; ill-feeling between, and Clinton, 339; his position at Yorktown, 340; surrender of, at Yorktown, 336; surrender, effect of, in England, 353

Courts of vice-admiralty, without juries, 134

Cowpens, battle of, 331

Crown Point, 37; importance of, 49; captured by Johnson, 50; evacuated by French, 81

Crown, supremacy of, 118, 122

Cumberland, Duke of, 5, 42

Currency, large issues of, 307; depreciation of, 308

Cushing discusses general congress with Franklin, 175

DANBURY, American stores destroyed at, by Tryon, 267

Dartmouth continues Hillsborough's colonial policy, 162

Dartmouth College established for the Indians, 183, 380

Davis, Isaac, 185

Deane, Silas, seeks aid in France, 219; sent by Congress to London as agent, 262; his extravagant negotiations, 263

Declaration of the rights of the colonies by the first Continental Congress, 177

Declaration of Independence, Jefferson's document adopted by Congress, 229; the popular reception of, 230; adopted by New York and New Jersey, 230; its character in the estimate of posterity, 231

Declaratory Act passed, 140; meaning of, 141, 142; effects of, 145

De Grasse arrives in the Chesapeake, 340; defeats the English fleet in the Chesapeake, 344

Delawares. *See* Indians.

Denominations, religions, 8, 378

D'Estaing, 392; fails to enter New York Harbor and goes to Newport, 301 *et seq.*; death of, at Savannah, 314

Detroit, 37; occupied by the English, 101; besieged by Pontiac, 102; relief of, 103

Dickinson, John, writes "Farmer's Letters," 147; his loyalty to England, 157; moves Pennsylvania to accept the proposition of a general congress, 171, 174, 181; argues for federation before separation, 229

Dieskau, career of, 41; at Crown Point, 50

Dissent in America, 9

Dominica captured by the French, 313

Drucour at Louisburg, 64

Dunbar, retreat of, from Fort Duquesne, 45

Dunmore, prorogues Virginia Legis-

lature, 172; flight of, to Williamsburg, 188; summons the House of Burgesses to meet at Williamsburg, 197
Dwight, Timothy, 386
Dyer, Oliver, on the Stamp Act, 134

EASTON, Indian conference at, 73, 101
Edwards, Jonathan, 387
England; her policy in America, 24, 25, 26, 37; successes at sea in 1759, 77; her conquests from France, 103, 104, 108; her naval supremacy, 104; her territorial expansion, 112; separation from America, 116; insufficiency of her constitution, 123; patronage in, 146; her view of the Mississippi Valley, 152; her diplomatic isolation, 155; liberal opinions in, 157; effort of the Bourbon powers to deprive, of her maritime and colonial powers, 349; practice of, in regard to blockade and contraband, 350; desires the alliance of Russia, 350; preparations for the second campaign of the war, 265
English ministry in sore straits, 303
Europe, the character of the American situation not realized in, 190
Eutaw Springs, battle of, 336
Express riders, system of, created, 177
Expenses of the Revolutionary War, 374

FAMILY compact of the Bourbons, 108
"Farmer's Letters," written by Dickinson, 147; answered by North's ministry, 155
Fireships of the French, 84
Fisheries off Newfoundland, 21
Fishing on the Banks forbidden, 181
Fisheries, Marbois's letter concerning, 362
Flag, the first American, 210
Forbes, character of, 61; expedition to Fort Duquesne, 71; illness of, 73; captures Fort Duquesne, 73; death of, 74
Foreign aid hastened, but did not determine, American independence, 261
Fort Bull captured by French, 53
Fort Duquesne, 27, 43, 71; capture of, 73; renamed Pittsburgh, 74
Fort Edward, 50
Fort Lee, captured by Howe, 245
Fort Le Bœuf, 37
Fort Loudon built, 54; captured by Cherokees, 101
Fort William Henry, massacre of, 57
Fort Stanwix, 269
Fort Washington captured by Howe, 244
Fort William Henry, 50
Fox opposes North's penal acts, 168
France, in America, 20, 23, 24, 25, 26, 37; losses in 1759, 80; in the following years, 103, 104, 108; her attitude toward American Revolution, 146; anxious to renew conflict with England, 147; interest of, in American affairs, 218; subsidy from, 262; volunteers from, 264; American vessels protected in ports of, 265; secret alliance with, 287; treaty with, ratified, 292; forces of, at Yorktown, 340, 346
Franchise, 11
Franklin, on internal and external taxation, 140; his loyalty to England, 157; his relation to the Hutchinson letters, 163; before the privy council, 164; discusses general congress with Cushing, 175; request of, for a hearing refused, 180; returns to America, 181; commissioned to create a post-office, 210, 213; becomes the rage in Paris, 263; his negotiations successful, 265; influence of, in France, 286, 292; American peace commissioner, 355; calls Jay from Madrid, 356; informs Oswald what the conditions of peace would be, 362, 387
Frederick the Great, 13, 39; in the Seven Years' War, 62, 76, 77, 104; hated by Pompadour, 107; his alliance with Russia, 109
"Freeman," of New York, on Stamp Act, 134
Freneau, Philip, 386
Freeman's Farm, battle of, 278

26

GADSDEN, Christopher, joins Lyttleton's expedition, 100; his broad plea for union, 137; opposes petitions of Congress, 138
Gage, his inefficiency at Niagara, 81; made governor of Massachusetts, 170; proposes savage auxiliaries, 175; sends a brigade to Jamaica Plain, 183, 186; expels the citizens of Boston, 187; recalled, 211
Gaspee, burning of the, 160
Gates, General, intrigues to supersede Schuyler, 267; army of, opposed to Burgoyne, 275 et seq.; his lenient terms to Burgoyne, 279; defeat of, at Camden, 318; replaced by Greene, 322
George I. and the Whigs, 4
George II., 13; death of, 105
George III., accession of, 105; his character, *ibid.*; his policy, 106, 107; the faction of his " friends," 106; his attitude concerning the Stamp Act, 140; becomes virtual prime minister, 146; efforts of, to raise troops in Europe, 211
George, Lake, 50
Georgia adopts the articles of the American Association, 206; overrun by the English, 313
German troops sold to George III., 212
Germain orders a concentration of the English forces in New York, 295
Germantown, Howe in, 273; the battle of, 280
Gist, Nathaniel, put in command of Indian forces, 294
Governments, colonial, 11
Grafton warns the king, 216
Grant's Hill, defeat at, 72
Grattan, the Irish agitator, 157
Gratitude, plea of, 121
Green, Jacob, writes the constitution of New Jersey, 225
Green Mountain boys resist the sheriff, 182
Greene, Nathaniel, at Boston, 187; Governor of Rhode Island, 207; taken by surprise at Fort Lee, 245; reorganizes the Southern army, 330; his defeat at Guilford by Cornwallis, 332; defeated at Hobkirk Hill by Rawdon, 335

Grenville, his theory of taxation, 119; secretary of state, 128; becomes prime minister, 128; supports Stamp Act, 139; his ministry falls, 139
Grenville, Thomas, negotiates with Vergennes concerning the independence of America, 357
Groton Heights, quarter refused by the British at, 333
Guilford, battle of, 332

HALE, NATHAN, hung as a spy, 242
Hamilton, Alexander, in the New York public meeting concerning first Continental Congress, 174; in command of an artillery company, 240; leads the assault at Yorktown, 344
Hancock, John, seizure of his sloop Liberty, 151, 184; excepted from amnesty, 200
Harvard College, 132, 380
Hawley, thinks internal and external taxation identical, 147
Hayne, Isaac, hanged by Rawdon, 336
Henry, Patrick, on Stamp Act, 134; on taxation, 134; a leader in Virginia, 155; marches with the militia to Williamsburg, 188
Herkimer, General, death of, at Oriskany, 270
Hessians, scandalous conduct of, in New Jersey, 252; the traffic in, 289
Hillsborough, his policy as colonial secretary, 148; issues warrant for Hutchinson's pay, 150; his instructions to Bernard, 150
Hobbes's Leviathan, 117
Hobkirk Hill, defeat of Greene at, 334
Holland, return of the Scotch brigade demanded of, 211; repudiate the commercial treaty proposed by Amsterdam, 352
Holmes, Admiral, at Quebec, 85; movements of his fleet, 89
Howe, Lord, character of, 61; death at Ticonderoga, 67
Howe, General, made commander-in-chief, 181; tradition of, at Mrs. Murray's, 242; his long journey to Philadelphia, 273

INDEX 403

Howe, the brothers, refused reinforcements, direct their attention to Philadelphia, 266

Hunter, James, leader of the North Carolina regulators, 159

Hutchinson, Thomas, lieutenant-governor of Massachusetts, 125, 157; the warrant for his pay, 149; Franklin and the letters of, 163; recalled to England, 170

ILLINOIS, county of, established, 306

Independence, feeling for, 123

Indians, and white settlers, 20; of Central America, 27; of the Gulf, 28; the Algonquin or Delaware, 28, 32; the Six Nations or Iroquois, 29, 30, 31, 32; the Dakotah, 33; alliances of, 33, 34; and English, 34, 113; and French, 35, 113; their outrages at Ticonderoga, 57; their discontent with the English, 101; their conspiracy under Pontiac, 102; Hillsborough's boundary to their territory, 152; in the Revolutionary War, 175

Indian brutalities under Burgoyne, 268; excesses of, avenged, 309

Institutions of English in America, 7, 12, 123

Ireland, English rule in, 16; Presbyterians in, 16

Irish emigration to the continent, 18; to America, 18, 19

Isle-aux-Noix, held by Bourlamarque, 8

JASPER, Sergeant, at Fort Moultrie, 224

Jay, John, chairman of New York committee, 171, 181; American peace commissioner summoned from Madrid by Franklin, 356; his position as to the treaty, 359; proposals of, to Shelbourn through Vaughan, 362

Jefferson, Thomas, a leader in Virginia, 155, 183; address of, to Dunmore, 197; his Declaration of Independence adopted with amendments, 229, 387

Jenkinson, author of the Stamp Act, 131

Johnson, Sir William, 36; captures Crown Point, 50; at Ticonderoga, 68; at Niagara, 80

Johnson, Samuel, Dr., 181

Jones, Paul, exploits of, 311

Judiciary, the English, 3; salaries of New York, 125; in New Jersey, Maryland and Pennsylvania, 126; appointment for life, 137

Jury, trial by, 137

KALB, Baron de, enlists in the American cause, 264

Kant foresees American independence, 114

Kaskaskia, settlement of, by Clark, 306

Kentucky, explored by Daniel Boone, 153; county of, recognized, 305

"King's Friends," faction of, 106

King's Mountain, battle of, 320; character of the fight, 321

Kittanning captured by Armstrong, 54

Knox founds the Order of the Cincinnati, 376

Kosciusko, 264

LAFAYETTE, enlists in the American cause, 264; the idol of the United States, 292; returns to France and brings back a fleet under Rochambeau, 324; in command in Virginia, 329, 337; retreats before Cornwallis, 338; before Yorktown, 340, 344

Laurens, Henry, negotiates a commercial treaty with the Dutch, 351

Lee, Arthur, in London, 262

Lee, Charles, won over to the American cause by Sears, and appointed major-general, 220; his popularity, 221; refuses to obey Washington's orders, 246; captured by the British, 249; exchanged for General Prescott, 249; his treachery at Monmouth, 297

Lee, Henry, captures Paulus Hook, 309

Lee, Richard Henry, his resolution in Congress, 225

Lee, William, an American agent in London, 351

Lévis arrives, 53; at Quebec, 85,

86; at Montreal, 88; attacks Ste. Foy, 96; retreat to Montreal, 97; surrender of, 98
Louis XV., 13
Lexington, the conflict at, 184; losses at, 186
Liberals, spirit of English, 139
Liberty, Sons of, on Stamp Act, 135
Ligneris abandons Fort Duquesne, 73; peculations of, 75
Lincoln, General, 275; surrenders at Charleston, 315
Literature of the Revolution, 385
Livingston, William, leads New York patriots, 126; his sympathy with Massachusetts circular, 150
Local prejudices as to the federal system, 233 et seq.
Locke's contract theory, 117
Long Island, battle of, 240 et seq.
Loudon, Earl of, 51, 52; withdraws from Louisburg, 56; recalled, 60
Louisburg, fall of, 64
Louisiana, 26; as a Spanish frontier, 152; and Florida lost to England, 307
Loyalty of the colonists, 20
Lyman at Crown Point, 50
Lyttleton quarrels with Cherokees, 100
Luzerne, his part in the treaty of Paris, 360

MAGNA CHARTA, principles of, 135
Macdonald, Allan and Flora, in North Carolina, 222; death of Allan, 224
Madison, James, calls for reprisal, 188; opposes the use of the word "toleration" in the Virginia declaration of rights, 224
Mandamus councillors, 169; their activity, 173; compelled to resign, 175
Mansfield's plea against the charters, 148
Marbois, letter of, respecting the fisheries intercepted, 362
Maria Theresa, 2
Marion, Francis, joins Lyttleton's expedition, 100; in South Carolina, 319
Maryland wants general congress, 171

Massachusetts, broadens her ground for resistance, 139; cautious in defence of her charter, 148; circular letter of her assembly, 150; her legislature dissolved, 150; her legislature refuses Bernard's salary, 156; her charter attacked by North, 169; Gage removes assembly to Salem, 170; chooses delegates to first Continental Congress, 173; petitions Congress for authority to organize her government, 207; directed to choose a house of representatives, 209, 381
McCrea, Jane, story of, 268
Mecklenburg, the town of, 194; declarations, 195
Meigs, Colonel, destroys English stores at Sag Harbor, 267
Merrill, Benjamin, leader of North Carolina regulators, 159
Mercer, Hugh, death of, 259
Methodist Church, the, 378
Middle States at the close of the war, 379
Military control of colonies, 125
Militia, colonial, 42
Ministers, responsibility of, 129
Mirabeau attacks the Landgrave of Hesse on account of the sale of troops, 289
Mississippi, the, as a bond of union, 23
Monmouth, battle of, 296
Montcalm, character of, 53; at Ticonderoga, 67; discouragements of, 76, 90; strength of his forces, 79; at Quebec, 82; policy of, 85; desperate condition of his army, 88; his defeat and death, 93, 95
Montesquieu, school of, 14
Montgomery abandons Fort Loudon, 100; death of, 204
Montmorency, Falls of, conflict near, 85, 86
Morris, Robert, raises money for Washington, 254; his success with the finances of the Confederation, 328, 373
Morristown, Washington establishes his headquarters at, 258
Moultrie joins Lyttleton's expedition, 100
Murray, General, at Quebec, 89; his defence of, 96

Mutiny Act modified, 133
Mutinies in the American army, 327
Mutiny of troops at Philadelphia allayed by funds furnished by Rochambeau, 344

NAVIGATION Acts, evasion of, 118; character of, 118, 124; enforcement of, 149
Natchez and other forts captured by Willing, 306
Navy, the American, during the Revolution, 210, 371
Netherlands, position of, with regard to England, 352
Newcastle ministry, 39, 40; fall of, 108; coalition of, with Bute, 127; its fall, 127
New England, shipping interests of, 124; her local prejudice, 137; her plea for charter rights, 138; her attitude toward "Quebec Act," 170, 171; her passive resistance to Port Act, 172; army, character of, 199; at Bunker Hill, 201; dwindles away, 202; at the close of the war, 380
New Hampshire, 36; Stamp Act in, 134; royal authority overthrown in, 207
New Jersey, college of (see Princeton); disavows Ogden's lukewarmness, 139; wants general congress, 171; adopts a constitution, 225
New Orleans revolts against Spain, 152
Newport, D'Estaing's expedition against, a failure, 301; abandoned by the British, 310
New York State, 42; demands free judiciary, 125; Stamp Act in, 134; her boundary claims, 152; her proposition for a general congress, 171; character of her delegates to first continental congress, 173; refuses to give full power to her delegates, 226
New York City, the Liberty Tree conflict in, 159; sends back tea-ship, 167; anomalous condition of affairs in, 220; entered by Charles Lee, 221; held by the British, 224; strategic importance of, at the opening of the war, 239; fortifications thrown up by Washington around, 239; English forces landed near, 240; evacuation of, 377; population of, 379
Niagara, Fort, 27; importance of, 49; resists the English, 49; captured by Johnson, 80
Non-importation agreements, 161
Norfolk captured by the Americans, 206
North becomes prime minister, 154; his penal acts, 168, 169, 170, 179; devises a compromise, 181; attempts conciliation, 216; ministry, fall of, 353
North Carolina, regulators in, 151; emigration from, 152; battle on the Alamance, 159; republic of Watanga in, 162; wants general congress, 172; Tories of, proscribed, 207

OFFICIALS of England in America, 125; their hostility to America, 148, 149; letters of, 163, 164; compelled to resign, 175
Ohio, valley of, 26, 45
Oliver, letters, 163; resigns under compulsion, 175; proposed savage auxiliaries, 175
Oriskany, battle of, 270
Orleans, isle of, 83, 84
Oswald, engaged to communicate with the American peace commissioners, 356
Oswego, captured by French, 53; recaptured, 70
Otis, James, his arguments against writs of assistance, 125; on the spirit of the Constitution, 135; thinks internal and external taxation identical, 147; removed from public life by an accident, 155

PAINE, THOMAS, his "Common Sense," 213, 387
Parliament, supremacy of, 118, 121; admitted by Stamp Act Congress, 138, 140; secured by George III as a principle, 145; corrupt elections and, 149; reasserted in the refusal to repeal revenue laws, 154; passes penal laws

406 INDEX

against America, 168; adopts conciliatory measures, 290
Parties in America, 158, 170
Partisan warfare, 59
Patriotism in America, 135, 139, 170
Patronage in England, 146
Paxton letters, 103
Peace commissioners, American, 355
Pelham ministry, 39
Penal acts demanded by the Tories, 179, 180
Penn, Richard, 196; arrival of, 210
Pennsylvania, 42; university of, 132; the proprietary government of, ended, 225, 226
Philadelphia, prevents landing of tea, 167; and the Boston Port Act, 172; Howe's army at, 281; occupied by Cornwallis, 294; evacuated, 295; Arnold in command of, 300; population of, at the close of the war, 379
Philip V. of Spain, 13
Pitt, William (the elder), 5, 6; plan for the French war, 40, 78; ministry of Newcastle and, 60; awakens American enthusiasm, 65; rejects Choiseul's offer of peace, 108; resigns with Newcastle, 108; relations to the Whigs, 128; holds American taxation unconstitutional, 39 (*see* Chatham)
Pittsburgh, founding of, 74
Point Pleasant, skirmish between the Indians and frontiersmen at, 178
Political theories, 117, 122
Political writers of the Revolution, 386
Politics, liberal, 5, 139
Pontiac, truce with, 101; conspiracy of, 102; his rebellion suppressed, 103
Population of the colonies, 9; of the United States after the war, 378 *et seq.*
Port Act, effect in colonies, 172
Post, Frederick, at Easton, 73, 101
Postage, reduction of, 133
"Presbyterian junto" of New York, 171
Presbyterian Church, the, in America, 379

Presbyterians, disabilities in Ireland, 17; as patriots, 174
Press, freedom of, 3; secured by Wilkes, 130
Price, Richard, his pamphlet on liberty, 211
Prideaux killed at Niagara, 80
Princeton College, 132, 380
Princeton, Cornwallis in, 248; battle of, 257
Prisoners, Howe consents to an exchange of, 260
Privateering authorized by Congress, 214; by Americans, 372
Providence, a, in history clearly evident in the origins of America, 348
Provincial and colonist, 118, 131, 168
Prussia. *See* Frederick the Great
Public meetings, inaugurated, 157; in New York, 171, 174
Pulaski, 264
Putnam, Israel, at Ticonderoga, 66; in Boston, 187; at Bunker Hill, 200

QUAKERS, their attitude concerning independence, 174, 379
Quebec, disposition of French forces near, 82; topography of, 83; surrender of, 95; Murray's defence of, 96, 97; relief of, 97; North's act concerning, 169; failure of the campaign against, 204
Quebec Act, object of, 177
Quesnay, 14
Quincy, Josiah, counsel for English soldiers, 158

RATIONALISM in England, 5
Rawdon, Lord, his cruelties in the colonies, 334; defeats Greene at Hobkirk Hill, 335
Regulators of North Carolina, 151
Religion, revival of, 5
Religious liberty in England, 3
Representation and legislation, 147
Representation and taxation. *See* Taxation
Requisitions on the colonies, 121
Revolution in continental politics, 2; in constitutional theory (*see* Constitutional revolution) of 1688 in America, 10; American, character of, 382; changes resulting from, 382

INDEX

Rhode Island ready to unite with Massachusetts to resist Port Act, 173; elects delegates to first continental congress, 173
Riedesel's memoirs of the retreat of Burgoyne, 279
Richmond burned by Arnold, 329
Rittenhouse, 213
Rochambeau enters Newport with French troops, 324; furnishes funds for the American troops, 344
Rockingham, leader of new Whigs, 128; his ministry, 139; his position on repeal of the Stamp Act, 140; fall of his first ministry, 142; helplessness of his followers, 149, 179; declares the act of Parliament a declaration of war, 180; ministry, the, 354; ministry, work of the, 358
Rodrigues, Hortales & Co., 262
Rogers, near Lake George, 55, 59; destroys Abenaki village, 82; occupies Detroit, 101
Roman Catholics, disabilities, 15, 16, 19
Rossbach, battle of, 63, 64
Rousseau, teachings of, 14
Ryswick, peace of, 2

SAINT LÉGER attacks Fort Stanwix, 269
Saint Lawrence, French in the valley of, 23
Saint Louis, settled by the French, 152
Saint Lucia seized by the English, 313
Saint Simon's army landed in Virginia, 341
Sainte-Foy, battle of, 96, 97
Salem made provincial capital of Massachusetts, 170; powder at, seized, 183
Savannah besieged by D'Estaing unsuccessfully, 314; evacuation of, 366
Schuyler, General, invades Canada, 203; sends reinforcements to Washington in New Jersey, 247; replaced by Gates in command of the department of the North, 267; fine strategy of, against Burgoyne, 268; hands over his command to General Gates, 270

Seven Years' War, 62, 63, 76, 104; effect in Europe, 112; effect in America, 112, 113
Shirley, at Niagara, 49; his plan to tax America, 51; removal of, 51
Slave-trade in America, 9; increase of, 133; Virginia revolutions concerning, 174
Shelburne, secretary for colonies in Chatham-Grafton ministry, 143; deprived of power in Chatham-Grafton ministry, 148; withdraws from it, 154, 179; ministry, the, 358; determination of, to divide the Americans from their allies, 363; fall of, 367
Shelby, Evan, defeats the Indians at Chickamauga, 306
Slaves in the Southern States at the close of the war, 378
Slavery after the war, 383
Smith, Adam, a friend of the colonists, 211
South Carolina, seizure of tea in, 167; proposes union for resistance, 171; royal authority overthrown in, 207; Cornwallis devastates, 317; opposed to the plan of supporting the army, 233; at the close of the war, 378
Sons of Liberty, 170
Spain declares war on England, 110; her losses, 110; her view of Louisiana, 152; revolt of New Orleans against, 152; refuses to join France in an American alliance, 287; in a serious crisis, 304; joins the alliance, 305; desires to regain Gibraltar, 351
Stamp Act, Jenkinson proposes, 131; revenue from, 131; passage of, 133; declared illegal in America, 134; its reception in America, 134; repealed, 140
Stanwix, at Oneida portage, 70; occupies the frontier, 80
Stark, John, at Ticonderoga, 66
State governments, success of, 284
Staten Island, the only available landing-place for the English at New York, 239; conference on, between Howe and a committee of Congress, 242
Stark, John, at Boston, 187, 254; victory of, at Bennington, 271

Sterling, Lord, retreats from Princeton before Cornwallis, 248
Steuben, Baron, made inspector-general of the American army in place of Conway, 293; raises an army in Virginia, 339
Stony Point, battle of, 277; capture of, 309
Sumpter, resistance of, in South Carolina, 318

TARIFF laid by Parliament on American imports, 145
Taxation of colonies by England, 41, 51, 118; internal and external, 119; and representation, 121, 134, 136, 138; legal argument for, 121, 122; officials plead for, 125, 163; held unconstitutional by English liberals, 139; Declaratory Act concerning, 140; revenue to be raised by, 144; by import duties, 145; of tea, 145; and revenue discussed by Otis, 147
Tea, tax on, 166; measures to prevent landing of, 167
Theories of colonists, 12, 147
Thomas, General, at Montreal, 204
Ticonderoga, held by French, 66; evacuated by them, 81; seizure of, by Ethan Allen, 189; taken by Burgoyne, 268; recaptured by the Americans, 276
Tories, the new, 3, 109, 143; American, 135; called loyalists, 170; design to enforce the Penal Acts, 179; in North Carolina proscribed, 207; treatment of, at New York, 239; hung in Philadelphia, pardoned in New Jersey, 300
Townshend, Charles, overthrows Rockingham ministry, 142
Trade, regulation of, 120, 133; diminution of English and American, 166
Treaty of Paris, 109; stipulations of, 111; unpopular in England, 111
Trenton, battle of, 253
Trinity, old, burned, 242
Trumbull, Governor of Connecticut, 207, 386
Tryon attacks North Carolina regulators, 151; at the battle on the Alamance, 159; action of, at New York, 239
Tucker opposes North's penal acts, 168
Turgot, 14; Stamp Act, 143; his death, 148

ULSTER, migration from, 16
Union, tendencies to, 7
United States, the date of the legal existence of the, 229; at the close of the Revolution, 378 et seq.
Utrecht, Peace of, 2

VALLEY FORGE, Washington's army in winter quarters at, 281
Vaudreuil, 41; braggadocio of, 76
Vaughan, 362
Venango, 37
Vergennes refuses to consider the English demands in the treaty, 361
Vergor in Acadia, 48
Vermont, 36; conflict between the Green Mountain Boys and the sheriff in, 182
Versailles, the peace of, the treaty, 364; secret clause in, 305; the agents of, 365 et seq.; final ratification of, 368
Virginia, 42; reception of Stamp Act by, 134; circular of her Legislature, 151; claims Kentucky and the Northwest, 152; her Assembly dissolved by Botetourt, 155; organizes intercolonial committees of correspondence, 162; her support of Boston and progress toward independence, 173; Legislature prorogued by Dunmore, 172; denounces writs of assistance and becomes a State, 225, 381
Voltaire, 13

WALPOLE, ministry of, 4
War between England and France, 52
Warrants, general, 130
Warren, Joseph, killed at Bunker Hill, 201
Washington, George, at Fort Necessity, 37; at Braddock's field, 44; at Cumberland, 71; at Fort Duquesne, 73; his sympathy with Massachusetts's circular, 150; a

INDEX 409

leader in Virginia, 155; his family and early life, 197 *et seq.*; appointed commander-in-chief, 199; at Boston, 199; at Cambridge 202; persists in his Fabian policy, 214; the sole respecter of Congress, 236; his supporters, 237; throws up fortifications around New York, 239; retreats from Long Island, 241; attempts to arrest the flight of his troops at Kip's Bay, 241; his headquarters at Morrisania, 241; retreats from New York, 242; retreats across the Harlem, 243; covers Greene's retreat, 245; invested with the powers of a dictator, 247; retreats across New Jersey, 247; masterly retreat over the Delaware, 248; effective force of, at the opening of the second campaign, 266; army at Brandywine, 272; cabal formed against, 282; collapse of the cabal, 293; description of the situation by, 302; pleads for long enlistments, 303; his foresight, 323; holds his communications with New England intact, 341; deceives Clinton and marches South, 343; revisits Mount Vernon, 344; allays the discontent of the army after the war, 375; resigns his command to Congress, 377; outlines the future policy of the country, 387

Wayne, General, conduct of, at Monmouth, 298; captures Stony Point, 309

Wesley, John, 5, 60, 190
West, jurisdiction of lands in, 137; colonization forbidden, 137
Western lands, claims to, by the States, 235
Whigs, policy of, 3, 118; division into old and new, 123; name American, 132; attack Chatham-Grafton ministry, 145
Whitefield, preaching of, 60
Whitefield, on the stamp act, 134
White Plains, the battle of, 243
William and Mary, College of, 132
Wilkes and freedom of the press, 130, 163
Winslow in Acadia, 48
Witherspoon, inspires the Constitution of New Jersey, 225; influence of, in the adoption of the Declaration of Independence, 229, 387
Wolfe, character of, 61, 79; at Louisburg, 64; defeat at the falls of the Montmorency, 86, 87; illness before Quebec, 87; his movements at Cape Rouge, 90, 91; lands and scales the heights of Abraham, 92; prepares for battle, 93, 94; his victory and death, 94, 95; effects of his victory, 115
Writs of assistance, 124
Wyoming, seizure by Connecticut, 162; the massacre of, 298

YALE COLLEGE, 132; 386
"Yankee Doodle," 385
Yorktown, invested by the French and American troops, 345; Cornwallis's surrender at, 337

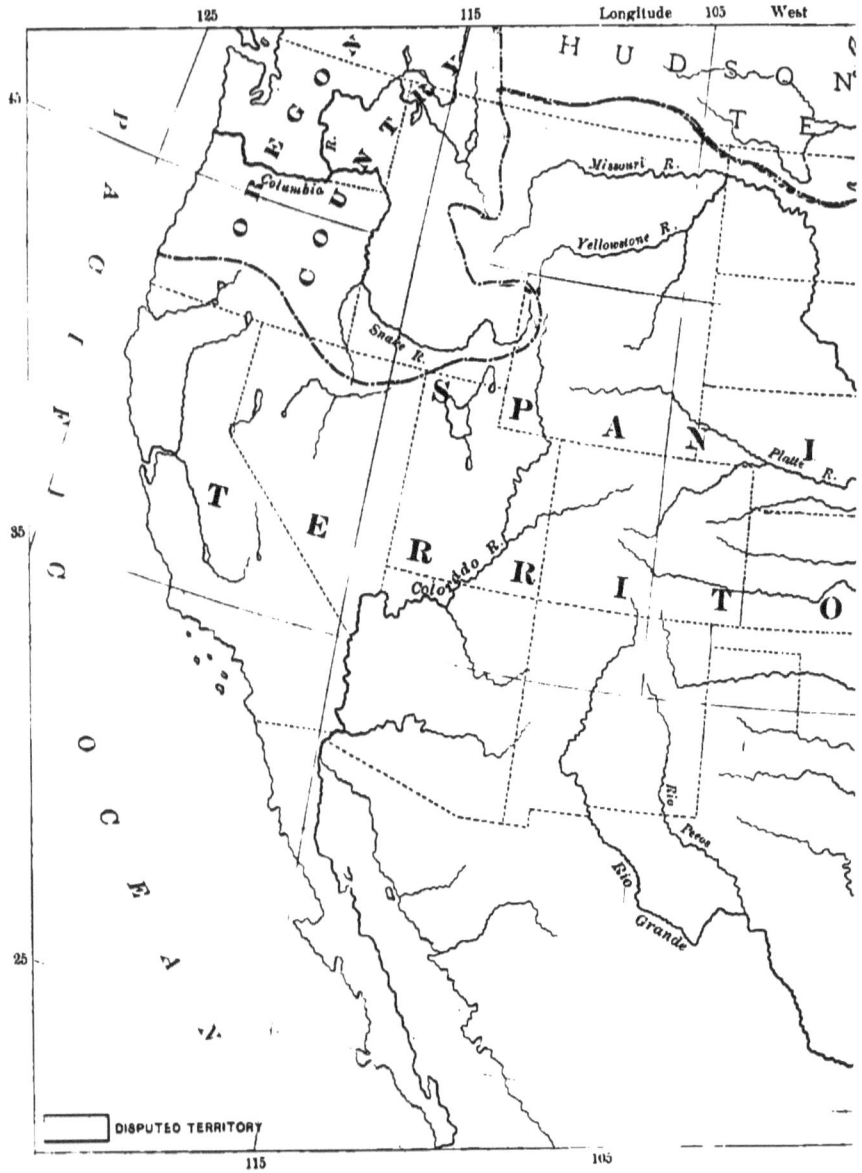

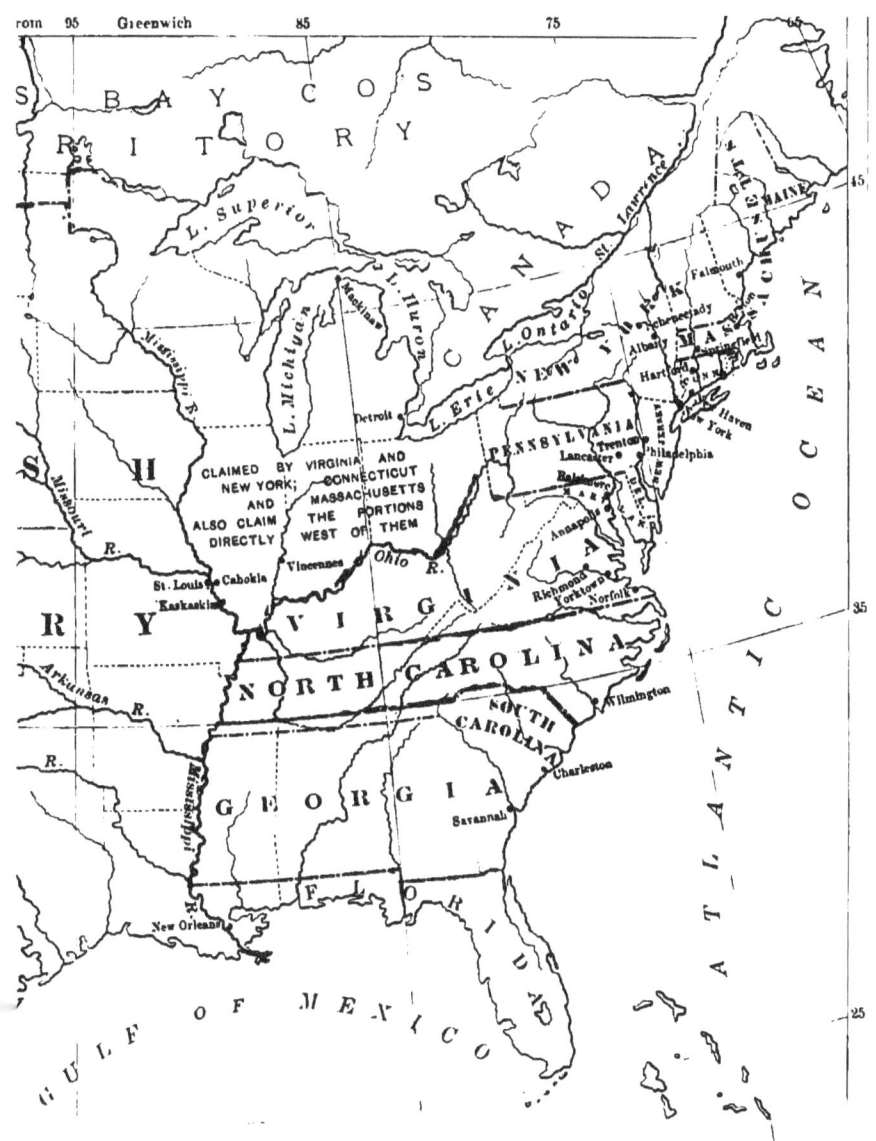

THE AMERICAN HISTORY SERIES.

THIS series, in a field in which so much important and original work is being done at the present time, forms a connected history of the United States, from the discovery of America to the present time. The whole period is divided into four distinct "Epochs," each comparatively rounded and complete in itself, and each treated by a special and eminent authority. It is designed to be eminently *history*, as distinguished from the chronicle of annals, and explain the significance as well as recount the course of events. Philosophic, rather than purely narrative, so far as may be without departure from its thoroughly popular and literary design, and dealing with causes and inferences as fully as with incidents, it will still make especially prominent the social picture of each epoch, and occupy itself with the manners, habits, beliefs, aims, and conduct of the great public, rather than the acts of individuals, however representative. It will be, in a word, a literary and philosophical history of the *people* of the United States.

The different volumes treat :—First, the epoch of discovery and colonization ; second, that of the French and Indian War and the Revolution—essentially forming one period as regards both the political current of events, and many of the actors therein; third, the discussion and adoption of the Federal Constitution after the successful issue of the Revolu-

THE AMERICAN HISTORY SERIES.

tion, and the growth in national consolidation of the different and at first discordant States; and fourth, the sectional conflict over the institution of slavery, from the rise of the slave-power to the end of the reconstruction period.

The initial volume entitled "The Colonial Era," by George Park Fisher, D.D., LL.D., Professor of Ecclesiastical History in Yale University, has been received with universal favor. "The French War and the Revolution," written by William M. Sloane, Ph.D., Professor of History in Princeton University, is now ready. The era of the adoption of the Constitution, and the subsequent national consolidation will be by Gen. Francis A. Walker, President of the Massachusetts Institute of Technology. The fourth period, on account both of its length and of its historic importance, will comprise two volumes, the first tracing the confederatizing of the Constitution under the influences of slavery, and the second, its nationalization under the influences of the Civil War and reconstruction. The author of these volumes is John W. Burgess, Ph.D., LL.D., Professor of History, Political Science, and Constitutional Law in Columbia College. It will be seen that for each of the works comprising the series the publishers have been fortunate enough to secure the co-operation of an author not only of national literary reputation, but of special authority upon the individual work he has undertaken. The five volumes will be published in 12mo, at $1.25 each, and each provided with maps and plans.

THE AMERICAN HISTORY SERIES.

PRESS NOTICES

Christian Union.

" The series promises to be one of great value."

New York Tribune.

" The new series is well begun and the reading public will look for the appearance of succeeding volumes with interest."

Boston Times.

"The series will be heartily appreciated by people who have neither the means nor the time to obtain their historical information from larger works."

Boston Journal.

" It promises to be a very useful series of monographs."

New England Journal of Education.

" The reputation and ability of the authors leave no room for doubting that this series will take first rank as an authority on our national history."

Chicago Journal.

" The series will make a very satisfactory presentation of their subject."

New York Press.

" The plan is a good one, and the series of volumes cannot fail to prove highly useful."

Boston Beacon.

" There is a demand for a competent survey of the subject on a scale not too great for popular instruction, and such a work is now to be supplied in the American History Series."

THE AMERICAN HISTORY SERIES.

THE COLONIAL ERA
By Prof. GEORGE P. FISHER

12mo, $1.25

PRESS NOTICES

Mr. M. W. Hazletine in New York Sun.

"We know of no other work which, in the compass of a single volume, offers so complete and satisfactory a conspectus of the subject."

The Critic.

"Prof. Fisher's work shows the hand of a master still in its strength. He seems to have a positive genius for clear, compact, and readable condensation."

The Independent.

"A book of great merit, brief without being bare, and marked with historic accuracy and philosophic grasp."

Hartford Courant.

"We do not know where so much information about our country is stored in so compact and readable form."

The Congregationalist.

"It is conspicuously complete, accurate, and clear. If the succeeding volumes equal this, the series will become a standard."

Philadelphia Telegraph.

"The style is direct, clear, and readable, and the author puts into succinct form just what most people will be likely to want to know."

Cincinnati Times-Star.

"The volume is full, well arranged, and interesting."

CHARLES SCRIBNER'S SONS

743-745 Broadway, - NEW YORK